American Silent Film

American Silent Film

WILLIAM K. EVERSON

DA CAPO PRESS • NEW YORK

Library of Congress Cataloging-in-Publication Data

Everson, William K.
   American silent film / William K. Everson.—1st Da Capo Press ed.
      p.   cm.
   Originally published: New York: Oxford University Press, 1978.
   Includes bibliographical references and index.
   ISBN 0-306-80876-5 (alk. paper)
   1. Motion pictures—United States—History. 2. Silent films—United
States—History and criticism. I. Title.
PN1993.5.U6E9   1998
791.43′0973—dc21   98-17185
                                                                    CIP

First Da Capo Press edition 1998

This Da Capo Press paperback edition of *American Silent Film*
is an unabridged republication of the edition first published
in New York in 1978, with three textual emendations. It is
reprinted by arrangement with Oxford University Press.

Published by Da Capo Press, Inc.
A Subsidiary of Plenum Publishing Corporation
233 Spring Street, New York, N.Y. 10013

Manufactured in the United States of America

To James Whale,
a director who never made a silent film,
but whose great love of the silents,
coupled with a unique approach to filmed theatre,
made him one of the supreme visual
and dramatic stylists of the Thirties

Acknowledgments

Especially grateful thanks are extended to James Card, George Eastman House, Rochester, Alex Gordon, Jacques Ledoux of the Royal Film Archive, Belgium, for their invaluable help in making rare prints available for screening, and to Kevin Brownlow for the loan of some outstanding stills from his collection.

And to the following film-makers, players, and scholars, my thanks for their patience and generosity of time and, in certain cases, the loaning of key stills: Lillian Gish, Blanche Sweet, Viola Dana, King Vidor, Henry King, Ben Carré, Paul Killiam of the D. W. Griffith Estate, Arthur Lennig, Richard Koszarski, David Bradley, and Michael Stolar.

Contents

1

A Survey

As if aware that future chroniclers would want to deal in neatly packaged periods of time, with traceable progressions of titles and dates,
the history of the motion picture conveniently managed to slice itself
up into a series of ten-year dynasties. Moreover, it even had the foresight to see that its key innovations and structural changes occurred
within the year prior to the beginning of a new decade—so that 1910,
1920, 1930, and 1940 could launch themselves without fumbling or
hesitation, their new image already fully formed. We are perhaps too
close to the fifties and sixties to extend that generalization to those
years as well, but it is an uncanny coincidence that it was the ninth
year of each preceding decade that produced the artistic, technological,
or commercial developments that were to shape and dominate the coming ten years.

In 1909, two short films by David Wark Griffith—*A Corner in Wheat*
(with its social criticism) and *The Lonely Villa* (with its advanced editing patterns)—laid the early blueprints for the full flowering of
Griffith's art with *The Birth of a Nation* and *Intolerance* a few years
later.

1929 was the year of the changeover to the sound film, a year in
which a whole new grammar of film had to be evolved.

And in 1939, following years of increasing Hays Office pandering to
"family entertainment" and rigid adherence to Production Code rules,
the movies suddenly took themselves in hand again. Such 1939 films as

John Ford's *Stagecoach* and Lewis Milestone's *Of Mice and Men* regained for the movies an adult stature that they had unknowingly renounced, and led us into 1940—and the films of Orson Welles and Preston Sturges.

But no one year planted and nourished so many seeds of change as did 1919. In that year, what was already big business began to be transformed into giant industry. Movies had already been grudgingly admitted to be "art"; now they were determined to prove that they were. Stars who had been happy to entertain their fans with perhaps four or five medium-length films a year now became impresarios in full charge of their own productions, determined to stagger audiences with only two (and soon, just one) productions annually, blockbusters of outsize proportions and length.

D. W. Griffith, who had wrought the screen's formal masterpiece *Intolerance* in 1916, but who had slipped somewhat thereafter, regained all his former glory with the unexpected commercial and artistic success of *Broken Blossoms*, the first genuinely poetic film. In Germany, Robert Wiene prepared the expressionistic *The Cabinet of Dr. Caligari*, and while its impact on American audiences and filmmakers would not be felt until its release in the United States in 1921, it obviously influenced other German directors. And the sophistication it gave contemporary German cinema would in turn have a marked effect on the content, if not the style, of the Hollywood film of the early twenties.

D. W. Griffith, Mary Pickford, Douglas Fairbanks, and Charles Chaplin, who had all been in nominal control of their films for some years but were in varying degrees employees of small or lesser companies, joined forces in 1919 to form United Artists, to give themselves total artistic freedom and greater profits. The smaller companies that had pioneered the industry's first twenty years had fallen by the wayside; Biograph, Edison, Lubin, Triangle, Essanay, and Thanhouser were no more.

Although there would never be stars bigger than Chaplin, Pickford, and Fairbanks (whose world-wide mass appeal was greater than the huge but more limited appeal of such later figures as Rudolph Valentino and Greta Garbo), the star system was still very much on the increase, fed by the fan magazines who not only helped create stars but frequently conducted polls among the fans to ascertain who all the current stars were. (Some of those early polls would be surprising today, with now almost forgotten names like Bessie Barrisdale and Dorothy Dalton constantly heading the popularity lists.) The stars names were used to sell movies, and the stars knew it, their salary requirements even then threatening to become the curse of the economy of film-making. Directors, too, had definite box-office standing, though it was usually achieved not so much through a recognition of artistic ability as though the demonstrated ability to turn out guaranteed audience-pleasing films. Thus, the names of Griffith, Cecil B. deMille, Maurice Tourneur, Rex Ingram, and Herbert Brenon meant both prestige and dollars and cents. Not until the late fifties, when movies became intellectually "in," and the Godards and the Truffauts joined such commercially reliable directors as Alfred Hitchcock and Cecil B. deMille, did the name of the film's director mean as much to the public—and to the box office—as it did during the twenties.

Because of their expanding length, increased physical size, and a sometimes smug awareness of their own importance and sophistication, the films of the twenties gradually and systematically took on a distinct physical "look." If one had to sum up this difference in a single factor, *lack of pacing* would be the choice. With certain obvious exceptions, the films of the twenties tended to slow down more and more as the decade wore on. They moved literally at a snail's pace by the end of the silent era, in sharp contrast to the speed of the earlier films.

The average film of the pre-1920 period was much shorter, five or six reels being deemed normal and acceptable for the average non-deluxe attraction. The tendency then was more to stories of movement: the acrobatic comedies of Fairbanks, the vehicles of Mary Pickford, which —whether comic, sentimental, or melodramatic—invariably packed in a maximum of plot and incident; the westerns of William S. Hart and Tom Mix. Furthermore, with the proven value of Griffith's innovative cutting techniques (the stupendous financial success of *The Birth of a Nation* was in itself sufficient "proof"), directors who had hitherto kept their cameras nailed to the floor and had rarely broken up scenes into successions of long, medium, and close shots, suddenly (and often pointlessly) strove to copy Griffith's style. The result was that films made between 1916 and 1919 really *moved*. As characters were introduced, there might be sudden flashbacks or cutaways to fill the audience in on their past life or to explain their association with other plot

Marguerite Snow

Photos of
Moving Picture Players
ON POSTCARDS

Price 25 cts. for 12 (assorted), by mail, postpaid

E. P. Sullivan

All the Most Popular Actors and Actresses

A complete set consists of about 175 of the most celebrated people in Moving Pictures, who play in the following companies: American, Keystone, Reliance, Solax, Thanhouser, Majestic, Kay-Bee, Comet, Biograph, Edison, Essanay, Kalem, Lubin, Pathé, Méliès, Selig, Vitagraph, 101 Bison, Gem, Rex, Powers, Crystal, Imp, Victor, Eclair, Nestor, Monopol and Pilot.

The cards are made of the best quality cardboard, are printed in sepia, and beautifully glazed.   The portraits are the latest and best of each player, and are true likenesses.

AMONG THE PLAYERS ARE

Mary Pickford, Henry Walthall, Mary Fuller, Marc McDermott, Alice Joyce, Carlyle Blackwell, Dolores Cassinelli, Frank Bushman, Octavia Handsworth, Paul Panzer, Ormi Hawley, Arthur Johnson, Kathleen Williams, Hobart Bosworth, Edith Storey, John Bunny, Edgena de Lespine, Irving Cummings, Pauline Bush, Warren Kerrigan, Virginia Westbrook, Herbert Rice, Mabel Normand, Fred Mace, Peggy Reid, John Adolphi, Blanche Cornwall, Darwin Karr, Mignon Anderson, James Cruze, King Baggot, Jane Fearnley, Mona Darkfeather, Virginia Chester, Pearl White, Chester Barnett, Mildred Brackan, William Ehfe, Barbara Tennant, Alex R. Frances, Louise Glaum, William Clifford, Florence Lawrence, Owen Moore, Marian Leonard, Billy Quirk, Elsie Albert, Edwin August, and a host of others equally as well known.

Do not fail to get a set of these pictures for your postcard album, the walls of your den, or to mail to your friends.

ADDRESS

HENRY LANG, 1815 Centre Street, Brooklyn, N. Y.

Billy Quirk

Alice Inward

characters. Love scenes would be broken up as the camera cut away to a pastoral vignette, a symbolic aside (the villain's thus-far hidden intentions might be telegraphed by a cut to closeup of a spider trapping a fly in its web), or reaction shots from other parties. Even the simplest shot would be covered from three or four angles, and in the editing stages the director, instead of selecting the best of the four takes, would use a portion of each. Action scenes—battles, chases, fights, last-minute rescues, flood, and fire—provided a logical reason for the creation of added suspense via skillful editing, and by intercutting between two parallel story-threads in the manner that had become so much of a Griffith trademark. The overall tendency in films of the pre-1920 years was to short scenes and many of them. Douglas Fairbanks, always much influenced by Griffith, sometimes outdid Griffith (and even the later Eisenstein) in the number and brevity of his shots. Fairbanks's 1917 western spoof *Wild and Woolly* moved at a fantastic pace, many shots running for no more than five frames. Even at the standard silent projection speed of 16 frames per second, his films raced and leaped, as was his intention. Shown today at the standard sound speed of 24 frames per second, they are frequently much too fast for detail of action to register.*

Speed of itself is not necessarily a virtue, but it was particularly suited to the kind of film being made in the teen years. And while a crackling pace can't hide a paucity of plot or a lack of directorial and acting talent, it can to a large degree compensate for it. It's hard not to be interested in a film that keeps on the move and constantly offers new and varied images. There were certainly many bad, naïve, and unimportant movies prior to 1920, but the proportion of *boring* movies must have been lower than in any period since!

With the twenties, the movies began to take themselves far more seriously. There was still a place for the western and the serial, but otherwise the physical action content of the average film grew less. Spectacle was on the increase, and massive sets and huge mobs were

* Strictly speaking there was no "standard" silent projection speed, but 16 frames per second is the "standard" speed imposed on that period by projection-machinery of the sound period. The majority of projectors were equipped to run at only one of two extremes: 24 frames per second for sound film, the speed necessary for accurate rendition of the sound track, and the arbitrary 16 frames for silents. However, *most* silents could be at least adequately run at one of those two speeds, or with utilization of *both* speeds.

considered best exploited in long shots which enabled the audience to see it all at a glance. (D. W. Griffith, it should be emphasized, did not fall into this new line of filmic thinking.)

Comedy, at the very beginning of the twenties, was at an awkward impasse, for Keaton, Chaplin, and Lloyd had still not made the transfer from shorts to features. Thus, the best sight-gag comedy was still to be found in the two-reeler, and a kind of unwritten snobbism decreed that it should remain there. Feature comedies were built more around situations than gags, and the almost desperate determination to keep physical-action gags out of them imposed an unnatural restraint, especially since this was before the importation of Germany's Ernst Lubitsch and the mining of Hollywood's rich veins of supplementary comedy: satire, farce, and romantic comedy.

This gradual slowing down of pace was by no means limited to the Hollywood film, although its effects are more obvious there. It is interesting, however, that European cinema too—and especially the cinema of Germany, Italy, and Great Britain—came to the end of the silent era on a parallel footing with Hollywood, making exactly the same kind of films, identical in content, directorial style, and self-indulgence in technique for its own sake. Undoubtedly this is partly due to those countries having copied successful Hollywood formulas; but it also points to the fact that other national cinemas experienced the same growing pains, perfecting their art almost to a point of stagnation.

In Hollywood, the slowing down of movie pace meant a temporary abandoning of much of the film grammar that had been built up in the preceding years, and especially the use of the moving camera. Even when Griffith had achieved such dynamic results in *The Birth of a Nation* by placing his camera on a truck to shoot running close-ups of galloping horsemen, there had been some critical protests. More than one reviewer regarded it as an arty trick, and claimed that such angles dispelled the carefully built-up realism, because the audience, now participant rather than spectator, was instantly made aware of the presence of the camera. At a time when the function of film editing was not properly understood, the criticism was more reasonable than it must seem today. In any event, the idea of shooting from a truck rapidly became standard in the grammar of film, especially in the chase scenes of westerns. The intelligent use of the moving camera for dramatic emphasis in non-action scenes also became standard. Much later in the twenties, and particularly after its over-emphasized use in several critically acclaimed German films, the pendulum swung to the other extreme, and Hollywood became obsessed by a need to move the camera constantly. Naturally, the moving camera was a valuable tool to directors like Griffith and (later) Alan Crosland and Michael Curtiz, to whom style and form were more important than content. Directors like Erich von Stroheim and Charles Chaplin, who were more interested in what they said than in how they said it, used the moving camera sparingly. Yet its effectiveness, when they chose to use it, demonstrates that they certainly understood the device and knew when it would work for them.

With the lessened use of the moving camera and of editing rhythms, the films of the early twenties concentrated more on beauty of camerawork and lighting—a beauty enhanced by the skilled utilization of tints and tones† and by the increased and soon perfected use of gauzes, filters, and glass shots.‡ Photographically, the film was at its height in the twenties, achieving a clarity and beauty which were to disappear with the coming of sound, and which would never—as a general standard, at least—be regained. It cannot be stressed too strongly that the sound motion picture was an entirely different medium from the silent motion picture, and not merely the extension of it. The difference between the two media is literally the difference between painting and

---

† At least until the late twenties, the black-and-white silent film was a rarity. A rich amber was the standard color, and to this were added different color stocks for appropriate moods or effects: green for scenes of terror, blue for night scenes, red for fire scenes, and often subtle combinations of stock. All of this was a matter of routine for the *average* film, apart from the constant experimenting in actual color photography and the hand-tinting of prints.

‡ What we term "optical effects"—variations of trick photography that are today almost entirely produced in special laboratories—were, in the silent period, shot *in* the camera during the course of normal production. Such work was slowly and painstakingly done, and was usually quite superior to equivalent work done by mattes and superimpositions in optical houses today. The glass shot was one of the major visual devices perfected by the cameramen of the twenties. It consisted of painting a foreground or background establishing material (a castle, a forest, a panorama of town and countryside) on glass placed in front of the camera lens. The actors, placed in correct perspective, would then be photographed through the glass, and the resulting perfect illusion would, for example, show them galloping up a long country road to a huge castle. Such scenes were not only flawlessly composed but also were rock steady and infinitely more satisfying than the back projection technique which largely supplanted the glass shot in the sound era.

photography, and the frequent unreality—or stylized reality—of much of the camerawork of the silent film was, artistically, one of its greatest assets. But this pictorial beauty became an end in itself, too. It pampered the vanity of stars who could monopolize the screen in long-held filtered close-ups, and it resulted in a plethora of theatrical scenes in which prolonged exchanges of dialogue (via subtitles) were played out against meticulously lit sets, usually in medium or long shot, as on a stage, and in which even action and spectacle were often presented as a series of tableaux.

Through the twenties, the virtuosity of the purely pictorial aspect of film increased steadily, reaching its apex in 1927 and 1928 with such films as F. W. Murnau's *Sunrise* and Josef von Sternberg's *Docks of New York*. It is this dominance of pictorial perfection that causes the films of the twenties to be something of an enigma. For quite certainly, the overall standards of the American film—both as entertainment and as art—were higher in the twenties than in any other period. It is in the twenties that we find the largest concentration of permanent classics of the American screen: Murnau's *Sunrise*, Stroheim's *Greed*, King Vidor's *The Big Parade* and *The Crowd*, Herbert Brenon's *A Kiss for Cinderella*, Griffith's *Isn't Life Wonderful?* and *Orphans of the Storm*, John Ford's *The Iron Horse* and *Four Sons*, Frank Borzage's *Seventh Heaven*, and so many others, to say nothing of the incredible comedy output from Buster Keaton, Charles Chaplin, Harold Lloyd, Harry Langdon, and Laurel and Hardy, and some of the best and most lavishly produced work of such impresario/stars as Mary Pickford, Douglas Fairbanks, and William S. Hart. To the student, coming fresh to the history of cinema, the twenties invariably seem overwhelming. The artistry, the size, the sheer variety—and, at the other but no less important end of the scale, the determination to entertain and give the customer his money's worth—is so stimulating that the twenties seem a treasure trove from which we may be retrieving gems for years to come.

Yet as one becomes more familiar with these ten years of peak film-making, one becomes strangely jaded. Nothing can ever dim the luster of the genuine masterpieces, whether *Sunrise* or Laurel and Hardy's two-reel comedy *Big Business*. But in view of the tremendous quantitive and qualitative output of those years, the percentage of truly great films is perhaps smaller than one would expect, given the technical mastery of film which had been achieved so early. As the twenties proceed, one finds a kind of standard formula being applied more and more; often this can be recognized instantly as a studio signature. Paramount, for example, was notoriously economy-conscious, often reducing the more exciting potentials to mere programmer level.§ MGM went to the opposite extreme, often spending a small fortune doctoring or remaking a completed film so that it would look exactly like an earlier successful film on the same subject. Fox seemed to have an obsession (not always misdirected) with sending the customer home happy, often tacking on spectacular wrap-up reels of action or melodrama to films that were managing very nicely without them. For all of their skill and production luxury, the entire group of silent Greta Garbo vehicles is without one *outstanding* production in a purely aesthetic sense. The tremendously successful Lon Chaney films, especially those done in collaboration with director Tod Browning, are vehicles in every sense of the word—the overlapping of incident and characters, and the repetition of plot content being extraordinary. Long unseen films from the prestigious directors of the twenties—James Cruze, King Vidor, Henry King, Rex Ingram—invariably prove disappointing as they become available again. They are skilled, slick, and yet somehow lifeless, adding nothing to our knowledge of those directors' works, and if anything, detracting from their reputations. One notable exception to this generalization is John Ford, the bulk of whose silent work has been missing for four decades. During that time, all that was available for general study (and only at archives, museums, and film societies) was his 1924 western epic *The Iron Horse*, while *Four Sons* (1928) was known to exist and had one or two occasional showings at archives only. Thus, one of the most prolific (and formulative) periods of one of America's finest directors has been a virtual blank; it is as though all that remained of Griffith was *Way Down East*. Fortunately, preservation and archival restoration programs in the latter 1960's uncovered most of Ford's silent work—long claimed by uninterested studios to

§ Though the term "programmer," a trade description, is more related to the films of the thirties, nevertheless it certainly applied to many Paramount films of the twenties. A programer lies midway between a "B" picture and an "A" picture. It is short and economical, but usually is just long enough or possessed of sufficient plot, star, or other values to find its own level in a theatrical program—as a support, as a co-feature, as a top-of-the-bill feature, or as a solo feature, depending largely upon the location of the theatre and the type of film.

have been destroyed in convenient fires. The rediscoveries included Ford's first feature, *Straight Shooting* (1917), his first film for Fox, *Just Pals* (1920), and such truly stunning (and totally forgotten) works as *Hangman's House* (1928).

When we are stimulated with the joy of discovery from some long unseen film of the twenties, it invariably proves to be a commercially unimportant one, or one made away from the formularized limits of a major studio. Stroheim's *The Merry Widow,* made for MGM, is an academically interesting but somewhat boring work, inflated and over-rated by virtue of its notoriety and its alleged "butchering" by the studio. But Stroheim's subsequent *The Wedding March,* made independently for Paramount release, and unexpectedly made available for study in the mid-1960's, is an incredible film: passionate, poignant, sophisticated in its use of the film-maker's tools, and quite possibly Stroheim's finest film, even if of less historic importance than *Greed.*

Universal Studios, a bread-and-butter company that rarely aimed at prestige works, was uncommonly successful in avoiding formula. Many of its films, considered little more than programmers in their day, stand the test of time remarkably well, not only because they have such human qualities and so effortlessly reflect the spirit and day-to-day living of their times, but because Universal freed its directors from assembly-line requirements. Standouts among Universal films of the twenties are *Smouldering Fires,* a beautifully acted (Pauline Frederick, Laura La-Plante) and directed (Clarence Brown) film that is human, under-played, and unobtrusively cinematic, with a plot that at MGM would doubtless have been turned into predictable soap opera; *Skinner's Dress Suit,* William Seiter's charming, witty, and still valid comment on family life, bread-winning, and "keeping up with the Joneses" in the social swim of the jazz age; and *The Cat and the Canary,* Paul Leni's Germanic, highly stylized, and quite definitive "old house" chiller.

The eternally frustrating aspect of the film output of the twenties is that we know there cannot be many more (if any) formal masterpieces awaiting rediscovery, nor is there much more time available for re-covery. The intensive preservation crusades by U.S. and world-wide archives quite certainly unearthed all the sizable caches of lost films, which still face the expensive procedure of copying for preservation. James Cruze's highly regarded *Beggar on Horseback* was one of the films thus saved—at least in part, for some of it had already deterio-

rated. But from the almost consistent stolidity and disappointment
which mark Cruze's work in this, his most prolific and acclaimed period
(*The Covered Wagon, The Pony Express, Old Ironsides, The City
Gone Mad*)—all 1923–26—one had the right to expect from *Beggar on
Horseback* notable content but rather dull execution—and this proved
to be very much the case. But against such disappointments, one can
fall back on films like *Smouldering Fires* or William K. Howard's notable *White Gold* (1927), a film that predates and blueprints the better-
known and bigger productions *The Wind* (by Victor Seastrom) and
City Girl (by Murnau).

Most of the *obviously* important films of 1921 (to take a date at random) are still with us: Fairbanks's *The Three Musketeers*, Germany's
The Cabinet of Dr. Caligari, and France's *J'Accuse* (both of these
European films were made earlier, but their U.S. release was delayed
until 1921), Chaplin's *The Kid*, and such lesser-known but still notable
films as Mary Pickford's *Through the Back Door* and William deMille's
Miss Lulu Bett. Yet a thorough perusal of one of the trade papers of
1921 shows that no less than 525 films were released that year. (That
total includes a handful of foreign imports and reissues, and undoubtedly does not include a negligible number of independent films and
quickies that were never honored with a preview for the trade press.
The figure, however, is reliable enough as a guide to the number of
films issued that year.) Out of those 525 films, only about 50 are known
to exist today—the more important ones generally available throughout
the world's archives, but many of the others represented only by a
single print in a studio vault or in the hands of a private collector. Obviously one cannot be dogmatic about the number of surviving films:
undoubtedly some of the missing may be lying, mislabeled perhaps, in
an abandoned vault or in the attic of a retired projectionist. But even
if the number of known surviving prints were to be doubled, it would
still represent but a fraction of the films released in 1921. True, many of
them must have been dull little programmers, westerns, actioners, or
comedies of no great importance. Yet if only ten had the imagination
and style of *Smouldering Fires*, then clearly there will continue to be
some gaps in our knowledge of the films of the twenties. And these figures are for but *one year*. The story is repeated every year, although
from 1925 on the proportion of salvaged and preserved films is, happily, somewhat higher.

Rather than bemoan the hundreds of missing film, perhaps we should thank a providence that has—despite incredible carelessness and almost criminal intentional obliteration on the part of Hollywood—preserved so much of the cinema of the twenties for us. Certainly we can trace highlights and trends, follow the careers of directors and stars, acknowledge the masterpieces and failures, and perhaps shatter a few myths. But while the history of the world is relatively safe from the sudden discovery of evidence that will cast new light on the achievements of Hammurabi or Alexander the Great, the much younger history of the film is always liable to reassessment through the reappearance of a single print. How could one attempt an evaluation of the American western without seeing *Law and Order* (1932), or of the pitfalls and achievements of the earliest days of sound without an intimate knowledge of Rouben Mamoulian's 1929 film *Applause?* Yet both of these films remained virtually unknown—too unknown even to be called forgotten—right through the thirties and forties.

No historian enjoys being proven wrong in his opinions or the completeness of his facts, but it would be nice to hope that the following chapters could be drastically revised twenty years hence, due to an interim discovery of films now lost.

2
The Beginnings

The movies began to flourish in America in the wake of the world-wide (though essentially British) Industrial Revolution, and while throughout the rest of the world movies were at least partially in the hands of the dreamers and the pioneer artists/inventors, in America from the very beginning the movies were an *industry*, firmly controlled by the businessmen. Well before the first Nickelodeon opened in 1905, the industry was trying to crush or minimize competition via lawsuits and injunctions, a modus operandi used increasingly as the industry grew and flourished. So active and complex is this aspect of movie industry history that a volume or two could easily be devoted to the legal battles involving infringements of rights, with additional volumes devoted to court cases involving censorship.*

The mechanical beginnings of the movies take us into an area of archaeology rather than history. If one passes by the *accepted* beginnings of the theory of illustrated motion—the old cave-man drawings in which multiple movements have been drawn for the legs—the tech-

---

* Throughout the history of the industry and right up to the present day, which can boast some outstanding practitioners of the art, many distributors, armed with partial rights to contestable properties, have garnered most of their income not from the exhibition of films, but from lawsuits against and settlements from others who claim rights in the same property. With copyright law as complicated and ambiguous as it is, especially in relation to film, it has proven a profitable field for some, and especially to the lawyers who have reaped rich harvests in fees whether they won or lost!

nique of movies began in 1640, with the development of the magic lantern. For some two hundred years, attempts were made to create an illusion of movement by combining the persistence of vision with a series of still pictures, via such devices as the Zoetrope, the Kinematoscope, the Phasmatrope, and many kindred inventions—most of which can be seen and operated in film museums and archives throughout the world. Except for the comic-strip-related consecutive pictures projected by the magic lantern, none of these devices sought to tell a story, but were content to convey either the illusion of reality or the illusion of movement—a busy square in daytime, suddenly transformed into a brilliantly lit night-time scene, with pinpoints of light against a blue sky; or (through the slit in the Zoetrope) the impression of a man continuously running and jumping, or of a bird flying. These were, and are, charming devices, imaginative in concept and delightful in execution, but essentially rich men's toys, designed for utilization by an individual, or at best a small group.

The first apparent breakthrough came in 1877, just two years after Alexander Graham Bell's invention of the telephone, with the still photography of horses in motion by Eadweard J. Muybridge. Actually, time and legend have been unusually kind to Muybridge, suggesting that he pioneered and persevered for years until he achieved success. To win a bet, Governor Leland Stanford of California wanted to prove that at some point in their stride, horses had all four hooves off the ground at the same time. Willing to back his convictions with cash, Stanford hired photographer Muybridge to provide visual proof. Muybridge, however, was not a particularly innovative man; his idea of shooting a series of consecutive still pictures proved difficult to carry out. Moreover, he was out of circulation for some time, due to his involvement in a murder trial. He was accused of shooting his wife's lover, and there was no doubt that he performed the deed. Nevertheless he was adjudged Not Guilty, disappeared for some time, and finally surfaced in time to renew his experiments for Stanford. The hiatus had brought no further inspiration, however, and the problem was solved only when John D. Isaacs, the chief engineer for the Southern Pacific Railroad, was brought in to study it. Knowing nothing of photography but a good deal about elementary physics and mechanics, he rigged up a system of magnetic releases to trigger a series of cameras. The system worked, and after having spent almost the amount that Griffith would later pour into *The Birth of a Nation,* Stanford had his visual proof and won his bet. Elated, Muybridge claimed credit for the success that had eluded him so long, and promptly took to the road—and the campus circuit—with the pictures, which he adapted to the Praxinoscope, the Zoetrope, and other "projection" devices. The series of still photographs were so close to motion that one would have assumed Muybridge would be tempted to explore further. However, he seemed quite content with the limited success (with Isaacs's spectacular help) he had achieved. To the initial horses he added elephants, dogs, cats, goats—and people. If he wasn't a visionary, he was certainly a showman; most of his people were totally and explicitly nude. Admittedly, there was genuine educational value in shots which showed clearly how the human body functioned as it ran, jumped, climbed, or played tennis. Nevertheless, the total exposure of the human body in what was still literally the Victorian era must have been decidedly startling. One cannot help feeling that Muybridge used his naked men and women as a come-on, the academic nature of his presentations providing a censor-proof front of respectability.

The one possibly cinematic spark in Muybridge's work was his occasional use of a skeleton figure, shot in a form of stop motion. But the very small percentage of such material suggests that Muybridge found it a lot of extra and unnecessary work, since audiences seemed fascinated with his fat elephants and plump ladies. There were some brief flurries of interest in a collaboration between Muybridge and Thomas Edison, with the intention of synchronizing sound with the pictures. There was no indication on Edison's part that he was aware of the possibilities of the pictures actually moving. Edison's own experiments with film began seriously in 1887, two years after Friese-Green had begun his experimental work in Great Britain. By 1889, Edison had perfected his Kinetograph and Kinetoscope. He was able to shoot movies and then show them on a combined projection-viewing machine, which limited viewing to a single person on a peep-show basis. Even when a number of the machines were assembled side by side in a parlor, the "audience" was obviously still very restricted. Even this initial development did not take place until 1894, indicating that even as a novelty, the movies were slow in catching on. The movies shown in the Kinetoscope parlors were very brief, often running no more than a few seconds. Even with the rapid customer turnover such brevity could produce, it was too cumbersome and limited a framework ever to become big business.

The major breakthrough came on April 23, 1896, at the Koster and Bial's Music Hall in New York City, when a few brief movies were shown on a large screen. They were cunningly selected, showing not only that the movies could *duplicate* the stage by the inclusion of some typical vaudeville acts, but also that they could do things that the stage could not—illustrated via travel scenes and seascapes. Above all, the presentation demonstrated the movie's need for audience: the *shared* wonder at the seeming magic of the movies, and the *shared* laughter at the comedy material, created an exhilaration that the single-viewer Kinetoscope could never hope to achieve. The Kinetoscope would remain as a peep-show novelty, especially in amusement arcades at seaside resorts, but the movies would now find their real home before increasingly large audiences: first in converted stores, then in small Nickelodeons, and finally in full-scale theatres, initially converted from theatrical houses and then constructed especially for movies. All of this, of course, took a great deal of time. The biggest audiences for the movies were provided by the vaudeville houses. The managers used the movies both to pad programs and as "chasers" to expedite turnover and prevent audiences from sitting through key acts again. It is a matter of record that key audiences for the new movies were the vast numbers of immigrants who had come to America. They learned about their new country—even to read, in some cases—from the movies. Yet as the first theatres came to be built, they were not built in the ghettos where these audiences proliferated. They were built in the better areas, and the ghetto audiences had to go to them. The indications are that from the very beginning, the businessmen had faith in the soundness of the *exhibition* side of the business, even if they could not anticipate the enormous financial and artistic advances of the *production* side.

With ten cents as the standard admission price—and in non-metropolitan areas often only five cents—the movies quickly established themselves as the cheapest form of mass entertainment, even though they were selling novelty rather than genuine or even prolonged entertainment and the vaudeville houses gave greater value for money. Nevertheless, producers of mass consumer goods (whisky, bicycles) seized on the movies as a means of publicizing their wares, and either financed commercials or contrived to have their product and its name brand prominently displayed in films. Another off-shoot of the interest in movies was a novelty introduced at the St. Louis Exposition of 1903 and eventually used as a traveling attraction across the country, a big money-maker for more than a year before the novelty of movies wore off. Hale's Tours, as the attraction was named, after its devisor, George Hale, consisted of a miniature movie theatre in the shape of a railroad coach. Using movies shot from a moving train, and projected onto a screen in front, Hall took his customers on scenic tours. Since the guard delivered a commentary and the train bell clanged frequently, sound was added to the presentation. Moreover, the little theatre rocked in simulated railroad motion, anticipating somewhat the special effect of "Sensurround" that was introduced in the 1970's. Max Ophuls's 1948 film *Letter from an Unknown Woman* contains a charming reconstruction of an immediate predecessor of Hale's Tours, in which painted backgrounds—the forerunner of the back projection screen—were rolled past the carriage windows. Interestingly enough, the idea was retained in Great Britain—always rather charmingly behind the times—through the thirties and forties as a special attraction in big department stores at Christmas time. Children and their parents would pay a small sum to enter a train, boat, or covered wagon "set" and be rocked or lurched through a tour of the Arctic or the Old West (sometimes shown via movies, though usually by the more economical and practical means of moving painted scenery). At the end of the journey, which usually took about five minutes, they would alight, to be met by Santa Claus and handed a small gift.

If the movies were a novelty, they were also a stunt, from the very beginning capitalizing on the kind of shock and sensation that could not be presented on stage. It can be argued that *The Kiss* (1896) was derived from the stage—and even used the original players, John Rice and May Irwin. However, the fact that only the kiss itself was used from the original play, and was done in a close two-shot for added intimacy, indicated that even this early there was the realization that actual or implied salaciousness could be box-office. The short film was considered provocative enough to bring demands for censorship. Undressing scenes occupied a surprising amount of screen time, as did violence—ranging from staged reconstructions of beheadings, assassinations, and executions to such films as Edison's *Electrocution of an Elephant,* which is exactly what it claims to be. This is a grisly piece of footage more because we *know* it is real than because of what it actually shows.

American cinema of 1896–1906 was actually far less enterprising than French cinema, which was unquestionably in the lead in terms of vitality and inventiveness. Both British and American cinema, the latter based largely in New York, were strongly influenced by the French, but in a surprisingly haphazard manner. The British did better than the Americans in imitating the semi-surreal street chases and comedies of the French. The strongest French influence on American cinema was via Mack Sennett and was delayed until *The Curtain Pole* (1909),† from which a direct line of French farce can be traced through to its initial climax in the first American feature-length comedy, *Tillie's Punctured Romance* (1914). There was a sense of exhilaration in the French films of the period, a delight in their own magic, a pride in the beauty that could be achieved via hand coloring and set design, and an almost mischievous determination to use the cinema to create the impossible. Even though America had no magical or comic genius to rival France's Georges Méliès, it could have copied his ideas. Instead it chose to duplicate the actual prints and "pirate" them around as original creations. The American attempts to copy Méliès's flair were limited to simple camera tricks and did not include the magical story-lines. Edison did some interesting work with animated titles, in which the letters, shot in stop-motion, re-arranged themselves on the screen, perhaps most interestingly in *The Dam Family* (1905), a visualization of a popular song. It was an amusing doggerel, designed to titillate with its rerefences to "the whole Dam family . . . and the Dam dog" and its thumbing-of-the-nose at censorship. Far more interesting than the animated titles, however, was the fact that the whole film was virtually a series of close-ups of the family, many of them framed by an iris. This was another example of a grammatical device being used because it was the *logical* mode of presentation. There was no awareness that the close-up, so effective here, could work just as well in another context.

If there was one common denominator to these films, it had two related aspects. First, movement itself was almost enough, so that there was no *need* to exploit comic or dramatic material. The result was

† See chapter 12, "Comedy."

that potentially very funny material was at best mildly amusing. Second, given the stress on movement, as many films as possible were shot outdoors. This not only gave rise to the chase (initially, in American films, more melodramatic than comic) as a movie staple but also led to the utilization of intensely cinematic devices in shooting those chases. *A Desperate Encounter Between Burglars and Police* is fully explained by its title. It is a street chase that concludes with a fight in a basement, and the editing is quite crisp in keeping it nicely on the move. *Bicycle Police*, made in 1905, only a year or two after New York City had instituted its motor-cycle police force, tells its story in only three shots. The first is an establishing shot showing the rescue of a little girl from the path of a reckless driver, and the last the arrest of the driver in the vicinity of Grant's Tomb. The intervening shot, and the bulk of the film, is a long, smoothly executed tracking shot up Riverside Drive, the camera mounted on a car to follow the bicycle police, who in turn are following the reckless motorist.

Interestingly, the tracking shot *from the rear* seemed to be accepted early and quite readily as a kind of documentary shot, allowing the viewer to be a casual witness to an apparently unstaged event. Putting the camera in front, however, though far more dramatic, automatically told the viewer that this was "staged" and therefore "unreal." This convention lasted for many years. In Great Britain, Cecil Hepworth, Griffith's predecessor and a remarkable, instinctive filmic narrator, made a fine little period drama, *John Gilpin's Ride*, in 1907. For the basic ride, a camera car was brought into play. However, it remained resolutely to the rear of the horse, whose nether portions, bobbing up and down before the camera, were far less dramatic than his head—flaring nostrils, flying mane—and the determined face of its rider would have been. Griffith certainly didn't *invent* the tracking shot, but he did recognize its potential and never wasted it by shooting from the back.

A further variation on the chase was *The Interboro Subway*, a newsreel made in 1904 to cover the opening of New York's first subway—an event of more than just local importance, since subways in America were then in their infancy and even in England had been in use for only a few years. The event seems to have been partially staged, since the passengers who alight and embark are clearly actors, the best-dressed ones being directed to walk out of the frame and then back into it again. But the newsreel was obviously shot just before or just after the official opening of the subway, and the mechanics are quite interesting. The camera was placed on an open car following the train. On an adjacent track, another car was equipped with high-powered lights to illuminate the train in its underground journey. All three conveyances were synchronized to run at exactly the same speed, and the light truck was sufficiently hidden by the vertical pillars between the tracks for its presence to be concealed from the camera. The lighting throughout is excellent, the picture clear and steady, as the camera follows the train through New York's underground until it reaches Grand Central Station, discharges its passengers, and goes on its way.

Motion pictures could hardly have been perfected, photographically speaking, at a more propitious time. At the turn of the century, the world was changing in so many ways, and the movie camera was there to capture it all permanently—from the great events of the international scene to the seemingly less important ones: the changeover from the horse and buggy era to the mechanized one of the automobile; the arrival of immigrants at Ellis Island; the images of faces from the worlds of politics, show business, and the arts—Theodore Roosevelt, Boss Croker, Buffalo Bill Cody, Lillian Russell, Edison, Mark Twain, Leo Tolstoy, Émile Zola. In Europe the cameras were there to record—in frustrating long shot—Queen Victoria as she rode in her Jubilee Procession and, a little later, a sadder procession, her funeral. But a few years after that, a whole battery of cameras, much closer to the scene of action, was able to record the funeral procession of Victoria's successor, King Edward VII, with some thirty heads of state walking in homage in the cortège—the last time so many kings and emperors would gather together before the face of Europe was changed by World War I.

In 1901, a "newsreel" of San Francisco consisted of a long, almost uninterrupted journey down Market Street, photographed from the front of a trolley car. Since much of Market Street has survived intact until today, despite the devastation of the 1906 earthquake, this is a particularly useful record. And when the earthquake hit, Edison's cameramen were rushed to the scene to capture the destruction and the still burning wreckage. The Edison reel opened with close-ups of the front pages of newspapers with their dramatic headlines, and used them to segue right into the remarkable photographic coverage of the event: one news medium giving way to another. Only a year before, cameras had been sent to Galveston, Texas, to record the scenes of destruction following the great storm there; one memorable shot to emerge from it was a literally 360-degree pan encompassing the wrecked waterfront. Recognizing the commercial value of the newsreel—though the term itself was not yet in use—enterprising film-makers were not averse to staging and re-creating "news coverage" from such far-flung battle zones as Cuba or the Boer war in Africa, the sheer distances involved making "instant" coverage impossible in those days prior to air travel. Audiences, believing that the camera could not lie, had no trouble accepting New Jersey-filmed scenes of the Boer war, despite the apparently charmed lives of the cameramen, who positioned themselves dead center in the action and got unprecedented pictures of the ebb and flow of battle, both sides advancing and retreating right past the camera lens, with winners and losers alike often finding time to throw a cheery nod or smile, and mortally wounded soldiers expiring conveniently close to the camera. Even the famous Battle of Santiago Bay, filmed on a New York rooftop by Vitagraph's Albert E. Smith with the most obvious miniatures, with cigarette smoke puffed into the scene to simulate gun fire, was accepted in most quarters as authentic. But in the face of all the actual footage that *was* being shot across the nation, especially in New York and its environs, the faking (including the reconstruction of sporting events) was relatively minimal, and the footage of urban life—of people, places, things, fashions—is today a rich heritage of inestimable historical and sociological value.

Although history (and the movies, via Spencer Tracy's portrayal of the inventor) has tended to paint Thomas Alva Edison as a great humanitarian and dreamer with little eye or thought for business, his involvement with the young movie industry seems to indicate otherwise. By 1897, Edison was already instituting lawsuits to protect his patents. The American Mutoscope and Biograph Company, the company with which Griffith would ultimately work, was a particular target of his ire. Then as now, however, lawsuits were long, drawn-out, and expensive. After extensive litigation, the courts agreed that Edison could patent his camera—but established that since Biograph's camera worked on different principles, there was no infringement. Nor was his claim accepted that the film stock itself had been infringed. Despite this initial set-back, Edison continued to instigate lawsuits against competitors—

The Master Mind
of the Movies

❡ Movie Fans the world over owe a debt of gratitude to Carl Laemmle, President of the Universal Film Mfg. Co., known to every one in the business as the "Dean of Moving Pictures."

❡ Mr. Laemmle fought the moving picture monopoly known as the "Trust" and beat it to a standstill. He established the first Independent Moving Picture concern, the initials forming the name of the well-known and popular brand, the "IMP." The mammoth organization known as the Universal is the outgrowth of the original "IMP" Company. Everything Mr. Laemmle fought for was in the interest of MOVIE PATRONS and BETTER PICTURES.

❡ Mr. Laemmle established at a cost of over a million dollars the first moving picture city in the world, and the only regularly incorporated city entirely given over to the making of moving pictures. Mr. Laemmle was the first to put the two- and three-reel pictures in the regular program without extra cost. There are literally scores of things Mr. Laemmle has done for the movie fans—entirely too many to be even mentioned here.

❡ Mr. Laemmle's latest and greatest achievement is the placing of a great Broadway Star or a great Broadway Play on the regular Universal Program at so slight an advance in cost to the Exhibitor that every fan everywhere should demand these wonderful features from his favorite theatre manager. He can get them for you and he will if you insist. Watch the advertisements in this magazine for the names of the great actors and the great plays that appear under the brand "Broadway Universal Features"—then demand them at your favorite theatre.

UNIVERSAL FILM MANUFACTURING CO.
CARL LAEMME, President

"The Largest Film
Manufacturing Concern
in the Universe"

1600 BROADWAY, NEW YORK

whose numbers were growing daily—with the same negative results. In perhaps the earliest film industry application of the philosophy "If you can't lick 'em, join 'em," Edison decided to join forces with Biograph. They would form, not a business merger as such, but the spearhead of a combine to protect the established companies and force the newcomers either to kowtow or get out of the business. On September 9, 1908, the Motion Picture Patents Company was launched, with Vitagraph as another key member. Its modus operandi, though legal, was not unlike the "protection" rackets that provided the plot lines for countless gangster movies. The Patents Company, or the Trust, would issue licenses to produce films, using the inventions and devices that they had patented. Initially, ten companies—eight leading American companies and two foreign producers (of Italian and French films)—were granted licenses by the Trust. Not all of the companies came in enthusiastically, the Selig Polyscope Company having been an early loser in a court battle over infringement. These ten producing companies formed a virtual monopoly.

Eastman Kodak made a deal with the Trust, guaranteeing to supply raw film stock only to Trust members. Kodak, of course, was the basic source of supply for film stock. The Trust took in royalties from every phase of the business—from manufacturers of projectors and equipment, from distributors, and from exhibitors, and since Edison and Biograph were the principal stock-holders, they pocketed the lion's share of the very considerable profits. A decidedly unethical advertising campaign was conducted to ensure that exhibitors booked only Trust-controlled films, although the advertisement reproduced does suggest that exhibitors had a choice. In actuality, if exhibitors dealt with non-Trust distributors, they faced the very real possibility of having their licenses revoked. The industry practice of "checkers" was introduced: the man who checks on a distributor, or stands by a theatre box office to tabulate the business being done, to ensure that accounts submitted are honest and reliable. The Trust consolidated and expanded for approximately six years of power and during that period gained about six million dollars—a firm indication that the ten-cent admission ticket represented a huge financial potential. Most of the competitors of the Trust were forced out of business, as anticipated. Only the strongest—Carl Laemmle and, later William Fox—survived, ultimately to become far stronger than any of the Trust companies that collectively had sought to suppress them.

The Motion Picture Patents Company was a well-knit business monopoly, uninterested in the artistic development of film and concerned solely with gouging every possible dollar out of the trade. However, this attitude bred a certain amount of dissension from within. Certainly Griffith, working at Biograph, was unwilling to go along with the purely monetary concept of the film industry. Also, since the Trust—and their lawyers and checkers—were situated primarily on the East Coast, its existence definitely spurred the eventual move to the West Coast—not only to remove maverick or rebel producers from constant supervision but to allow them to beat a hasty retreat across the Mexican border, should litigation catch up with them.

The harm done by the Trust may have been considerable. It extended its influence over the entire formulative period of the *art* of movie-making, and because it promoted commerce before art, it literally made the development of that art somewhat of a monopoly too. Power was concentrated in the hands of one man, D. W. Griffith, who, perhaps fortuitously, *was* working for the Trust. On the other hand, while the Trust discouraged independence, it did successfully kill off many fly-by-night companies with mediocre rosters of talents. It maintained a competent if standardized level of performance, and was *not* strong enough to kill off fiercely determined individualists like Carl Laemmle, William Fox, and Mack Sennett, who bucked the Trust and ultimately won out. Too, by investigating all of the money-making aspects of the industry, the Trust established basic methods of operation which were either proven sound, and further developed in later years, or proven legally insupportable and jettisoned or revised.

3

The Birth of Film Grammar

By an incredible stroke of luck—the kind of luck that rarely smiles on the formulative years of any art or industrial process—the evolution of film language can be told through the work of two men, Edwin S. Porter and David Wark Griffith. In a sense, all of the pioneering work of the years 1903 to 1912 can be encapsulated in the films of these men: Griffith representing an instinctive and experimental approach to film-making, Porter (though it is extremely unfair to categorize him so simply) the mistakes and the caution. Moreover, these two men worked with companies (Griffith for Biograph, Porter for Edison) whose films not only represent extremes of both ambition and achievement but have also been well preserved. This preservation has to do with not only quality—much of the material now available for study is taken from the original 35mm negatives, and thus is fully representative of original pictorial quality and completeness—but also quantity. Virtually all of the key Biograph films seem to exist, and an astonishingly large cross section of the Edison films as well.

Since, in the early days of film, technical mastery was a prerequisite to artistic advance, it is reasonable to assume that most of the worthwhile films *had* to come from the bigger, better-established companies—which necessarily meant companies operating within the Motion Picture Patents Company. From its beginnings until its loss of power in 1915, the Patents Company at one time or another counted these producing companies among its members: General Film Company, American Biograph, Essanay, Edison, Kalem, George Klein, Lubin, Méliès Company, Pathé, Selig, and Vitagraph.

Obviously, one cannot discount work done by non-Patents Company studios. However, for the most part, these were undercapitalized, often transient and short-lived companies, enjoying none of the production advantages of the bigger companies or, because of the enforced exhibitor antagonism toward them, able to afford top talent. Even Carl Laemmle's IMP company, the most tenacious of the "rebel" companies, and ultimately the most successful when it evolved into Universal Studios in 1912, makes a singularly unimpressive showing with its surviving films. The Mary Pickford films it made are incredibly primitive, especially in comparison with the one-reelers Pickford had made earlier for Biograph. Of all the Patents Company affiliates, today *only* Biograph and Edison are represented by a major and reliable cross section of their output. Enough exists of Vitagraph product for us to assume that it was an exceptionally vigorous and adventurous company. Essanay can be judged only by the Chaplin shorts and the occasional surviving feature (all from a later period), and by the pitifully few early Broncho Billy Anderson westerns that survive. The early material from Kalem, Lubin, and Selig is almost as sparse. If Porter had chanced to work for Kalem and Griffith for Vitagraph, then our knowledge of early film history would be inadequate indeed.

However, no two companies could be more representative of the pre-1912* era than Edison and Biograph. For the Edison Company, financially successful and artistically unambitious, movies were merely an adjunct to and an off-shoot of such other Edison inventions as the electric light or the phonograph—and were ground out as efficiently and soullessly. Biograph in 1908, the year Griffith joined, was financially unsound. In fact, it had been taken over by J. J. Kennedy, an executive of the Empire Trust Company, who had decided to try to salvage the company as a way of recovering an otherwise irretrievable bank loan. It was Griffith's instinctive flair for film and narrative that did indeed put Biograph back on its feet and propelled it into a position of preeminence and leadership, despite the controls and frustrat-

---

* 1912 has been selected as the cut-off date for this consideration of early narrative film since that year marked the beginning of the changeover to the feature-length film of four to six reels.

ing restrictions placed upon Griffith by Kennedy and the other Biograph executives.

Nothing could illustrate better the Edison and Biograph approaches to narrative problems than their scripts. Once Griffith had established himself at Biograph, scripts were not used. He worked from original stories and synopses and bypassed the script process entirely, working intuitively. That there were certain shortcomings to this method cannot be denied. The action stories, depending on chase and the building of suspense via intercutting, tended to work much better—even from the beginning—than the purely dramatic stories, in which motives often seemed ambiguous or unexplained and climaxes often were flat. On the other hand, the script method at Edison tended to turn everything—chase film, mystery, romantic drama—into an assembly-line product, devoid of dramatic highs and lows, and with little or no direction. An Edison "script"—and they were all uniform—consisted of two or three letter-size sheets of paper, broken down into shots, each of which was given a line or two (at most) of description. There were two basic problems: a lack of communication in conveying the ideas of the original story through the script to the director, and a lack of imagination on the part of Edison's directors. Whoever took those original stories and broke them down into script form obviously felt that if he, she, or they understood the intent of the story, then such understanding would be automatic in their shot breakdown. This was the initial mistake; many key plot elements, and particularly character motivations, simply were lost between original synopsis and script. The second, and greater, mistake lay with the singularly uninspiring collection of Edison directors, who saw it as their function to *illustrate* the script rather than *develop* it. The scripts were no more than bare bones. They gave no indication of a character's motives or background, or how he should think or dress; they gave no hints as to how a set should look, or what mood the lighting should strive for. Finally, if the action described was to be accomplished via cuts and close-ups and changing of camera position, one would never know it from the script, which described every shot as though it were a forerunner of Hitchcock's ten-minute take. *Instinctive* directors like Griffith would have added bits of business—comic or pathetic—to round out the characters and reduce the tableau-like effect, and would have given thought to lighting, clothing, appropriate furniture, and the strategic use of extras. Extras and bit players were present in Edison films only to serve the needs of the narrative, never to provide atmosphere or a sense of casual reality. Strange characters would suddenly be introduced in a close-up, looking as bewildered as the audience. Already minimized suspense would be lessened further by titles that telegraphed the action before it actually happened. The lack of an editorial structure caused the films simply to end, when they had run their last scene, rather than build to a climax.

Edison film-makers also simplified their job by writing lengthy footage-eating titles into the narrative. Detective films were especially welcome, since they provided a logical excuse for questions and lengthy answers. In fairness, it must be admitted that this method was not restricted to Edison, and that many other small studios were turning out films equally obscure in narrative and equally lacking in drama. The annoying aspect of the Edison films was that they *looked* good: cleanly photographed, often with well-chosen locations, and sometimes replete with smoothly done dissolves and other effects. However, the talent roster was weighted far more in the direction of technical skills than creative ones. Far fewer noted talents came out of apprenticeship with Edison than with Biograph or, later, Ince. Since there were more players employed than directors or writers, one would assume a correspondingly greater proportion of notable graduate actors, but even here the ratio is disappointingly small. Only Viola Dana and Shirley Mason, sisters appearing under their decidedly non-marquee-oriented real name, Flugrath) became major stars. Others players, such as Robert Walker, Johnny Walker, Edward Earle, and Frank McGlynn achieved modest fame, but hardly compared with the Biograph graduates—Lillian and Dorothy Gish, Jack Mulhall, Lionel Barrymore, Harry Carey, Mary Pickford, Mae Marsh, Blanche Sweet, Henry B. Walthall, and so many others. Among directors, the single film acted in by D. W. Griffith and the scenarios written by Alan Crosland hardly constitute an "apprenticeship" which those later notable directors can ascribe to Edison. Indeed, until the mid-1970's, with the rediscovery of the totally forgotten John Collins,† one would have felt justified in claiming that

† John Collins, of whom much more when we reach the post-*Intolerance* years, joined the Edison Company in 1904 as an all-around handyman, whose duties for a while included those of casting director. Eventually he became a director for Edison, making some of their few really distinguished films before leaving to join Metro, which offered him far greater opportunities.

with the single exception of Edwin S. Porter, the Edison Studios never turned out a notable director, or even one above average.

Nor did the Edison films show the sense of dynamic progress that one gets from studying the Biograph films on a year-by-year basis. On the contrary, there is a sense of stagnation. In 1914, Edison made a rather charming short entitled *'Twas the Night Before Christmas,* obviously intended for Christmas week release, and concluding by wishing season's greetings to the theatre audience. It was a pleasing little tale about a boy who is dismayed that there is no one to fill Santa's stocking, and who, after hitching a ride on Santa's sleigh, contacts children from around the world—Italy, England, even Alaska—and persuades them to give the toy they all love best, as a surprise for Santa. It was a charming film in its own way, with simple but effective special effects and exceptionally good lighting in the scenes of Santa by the fireplaces, filling stockings. But if one places it side by side with an earlier (1906) Edison title *The Night Before Christmas,* the earlier film wins hands down, taking a far greater delight in its own magic and using extensive and very accomplished table-top miniature work of Santa and his reindeers traveling through the skies and over rooftops. Generally speaking, the earlier years produced by far the most interesting Edison films. It is frustrating that the directors of these films were usually not credited and frequently not listed in surviving company records.

One Edison film of 1904 might well lay claim to being the screen's first genuinely lyrical film, as well as one of the finest ever produced by the studio. Virtually unknown today, *The Land Beyond the Sunset* was produced with the collaboration of the Fresh Air Fund, a charitable group organized to take slum youngsters for outings in the country. (Edison was particularly fond of tie-ins with industrial groups, the Red Cross, and other organizations, and many of the resulting films have considerable documentary value today because of their location shooting in hospitals, factories, etc.). *The Land Beyond the Sunset* begins with officers of the Fresh Air Fund meeting to plan their next outing. We then see one of the most unfortunate of the slum children who has received an invitation. He is a boy in rags, who works hard in the streets of New York, selling papers and doing whatever odd jobs he can, to be rewarded with beatings from his drunken slattern of a mother. Knowing she would refuse him permission for the outing, he has to sneak away while she is in a drunken stupor. For once, the prosaic Edison script wound up in the hands of a director—or, more likely, cameraman/director—who had an eye for pictorial composition and who, since the bulk of the film takes place out of doors, seized the opportunity to frame his shots with both symmetry and beauty. The shots of the slum lad walking through the busy New York streets look almost like a modern counterpart of Dickens, and in view of the beauty and reality of the rest of the film, it is a pity that the shots of the children meeting at the station and going through the barrier to board their train are done with studio flats and a painted backdrop. Once into the country, however, the beauty, mixed with a sense of exhilaration, returns. The first shot is of an empty field, picturesque with flowers and trees; from behind the camera, the children suddenly rush into the frame, communicating a feeling of joy and wonderment. After several shots of the children enjoying themselves, a group of them settle down, to be told a story by the priest in charge of the outing. The camera dissolves to a re-enactment of the story: a little boy, mistreated and unhappy, is taken in hand by fairies, who place him in a boat and send him out to sea, to the land beyond the sunset, where he will know only peace and happiness. The story over, the priest collects his flock to return to the city. The slum boy elects to stay behind and eludes the priest all too easily; indeed, he is not even missed. (This was a weakness of so many early films: in trying to give the audience the "entire picture" within a single shot, and without cutting, it over-simplified and made unrealistic potentially dramatic or exciting scenes.) Alone, the youngster emulates the boy of the story: he finds an abandoned rowboat and pushes himself out to sea—to his death, but also to an escape from pain and cruelty in "the land beyond the sunset." These final shots are beautifully composed, the initial near-shore scenes framed by trees and foliage, the reflection of the moon glittering on the water. Furthermore, these scenes astonishingly pre-date the final scenes of Erich von Stroheim's *Greed*, in which the camera retreats farther and farther back from the lone figure of McTeague, awaiting death on the desert. Here, however, the situation is reversed: the camera stays in the same position on the sea shore, while in a series of cuts the boat is shown farther and farther out to sea, until it disappears into infinity. In Edison films such poetry was extremely rare, and even in the Griffith Biographs (such as *Lines of White on a Sullen Sea* or *The*

Mender of Nets) tended to be more a matter of outstanding individual compositions than an overall concept.

Edison's key cameraman/director, Edwin S. Porter, was to the American film what George Méliès was to the French—its first recognized director. *The Great Train Robbery* was far from being the film that "introduced narrative to the American screen," as has often been claimed, but in 1903, it was certainly the first American film in which a narrative structure (in this case, the classic western formula of crime, pursuit, and capture) was *recognized,* and in which the name of the director was acknowledged. Porter is one of the enigmas of the American screen. Had he capitalized on the success of *The Great Train Robbery,* investigating and expanding the story-telling methods he had used in that film, he might well have become a father of American film, assuming leadership before the arrival of Griffith some five years later. On the one hand, he has been hailed as an instinctive genius, a reputation which he certainly never claimed, and which was later artificially supported by the re-editing of some of his earlier films on a more sophisticated level. On the other hand, he has been maligned because none of his later films seem to bear out the instinctive understanding of cinema evidenced by *The Great Train Robbery.* Indeed, his post-1912 features (*The Count of Monte Cristo, Tess of the Storm Country*) are extremely primitive, lacking the crude energy of his early one-reelers.

Porter was essentially a cameraman and a technician, who delighted in tinkering and solving narrative problems via mechanical means. Often he did not realize that those mechanics overlapped into art and could be formulated into a language of film. Some of his early pre-narrative films, such as *Jack and the Beanstalk,* display astonishingly skillful and advanced production techniques. The success of *The Great Train Robbery* propelled him, much against his will, into becoming a director. Actually, until the advent of D. W. Griffith, the "art" of direction was hardly an art at all, but merely an adjunct to camerawork. "Director" and "cameraman," as in Porter's case, were usually one and the same, with the main attention being given to the photographic image. Porter was unhappy with the importance thrust upon him and would have much preferred to remain primarily a technician—an inventor, perhaps, of techniques to be used and exploited by others. Despite the simple but effective editing of *The Great Train Robbery,*

Porter saw it only as the obvious way to tell that particular story. He understood neither its principles nor the enormous possibilities of its application to other stories. All of his subsequent films are weakened by two elements that became increasingly important in the telling of stories on the screen: editing and the ability to handle actors. *The Great Train Robbery* deals with *groups* of people, primarily the band of outlaws and the pursuing sheriff's posse. Occasionally individuals are thrust into the foreground: the man on the train who is shot while trying to flee from the holdup; the dude in the saloon forced to dance by local roughnecks; the little girl who discovers the stricken telegraphist. These people are, in essence, used to "establish" shots, to provide punctuation, or to link scenes. They are not used as individuals, and the camera rarely moves close enough for their facial expressions to be recognizable. The little girl comes off best, since she is alone on screen with the body of the telegraphist; her pantomime of distress and prayer is perhaps the only example of acting in the entire film. Otherwise, the shots one tends to remember are those which utilize some kind of primitive technique or mechanical trickery: the fairly long, smooth panning shot following the robbers as they leave the train tracks; the fight in the train's coal-tender, where an effective jump-cut allows the substitution of a dummy for the struggling engineer just before he is thrown from the train; or a quite adept forerunner of both the matte-shot and back projection, in which the arrival of the train outside the signal box is printed in.

This tableau-like kind of narrative, even more evident in Porter's *Uncle Tom's Cabin*, where a presumed audience awareness of story and characters resulted in a series of highlight scenes linked together without any attempt at being "fleshed out" or built by the editing process, probably represented the peak of Porter's story-telling abilities. His *Life of an American Policeman* (1905) was so loosely connected that later editions of the film were able to rearrange its scenes quite drastically without in any way harming its continuity!

From the very first scene, the film's point of view is ambiguous. We are introduced to a policeman's family having breakfast at home; it is a seemingly happy family, complete with small baby. But the camera keeps us at arm's length throughout. The "intimate" scene is played as though on a stage, with the camera picking up the action from so far back that we never once get a chance to see the father's face. As a result, we never know whether we are following *his* specific activities during the day, the film thus being a kind of hour-by-hour record of a policeman's duties and problems, or whether the family is shown as a means of humanizing the police force in general, and the ensuing film a composite picture of overall police activities. In view of the many changes of location, the latter seems more likely. From the family breakfast table, the film cuts to the squad of policemen leaving their precinct headquarters, and again the camera keeps its distance, giving no clue as to whether we are still supposed to be concentrating on *one* policeman. The initial sequences of the policeman on duty in downtown New York, helping a lost child and supervising busy traffic, have both charm and documentary value.

The next sequence, however, underscores Porter's basic lack of understanding of the power of editing. A potentially dramatic situation is shot in one long-held, static long shot. With the camera seemingly positioned in mid-river (though probably on an adjacent wharf), a woman walks into the frame and throws herself into the river in an attempted suicide. With no build-up whatsoever, or even a close-up of the woman's anguished face, the audience is totally unprepared for such a dramatic event. Almost immediately, with unlikely speed and in even more unlikely numbers for such an isolated location, a number of policemen arrive and attempt her rescue. One dives into the water to support her; another clambers down over the pilings to lend a hand. A ladder is produced from somewhere and lowered. The maneuvers are not easy, and it takes a long time to get the woman into position. She is apparently quite heavy, and hoisting her up is laborious and slow. The woman's long immersion in the water has caused her skirt to become disarrayed, and at one point, as she is being hoisted up the ladder, a knee is momentarily exposed. The "unconscious" woman's hand immediately repairs this immodesty—although with the extreme long shot from which the scene was taken, the indecorum would surely have passed unnoticed. Finally, the woman is pulled back on the wharf and given artificial respiration. Only then is there a cut, to a shot of the arriving horse-drawn ambulance. The most elementary understanding of editing should have dictated that that shot be cut into the interminable ladder sequence, not only speeding it up but also eliminating the unfortunate knee shot. But every foot of the sequence is retained, with the camera maintaining its aloof distance throughout.

The film's next sequence, entitled "A Runaway in the Park" is at least broken up into several shots, and the action itself gives it some momentum, but the editing is still static. An automobile in the park startles a horse and causes it to run away—none too convincingly, since the female rider is clearly urging it to greater speed. A mounted policeman (on foot) sees the runaway coming and gives it time to pass him before he somewhat laboriously climbs into the saddle. From that point on, the framing and editing are singularly unimaginative. The camera is placed at a vantage point in the left bottom of the frame, taking in a long expanse of park roadway. The two riders gallop into the frame, up to the camera, and out of the frame. This shot is repeated from several similar vantage points, until the policeman overtakes the runaway and stops it. The constant "jumping ahead" of the chase is not only predictable but removes the spectator from any sense of involvement. Even if there had been a reverse angle of the riders from the rear, after they had exited the frame, there would have been a token sense of continuity and realism. But the angle remains rigid throughout, and there was apparently no thought given to either trucking or panning— even though such devices had been used in earlier Edison films.

The final sequence is not only equally unimaginative but even confusing. Titled "A Joke on the Roundsman," it winds up its semi-documentary tribute to the New York policeman with a humorous vignette which might have been intended to humanize the policeman a little after so much dedication and heroism. A mounted policeman slips into the stables of an Upper Fifth Avenue mansion for a quick drink. Unfortunately, his minor dereliction of duty is ill-timed; his superior is waiting outside for him to report. The policeman unsaddles his horse and hides inside the cab. The ostler attaches the harness of the small cab to both horses, and the cab makes its exit, past the unsuspecting supervisor. Around the block it stops; the policeman hops out, saddles up, and rides casually to report to his superior. As they converse, the cab trots around the corner, now drawn by only one horse. The supervisor scratches his head in bemusement. At best, it is hardly an earth-shattering joke, but as it stands, there is no joke at all. Undoubtedly the joke was clear to Porter from the original synopsis, but he is unable to convey it to the audience. One subtitle might have done the trick, or perhaps a close-up of the supervisor looking at the two horses, and then later a repeat close-up as he looks at the one horse.

As it is, the audience is kept so distanced from him that his mild expression of bemusement is all but lost.

Porter's inadequacy at conveying key story points is further emphasized in *The Kleptomaniac* (1906). Here is a mature little film making a valid social point—the inequities of one law for the rich and another for the poor. First, it tells the story of a woman who steals food from a store front to feed her starving child. (The antagonism of the passers-by who witness her act is quite startling.) Second, there is the story of a rich kleptomaniac who steals much more valuable merchandise from a store, but on impulse. The two women are brought into court, following a momentary comedy break in which a (presumed) prostitute is sentenced and goes off gaily to prison, waving at the audience. The woman who had been forced to steal is given a stiff sentence; the woman who stole on impulse is reprimanded and let off. The final shot of the film is a drawing of the figure of justice—a copy of the figure seen throughout the courtroom scene behind the judge's chair—with the blindfold appropriately over its eyes but its scales off-balance, one weighed down by a bagful of dollars. It is a statement both outspoken and sophisticated for a film made in 1906. The film itself is quite well made, and though the transition between the two stories is rather abrupt, it is not confusing. The flat studio backgrounds of the interior scenes (slum apartment, Macy's department store, the courtroom) are rather jarringly juxtaposed with genuine street exteriors, including those of Macy's, and pictorial continuity did not yet seem to have been a major concern (some scenes were taken after a heavy snowfall, others while the streets were clean). But these are minor shortcomings compared with one major one: Porter does not provide a close-up, or even a medium shot, of the rich woman as she commits her crime. The interior shot of the department store is so "busy," with so many identically dressed women bustling around in a protracted long shot, that the audience is given no guidance at all as to where to look or what is going on. In fact, the film's title, *The Kleptomaniac*, is the only clue to this vital piece of action. Further, Edison was presumably worried that that title might not be understood, and issued prints bearing the alternate title *The Thief*. It is quite possible that audiences seeing it under the simpler title might have been as confused as they were over that joke on the roundsman.

Porter apparently saw film narrative only in terms of plot, never in terms of people. None of his Edison one-reelers indicate an ability to handle, control, and guide actors, and even in his later features, direction of the players seems to have been his least concern. Admittedly, one tends to expect more of Porter because of his mechanical skills and the instinctive way he seemed to solve certain narrative problems. Perhaps one should remember that he didn't want to be a director and made no claims to being one. Undoubtedly, too, the Edison front office was easily satisfied, and as long as the films were slickly photographed, no complaints were made about poor direction, illogical stories, or such classic gaffes as an up-to-date New Jersey sewer appearing immediately outside the main gate of a cavalry fort in the Old West (*The Corporal's Daughter*, 1915). Directors seem to have been neither praised nor criticized, and actors were left pretty much to their own devices. Even the good actors in the Edison films—Edward Earle, Frank McGlynn—failed to turn in the subtle and often outstanding performances found in contemporary Biograph shorts, and had to await their post-Edison periods to establish their reputations.

The Biograph films made prior to Griffith's arrival were not markedly better. Thanks to chief cameraman G. W. Bitzer, they were often better composed, and in a technical sense—brightness, clarity, sharpness of focus—they were excellent. But Bitzer was not an *inventive* mechanic, as Porter was, and the Biograph shorts trailed behind the Edisons in trick work and camera magic.

The paths of Griffith and Porter crossed just once, when, in *Rescued from an Eagle's Nest* (1907), Griffith acted in an Edison one-reeler under Porter's direction. It was a charming and naïve little melodrama, highlighted by a trick shot of an eagle swooping down and flying off with a healthy-sized baby. (The eagle was fake, the baby very real.) As in *The Kleptomaniac*, the juxtaposition of real exteriors (woodland and cliffs) with painted studio sets was not very convincing. Griffith's performance was energetic at times but basically wooden, and Porter's camerawork/direction seemed unable to exploit even the limited dramatic potential the subject offered. In the climactic fight between man and eagle, both protagonists were so far to the left of the screen that one saw only flailing arms and fluttering wings, and even these were totally lost when the film later showed up on television screens.

Griffith, a playwright with one modest success and an actor (if he couldn't succeed as a writer) who respected the theatre but not the movies, could hardly blame Porter's poor direction—or lack of direction—for his own inept performance. When Griffith subsequently moved to Biograph as both an actor and a writer of stories for their one-reelers, his performances under Biograph directors in films like *The Crossroads of Life* were no better. If anything, the constriction of the smaller sets made them even worse, and Griffith was wont to pose and pantomime in a stiff, self-conscious manner. However, he was a handsome man and looked more at home in a dress suit than he had in woodsman's garb. When, after a very short period with Biograph, Griffith was offered the opportunity to direct (through the indisposition of another director), he was reluctant. He knew nothing about making movies, and in common with most theatre people, looked down on them. He accepted because he and his wife, actress Linda Arvidson, needed the money, and on the assurance that if he failed, he could still count on employment as an actor and a writer.

Griffith's first film, *The Adventure of Dollie* (1908), was less than one reel in length, but like so many first films by major directors, it showed a remarkably intuitive understanding of the medium. It was a cleanly put-together film, photographed entirely outdoors. The acting was performed mainly in long or medium shot, with no opportunity for real subtlety, yet with less gesticulating and posing than there had been in Griffith's own film acting to date. The plot dealt with a little girl kidnapped by gypsies and concealed in a barrel—which drops off the gypsy wagon as it crosses a river, is swept down over a very minor waterfall, and permits the child to pop out, quite unhurt, into her distraught father's arms. Although not really "edited," the shots were neatly linked together, with some particularly important scenes played right in front of the camera lens for added emphasis. It was as good as most films made by veterans of five years of direction, and better than many. With its casual blueprinting of the climax of Griffith's 1920 *Way Down East*, it was both an auspicious and an appropriate beginning to Griffith's career. Griffith himself was both surprised and pleased at how well it had turned out, and announced his willingness to continue. Within a year he dominated Biograph production, earning the company both prestige and dollars. Between 1908 and 1913 he directed more than 400 films, primarily one-reelers, though with increasingly elaborate two-reelers taking over toward the end. Within those five years, Griffith, helped immeasurably by cameraman Bitzer, created the whole language of film—taking the discarded or unexploited devices invented by others, creating new ones, experimenting with lighting, using the frame to its fullest—and suggesting action in off-screen space—creating a subtler, more underplayed form of acting. To do this, to "photograph thought," he used primarily younger players who did not have to unlearn stage techniques. He constantly moved the camera closer to them—contrary to prevailing standards, which expected the "whole" actor to be on view throughout the entire short, as on the stage—so that the nuances of expression on their faces could be captured. Most of all—and most importantly—he concentrated on pacing, on editing, and such devices as the flashback and the cross-cut.

It is easy enough to trace Griffith's progress from year to year; he himself made it easy, by constantly reusing and refining the same themes and even the same plots. The last-minute rescue affords an obvious example. *The Fatal Hour* (1908) was a lively little melodrama about Chinese white-slavers who kidnapped girls in New York and transported them to Fort Lee, New Jersey—the very opposite, one would have thought, of a normal commercial modus operandi. The climax finds the heroine tied and helpless in a shack, menaced by a revolver attached to the mechanism of a clock and due to go off at a specific time. The situation itself is sufficiently absorbing, and not too much is made of the successful rescue attempt. *The Lonely Villa* (1909) extends the climax both in time and in scope. A mother and her daughters are menaced by burglars; by chance, the father phones in at just the right moment and learns of their predicament. His car has broken down, and he commandeers a gypsy caravan to race to the rescue. The cross-cutting between besieged household and rescuers is much further developed than in *The Fatal Hour,* but it is still relatively superficial. There is no camera movement within the film, and the intercut shots do not get shorter and more dynamic as the climax approaches. As mother and daughters are about to be manhandled, the rescuers burst in—a fairly tame climax, deprived of shots of the rescuers almost at their goal.

In *Her Terrible Ordeal* (1910), Griffith stretches the suspense out over almost the entire reel: the heroine is trapped in the company safe, facing suffocation, while her boss has just left for the weekend. One of Griffith's delaying tactics in this film was to include a long shot of a top-hatted, elegantly cloaked gentleman waiting on the platform of a railway station. The audience presumably anticipated that this was the boss, and that he was about to be apprised of his secretary's danger. But the figure moves into closer camera range and even beams at an off-screen figure, or the audience itself. It isn't the boss at all, but Griffith himself in a Hitchcockian bit, leading the audience up the garden path.

The Lonedale Operator (1911) was a beautifully made little chase film which snares audience interest immediately by the humanistic touch displayed by Blanche Sweet—her delicate balancing on the railroad line as she walks along chatting to her boyfriend. Burglars try to break into her telegraphist's office to steal a waiting payroll, but she gets a message out, and from a few miles down the track, a train rushes to her rescue. About a third of the film is devoted to cross-cutting between the heroine's predicament and the rescue train. The cuts are far more polished and more varied than in *The Lonely Villa*. The camera is placed in the cab of the train, and later at a low angle by the tracks, so that the train rushes into and fills the frame. For all of its advances, however, the film is still missing one final refinement: the camera does not move with the action.

Within a year, Griffith refined the camerawork by literally remaking the same story, this time calling it *A Girl and Her Trust* (1912). The new story is literally all chase, even to sacrificing some of the charming bits of establishing business, such as the walk along the single rail. The climax of *The Lonely Villa*, the siege in the telegraphist's office, becomes the midpoint here. The thieves do break in and steal the payroll, but so tenacious is the telegraphist in her attempts to fight them off that they have to take her with them aboard their getaway vehicle—a railroad handcar. The chase is thus between the fleeing robbers on the handcar, and the pursuing locomotive. Griffith mounts his camera on a vehicle immediately in front of the handcar, to catch the full facial expressions of robbers and hostage while they are in motion, on the locomotive, and on an automobile running adjacent to the railway tracks. This last position not only increases the sense of involvement in the chase but also produces some stunning imagery that enhances the sense of speed. Houses, trees, and telegraph poles all appear as separate planes of reference between locomotive and camera car, creating a blurred effect as the camera rushes by. This means of emphasizing high speed would seem to be an obvious one for chase sequences, but it is usually one that only editors-turned-directors employ. One example is Joseph H. Lewis, who in "B" westerns of the forties often selected a stretch of road containing a low white picket fence. That long white line, dashing across the screen between two groups of horsemen (often on differing levels, with the camera perhaps on a third), was a direct descendant of the buildings and trees that hurtled across Griffith's landscape.

Griffith became so immersed in the possibilities of editing in *A Girl and Her Trust* that he forgot one important aspect—screen direction. The bulk of the action rushes across the screen from left to right, but there are occasional intercuts from right to left. However, while maintenance of screen direction is a basic rule of film editing, it is not an unviolable law, and is frequently broken to good effect. John Ford broke screen direction justifiably in his magnificent chase in *Stagecoach* (1939) and even perversely in *Fort Apache* (1948). The chase in *A Girl and Her Trust* leaves the audience almost as exhausted as the winded would-be robbers on their handcar, and Griffith winds up with a neat piece of romantic-comic "business." If the conclusion of the chase can be considered a semi-colon, then Griffith adds one short sentence to conclude his story. Telegraphist and boyfriend (Dorothy Bernard and Wilfrid Lucas) hop on the cow-catcher of the rescuing locomotive to hold hands and eat a sandwich. The train reverses, pulling away from the camera, and as the figures recede and become smaller, steam from the engine envelops the image to form a natural fadeout.

In terms of assembling all of the editing and other techniques necessary for the chase, *A Girl and Her Trust* almost represents the zenith of Griffith's experiments at Biograph. All that remained was to adapt it to an expanded and more sophisticated usage, which Griffith did in some of his last and most elaborate two-reelers at Biograph: *Massacre* (1912), a loose reworking of the story of Custer's Last Stand, and *The Battle of Elderbush Gulch* (1913), a large-scale, complex western with Lillian Gish, Robert Harron, and Mae Marsh that was virtually a blueprint for the climax of *The Birth of a Nation*.‡ Griffith's methods were

‡ Calling a film like *The Battle of Elderbush Gulch* a two-reeler, which it was, is in a sense misleading. Because the one- and two-reel lengths of films were growing increasingly irksome to Griffith's ambitious concepts, he shot at a slow camera speed, getting in far more plot and action per foot than did most of his contem-

also being studied and used, though not always instinctively understood, by his subdirectors. *The Telephone Girl and the Lady* (1913), another variation on the *The Lonely Villa/A Girl and Her Trust* chase theme, was prepared by Griffith but actually shot by an assistant, Tony O'Sullivan, while Griffith was on the West Coast. All of the ingredients are there—the cross-cutting, the use of the moving camera in some extremely good running inserts of mounted policeman-hero Alfred Paget riding to the rescue, and a well-done fight between Paget and villain Harry Carey at the climax—but somehow, it does not flow as it should. Certain cuts are awkward, and devices to prolong suspense are held too long.

But taking an ingredient as elementary as the chase, and studying Griffith's refinement of it from 1908 to 1913, is almost too easy and simplified a process. Fortunately, most of Griffith's Biographs have survived, if only in the paper-print form preserved by the Library of Congress. One can (as certain university courses on Griffith have been doing) literally study his work in depth, a year at a time, and see how, within any given year, the refinements—almost imperceptible at first—develop and progress.

In a loose sense, one can divide the Griffith Biographs into three groups. First and foremost, there are the action films with chase climaxes, which are used primarily to develop editing and photographic techniques. These included some bizarre "city" crime films, including *The Miser's Heart* (1911), in which a tot is suspended from a window by a rope, with robbers slowly burning through the rope with a candle to force the captive miser to open his safe, and *A Terrible Discovery* (1911), a curious forerunner (in spirit) of Lon Chaney's

---

poraries. An Edison and even the much higher-quality Ince film would use a faster camera speed and incorporate less plot material; thus, Edison and Ince shorts *can* be shown at the standard sound speed projection of 24 frames per second —or 10 minutes per thousand-foot reel of film—without seeming too fast. While Griffith's camera speeds varied, he tended to work at around 12 frames per second —which would turn the action into an incomprehensible frenzy if projected today at sound speed, as unfortunately his films often are. *The Battle* and *The Battle of Elderbush Gulch*, shown at the accepted (though arbitrary) silent speed of 16 frames per second, still seem much too fast. Properly projected at around 12 frames per second, they would run much longer than the standard one- and two-reelers. In its day, *The Battle of Elderbush Gulch*, properly projected, would have run close to 40 minutes, and so, with its size and spectacle, would have had almost the impact of a full feature.

The Unholy Three, with a paroled criminal returning to town disguised as a woman, so that he may gain entrance to the home of the district attorney who convicted him, and murder him. *The Lesser Evil* (1912) transposed a standard western plot to the sea. The heroine (Blanche Sweet) is captured by gun runners, and not knowing that help is on the way, is prepared to kill herself rather than fall into the hands of a mutinous and lecherous crew. As in many of his melodramas of the period, Griffith's nominal villain—played here by Alfred Paget—is something of a "good bad man," his basic decency causing him to take a stand in the girl's defense and allowing her to escape unscathed at the end. As in *A Girl and Her Trust*, one of its most interesting aspects is its final "sentence": with boy and girl reunited, Griffith shoots into the sun for his final low-key romantic image. But the bulk of the Griffith melodramas designed to exploit the chase and the rescue tended to be outdoor melodramas (*The Revenue Man and the Girl*), westerns (*The Last Drop of Water*, a 1911 one-reeler that was quite majestic in its creation of the epic qualities of a *Covered Wagon* in a single reel), and Civil War stories (*The Battle*, also 1911). For the most part, the Civil War stories were done in the East, where the New Jersey and New York terrain was appropriate, while the best westerns awaited Griffith's yearly trips to the West Coast and benefitted a great deal from the still rugged grandeur of the wild country surrounding (and in some cases, part of) Hollywood.

The second, and far more varied group of Griffith's films, might be termed the "story" films—stories designed to exploit a specific player (as a *type*, rather than as a star), stories of social comment, or stories based on or suggested by the classics. Although content and technique did sometimes overlap, occasionally suggested by the original material,§ the "story" films tend to be less adventurous in terms of technique, though not necessarily less satisfying. Griffith's attempts to elevate the content of story films ranged far beyond the Jack London-James Fenimore Cooper level, although he did his share of them. He used Dickens and Tolstoy openly—his 1909 *Resurrection* was a remarkably concise distillation of that complex novel into a single reel—and other authors less openly. *The Battle* was quite obviously influenced by Stephen

§ Griffith's 1909 *A Corner in Wheat*, from the Frank Norris story "The Pit," was a remarkable social essay, but much of its filmic technique, including the cross-cutting between rich and poor, is an essential ingredient of the original, too.

Crane's *The Red Badge of Courage; The Sealed Room* seemed to draw (as did many silent melodramas) on Poe's *A Cask of Amontillado;* even the Civil War story *The House With Closed Shutters* seemed inspired by Hawthorne's *The House of the Seven Gables,* and the title partly confirmed it. *A Drunkard's Reformation* paralleled a play based on Zola.

If plot is dominant over technique in these films, the result is sometimes a bonus in terms of pictorial poetry or subtlety of acting. Griffith's various films dealing with the people of fishing communities—ranging from *Fisher Folk* to *The Sands of Dee, A Mender of Nets, Lines of White on a Sullen Sea* (an example of the poetic and evocative titles that Griffith frequently used) to *Enoch Arden*—tended to be more leisurely, to give time for the shots of the fishing boats lying at anchor or lovers walking along the sands or up the cliffs. Not that these films had seascape beauty and nothing else. *A Mender of Nets* is almost an embryonic *An American Tragedy,* with Mary Pickford giving a particularly fine performance as the fisherman's daughter who sacrifices her own happiness by refusing to marry the man who has made another girl (Mabel Normand) pregnant, and who is forced into a loveless but "necessary" marriage to her. The film closes with a particularly lovely close-up of Mary Pickford, smiling as she works with her father, facing a lonely future, and philosophising, "After all, *somebody* has to mend other people's broken nets." The emotional stories such as these, or *Thru Darkening Vales,* also give Griffith a chance to use landscape both dramatically and symbolically, a nicety that there was often little time for in the one-reeler, but that later proved to be an integral aspect of such Griffith features as *The Greatest Question* and *Way Down East.*

Griffith's "story" films also included some wildly melodramatic tales that in later years would have been labeled "exploitation" films. *The Voice of the Violin* (1909), years before the Russian Revolution, was already telling Americans that Communist agents were at work in their midst, spreading dissent and causing labor disputes, while *For His Son* was the incredible saga of a soft-drink manufacturer who spiked his product with cocaine to produce "Dopocoke," a drink that led to madness and death! Griffith also made several straightforward temperance films, the most moving of which was titled simply *What Drink Did.*

The third group of Griffith Biographs were the films designed neither to tell worthwhile stories nor to further narrative experimentation in terms of editing or camerawork, but were ground out purely to meet the required quota. If films of only this category survived—films like *Confidence,* with Owen Moore—Griffith's reputation would be considerably less than it is. Fortunately, and perhaps significantly, there are relatively few films in this category, indicating that Griffith's enthusiasm rarely flagged. Also, as we see more of Griffith's Biographs and understand his methods, more of the apparently uninteresting aspects of some of the films fall into place. For years, one of the most consistently available Griffith Biographs was *The New York Hat,* a simple romantic story given distinction by its cast (Mary Pickford, Lionel Barrymore, and in minor roles, Mae Marsh, Lillian Gish, and others) and by the fact that it was written by Anita Loos. Although a pleasing subject with some nice human touches, it inevitably disappointed with its lack of obvious technique, and its apparent lethargy at times, especially when relatively few other Biographs were available for comparison. In all of the shots of Mary Pickford's home, for example, the camera was always placed in exactly the same position in the street outside the garden, and players always made their entrances and exits in the same way. At first, it looked at though Griffith merely shot, in one session, all the scenes involving that location without once bothering to move his camera. Such economy in time shouldn't necessarily be discounted as the reason for those scenes. On the other hand, as one gets more and more into Griffith's rural films, such as the lovely and only recently rediscovered *The Country Doctor,* one finds out how important the home is as a symbol to Griffith, and how he frequently shoots it deliberately and rigidly from one angle to impress the audience with its stability and consistency. (This certainly applies to the way Griffith shoots the two basic exterior and interior views of the home in *The Birth of a Nation.*) Establishing roots and permanence was apparently very important to Griffith. *The Country Doctor,* for example, begins with a pan across the countryside in which his story takes place. That story (a partially tragic one) told, Griffith concludes by going back to the beginning, and reversing that pan over the countryside.

Perhaps there is a fourth group of Griffith Biographs that one might consider, though admittedly, it calls for conjecture and supposition. However, there is a curious stress on what one can only term forerunners of the *film noir* school, which, while present through most phases of film history, really developed only in the thirties and reached its stylistic peak in the immediate post-war years. Griffith's *films noir* probably began with the grim *In the Watches of the Night* in 1909, and they are more than just films with tragic or unhappy endings. Before the star system evolved, audiences were not necessarily dismayed if the ending was sad or the protagonist died. In fact, Thomas Ince used the tragic ending as a shock gimmick, much as Griffith used the last-minute rescue. But Griffith's *films noir* had a sour, defeated feel to them, as though they were personal statements by a man who was disappointed at the way the world had gone. Griffith's own espousal, well into the twenties, of Victorian-era codes and virtues seems to confirm this. It is known that Griffith's Biograph bosses were not happy with films like *In the Watches of the Night*. They could accept the melodramatic tragedy of *The Usurer*, but not the gloomy and often psychological defeatism of *Through the Breakers* or *The Restoration*. If he had not been watched and checked, one wonders whether Griffith might not have added far more *films noir* to his Biograph schedule. Indeed, if he had been able to direct features into the late thirties and forties, whether he (like John Ford, whose attitudes and regrets were parallel) might he not have devoted his final years to a sadder look at the past, perhaps making a final statement on the Civil War that might compare with *The Birth of a Nation*, much as Ford's *The Man Who Shot Liberty Valance* has been compared with his own *Stagecoach?*

It is interesting that Griffith's *noir* Biographs seem clustered mainly in the early years. As the fiftieth anniversary of the Civil War approached, his spirits seemed to lift somewhat, as he (and, of course, other producers) catered to the renewed interest in Civil War stories not only by making more of them but by giving them preferred treatment. The scale of the battle scenes, the attention to minute detail, and the sheer numbers of uniformed extras (in, for example, *The Battle*, a one-reeler of 1911) is incredible. In terms of production values, *The Battle* is a bigger picture than many features of the forties and fifties. And in view of the criticism that would fall on Griffith following *The Birth of a Nation*, his attitudes in these films are especially interesting. Most of them take the Northern point of view rather than the Southern—or, to be more specific, take no point of view at all, but deal sympathetically with Northern protagonists. The problem of Negro slaves is dealt with from a sympathetic Southern viewpoint in *His Trust*, which, with its sequel, *His Trust Fulfilled*, somewhat anticipated *Gone With the Wind* in being a two-part saga of the Civil War and its aftermath. Here, though, the protagonist is a black hero, a former slave, who guards his master's family after the former's death in battle, protects the wife, and ultimately pays for the child's education. Although racial slurs (not even considered slurs) were commonplace in film titles and subtitles of the period, one never finds the words "coon," "darkey," or "nigger" used in any of the Griffith Biographs or their synopses—though one does betray a certain prejudice by referring to the tears that stream down a Negro's "black but honest cheeks," as though it was almost a contradiction in terms.

Griffith's Biograph films became the yardstick by which all others were measured, critics referring to competing films as being "up to" or "below" Biograph standards, or employing "Biograph lighting." Their immediate influence in America seems to have been slight, since Griffith's methods were not fully understood, and competitors found it easier to copy theme than to emulate style. It seems fairly safe to assume that Edison would never have made a philosophic little whimsy like *Annie Crawls Upstairs* if Griffith had not first made *Pippa Passes*. European influence is more obvious but hard to pinpoint, since the best of the later Biographs may well have been cut off by the First World War. But certainly, many little French Gaumont one-reelers, such as *The Widower*, have an unmistakable Griffith-Biograph "look" to them.

The best Griffiths of 1912–13 are not merely milestones of technique on the way to a final development but outstanding little films that need no apology for age. *The Musketeers of Pig Alley* (1912) has compositions that Eisenstein and Tisse could have been proud of a decade later. The remarkable *An Unseen Enemy*, also made in 1912 and used to introduce Lillian and Dorothy Gish, has a surreal, nightmare quality to its melodrama that almost certainly influenced the images in the French serials of Feuillade. And best of all, the mature, often almost Freudian *The Mothering Heart* (1913), with a superb performance by Lillian Gish as a mature wife and mother, is a totally modern and valid film today, with erotic symbolism in its last scene so advanced for its day that one would almost think it accidental, if not for the lingering close-up that Griffith utilizes to underline the point and assure us otherwise.

One can appreciate exactly how far in advance of his time Griffith really was, and how almost singlehandedly he had created a language and grammar of film, by comparing a Griffith-Biograph genre film (western, Civil War, crime) with a similar genre film by another contemporary, or even later, film-maker. A particularly apt comparison can be made between *Fighting Blood*, one of the best of Griffith's westerns, made in 1911, and Edison's *The Corporal's Daughter*, very similar in theme and structure, yet made in 1915. The Edison film gives no information or background about its characters, but merely throws them on screen. Titles telegraph the solution to suspense sequences even before they are under way. Moreover, the images frequently do not reflect the information conveyed by the titles. At one point, we are told that the cavalry is "gallantly fighting back against overwhelming odds," and are then shown a well-equipped body of men, strategically placed atop a hill, with plenty of rocks for cover, shooting *down* at an exposed and numerically inferior group of Indians! Cross-cutting in the rescue ride is kept to a minimum. In fact, once it has been established that help is on the way, no further reference is made until the rescuers arrive. And since that wraps up the story, no time is wasted on humanistic, comedic, or romantic touches before the "End" title is flashed on the screen.

Griffith's *Fighting Blood*, on the other hand, takes time to establish the appeal of the family about to be besieged by Indians. The byplay of the smaller children is not only beguiling but is guaranteed to involve audience concern. The action starts early but methodically, gradually building in size and ferocity, the shots getting both bigger—taking in more panoramic territory—and shorter. In extreme long shot, the rescuing posse rides horizontally across the back of the screen, disappearing off the right frame line, and while those riders are still in view, a fresh group rides *into* the frame, also from the right but much nearer the camera, a shot that is not only exciting but indicates *more* riders and more activity off-screen. (Griffith knew precisely what he was doing here, and was to repeat this shot in other films, most recognizably, in an identical context, in his 1924 *America*.) The inevitable fluffs that can happen in an ambitious film of this kind *do* happen—and are adroitly overcome. At one point, Robert Harron has to mount his horse and ride for help—but the horse, obviously scared by all the noise, rears up and then shies away. Griffith waits until he reaches a point where Harron is heading in the horse's direction, cuts away to another piece of action, and then cuts back to Harron, safely mounted. (This is in contrast to the long-drawn-out, earlier-discussed suicide attempt in Porter's *Life of an American Policeman* or the blatant revelation of the modern sewer in *The Corporal's Daughter*, which a cut would have eliminated or a change of angle obscured.) The prolonged cross-cut climax of defense and rescue is beautifully sustained, almost mathematically precise in its cutting. Then, too, at the end of the film, Griffith allows the audience time to unwind. There is a reconciliation between father and son, and cheerful shots of the cherubic youngsters crawling out, smiling, from their hiding place under the bed. The incredible thing is not that *Fighting Blood* and *The Corporal's Daughter* could exist side by side (in fact, they didn't) but that four years after *Fighting Blood*, and the same year that Griffith made *The Birth of a Nation*, a mediocre film like *The Corporal's Daughter* could be deemed acceptable by its producers, the exhibitors who booked it, and the audiences that saw it.

Griffith was well aware of what he had done for Biograph, and he wanted recognition, partly financial, but mainly in terms of freedom to make longer, better pictures. He asked for a share of the company's profits, which was denied, and to be allowed to explore beyond the two-reel film, which was also denied. He hit back, hoping to prove his point, by turning *Judith of Bethulia*, intended as a two-reeler, into a four-reel film. Shot partly on location at Chatsworth, near Hollywood, and partly in the studio, it alegedly cost over $36,000. If the figure is accurate, and records indicate that it is, Biograph's concern was at least understandable. Compared with the results that Griffith achieved on small budgets for one- and two-reel films, neither the cost nor the results seem warranted. The Biograph executives may well have been unimaginative and short-sighted, but as businessmen, they can't altogether be faulted for objecting to Griffith's budget or to his high-handed methods. They offered him the alternative of continuing to direct short films, or supervising other directors—or getting out. He chose to leave, and with his key players and, of course, G. W. Bitzer, headed for the West Coast and—ultimately—*The Birth of a Nation*.

4

The Early Features

Few periods in film history are as sparsely represented as those years between 1912 and *The Birth of a Nation* in 1915, when the feature-length film (of five reels or more) replaced the two-reeler as the staple program ingredient and restructured both the art and the economics of film. Many film historians see this period as essentially one of commercial rather than artistic growth. It is certainly true that these years were marked by the mass creation of stars, the founding of the great production-distribution combines to come (Universal was formed in 1912, and Paramount, Fox, and Metro shortly thereafter), and the gradual construction of more imposing—and certainly much larger—theatres to showcase the new, bigger, and longer product.

The parallel with the coming of sound some fifteen years later is quite astonishing. In both cases, the established directors and the leaders of the art as it then existed were unwilling or unable to forge ahead to the new medium. The experimenting was done by the second-raters, or in some cases by the stars, who saw the added length (or later, the added dimension of speech) as essentially a commercial and mechanical novelty rather than as an artistic advance. The first efforts were crude and simple, but because they were novel and caught the imagination of the public, they made money and thus seemed, for a while, capable of reshaping the whole structure of film. But both the very early features and the very early sound films, even on their own limited levels, were quickly made obsolete by rapidly advancing technology. And once the better directors were able to turn their attention to them, the initial endeavors became even more outdated. Just as there were no commercial or artistic reasons for sound films of 1928–29 to be exhibited after 1930, so too were the initial feature-length films of 1912–13 forgotten by 1915. They were swept aside, the few good along with the many bad, and later historians were forced to generalities rather than specifics in covering this period.

The generalizations on the whole are not unreliable, but they do perhaps lead to false assumptions. The early features *were* crude, reverting to the techniques of the stage and usually ignoring the great lexicon of film language built up at Biograph by Griffith, since his methods were not (by 1912) understood, indeed, nor even at their final fruition. More importantly, they had not yet been vindicated by overpowering commercial success.

Griffith was able to make a tentative entry into feature production only with one transitional-length film in 1913 and a more ambitious group of features in 1914. It's all too easy to look at the tableau-like content and style of feature films in 1912 and 1913, skip to 1915, and then demonstrate the tremendous influence of Griffith on other filmmakers in that year, when the fantastic success (financial as well as aesthetic) of *The Birth of a Nation* changed the physical look and pace of films for at least the next five years. One is tempted to equate the success of such notable 1915 films as Ralph Ince's *Juggernaut, Second in Command* (a Francis X. Bushman vehicle, with some of the most deliberate and sustained use of the mobile camera of any American film of the pre-1920 years), and Allan Dwan's *David Harum* with their directors' espousal of Griffith's methods. The next step is to conjecture that but for Griffith, film might have remained on its new path of imitating the stage and evolved a glossy but theatrical style that would have culminated with directors like George Cukor and John Cromwell rather than Griffith and John Ford.

The conjecture is not unreasonable, but it is also unfair to directors of stature prior to Griffith who did *not* see film as a parallel to theatre. Directors like Maurice Tourneur and George Loane Tucker were not dynamic enough to produce any radical change in film-making methods. And too, they did arrive on the scene *after* Griffith had made his major contributions to film language in his Biograph films of 1908–12. It is obviously impossible (and pointless) to imagine American film without Griffith, or to estimate the delay in the development of American film art without the catharsis of *The Birth of a Nation* and *Intolerance* in 1915–16, and their influence on virtually all of the major American film-makers of those years: Ford, Stroheim, Raoul Walsh, Sennett, Fairbanks, and Henry King. On the other hand, in 1913–14, Tucker and Tourneur were doing things that were cinematically subtler than Griffith had done (or had been allowed to do) up to that time. Thus it is not unreasonable to assume that, given time, such directors would have made a similar contribution. (They were not alone; one should add Herbert Brenon, Cecil B. deMille, and, of course, a major if scattered concentration of talent in Europe.) Moreover, European features, especially the Italian spectacles, such as *Quo Vadis?* and *The Last Days of Pompeii*, were being profitably exposed to American audiences from 1913 on. While their sophistication might be debatable, they did have size and relative splendor. Moreover, they used optical tricks and effects quite ingeniously, so that pictorially they were far more imaginative than their closest American equivalents, and ultimately had a stimulating effect on American film-makers.

There was no conveniently sudden and spectacular breakthrough to the multiple-reel silent feature, as there was to be with sound via *The Jazz Singer*. In any case, the waters have been sufficiently muddied with false claims, including Griffith's *Judith of Bethulia* (1913) and, incredibly, *The Squaw Man* (1914), not only frequently touted as the first American feature film but also referred to solely as a Cecil B. deMille production, when in actuality it was co-directed by deMille and the prolific actor-executive-director Oscar Apfel. Its only historic claim (apart from its more tenable artistic ones) can be that it was the first feature made in the area now known as Hollywood.

Longer features of five reels or more began to proliferate in 1912, two years before *The Squaw Man*, though often they did not run as long as their physical footage might suggest. A Griffith one-reeler from Biograph, with its fast action and rapid editing, might be shot at a rate of 12 frames per second and projected at around 16 frames per second, already giving it a slightly faster pace than life. Cramming so much plot into a thousand feet of film obviously meant more work for Griffith, but the slower projection speed gave him an additional five minutes in which to develop stories properly without the cost of extra footage. A thousand feet of film, depending on the intent of the director and photographer or the whim of the projectionist, could take less than ten minutes to project or more than fifteen. The initial features, however, of which Helen Gardner's *Cleopatra* (1912) is typical, were devoid of physical action and told their stories via tableaux-like posing and long narrative titles in very static form. Its camera speed must have been close to 24 frames per second, so that even when run at that standard sound-speed rate its action does not seem very fast. Had it been projected at the standard silent rate of about 16 frames per second, it would not only have been dramatically boring but also would have lost the persistence of vision and seemed unnatural, with a flickering, slow-motion effect. The average five- or six-reel feature like *Cleopatra* thus ran for about one hour.

One wonders why the novelty of length was enough to offset the lack of excitement. How could audiences, in the same year, sit through Griffith's *A Girl and Her Trust*—one thousand feet of melodramatic excitement, most of it pure chase, full of sweepingly fluid mobile shots, splendidly cut, and set almost entirely out of doors—and then turn to *Cleopatra*, with its static posing, lack of action, and cardboard interior sets? Even though Helen Gardner's studio was situated in Tappan and adjacent to the Hudson River, there was no attempt to make use of the river as a substitute for the Nile. Admittedly, New York rocks and foliage might not have suggested an authentic Nile, but authenticity was hardly an aim of most films at that time. In any case, careful angling of the camera could have made their river look passably Eastern, just as it was made to look passably Western for the Pearl White serials. As it was, the majesty of Cleopatra's arrival by barge, and the spectacle of battles on the water, were achieved mainly by subtitles, smoke pots, and a mast or two bobbing up and down behind a painted dockside—effects far inferior to anything the stage had to offer. (In fact, the stage at that time was trying to outdo itself with spectacle and pictorial effects. The cinema made no attempt to realize its own potential by showing just what it could do that the theatre could not.) The only relaxed, human moment in *Cleopatra* is when a dog—whether Cleopatra's pet or merely a curious visitor is never made clear—ambles into her courtroom, sniffs at a few props, and generally displays a naturalness that none of the actors can duplicate. Since Helen Gardner was a movie actress, formerly with Vitagraph, and an interesting actress with some legitimate claims to being the first movie vamp, she obviously was not trying to recapture a stage aura with such a blatantly non-cinematic exercise.

That excuse, at least, can be made for Adolph Zukor's attempts to present "Famous Players in Famous Plays," beginning with the importation of Sarah Bernhardt's French *Queen Elizabeth* and continuing through the filming of American stage actors in their most famous roles: James K. Hackett in *The Prisoner of Zenda* and James O'Neill in *The Count of Monte Cristo.* The blatant artificiality of the sets may have been a deliberate attempt to provide the proper backing for actors associated with the stage. However, it seems unlikely. When genuine exteriors or seascapes are locally convenient, they are thrown in regardless of how much they clash with the dominant stage sets. Griffith, in filming Tolstoy and Dickens earlier, had used outdoor locations wherever possible—even if it meant using an ornate Central Park fountain to suggest Verona, or putting up a prop Russian sentry box in a snowy New Jersey wood to indicate the wilds of Siberia. The use of stage sets in the Zukor films is entirely without the stylization that made patently (and intentionally) artificial sets work in *The Cabinet of Dr. Caligari* (1920) or *Henry V* (1945). More important, the Zukor films have neither theatrical nor filmic grammar. The lighting of a stage set, the build-up to and handling of entrances and exits, and most of all, of course, the performances of the actors—which, in a sense, provide a kind of editing in the way they shift audience attention—are all elements that *can* be manipulated on film (and never better demonstrated than in the talkies of James Whale). But Edwin S. Porter, who directed *The Count of Monte Cristo,* knew nothing of stage technique, was inept at handling actors, and probably didn't even fully understand the quite remarkable tricks and devices he had explored and in some cases created in his earlier one-reelers. *The Count of Monte Cristo,* a 1913 release, isn't really directed at all. A number of sets are provided and the actors let loose to go through their paces. The only close-up in the entire film is of a locket—not from dramatic choice but out of necessity, since it is a key prop and can be recognized by an audience only via a close-up. For the rest, any kind of dramatic interest in the well-known story is minimized by its lack of film grammar and its uninteresting sets. Reading the novel, and letting one's imagination loose on its colorful characters and exotic locales, must inevitably have been a far more stimulating experience. Since the whole art of constructing features—

let alone writing original material for them—was so new, most of the
1912–13 features did fall back on well-known, pre-written classics of
literature or popular hits of the stage. In almost every case, the films
must have seemed a poor substitute for the originals. The most notable
exceptions were such westerns as *The Squaw Man* and *The Virginian,*
which, by 1914, were being shot far more out of doors, and did bring a
spectacular dimension denied to the stage versions.

But in the one area in which they were being most heavily promoted—that of famous players in their best roles—these early examples
of filmed theater failed badly; they were totally inadequate and even
harmful records of the stars they sought to immortalize. The lack of
sound was, surprisingly, not a major handicap. John Barrymore was a
superb and subtle actor, possessed of a magnificent voice, and some of
his finest acting is to be found in the sound films of the early thirties.
But had he never made a sound film, his genius would have been accurately recorded by the silent film. Hackett, Bernhardt, and O'Neill
came to film at the wrong time, however, as did Sir Herbert Tree and
DeWolfe Hopper. They were already past their prime, and the early
cameras and film stocks, far from flattering them, merely made them
look older. Furthermore, directors like Edwin S. Porter (unlike Alan
Crosland, who directed some of Barrymore's best silent vehicles) did
not understand their medium well enough to present their stars in anything but aloof, long-distance pantomime.

James O'Neill had been playing Edmond Dantes for some forty
years; it was his whole life, just as the role of Sherlock Holmes had become a way of life for William Gillette. (Gillette made a Holmes film
in 1916, but it appears not to have survived.) Even though O'Neill was
well past his prime, presumably the expertise he could have brought
to the role of Dantes would have been a joy to watch. But virtually any
of the Biograph players, from Wilfred Lucas to Walter Miller, could
have made a better *film* Dantes than this stage actor who had devoted
his life to the role. Seen only in long, medium, and full-figure form, as
on the stage, and having no understanding of the requirements of film
anyway, his performance is reduced to an arm-waving, stiffly posing
pantomime, with never a good look at his face, let alone the opportunity for that face to register nuances of emotion. When Sir Laurence
Olivier, about to play James O'Neill (Eugene O'Neill's father) in *Long
Day's Journey into Night,* heard of the existence of *The Count of*

Monte Cristo, he eagerly borrowed a print to screen for his National Theatre company. However, it is doubtful that it was of much practical help to him in observing mannerisms and traits that he could incorporate into his own performance.

The immediate popularity of films like *Cleopatra* and *The Count of Monte Cristo,* while hard to justify, is at least understandable. They did have the novelty of length, and to the generally unsophisticated American audiences that flocked to them, they were undoubtedly easier to understand than, for example, the early films of Maurice Tourneur. Tourneur's *The Wishing Ring* (1914) appears to be such a slight piece of whimsy that it is easy for one's attention to wander. And when attention is no longer paid, one not only misses the surprising subtleties of plot but the incredible sophistication of camerawork, lighting, and editing. If it is possible for today's audience to react that way—invariably, even with film students, the revelations of that film come with the *second* viewing—one can well understand that 1914 audiences just weren't ready for it, and that the simpler, clearly stated tableaux of *The Count of Monte Cristo* were easier to assimilate. It is becoming increasingly clear, though, that films like *The Wishing Ring* were not altogether unusual. Every film of like status, such as *Traffic in Souls* and Thomas Ince's *The Italian*—films recovered during the 1970's—confirms a growing suspicion that 1913/14 may be one of the great lost frontiers of film scholarship, likely to reveal more examples of modernity and sophistication in film-making than historians have ever suspected.

Before delving further into American film of this period, however, it is perhaps only fair to stress that the most *advanced* feature films were those being made in Denmark. It is significant, perhaps, that Denmark was a small country with a potentially small income from film. Thus, its film industry tended to attract not the merchants and those who saw the movies as a way of turning a quick profit but artists sincerely interested in the future of the medium. Ironically—and this has seldom happened since—the artistry of the early Danish short films, coupled with astute showmanship, was so high that they did achieve worldwide commercial success. At one time, Denmark's Nordisk Films was second only to France's Pathé in worldwide distribution and profits. Unfortunately, the success did not continue when the transfer to features was made. There was less of a chance for longer films to compete with

American films, with their increasingly popular stars. In any event, the First World War disrupted and delayed the progress of many European film-producing countries.

The early Danish features benefitted not only from creative and innovative directors like Benjamin Christensen and August Blom but from audiences that did not look down on the movies. Danish films attracted the attention—and the services—of the finest and most popular stage actors and actresses, and the mutual respect between audience and film is quite apparent. Several of these early Danish masterpieces still exist in pristine 35mm prints, and the mystery is not so much how these sophisticated films came to be made as why they have been so long neglected. Neither *Atlantis* (1913) nor *The Evangelist's Life* (1914) are even referred to in one of the "definitive" books, Forsyth Hardy's *Scandinavian Film*. In maturity of content, in strong psychological themes, and in the smooth lyricism of the camerawork (this applies as much to a spy film like *The Mysterious X* as it does to the much more complex *Atlantis*), these films are indisputably in advance of anything being done in the bigger film-making countries: the United States, Great Britain, Germany, France, Italy. But quite apart from questions of technical skill, the one major difference between the Danish feature and the American, and the one that impresses the most, is the respect given to both the actor and the audience. Actors are given time to think and reflect, instead of being at the mercy of a narrative that propels them from one scene to the next, as was the method in most American films. If the thought process is a lengthy one, then other action is placed at the back of the frame to keep the scene from becoming static. Tho actors even seem to look *past* tho camera, to ignore it. It does seem quite revolutionary—although it shouldn't, even in this early period—to see actors taking time on screen to ponder their decisions, instead of being merely tools to keep the narrative flowing.

Yet for all their sophistication, the Danish films did have one basic weakness which the American film, perhaps from its assembly-line methods and from knowing its audience, instinctively avoided. The Danish works suffered from a combined lack of construction and lack of elementary showmanship. They didn't have the narrative drive, or the sense of building to a climax, that was characteristic of the American film. *Atlantis* is typical. A lengthy shipwreck sequence (virtually a documentary, since a real ship is used) is obviously the climax of the film. It disposes of some of the characters and is surely intended as a prelude to the wrap-up. Yet the film ambles untidily on, tying up its loose ends, and obviously never able to regain the dramatic excitement of the shipwreck sequence. One of the lesser characters is an "armless wonder" (similar to the Lon Chaney character in *The Unknown*), an extraordinary individual who does everything—eating, smoking, writing, drinking—with his feet, so efficiently that one soon regards his remarkable feats as being quite normal. We meet him only casually, early in the film. Later, after the shipwreck, the film comes to a halt for virtually a reel while he, one of the survivors, opens his act in a New York vaudeville theatre. It's a superb and engrossing act, but one senses that an American director would instinctively have shown it to us (perhaps at a ship's concert) prior to the wreck. Placed where it is, its effectiveness is lessened, and it further delays the conclusion of the narrative.

Although *Atlantis* was released in the United States, most of the early Danish features appear not to have been, and attempts to assess their influence on American directors are pure speculation. The Maurice Tourneur-Clarence Brown *The Great Redeemer* (1920) seems very similar in content and style to *An Evangelist's Life*, and presumably Tourneur could have seen it in Europe. The naturalism and acting styles of Ince's *The Italian* likewise suggest a knowledge of the Danish films. However, *The Italian* is far too good a film to be merely a copy, and it is probably unfair to suggest influences based only on conjecture.

In any event, the emerging pattern from these recovered 1913–14 American films (and one fervently hopes that there will be many more of them) indicates that, as in Denmark, a few directors were attracted to the American film because of excitement and enthusiasm for the medium, not for its profit potential. It also indicates at least some of these directors did *not* depend on the methods of D. W. Griffith, and in fact, to the contrary, were far more concerned with content and with *concealing* technique rather than exploiting it for its own sake.

The 1913 film *Traffic in Souls* is far more famous for its subject matter (an exposé of white slavery) and for the conditions under which it was made (secretly, and without the knowledge of the studio front office) than for its usually derided qualities as a film. As recently as

1975, the British Film Institute—which should certainly know better—referred to it as "laughingly melodramatic," while the Museum of Modern Art in New York City almost invited disrespect in its condescending program notes. Yet unlike so many features of the immediate post-1912 period, *Traffic in Souls* is never stagey. There's no conscious "art" about it either; all of the sets are naturalistic and the framings uncomplicated. They do their job, the actors walk in and out of them without bothering about their own positioning, and the camera merely records. The film, in fact, has much of the casual realism and unobtrusive self-confidence of the Warner Brothers crime films of the early thirties. Its documentary values are enhanced by much location shooting in New York. Very little is known about the work of its director, George Loane Tucker (who spent much of his short filmmaking life in England, where he married actress Elisabeth Risdon), apart from surviving fragments of *The Miracle Man*. His instinctive grasp of film-making here suggests that he may well have been one of the major talents of those early years. Even more notable as an example of early naturalism—and a film that can in some ways be favorably compared with Erich von Stroheim's *Greed* (1924)—is Thomas Ince's *The Italian*, directed in 1914 by Reginald Barker (although Ince's fondness for assuming screen credit himself managed to deprive Barker of recognition for this remarkable film until much later).

The Italian is the story of a farm-worker who leaves his native soil to make good in America. Although confident that he will do so, he is under a certain amount of pressure. If he doesn't succeed within a year, the girl he loves (and who loves him) will be forced into marriage with another. This plot contrivance is, however, merely that—a contrivance, to inject suspense into the earlier sequences and to permit the luxury of picturesque farewells and subsequent cross-cuttings of the two lovers separated by thousands of miles of ocean. The early portion of the film is romantic in the extreme, with California countryside and missions substituting quite satisfactorily for the Italian equivalents. The canals in the Venice area of Hollywood are also pressed into service. In this "prologue," there is a great deal of smooth camera movement and many striking images, such as that of the lovers silhouetted at dusk on the side of a hill. The immigrant's departure is also extremely well done, some cunning editing and mobile camerawork managing to suggest quite convincingly the departure of a ship loaded with immigrants.

The immigrant's destination is of course New York; but the slum and ghetto areas where the bulk of the film then takes place were actually shot in San Francisco, since Los Angeles' slums looked a shade too prosperous to double for New York. The grime and the disillusionment that the hero finds in "Little Italy" is depicted in a grim and utterly realistic manner, suggesting that the perhaps excessive romanticism of the Italian scenes may well have been deliberate for purposes of contrast. Although hardly finding the new land the paradise he expected, the immigrant works hard as a boot-black and saves his money. He also wins the (temporary) favor of the local political boss, who uses him to win the votes of his "Wop friends." The immigrant does manage to send for his fiancée, and they are married.

The remainder of the film however, somewhat backtracks from its traditional "Land of Opportunity" view of America to present an unrelentingly grim picture of grinding poverty that must have been disconcerting, to say the least, to the immigrants who formed a large part of the film's contemporary audience. Things go badly for the couple in New York, especially after the birth of a child. The child, weak from malnutrition, is dying from that and related causes of ghetto-living, including the heat: infant mortality from heat alone ran high in New York's "Little Italy" at that time. Going out to buy milk, the father is robbed of the little money he has. Searching for his assailants, he finds them, begs for the return of the money, is beaten—and then arrested by the police. While he is in prison, and unable to get in touch with his wife, the baby dies. This middle portion of the film seems honest, touching, and incredibly realistic. The beating in the street, though brief, has a savagery and a desperation not encountered in films of that period, and director Reginald Barker is adept at utilizing the naturalistic lighting of streets and alleys for dramatic emphasis. When the husband is left unconscious in an alley, his body is concealed by shadows, but his face is highlighted by a shaft of light as the sun shines through slats and broken fences.

The final third of the film takes a novelettish turn (although only in contrast with the controlled realism of the middle portions), and the last scene is a disappointment. Perhaps for prestige purposes, to suggest a major literary origin that the film did not in fact possess, the story is told within the framework of noted actor George Beban, resplendent in dressing gown and in a palatial home, sitting down to read the manuscript. (This also serves to stress the versatility of Beban in transferring from matinee idol image to that of the shabby Italian immigrant.) The last scene, however, is an intensely emotional wrap-up to the story, with the Italian by the grave of his child, and both the scene's content and motivation are conveyed by a page of text from the book (which then closes to provide "The End"), as though Ince was dubious that director Barker and actor Beban could carry that scene visually—although all indications were that they certainly could have.

However, criticizing *The Italian* for not being quite ambitious enough in certain areas is patently unfair, in view of its otherwise towering achievements. Quite apart from its realism and its willingness to take a chance on what must, even then, have been an unpopular and commercially doubtful theme, its technical virtuosity is quite extraordinary. The photography, from its lyrical style in the romantic opening to its anticipation of neo-realist methods in the slum sequences, is both artistically and technically well in advance of its period. The constant mobility of the camera also includes one or two hand-held shots so that—in at least one instance—the camera is able to assume a subjective view-point and literally go off at a tangent in mid-action as the character involved abruptly, and without warning, changes his course of action.* Too, there are frequent dissolves as the Italian recalls the past or dreams of his girl back home. Dissolves in Ince films were not new, and had always been unusually smooth. In fact, the very skill with which they were done may well account for the number of times Ince injected this device into his film. But while they were not really novel in 1914, they were not always well executed. Some of Griffith's dissolves in *The Birth of a Nation* a year later still had a certain jerkiness to them, and the French spectacle *The Miracle of the Wolves* (as late as 1924) seemed, somewhat perversely, to use the dissolve as a transitional device, even though it caused a jarring conflict between the two images.

---

* Use of the subjective camera, a valuable dramatic device, is all too frequently made less effective because of an insistence on smooth and basically unreal movements to dovetail with the Hollywood gloss of the rest of the film. *The Lady in the Lake,* a 1946 Philip Marlowe mystery, tried the interesting (though very quickly dated) experimental technique of telling the whole story through the eyes of the thus largely unseen detective. But the camera movements remained stately tracks or swish-pans—movements of the *camera* rather than those of the human eye. The subjective shots in *The Italian* are brief, but they have a spontaneity that such shots very rarely achieve.

But in *The Italian,* superimposition is perfect, and one image flows as smoothly and naturally into the next as in the dream that it serves to duplicate. The validity of *The Italian* is underscored by Francis Ford Coppola's use of it as a basic model and constance reference while making *The Godfather* (1972); in fact, one might even conjecture that Robert de Niro was in the film because of his resemblance to George Beban.

One might further conjecture on the influence of Beban's performance. For 1914, it is an astonishing performance—especially for a stage player working in film, and *under-* rather than *over-*playing. One cannot know whether Beban saw any of the Danish films of the period, but certainly he has that propensity typical of Danish screen actors of the period of projecting intensity of thought, and of seeming to act *beyond* the reaches of the camera, as though it were not there at all. De Niro's performances in *The Godfather,* and especially in the later *The Last Tycoon* (1976), certainly *seem* to have their roots in Beban's performance in *The Italian.*

It is unfair to arbitrarily list *The Italian* as Reginald Barker's finest film; the mere fact that *it* was virtually unknown until a few years ago should caution against such a rash assumption. But it is certainly reasonable to assume that it is Barker's most important film, though the extent of its influence on other film-makers awaits substantiation from further re-discoveries. Barker himself became best-known for virile yet mature action films, and like so many major silent directors (James Cruze, Karl Brown, Herbert Brenon, Irving Willat), wound up at Monogram or Republic (in his case, at *both* studios) in the mid-1930's, turning out unimportant but still expertly-made programmers.

If *The Italian* represented a major break-through in its naturalistic approach to both form and content, then Maurice Tourneur's *The Wishing Ring,* also of 1914, must be considered an equally major landmark in both its lyricism and its attempts to weld the diverse elements of cinema and theatre. The movies both respected the stage and emulated them—hence, the recurring descriptions of movies as "picture plays" or "photo plays"—but Tourneur, in particular, tried to evolve a language of film built rather more on pictorialism than on grammar. He certainly understood the principles of editing, and there is some extremely subtle cutting in *The Wishing Ring*—so subtle that it disguises rather than calls attention to itself. Moreover, in his early interviews, Tourneur named Griffith as his inspiration—but this seems essentially a graceful rather than a realistic gesture. There are certainly traces of Griffith in Tourneur, especially in his post-1916 films, but *The Wishing Ring* owes Griffith no particular allegiance, and in fact is a more sophisticated film than any of the pre-*The Birth of a Nation* features made by Griffith. Its performances are charmingly relaxed and casual, and the atmosphere of England is so well re-created that for many years normally astute historians assumed it was a British film. This in itself is no minor achievement, since it was made in Fort Lee—in 1914 certainly a more pleasant and picturesque area than it is today, but still unmistakably New Jersey. Ingenious directors could *adapt* its fairly open but clearly "tamed" landscapes to suggest the West or Russia, but there were always tell-tale signs to give the lie to it. Tourneur's unerring eye, however, found the buildings that had an English "look" to them, and by additional construction, or a few rose bushes, made them *thoroughly* English. At one point he needed a high "English" cliff and found it along New Jersey's Palisades—building a small, church-like edifice into the landscape solely to obliterate a view of the Hudson River, which would be both familiar to American audiences and would invalidate the location in England, where rivers of the size and breadth of the Hudson just aren't found in rural areas!

Tourneur's means of reminding audiences that *The Wishing Ring* was a kind of play were both obvious and subtle. The obvious method was to open on a stage; a group of attractive young maidens trot daintily across it to address the audience, and then pull the curtains open so that the play may begin. At the end of the narrative, all of the characters are seated at a feasting table for their "curtain call," and the camera pans from left to right, giving the audience a last glimpse of the players—in order of their importance—before the young ladies reappear to draw the curtains across the stage. In between, however, Tourneur uses almost subliminal means to implant the suggestion of theater. One of his favorite devices (developed to a surprising degree of sophistication over the ensuing years) was to photograph genuine outdoor scenes through a kind of proscenium arch—the silhouette of a cave-mouth, the framing of branches, or perhaps even a genuine arch. If the latter looked *too* genuine, he would sometimes back up, adding a patently artificial arch to the foreground, through which he would photograph the action and the genuine article.

Yet despite these attempts to create an artificial frame, the action within that frame was both realistic and *un*theatrical. Tourneur and his great cameraman, John Van Den Broek, were probably the first film craftsmen to insist on a logical light source on the screen. (This was to become a major concern later on to important cameramen like James Wong Howe, but it was often ignored by directors. Griffith was notorious for being concerned only with the immediate effect of the individual image, not caring whether its lighting or composition meshed with the preceding or succeeding shots.) Every single shot in *The Wishing Ring* has a clearly indicated source of light: a window, a fireplace, a gypsy campfire, the moon. Not only is each shot composed with the light-source in mind, but many of the shots are distinguished by an unself-conscious form of symmetry. Tourneur studied painting before he turned to film, and it shows; yet the most symmetrical compositions in his films (and there are many, as early as *The Wishing Ring*) are always the briefest and the most animated. As if aware that these compositions might freeze into picture-postcard tableaux if held too long, Tourneur rushes them off the screen almost as soon as he places them there—and their few seconds on screen (three girls daintily crossing a stream on stepping stones, or leaning, laughing, over a fence, one head in full close-up, the other two receding toward the rear of the frame) look entirely unforced, as though a candid camera had happened to catch them by accident.

The Wishing Ring has a fragile little story combining whimsy and romance with a good sense of fun and pace. To outline its plot would do a disservice to its charm. Suffice to say that its comedy still provokes chuckles, and that the film as a whole still radiates warmth. The prints in circulation today almost all emanate from the American Film Institute, which made a 35mm blow-up negative from an old British 16mm print and then made reduction prints from their new negative. Even having gone through this grain-inducing mechanical process, and losing the richness of the original color tones, the photographic quality of the film still impresses.

After such an auspicious beginning, Tourneur's subsequent films are perhaps disappointing, filled with stunning images but not always accompanied by the dramatic unity that went along with those images in *The Wishing Ring*. True, many of the films from his peak period—such as the 1920 *Treasure Island*—no longer seem to exist. Fortunately, *The*

Blue Bird (1918), the finest film of Tourneur's earlier period, does still exist. By far the best of the three adaptations of the Maeterlinck fantasy, it was also the most stylized collaboration between Tourneur and his great art director, Ben Carre, combining charming narrative naïveté with a pictorial sophistication that exploited color, silhouettes, deliberately fanciful sets, and unique costuming.

During the war years, the New York/New Jersey film-making center sheltered and nourished a number of refugee/émigré film artists from France. Many of these deliberately employed themes of French locale in their stories, or French theatrical design in their sets, to make the propagandist point that French culture was still flourishing and expanding beyond the war zone. *The Blue Bird,* dominated by the French theatrical, pictorial, and even acting styles that Tourneur and Carre had brought with them, is one of the best surviving examples of this unique French colonization within the American film, as well as being one of Tourneur's loveliest films.

Tourneur in his later Hollywood career was plagued by inadequate budgets and having to accept subject matter of no particular interest to him. The film that might well be considered his masterpiece, the 1920 *The Last of the Mohicans,* was substantially shot by his protégé, Clarence Brown, due to his own illness at that time—though Brown himself has been quick to allocate credit for the film's conception and design to Tourneur. Tourneur left Hollywood in the 1920's and returned to Europe, where he worked steadily until his death (in his eighties) well after World War II. His late silent and sound films included co-productions done in England and Germany, and all were marked by rich pictorial qualities. His late silent German film, *Ship of Lost Men* (1929), had such astonishing visual stylistics that even the young Marlene Dietrich was overshadowed by them, while one of his last films, *Le Main du Diable* (*The Devil's Hand,* released in the United States as *Carnival of Sinners*), made in 1942 under the German occupation, contained an entire reel of stylized lighting and exaggerated silhouettes that was not only one of the finest single pieces of film he ever made but an obvious homage to the art of the silent film. His son, Jacques Tourneur, carried on his strong pictorial sense in the sound period via such traditional Hollywood forms as the horror film (*Cat People* and *Curse of the Demon*) and the western (*Wichita, Stars in My Crown*).

In 1977, one has little hesitation in assuming that *The Wishing Ring* and *The Italian* represent the peak of sophisticated American film-making in 1914; yet five years earlier, before the re-emergence of *The Italian*, one would have felt safe in making such a broad claim for *The Wishing Ring* alone. Pending (hopefully) further discoveries, all one can say now with confidence is that while D. W. Griffith may have been the great innovator in earlier years, and would become so again, artistic leadership of American film had, in 1914, temporarily passed into other hands. And while it is perhaps the artistic aspect of these films that seems of paramount importance today, one should not forget that the *commercial* success of these early features reshaped and up-graded the merchandising and money-making methods of the film industry. The Italian import *Quo Vadis?* played at New York's Astor Theatre to a one-dollar admission charge (a new high, then) and was booked on a percentage basis, with 10 percent of the receipts being returned to the distributor.† Within a very short time, this became the standard practice, at least for key theaters in metropolitan centers, and the exhibitor had the choice of paying a stiff flat rental, often in the neighborhood of $700 a week (which meant that if he was lucky, or exploited the film well, he *could* make a very substantial profit), or of playing on percentage—which reduced the risk but, on a really success-ful engagement, also reduced the size of his profit. Prior to the really big box-office returns ushered in by *The Birth of a Nation*, the features of this period were capable of grossing between a hundred and two hundred thousand dollars—small potatoes by contemporary standards, but not so in a proportionate sense, when films could be made (or bought and imported) for a few thousand dollars.

In the long run, however, what impresses most about the best of the 1914 features is how rapidly they had reached maturity. It is amazing to realize that less than twenty years separates Edison's *The Kiss* from *The Wishing Ring*. (Quite certainly, no such striking progress exists on *any* level of film-making in the *past* twenty years—unless, on a purely moralistic level, one compares the sexual innocence of films of the

---

† The percentage demanded of an exhibitor steadily increased through the years and was often boosted by the importance of a specific film. "Sliding" scales were established so that over a given figure, the percentage would be increased. Today, with a well-advertised, pre-sold major movie, it is not at all uncommon for the distributor to demand, and get, a percentage from the exhibitor as high as 70 percent!

1950's with the no-holds-barred pornography that can be exhibited publicly in the 1970's, and there is certainly reasonable doubt as to whether that can be termed "progress"!) True, it is unfair to equate the development of the cinema with the gap between the invention of the wheel and the merchandising of the automobile, or the centuries between the first cave drawings and the mass availability of art masterpieces. In such cases, ideas and art had to wait for mechanics to evolve, for execution to catch up with inspiration. And the movies, of course, being an amalgamation of all the other arts, had certain built-in shortcuts in that they were able to capitalize on the accumulation of modes and methods of those other arts through the centuries. Yet although they were drawing on pre-existent arts, the movies still had to find their own language. The theater had existed for centuries as a popular and flourishing art, yet it wasn't until the 1800's that the curtain was first used to end acts, and by its lowering to create time lapses and geographic changes. (Prior to that time, the curtain was never lowered during the performance, scene changes taking place in full view of the audience.) Yet within a year or two, the movies were solving that problem, first, by the information-purveying sub-title, and shortly thereafter, by the fade-out, the iris-out, or the dissolve. By 1914, the movies still had a long way to go and a lot to learn, but they were out of the "crawling" stage and into a healthy adolescence. They had earned the right to be called an art.

5

Griffith and
"The Birth of a Nation"

Griffith's *Judith of Bethulia*, made in 1913, is usually designated as the climax of his Biograph period. In fact, it is more properly a tentative beginning of his transference to the feature-length film. Because of Griffith's eminence, film history has tended to magnify the importance of *Judith of Bethulia*. It has often been called the first American feature; it was neither that nor the longest American film to date. At four reels, it was still a transition film in terms of length, though admittedly, the silent speed of projection gave it a running time of about an hour. (This was still too long for the conservative Biograph Company, which, despite ample audience proof to the contrary, refused to believe it was commercially viable and held off its release for a year. Later, out-takes and additional titles were inserted to pad the length, and the film was reissued under the non-Biblical title *The Unpardonable Sin*, to cash in on the enhanced reputation of Griffith and its stars.)

As a climax to the Biograph films, *Judith of Bethulia* inevitably disappoints. The increasing subtleties and clarity of story-telling that had been apparent in Griffith's last one- and two-reelers for Biograph appear to have been sacrificed almost entirely to a length that the film does not really need. Placed side by side with another 1913 Griffith Biograph, the two-reel *The Battle of Elderbush Gulch*, its inadequacies are especially apparent. Both films are in a way related, since they deal with one specific "military" engagement and its solution. But even allowing for Griffith's greater affinity for the western, the two are miles apart in technique. The western is lean, clean-cut, and builds steadily to a climactic crescendo of excitement. The Biblical feature is confused and protracted, and since the climax is essentially a dramatic/emotional one, the action scenes that follow it—no different from those that precede it—are merely anti-climactic. Admittedly, there are extenuating circumstances. The movie was not conceived as a feature, and Griffith's decision to film it that way not only meant reshuffling and expanding a fairly tight continuity but working with an inadequate budget. Too, all of the exteriors were shot on drab Chatsworth locations, which gave Griffith no opportunities for dramatic use of landscape, let alone symbolic or lyrical treatment. Chatsworth has always been a convenience for Hollywood rather than an asset. Its close proximity to the studios has meant that production units could commute back and forth every day; its terrain may be dull, but it does encompass open plains, rocks, hills, trails, and a small lake. Quickie producers could shoot an entire film on its acreage without any problems. The nondescript quality of the scenery has allowed it to be used for the Old West and Old England, desolate terrain in some post-atomic age, the moon and various planets, Africa, Iron Curtain countries, and, of course, both prehistoric and Biblical terrain. From the 1950's on, an increasing use of color spruced up the drabness somewhat, but it has always remained an uninteresting location which eventually found its true level as a background for half-hour television series. Its function, if any, was to enable good directors to film odd inserts or pickup shots that had been neglected on expensive location jaunts to more picturesque locales. It fulfilled this function for John Ford in many films, notably *Stagecoach* and *Fort Apache*.

Griffith, however, had neither color, other than toned stock, nor panchromatic film, so that to the drabness of rocky scrubland was added the gray, washed-out look of sky and horizon. The garb of the opposing armies was virtually indistinguishable, and the action scenes became directionless skirmishes in which identical extras were absorbed into a background of dust, rocks, and sun-dried grass and foliage. The Chatsworth location wasn't all that was wrong with *Judith of Bethulia*, but it is significant that Griffith had rarely used it before (and then for his prehistoric duo, *Man's Genesis* and *Brute Force*, where he obviously wanted a nonrecognizably California locale) and never used it again on a major film. And just as the perfectly constructed *The Battle of*

Elderbush Gulch might well have been spoiled had its length been doubled, so might *Judith of Bethulia* have been improved had its length been halved. However, it is not entirely without merit or interest. Griffith's genius for using space and suggesting size is evident from the way a few very economical sets form a convincing walled city. Best of all is the acting—the dignified underplaying of Henry B. Walthall as Holofernes and the rich, often subtle, always passionate performance of Blanche Sweet, a performance which is valid today and deserves a better showcase but which must have seemed outstanding in its day. *Judith of Bethulia* certainly shows far less control and instinctive understanding of the medium than the best of Griffith's Biograph films, but it was a useful transitional step, enabling Griffith to encounter the problems of feature length before he segued into full-scale feature production.

With his Biograph ties severed, Griffith took G. W. Bitzer and the best of his Biograph acting troupe and moved to Hollywood, to join Reliance-Majestic. Without his leadership, the talent he attracted, and, of course, the quality of the Griffith-directed films, Biograph floundered. They held on for a year or two by making imitation Sennett comedies and imitation Griffith melodramas—the latter often looking more like parodies—and by making a handful of films of genuine (if not particularly cinematic) interest that starred such Broadway personalities as Bert Williams. But Biograph, still refusing to explore beyond the boundaries of proven formulas, could not hope to survive indefinitely on a continuation of their one- and two-reelers. Within a year or so, the company that had once been considered the leader of the film industry became first obsolete and then extinct.

Griffith's arrival at Reliance-Majestic did not at once produce startling results. His immediate aim was to keep the studio going and to meet the payrolls, and to do this he turned out a quartet of very presentable features utilizing Henry B. Walthall, Mae Marsh, Blanche Sweet, Robert Harron, and Lillian Gish. All of them were better than *Judith of Bethulia*, and the best of them, *The Avenging Conscience*, a film that Seymour Stern once appropriately described as "an Edgar Allan Poe *mosaic*," was quite remarkable in many ways. However, none of the four could be said to equal the best feature production of the day. Still, Griffith knew that he was marking time, and as features designed purely for commercial needs and to make an immediate profit, they were well above average standards. Perhaps of more interest—now, in retrospect, if not then—were the one- and two-reelers being produced by Griffith's protégé directors. So well did these men understand Griffith's methods, and know what would meet with his approval, that the one-reelers seemed almost like polished extensions of the Biograph shorts, while some of the two-reelers even seemed a blueprint of elements in Griffith features yet to come. Today, it is difficult to know for sure exactly how much personal supervision on Griffith's part was involved. If one can accept the similar period of Triangle in 1916 as a criterion, however, it is highly possible that, despite his busy schedule, Griffith did in fact find time not only to approve stories but also to involve himself in shooting and editing. It is also possible, however, that his directors were by now so skilled at making films in his image that Griffith had enough confidence in them to afford them relative autonomy, and even at times to benefit from their initiative and incorporate some of their ideas into his own work.

A good example of work by a Griffith protégé is *The Doll House Mystery*, an unusually expert little melodrama co-directed by Chester and Sidney Franklin. On the surface, it was almost a definitive Griffith two-reeler, building suspense steadily, opening up the chase in the final sequences to include a locomotive and an automobile, and climaxing with a shoot-out in a deserted cabin, its location allowing for extensive overhead panoramic shots. Yet, unlike similar Griffith shorts, the story was not just an excuse for an exercise in excitement and editing skill. It is important in its own right, and more time than usual is spent in establishing the story and its characters before the plot gets underway. The characters, particularly a socialite wife (played by Marguerite Marsh, Mae's sister) and the son of an ex-convict, well played by the child actor George Stone, are far more rounded than the average protagonists of the earlier Griffith Biographs. The final chase scenes even involve some locations and specific camera placements that Griffith copied precisely in the climax to the modern segment of *Intolerance*. Not many of the Reliance-Majestic shorts from this period survive, but those that do are indicative of a rapidly advancing sophistication. Even the comedies, despite the proven popular appeal of Mack Sennett's frenzied slapstick, are relatively gentle, human, and even satiric. *Cupid Versus Cigarettes* is not only a pleasing little comedy on its own terms but also remarkably up-to-date on two counts—as a hard-hitting if genially presented attack on the physical harm of cigarette smoking and as a staunch advocate of equal rights for women.

It would be quite fair to suggest that the short films made under Griffith's supervision at Reliance, and directed by men like the Franklins, represent some of the most sophisticated technique on view in 1914, whereas the features directed by Griffith personally in that year must be considered less advanced than those of Maurice Tourneur or Cecil B. deMille. On the other hand, Tourneur selectively and de-Mille prolifically (he directed seven full features in 1914 and was to accelerate his pace to twelve in 1915) were working at the peak of their artistic capabilities for that time. Griffith, on the other hand, worked hurriedly, efficiently, but without marked artistic inspiration in the first half of 1914, so that he could devote his full energies to *The Birth of a Nation*. *The Battle of the Sexes* was followed by *The Escape*, for many years now an apparently lost film. Even if Griffith used this film to mark time, it is perhaps indicative of his faith in the medium and of his over-generous estimation of audience intelligence and taste that he would have selected this story—from a Paul Armstrong play—as having commercial potential. For *The Escape*, despite an ultimately happy ending for two of its protagonists, is an almost unrelievedly sordid procession of brutality, madness, sex, disease, and death—the last including both a baby (crushed to death by its drunken father) and a kitten. If nothing else, *The Escape* might well qualify as the first feature-length *film noir*, just as Griffith's 1909 one-reeler *In the Watches of the Night* might be considered the very first foray into what is generally regarded as a filmic style of the forties.

Home Sweet Home, which followed *The Escape*, was an all-star film—Lillian and Dorothy Gish, Mae Marsh, Henry B. Walthall, Robert Harron, Miriam Cooper, Owen Moore, Blanche Sweet, and most of the other Griffith players. It was a naïvely symbolic tale, too consciously striving for "meaning" and artistic pretension, a weakness that was to mar such later Griffith films as *Dream Street* (1921). However, audiences liked the film far more than *The Escape*, and critics were kindly disposed toward its somewhat over-wrought filmic poetry. In at least three ways, the film resembled elements of the later *Intolerance*. It was an episodic film, its separate stories linked by a none-too-sturdy device—a much exaggerated and even falsified account of the life of John Howard Payne, writer of the lyrics of the title song. (In *Intolerance*, the titular theme was the linking device, even though the film was only partially about intolerance.) And as in *Intolerance*, the Mae Marsh-Robert Harron-Miriam Cooper sequence was actually planned (and even released) as a separate entity, then recalled, reshaped, and inserted into the body of a more ambitious film.

The last of Griffith's 1914 quartet, *The Avenging Conscience*, is one of the most fascinating and bewildering of films, by turns innovative and mature, naïve and listless. Some of the usage of Poe material is justified, other material pointlessly dragged in. The film does substitute psychological tension for physical action; the ghostly apparition that accompanies the killer's guilt pangs is smoothly done; cross-cutting for emotional suspense rather than thrill is often quite creative (especially in a Raskolnikov/Porfiri-like encounter between a detective and the man he is sure is a murderer); and at times, the film has much of the doom-laden power of the celebrated German films of the twenties. Its dream ending is quite modern, too, and much in the manner of Lang's *The Woman in the Window* (1944); the nightmarish story is brought to a conclusion, with all the loose ends wrapped up. The revelation that it was all a dream—a less common device in 1914—provided an appropriate sense of relief but was in no way merely a convenient resolution of an otherwise insoluble plot dilemma (as was frequently the case in melodramas in the forties).

The main problem with *The Avenging Conscience* is its lack of cohesion and general untidiness. One would like to think that the film's strongest element, its brooding power, is there by design. But if so, then the shortcomings of the rest of the film are inexcusable. In any event, if it is not quite the milestone film that Griffith's admirers would like it to be, its flaws at least throw into stark relief the enormous advances made by Griffith during the latter part of 1914. When *The Avenging Conscience* premiered in New York on August 2, 1914, Griffith, Bitzer, Lillian Gish, and Mae Marsh were already at work on *The Birth of a Nation*.

It is virtually impossible today to appreciate fully the impact that *The Birth of a Nation* made on audiences, on film-makers, and on both the art and industry of movies when it premiered in February 1915. So controversial has it always been because of its racial content—a controversy often artificially created and sustained—that its artistic and

innovative qualities have frequently been acknowledged almost grudgingly, as a lesser asset that did not compensate for the film's inflammatory qualities. Yet no other single film in movie history has ever done
what *The Birth of a Nation* did: established movies as an international
art and an international industry almost overnight, and influenced the
manner of narrative story-telling in American films for at least the next
six years. Griffith's methods were not new, but prior to *The Birth of a
Naiton* they were neither understood nor considered important enough
to be worth copying. The incredible financial success of the film "justified" Griffith's techniques, and at least through the end of 1920 the film
was copied (lazily) by the lesser directors and instinctively—and out of
a sense of homage—by the newer and more talented directors (John
Ford, Henry King). Probably more acting and directorial talent was
nurtured among the film's cast and crew than that of any other film,
with the possible exception of Griffth's own subsequent *Intolerance*.

The film established and justified the practice of raised admission
prices, taking the motion picture forever out of the ten-cent category.
It has almost certainly become the industry's top-grossing box-office
champion. While this claim is not necessarily a criterion of artistic
achievement—many of the industry's top grossers are of singularly negligible value artistically—it is an incredible achievement for a film that
was made in 1915 and has been in constant exhibition, including commercial exhibition, ever since. Admittedly, it might be a hard claim to
support in terms of dollars and cents. Existing financial records can
only prove a minimum income from the film, since Griffith did not have
national distribution in 1915 and sold the film on a state's rights basis.
This means that records exist only on the flat or percentage payments
made to Griffith for distribution rights to given territories, not on the
gross income from those territories. Nevertheless, existing figures do
indicate a minimum return over the years of 50 million dollars.* If it
were no more than that, it would be an incredible profit for a film that
was estimated to cost between $65,000 and $112,000. These two figures
represent production cost and the final cost up to presentation, including a substantial sum for advertising and such added niceties as a full,
live orchestral score. Grosses in terms of dollars mean very little any-
more, when contemporary grosses are invariably inflated by the casual
use of the $5 admission charge. The only fair estimate of a film's suc-

* This figure has now been disputed by the trade journal *Variety*; there is further
discussion on this point in the final chapter of the book.

cess, in the long run, should be the *number* of paid admissions, an unchanging guide to a film's popularity. On that score, there can be no question of the leadership of *The Birth of a Nation*. In the first six months of its release, it was seen by more people than had attended *all* the plays presented in the United States in the previous few years! It was this obvious competition and commercial threat that caused the theatre to hit back by coining the phrase "the legitimate stage" as a deliberate insult to the medium of film.

At twelve reels, or a running time of three hours, *The Birth of a Nation* was at least twice as long as that of the average American feature of the day. It represented the tremendous faith of Griffith, who was forced to subsidize the film by raising completion money himself, when the estimated budget was depleted.

Part One (slightly more than a third of the total film) dramatizes the events leading up to the Civil War of 1861–65 and the war itself, including the surrender of Lee and the assassination of Lincoln. Also included in this section is a prologue depicting the introduction of slavery into America in the 17th century and the rise of the Abolitionist movement 150 years later. Despite the brilliant crescendo of cross-cutting in the climax of the second half, the first half is certainly better. It is here that Griffith's ability to humanize history is seen at its best. His story is told through the interaction between two families, one Northern and one Southern, showing the heartbreak of the Civil War in personal as well as ideological terms. The head of the Northern family, Austin Stoneman (played by Ralph Lewis), is actually a thinly disguised portrait of Thaddeus Stevens, a prominent Radical Republican Congressman proponent of harsh approach to Southern Reconstruction, while such key figures as Lincoln, Lee, Grant, John Wilkes Booth and Senator Charles Sumner naturally appear under their own names. So adept is the interweaving of factual and fictional characters that it would be quite possible to edit out most of the romantic and fictional elements of the film and still be left with a virtual documentary.

Many of the most striking images occur in the first half: the tragedy of war is as poignantly portrayed by a single shot of a dead soldier, half curled up as if in sleep, and preceded by the subtitle "War's Peace," as it was to be later by that bravura crane-shot pullback of the entire Atlanta square filled with the dead and dying in *Gone With the Wind*. One of the first outstanding examples of "painting with light" in film can be seen in the brief sequence of Sherman's march to the sea. A small group of refugees (probably a family whose home has been burned) huddle at the left of the screen in a stylized and partially painted set suggesting the wreckage of a house. The camera moves across to a panoramic overhead long shot of Sherman's troops marching away from the camera, past a burning building. There is an insert to a closer view, then a cut back to the end position of the previous pan, and the camera retraces its move back to the pathetic refugees. Within a few seconds, apart from the narrative point made by the poignant scene, one sees the welding of stylized and harshly documentarian styles, close-shot and extreme long shot separated by two kinds of lighting and composition, yet linked emotionally by a cause-and-effect motif and physically by a camera movement.

Another superb moment in Part One is the homecoming of Colonel Cameron (Henry B. Walthall) to his mother (Josephine Crowell) and sister (Mae Marsh) after capture, imprisonment, and a sojourn in a military hospital. In the scenes immediately prior to the reunion, Griffith creates a mood that is first joyful (the happy preparations for his return) and then sad (the realization of the poverty thrust on them by the South's defeat). The reunion itself, starting with a long shot of the tattered soldier entering the frame at the end of the street and climaxing with his embrace of his sister at the door, and then being drawn into the house by the arms of his mother (who is otherwise not shown) is a beautifully tender and underplayed scene. Further, it indicates a great respect for the audience's ability to inject its own emotions into a scene, to accept suggestion rather than outright statement, and to imagine actions (and the conclusion of the scene) taking place off screen. Although this scene has been imitated (knowingly and otherwise) many times, perhaps most effectively by John Ford in a 1933 talkie, *Pilgrimage*, the original has somehow never been surpassed; even out of context, as a film "clip," it still has the power to be intensely moving. Incredibly, the superb underplaying and meticulous timing of this sequence were achieved through careful rehearsals designed not so much to perfect the actors' performances as to get the scene completed within a specific time. This occurred partly because, even while shooting, Griffith could envision the rhythm of the completed film, and partly because of economics; he could not afford the luxury of reshooting.

Towering over all else in Part One of *The Birth of a Nation* were the monumental battle scenes (shot in the area now totally covered by Universal Studios), which may since have been surpassed in terms of sheer size but have certainly never been equalled in terms of realism or excitement. Deliberately patterned after Matthew Brady photographs, subdirected by a group of unit directors who were able to turn the "huge" armies† into masses of individuals rather than tableau-like mobs, these battle scenes, staged with extreme camera mobility and the usual Griffith juxtaposition of close detail shots with panoramic long shots, have vitality, savagery, and an incredible sense of spontaneity. No matter how many times one has seen these sequences, one tends to jump along with the extra, who is clearly surprised when a mortar bomb explodes behind his back, or to be moved by the destruction of a tree hit by a shell. (Griffith had an astonishing ability to crystallise the awful, massive destruction of war into shots of simple symbolism or metaphor. Despite the grimness of the often authentic war scenes in his World War I film *Hearts of the World*, its most moving single shot is of a brace of swans, with their cygnets, swimming away from the ripples in their pond caused by falling dirt from a bomb explosion.)

Part Two of *The Birth of a Nation* traces the exploitation of the newly emancipated Southern Negroes by Northern bankers and industrialists (carpetbaggers) and by political fanatics of both North and South (scalawags). It dramatizes the struggle against, and ultimate defeat of, a vengeful movement by these elements to "crush the White South under the heel of the Black South" (quoting from Woodrow Wilson) and to rule the defeated South through a Northern-controlled economic, political, and racial dictatorship. It was this second portion of the film, with its glorification of the Ku Klux Klan of that period, that has caused most of the film's problems. Not only does this section of the film draw heavily on the writings of Thomas Dixon but because of the elimination of most of the authentic historical characters, and the involvement of the Thaddeus Stevens parallel in much of the fictional melodrama, it is more open to questions of historical distortion.

† Despite their size, these "huge" battle scenes rarely used more than 300 extras. As Lillian Gish has pointed out, any director could make thousands of extras look like thousands of extras. Only Griffith could make 300 men look like thousands. Yet frequently good and reliable writers, unimpressed by press agentry and familiar with its claims, casually refer to the "thousands" deployed in these scenes, quite honestly believing the apparent evidence of their own eyes.

It was, of course, the dynamic quality of *The Birth of a Nation* that caused—and still causes—the film problems on racial grounds. No movie with such imagination and persuasive power had ever been seen before. With no disrespect to the remarkable early films of Tourneur and others, it was as if an audience familiar only with comic strips had suddenly been introduced to the works of Tolstoy, and in a way that they could understand. Yet audiences were, understandably, not yet sophisticated enough to understand film technique, or how it was manipulating them. It is extremely unlikely that even Griffith fully understood the awesome power of the film medium. In Griffith's eyes, *The Birth of a Nation* did tell the truth; however, it was only one side of a truth. The assertive style of the film left no option for another side. Audiences, confronted with an overpowering flow of images, often connected by fully documented and undeniably accurate titles, had no way of knowing how the linkage and arrangement of shots could lead the spectator to the film-maker's point of view. Thus, Griffith introduces a sequence, backed up by historical references, showing the passage of a bill permitting the inter-marriage of blacks and whites. But he follows it with a quick shot of a young black looking up lecherously, and then a shot of a white girl and her companions (presumably parents) shuddering and drawing back as they watch the proceedings from a balcony. There is nothing in the film to prove that the black man is looking at the white girl, yet from the arrangement of shots, the implication is obvious. Here, historical reconstruction slides unobtrusively into pure editorializing. At another point in the film, the mulatto villain Silas Lynch (played by George Siegmann) confronts Colonel Cameron on the street and tells him, "The sidewalk belongs to us as much as to you, 'Colonel' Cameron." There is nothing unreasonable in his statement or even in his manner, but the insertion of the quotes around the word "Colonel" in the title immediately injects a note of insulting derision.

Ironically, the use of the same filmic method that Griffith evolved to tell his story has been in part responsible for the effectiveness of the campaign against the film ever since. A David Wolper television documentary of the 1960's, *Hollywood, The Golden Years,* told the history of the silent period in superficial but generally acceptable terms, considering the non-scholastic mass audience it was aimed at. However, it sustained and enlarged on the myth of the riots that were supposed to have greeted *The Birth of a Nation* on its initial showing in Boston.

(There were protests and demonstrations, but of a small-scale and well-controlled nature.) After the narrator set up the "massive" nature of the protests, the screen was filled with montages of newspaper headlines, some of which may even have been authentic, but superimposed over unidentifiable shots of huge rioting mobs sweeping through city streets which definitely had no connection whatsoever with the opening of the film in Boston. Yet, quite logically, audiences assumed it to be a bit of "truthful" reportage.

Through the years, *The Birth of a Nation* has constantly been harassed by the NAACP, which has bombarded announced showings of the film with masses of "protest" letters, evenly divided into three different and always word-for-word styles, indicating that the writers had never seen the film they were protesting so vehemently. Griffith himself stated, in a filmed interview that accompanied a reissue of the film in 1930, "The *original* Klan was needed." Whatever its shortcomings, it did what it felt was its job, and disbanded. Later revivals of the Klan could not lay any claims to necessity or expediency as a reason for their existence, which were simply to propagate racial hatred and terrorism. The blind bigotry of the later Klan has always had an adverse effect on the depiction within *The Birth of a Nation* of the original Klan.

The main thrust of the attacks against *The Birth of a Nation* is that Griffith was a racist, using the screen deliberately for inflammatory purposes. Actually, even if he *had* been a racist, *The Birth of a Nation* would still have to be accepted as a masterpiece, just as *The Triumph of the Will* is unquestionably a masterpiece despite being a propagandist paean of praise to Nazi ideology. But the facts concerning Griffith and his attitudes are otherwise.

When the film went into release in 1915, it carried an opening credit (missing from all subsequent prints) in which Griffith expressed the view that none of the standard history books had ever presented an impartial view of the South's role in the American Civil War. This film, he said, *was* to present an accurate and impartial account of that role from a Southern viewpoint. In itself, that avowed aim is perhaps a contradiction in terms, and stresses the problems involved in putting both realism and truth on the screen. Novelist Howard Fast, motivated as much by his sincerely held Communist beliefs as Griffith was by his Southern beliefs, wrote a novel, *Freedom Road,* based on the same historical records that Griffith consulted. Yet Fast's approach was so completely different that his hero was the same Negro used by Griffith for his nominal villain, Silas Lynch.‡ Of the two approaches, one is inclined to put a little more credence in Griffith's, since he had grown up in the post-Reconstruction era. His father was a colorful Confederate participant in the Civil War, though it seems probable that the Griffith family somewhat exaggerated his exploits and deliberately created a semi-legend concerning his wartime valor.

Griffith's own subtitle—that the film was to depict an impartial account of the Southern viewpoint—is in itself an explanation for a film which certainly does shows the Negro in an unflattering light. Early in the film, another title refers to life running "in a quaintly way that is no more," but in Griffith's own home area—Crestwood and LaGrange, in Kentucky—life still does run very much in that "quaintly way," and inborn attitudes toward the Negro have not changed. In a late 1950's tribute to Griffith, at ceremonies by his grave in Crestwood, one of those present was Griffith's Negro chauffeur—and close friend. By rights he should have been one of the honored guests there, but the condescension toward him was obvious and the respect grudging.

The events that Griffith was reconstructing in *The Birth of a Nation* were by no means ancient history. Scarcely half a century had gone by since the Reconstruction period, and many veterans of the conflict worked with Griffith on the film. If the film appeared to be anti-Negro at times, it can be understood why it was so, for the Confederate soldiers and officers who advised Griffith had strong obvious opinions on the war and on blacks, too. Nobody has ever accused Lewis Milestone of being anti-Japanese for making *The Purple Heart* because it dealt with a contemporary (World War Two) period when the Japanese were enemies, and when it was fashionable, understandable, and perhaps even propagandistically necessary, to dislike them. Yet viewed objectively, *The Purple Heart* is one of the most racially slanted films ever made. Possibly if Griffith had been able to make *The Birth of a Nation* fifty years earlier, during the Reconstruction period itself, it would have been seen as a reflection of its times (as we now see the World War Two films), and no such accusations would have been

‡ There was only one genuine villain in *The Birth of a Nation*, the renegade Gus, played by Walter Long. But even with him, as with the other unsympathetic blacks, Griffith was careful to place the blame for his behavior on the white carpetbaggers who had manipulated the Negroes for their own ends.

flung at him. (There are also many later American films with, intentionally or otherwise, far stronger anti-black attitudes than *The Birth of a Nation.* Yet because they are lesser films, often forgotten and non-influential, they are accepted with amused tolerance.)

As it is, Griffith displayed considerable restraint in controlling Southern prejudices and in being fair to the Negro. No such restraints are present in Thomas Dixon's novel *The Clansman,* a vicious, incredibly bigoted work on which *The Birth of a Nation* is largely based. One whole chapter is devoted to a discussion of the Negro's place in American society, with Dr. Cameron exclaiming that ". . . for a thick-lipped, flat-nosed, spindle-shanked Negro, exuding his nauseous animal odor, to shout in derision over the hearths and homes of white men and women is an atrocity too monstrous for belief." On the question of equality, Cameron states that "we sink to his level if you walk as his equal in physical contact with him. His race is not an infant, it is a degenerate." The whole book is so filled with stomach-turning vitriol of this nature that hatred appears to be the raison d'être for its existence. The natural melodrama of the theme, enlarged to magnificent proportions of historical tableaux by Griffith, is so minimized by Dixon that Griffith's entire three-reel climax is dismissed by Dixon in one line, and even happens "off-page." None of Dixon's racial hatred is utilized by Griffith, although had he been so inclined, he could certainly have used—and excused—it on the grounds that he could not tamper with the thoughts and writings of another. However, one has many concrete examples of Griffith's toning down of Dixon's bias, most specifically in his handling of the Little Sister's suicide.

In the film, Mae Marsh jumps to her death to avoid rape at the hands of an individual Negro. In the novel, the girl *and* her mother, already assaulted by an organized group of Negroes, later commit suicide together because of "the shame that neither they nor the world can forget." All that Griffith used of this ugly chapter is the final sentence—"Hand in hand they stepped from the cliff into the mists and on through the opal gates of death"—which he translated into the title, "For her who had learned the stern lesson of honor, we should not grieve that she found sweeter the opal gates of death." Actually, even in this grim sequence, the threat of rape is only implied, for the audience has been pre-conditioned to Gus's bestial nature through earlier sequences. In the context of that sequence alone, Gus's conduct is not totally unreasonable. He does approach the girl with respect, and proposes marriage: admittedly, to the Southern mind of that particular time, probably a greater crime than rape! But in contemporary terms, if the girl chose to flee from him in terror and commit suicide, it was her problem rather than his.

One of the weakest thrusts still made against Griffith's alleged racial bias is his use of white actors in Negro roles, the assumption being that prejudice prevented his hiring Negroes for prominent roles. This accusation is easily disposed of, and boils down to a simple matter of economics, Griffith's production methods, and the fact than in 1915, most of the acting opportunities for blacks were on the East Coast rather than the West, and the number of Negro actors situated in Hollywood was minuscule. (Further, one can appreciate the ready reluctance of Negro actors to appear in any film known to be based on the works of Thomas Dixon.) To save costs, and to make the most of actors familiar with his methods, Griffith frequently used the same actors in a number of roles within a given picture. With make-up, whites could effectively play blacks, but obviously the process could not be reversed. Thus, Walter Long, who appeared in the guerrilla raid in Piedmont early in the film as "the scalawag white captain," later became Gus, the black renegade; and following his death on the battlefield as a Union soldier, Robert Harron re-emerged as one of the Negro militia. In lesser roles, many Negroes do, of course, appear. In any case, the white actor in black-face was very much a tradition of the theatre at that time, and many actors, such as Tom Wilson and Jules Cowles, made a virtual career of such roles. Indeed, many fair-skinned Negroes even donned black make-up to maintain the theatrical stereotype of the minstrel black. Griffith was much hurt by the reaction to the film's racial content, and especially by allegations of his own racism, which he denied vehemently. It may be that his oft-proclaimed warmth for and friendship toward the Negro, though genuine, was still shaped by the Southerner's traditional concept of the Negro's "place" in society. The "good" blacks in his films far outnumbered the "bad," but their goodness and virtues—including loyalty, bravery, and self-sacrifice—arise out of their servitude and devotion to white masters in stories of the days of slavery, or white superiors, in contemporary settings.

Anti-Griffith factions have constantly striven to prove that Griffith, chagrined and conscience-stricken over *The Birth of a Nation*, made his subsequent film *Intolerance* (1916) as an "atonement." From his point of view, *Intolerance* was an angry (if not always logically presented) cry of protest against the meddlers and would-be censors who would limit Griffith's freedom of expression on the screen. Had he wanted to "atone," *Intolerance* surely would have been an ideal vehicle. But of the various forms of intolerance utilized and condemned in the film, *racial* intolerance is conspicuously absent. In fact, apart from the Ethiopian contingent of Cyrus the Persian's armies, there are no Negroes at all in *Intolerance*—not even in the Utopian world of the future, where wars and hatred have been abolished and Christ's love reigns over all. Nor is there a marked change of attitude in any of Griffith's subsequent films. In *The Greatest Thing in Life, The White Rose, America, The Greatest Question* and even in his talkie *Abraham Lincoln* (1930), blacks are treated amusingly, sentimentally, sometimes seriously, usually affectionately, but always with a degree of condescension. *Never*, however, with hostility.

In terms of film history, Griffith's opinion and treatment of blacks is not all that important. But inasmuch as *The Birth of a Nation* is quite possibly the single most important film of all time, and a film that is rarely regarded objectively *because* of its racial content, it is important to clarify Griffith's *intent* and to stress that, while difficult, it should be shown in an atmosphere that tries to separate form from content. (Too many colleges and universities today pay only lip service to its innovations and present the film under a cloud of apologies.) There is no question about the fact that it remains very controversial racially, and its *theatrical* revival, to uninformed audiences, is perhaps both dangerous and unwise. It is no small tribute to the film's astonishing power that it *can* still sway audience emotions more than half a century after its production.

The Birth of a Nation, odd acting gestures and minor mechanical imperfections apart, does not date. No mere archival milestone, it is a living work, its acting often subtle, its photography incorporating both lyrical and documentarian values. A good print, properly presented at the right speed, and with an appropriate musical score, can bring it to roaring life again—building to a tremendous crescendo of excitement in its closing reels, where the increasingly rapid cross-cutting between two different locales of action, and not one but two "rides to the rescue," forms a climax still unparalleled in blood-quickening excitement. As both an entertainment and as the first major work of screen art, it enriches anew with each repeated viewing, and while its weaknesses become more apparent on re-viewing, they take a long time to surface and are usually quite insignificant.

One weakness in the film is perhaps Griffith's use of a kind of shorthand body language to avoid lengthy titles or expository scenes. One such moment occurs midway in the film, when the mother goes to a military hospital to visit her wounded son. After a title stating that secret elements have condemned her son to be hanged as a guerrilla, we see an Army surgeon conveying this information by a quick flick of his wrist in the region of his neck—pantomiming the act of execution by hanging. In one sense, the whole sequence is absurd. The son was captured in battle, where he had in fact been cheered by the enemy for his heroism in ministering to their own wounded. No possible circumstances could justify the intervention of sinister secret influences or the regarding of a Southern colonel as a guerrilla. Even less likely is that a surgeon, presumably by his very calling a humanitarian, would be so indelicate as to pass such information on to a grieving mother in so callous and coarse a manner. To Griffith, the sequence is clearly only punctuation. He is merely laying, as quickly and economically as he can, the groundwork for a longer and more important sequence in which the mother goes to a harassed President Lincoln, who still finds time to listen to her appeal and grant a pardon. So instinctively right was Griffith's pacing, and his anticipation of audience reaction, that the scene, for all its absurdity, works and even passes unnoticed on initial viewings. (So does a similar piece of body language at the climax of *Intolerance*, when the distraught wife [Mae Marsh] seeks from a priest the confirmation that her husband will not be hung, and signals her inquiry by pantomiming the yanking up of a rope, while she shakes her head hopefully, yet questioningly.) While these uses of body language take on a ludicrous quality when studied and analyzed, in their initial context they work well, and compress a wealth of meaning and emotion into a minimum of gestures and expressions.

While *The Birth of a Nation*'s immense power as entertainment was grasped immediately by the critics, not all of them were as enthusiastic over its innovations: a veritable textbook of cinematic grammar, style, and devices that would remain intact until the coming of sound, and even thereafter be of continuing influence. Some critics felt it absurd

Cripple Creek Bar Room (Edison, 1898)

An early "mobile" camera for documentarian rather than dramatic purposes

The Great Train Robbery (Edison, 1903)

Typical harsh early studio lighting

Typical Griffith use of
landscape in *Ramona*
(1910)

Griffith's *The Lesser Evil*
(1910) with Blanche
Sweet and (at right)
Alfred Paget

Griffith's *A Girl and Her
Trust* (1912) with Charles
Mailes, Alfred Paget, and
Dorothy Bernard

Early comedy stars: John Bunny and Flora Finch in *A Cure for Pokeritus*
(Vitagraph, 1912)

An early full-length feature: Sidney Olcott's *From the Manger to the Cross*
(1912) with R. Henderson Bland and Alice Hollister

The Deadly Turning, an episode from the serial *The Perils of Pauline* (1914) with Pearl White and Crane Wilbur

Assembly-line shooting methods at Thomas Edison's Menlo Park, New Jersey, studios in 1915.

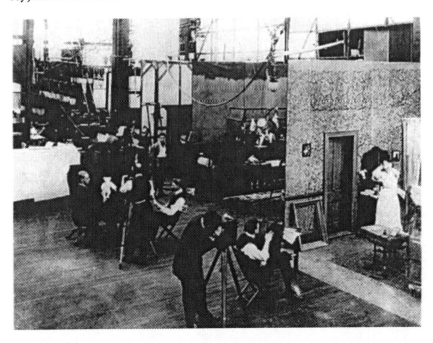

Major figures of the new Lasky Feature Company, Hollywood, 1913: Cecil B. deMille and Oscar Apfel, co-directors of *The Squaw Man*; Dustin Farnum, star of that film, Edmund Breese and Edward Abeles, stars, and, seated, Jesse Lasky.

Thomas H. Ince

The Wishing Ring (1914), directed by Maurice Tourneur, with Vivian Martin and Chester Barnet

Battle scenes for *The Birth of a Nation* (1915), shot on the present site of Universal Pictures

The assassination of Lincoln from *The Birth of a Nation*

Intolerance (1916)—the feasting and
celebrations in Babylon

Intolerance—Lillian Gish rocking the
cradle behind a linking title

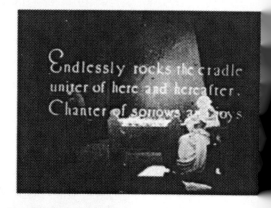

Intolerance—Mae Marsh in the modern
story

The Romance of Happy Valley
(Griffith, 1919) with Lillian Gish

The Wharf Rat (1916) with
Mae Marsh

Hell's Hinges (1916) with William S. Hart

George Beban, star of the notable earlier *The Italian*, being directed by Maurice Tourneur (right) in *The Pawn of Fate* (1916)

John Davidson (seated), George Beban and Doris Kenyon (standing), in *The Pawn of Fate*. Crew includes Jan Van Den Broek (behind camera), Maurice Tourneur (holding script), and Clarence Brown (standing below camera)

Harry Carey (arms upraised) in *Straight Shooting* (1917), John Ford's first feature. Ford returned to this familiar location frequently, for *The Iron Horse, Stagecoach*, and other films.

Anita Stewart, a major star for Vitagraph and later MGM, in the teens and early 20's.

Wild and Woolly (1917) with Douglas Fairbanks

that the use of the moving camera in the battle and chase scenes placed the audience in the "confusing" position of being absorbed into the action, resolutely holding to the theory that the audience should remain firmly separated, as a spectator only, in the tradition of the theatre. The shaping of the screen into iris, vignette, and other forms—even the use of horizontal panels, anticipating the CinemaScope image—likewise confused those critics who still regarded the film as an alternative to the stage. But the basic construction of the film—a methodical beginning; the establishment of time, place, and characters; the building up to an initial climax; the relaxing of tempo to repeat the process and build up to a second, longer, greater climax; the mathematical precision of editing within that climax, even to throwing in a brief, seemingly unintended "joke" so that audiences could relax, release their pent-up tensions, and draw greater excitement from the remainder of the film's climax—all of this became a model on which the structure of American film was to be based for the next half-decade. It was to reach its purely academic peak in *Intolerance,* a commercial failure. But so great and long-lasting was the commercial success of *The Birth of a Nation* that even the failure of *Intolerance,* considered an artistic indulgence, was over-ridden by the phenomenal box-office success and artistic influence of what is still one of cinema's peaks: *The Birth of a Nation.*§

§ The incredible influence of the film on European dictators, particularly on Stiller in Sweden, has deliberately been omitted here. This influence was somewhat delayed by the intervening war years, and reached its peak in the twenties, when Griffith's influence and prestige at home were on the wane. It will be discussed more fully in a later chapter on the twenties.

6

"Intolerance"

Griffith's own hopes and plans for a follow-up to *The Birth of a Nation* were never announced. That film had so wholly consumed his time and energies—not only in production but in the constant seeking out of new capital—that thoughts of the future could only be dreams rather than planned realities. Moreover, Griffith had no conception of the incredible financial success that awaited *The Birth of a Nation*. The possibilities of capitalizing on success were there, but so were the equally strong probabilities of having to retrench and recoup possible losses. When *Intolerance* (1916) did emerge as the next Griffith film, it was the result not so much of a desire to top the spectacle of *The Birth of a Nation* as to provide a weapon against the critics of the Civil War film and to justify the movie medium's right to freedom of expression by proving that with freedom came artistic expansion.

Griffith described his conception: "The purpose of the production is to trace a universal theme through various episodes of the race's history. Ancient, sacred, medieval and modern times are considered. Events are not set forth in their historical sequence or according to the accepted forms of dramatic construction, but as they might flash across a mind seeking to parallel the life of the different ages."

As his base, Griffith took the already completed *The Mother and the Law*, a modern story with strong elements of social criticism, with Mae Marsh, Robert Harron, and Miriam Cooper in the leads. Started before *The Birth of a Nation*, it was—and is—one of Griffith's most mature works, although it would not be seen separately from *Intolerance* until 1919. To this film, Griffith added a story of ancient Babylon at the time of its overthrow by Cyrus the Persian; a story of France in the Middle Ages, climaxing with the St. Bartholomew's Day massacre engineered by Catherine de Medici; and a fourth story, utilized mainly for counterpoint, dealing with Christ and His crucifixion. This Biblical story was the shortest of the four, and unlike the Babylonian and French episodes, contained no fictional characters or elements interwoven with fact. All four stories were linked by the symbolic image of a woman (Lillian Gish) rocking a cradle, a visualization of Walt Whitman's lines, ". . . out of the cradle endlessly rocking, Uniter of Here and Hereafter."

Griffith further explained his method: "The stories will begin like four currents looked at from a hilltop. At first the four currents will flow apart, slowly and quietly. But as they flow, they grow nearer and nearer together, and faster and faster, until in the end, in the last act, they mingle in one mighty river of expressed emotion."

While this analysis clearly and accurately describes the structure of the film, it is most likely *not* Griffith's own wording, though it is always ascribed to him. His prose was often clumsy and heavy-handed (though not without a certain rough-hewn poetry), so it seems dubious that he could, or would, have described such a monumental venture in such restrained terms. Almost certainly, his own description would have been more florid. The use of the river as a symbol was to remain a favorite device of his, to be returned to frequently in such films as *The Greatest Question* and *Way Down East* (both of 1920).

Intolerance has been termed the movies' only film fugue—which it probably is—and the only film capable of being regarded as a separate, independent work of art, comparable with the works of a Rodin, a Michelangelo, or a Beethoven. This latter summarization, though understandable at the point in film history at which it was made, is hardly supportable, since it implies the same artistic perfection ascribed to the works of painting or music with which it has been equated. While *Intolerance* is an innovative masterpiece, and in many ways one of the formal masterpieces of all cinema, it is still very much of a flawed masterpiece—a contradiction in terms that somehow seems justifiable in the world of film if not in the other arts.

In terms of sheer size, scope, and the splendor of its sets, *Intolerance* has probably never been equalled. The huge Babylonian set sprawled over more than 250 acres of Hollywood at the junction of Hollywood and Sunset Boulevards—a landmark later partially taken up (in the twenties) by the Charles Ray Studios, which eventually became the Monogram/Allied Artists Studio and was finally turned into a television station. Much of the interior work was done at the old Fine Arts Studio, and stretches of studio wall and the studio gate can be seen in the industrial and strike sequences in the modern story. (The Fine Arts Studio was later absorbed into the Columbia Pictures complex and eventually burned down.) Incredibly, the massive battle scenes (which include a couple of beheadings, one obviously "rigged," the other less so) were organized and staged without the participation of second unit directors or experienced stunt men, and despite all the carnage and the falls, no one was injured. But the physical size of the production is perhaps one of the least imposing of its many accomplishments. In terms of technique—both the innovations of Griffith and the mechanical means to implement those innovations—the film is a virtual textbook, containing forerunners of glass shots, an ingenious improvised camera-crane which even foreshadowed the effects of the zoom lens in certain shots, the most sophisticated use yet of toning and tinting, coupled with mood lighting, for dramatic effect; some astonishingly "modern" performances, especially from Mae Marsh and Miriam Cooper; and, of course, a pattern of editing, or montage, which was to be of profound influence on the Soviet films of the twenties.

Certainly the most astonishing, if not the most important, aspect of these innovations is that Griffith shot and cut the entire film instinctively, without recourse to either script or notes, and did it while maintaining his responsibilities as the third arm (the others: Thomas Ince, Mack Sennett) of the Triangle Studio, the new production/distribution complex that Griffith had just joined as a partner. In 1916, the year of the release of *Intolerance*, Griffith was also responsible for the production of some fifty other full-length features, including a dozen Douglas Fairbanks films. Admittedly, in many cases his responsibility was limited to suggestions and decisions rather than physical participation; on the other hand, several Triangle releases of that year clearly show signs of his personal supervision. *Hoodoo Ann*, a charming Robert Harron-Mae Marsh romance, was even written by Griffith under the pseudonym Granville Warwick, and contained enough authentic Griffith touches to confirm his personal involvement in production. *Any* distractions from the task of conceiving and controlling a project such as *Intolerance* would be notable; the "distraction" of running a studio and providing a solid year's output of films (many of them of real quality) is almost inconceivable.

The editing of *Intolerance*, both cumulatively and within individual sequences, remains a tour de force. Griffith seems to have learned a great deal about the successful structuring of a film just by studying his own *The Birth of a Nation*, which started slowly and methodically, built to its first climax, relaxed, and then built to a second, greater, and more prolonged climax. *Intolerance*, though of the same length, rearranges the structuring to its advantage. It starts in the same methodical way, introducing its characters and establishing its theme. It withholds the Babylonian sequence until substantially into the early portion of the film, the size of its set—introduced via an iris from the bottom left of the screen, slowly opening to reveal the exterior walls of the city—renewing audience interest in a film that seemed to be taking its time getting down to business. (However, Griffith cannily *still* withheld the most overpowering shots of Babylon—those overhead shots taken both from a camera-crane and a moored balloon—until the bachannal sequence in the second half of the film, thus providing new visual thrills right after the midway battle sequence, when the audience must have assumed that the film had reached its spectacular zenith and was now being wrapped up.

Moreover, while *The Birth of a Nation* (perhaps of necessity, because of the chronological sequence of events) placed its slowest section at the beginning of the second half, spending some three reels establishing milieu and historical background before building to the second climax, Griffith, in *Intolerance*, places all of the historical and other background data in the early portion of the film. Thus, the first climax, of Babylon's initial victory over Cyrus the Persian, comes two thirds of the way through the film. Part Two very quickly picks up the threads of all four stories, and within one reel marshals them into position for the bravura climax—some three reels of sustained action in which Griffith cuts from story to story and period to period with increasing rapidity, at first continuing to use the Woman Rocking the Cradle as a linking device, and then dispensing with her entirely so that all four stories erupt and pour across the screen simultaneously—

cutting from long shot to long shot, from chariot wheels to train wheels, in a display of editing that could not have been more precise had it been mathematically planned on a story board.

No matter how many times one has seen *Intolerance*, these climactic reels leave one spent and exhausted. Even if one is able to detach oneself from emotional involvement, the sheer pace and fury of the images themselves is enervating. The three historical stories have tragic endings, the modern story a happy ending—though it is by no means predictable, and since the traditional "happy ending" is not yet a Hollywood formula in 1916, its outcome still engenders tremendous suspense, which Griffith milks to the last frame of the last shot. (Even when the pardon is clearly about to be granted, the executioners' hands tremble as they hold their knives a fraction above the ropes that, when cut, will send the doomed man through the gallows' trap door!) Griffith's epilogue, depicting a future Utopia in which wars will be no more, and wherein "flowery fields bloom in place of prison walls," is a valid part of the film's structure. Griffith believed in his message sincerely, and felt that the universal language of film could help to bring about such an enviable (if unlikely) world state. But regardless of the validity—or naïveté—of his philosophy, one needs those few minutes of placid, ambiguous epilogue to unwind and regain one's composure after such a sustained barrage on the senses and emotions.

In the face of such a virtuoso piece of film-making—film-making that would be incredible *today*, if anyone had the vision and imagination to attempt it, but that was truly astounding for a period as early as 1916—and particularly in the face of its remarkable visual beauty (G. W. Bitzer again photographed, with Karl Brown as his assistant, and most of the big scenes were covered with only one camera), it is almost blasphemous to have to admit that this Bible of filmic grammar and technique has a *lot* of things wrong with it. Its initial problem is that, the French episode apart, it really has nothing to do with intolerance at all, and Griffith even seems subliminally aware of this by dragging the word in whenever he can to underline his theme. (The law court is referred to as "a sometimes House of Intolerance," and the young husband sent to prison is "intolerated away for a term.") As in *The Birth of a Nation*, the treatment of history rarely admits that there could be two sides to any question. Statements from politicians and historical figures, often quite genuine, are occasionally presented out of context and their subtitles underlined, to stress their infallibility. As in *The Birth of a Nation*, Griffith frequently injects his own editorializing into historical matter, giving the audience little opportunity—or time—to separate fact from opinion. Griffith's handling of the Babylonian sequences is masterly. Remarkably little is known about that civilization, even less certainly in 1916 than today. Yet by using instinct and imagination, and by incorporating interesting, if not entirely relevant documenary data (". . . to the Babylonians we owe the division of the hour into sixty minutes"), Griffith builds up an astonishingly convincing picture of Babylonian life. (Showmanship was added to what little was known of Babylonian architecture and weaponry: the elephants, as a design motif on the walls, were an element added by Griffith, as was the decision to give the Babylonians a flame-thrower to aid in their battle against the Persians.) We really get a sense of how Babylonian nobility and peasantry lived, loved, relaxed, and celebrated. Universalizing his fictional characters—giving his Babylonian heroine the coquettishness of a modern American girl, and having her worry about getting a new dress—made Griffith's history warm, human, and somehow contemporary, while the tableau-like re-enactments of actual events, and the frequent citing of historical authorities, gave it an underlying scholarship, too. But Griffith's Babylon is just that, our limited knowledge of its history somewhat "revised" to support Griffith's theme. His nominal hero in this sequence, Belshazzar, is depicted as a democrat and a liberal thinker, unwilling to restrict his people's liberty in any way. Yet in contemporary parlance, he would be considered something of a "swinger," his Babylon not too far removed from Sodom and Gomorrah, and thus ripe for downfall. Conversely, Griffith's villain, Cyrus the Persian, with his battle cry of "Kill! Kill! Kill! And to God the Glory!", is depicted as a pure tyrant. Yet Cyrus was no more wholly evil than Belshazzar was wholly good, and in fact his conquest of Babylon brought with it many cultural advantages. Griffith's casual use of history for his own ends also leads to distortion in other ways: he quotes Hammurabi's code of justice—"An eye for an eye, a tooth for a tooth"—as though it were purely a code of vengeance, thus minimizing a remarkable early figure whose achievements included a school system, socialized medicine, a drainage system, and a sophisticated judicial procedure.

While *Intolerance* has some brilliant performances, it also has some very bad ones. Josephine Crowell, who was so moving and restrained as Mrs. Cameron in *The Birth of a Nation,* is positively grotesque as Catherine de Medici—and the fault is Griffith's as much as hers. In many ways, too, *Intolerance* is an untidy film, though this may be an unfair criticism since it obviously had to be edited quite ruthlessly to bring it down to its still substantial thirteen reels. Certain awkward pieces of cutting, or unexplained facial expressions, suddenly make sense when one sees *The Mother and the Law* or *The Fall of Babylon** in their full separate versions. For the most part, what Griffith was forced to excise *was* extraneous, but its elimination nevertheless upset the editorial flow of the film. (When we first see the great gate of Imgur-Bel, we get quick flashes of the gate in operation, but each shot is too short, an upward pan obviously being cut off before its conclusion. Later, fairly lengthy discussions of religious freedom between Belshazzar and his High Priest are condensed to a quick exchange of glances, with no explanation as to why the High Priest is suddenly scowling and displeased.)

Many cuts may have been dictated by the inevitability of ultimate protest: at one time, for example, the financier was very clearly meant to be accepted as Rockefeller! And frames of the initial version of the film, deposited with the Library of Congress, indicate that some scenes were included solely for the opportunity they provided for Griffith to attack various forms of corruption and sexual depravity. Finally, well into the release of not only this but all of his films, Griffith was wont to tamper with his original editing. Even in the 1940's, when much of his material was being revived theatrically, adverse audience reaction to a given scene would tell him that it was cut wrong—and up he would go to the projection booth to correct it! Many of the prints extant today may well have been tampered with by Griffith in just such a fashion,

---

* *The Fall of Babylon* was released as a separate feature in 1919, with all the deleted material, including one or two complete sets, not otherwise seen in *Intolerance,* restored. Since the film was now essentially an "entertainment" and a "spectacular," its unhappy ending was inappropriate, and Griffith shot additional footage to build up the romance between Constance Talmadge and Elmer Clifton, eliminate her death scene, and give them a happy future in exile "in distant Nineveh" (which in actuality had been destroyed some 200 years earlier!). In the intervening years, Talmade had become a big star, primarily in romantic comedy, and her added sophistication and grooming stressed rather clearly which scenes were old and which were new.

their "untidiness" due not to initial mistakes but to re-cutting four decades later. In many ways, however, *Intolerance* does represent the peak of Griffith's editorial practices. Thereafter, vanity and lethargy combined to reduce the effectiveness of his cuts. His conception was often brilliant, but the execution frequently lazy and slipshod.

Apart from the overall conception of *Intolerance*, inevitably bound up with its editing patterns, individual sequences illustrate some of the most complex cutting seen in any film to that time. The murder sequence (Robert Harron fights with Walter Long after rescuing Mae Marsh; Miriam Cooper shoots Long from a ledge outside the window and escapes; Harron is arrested by the police) is an incredibly frenetic barrage of images, some of them of only a few frames' duration, which must have proved as bewildering to 1916 audiences as it was to prove stimulating to Eisenstein and other Soviet directors.

The power of Griffith's work, however, is such that one usually doesn't notice the mistakes of the non-matching shots until one is intimately familiar with it. Historian Arthur Lennig made a minute study in 1975 of the three versions of *The Mother and the Law*, the modern story of *Intolerance*. First was the version shot in 1914; second, the partially revised version incorporated into *Intolerance*; third, the original but revised and partially re-shot version ultimately released on its own in 1919. Lennig was able not only to pinpoint the cunning disguise and re-use of sets within the film but also to note specific differences in sets, furniture, hair-styles, clothing, and even players. The final print constantly intercuts shots from all three versions, and even the "middle" cut, as represented by *Intolerance*, has some striking lapses in continuity. Yet until Lennig drew attention to them, these all passed unnoticed; and even knowing of them, the power of the film is still so great that one is unaware of them unless specifically looking for them.

Not unexpectedly, *Intolerance* failed to duplicate the great popular success of *The Birth of a Nation*. Initial reviews, and box-office figures, were promising. But once away from the metropolitan centers, the film seemed to have little appeal. Not only were audiences confused by its style, but increasingly they disagreed with its pacifist message. More and more it seemed that America would be drawn into the First World War, and the gradually increasing number of "anti-Hun" melodramas excited audiences far more than this appeal for brotherly love and peace. Even the more substantial British success of the film was minimized by that country's involvement in the war. The film's failure consumed most of Griffith's profits from *The Birth of a Nation* and caused him to re-trench and follow a policy that, alas, other directors of integrity, such as Erich von Stroheim, never had the acumen to emulate. Following *Intolerance*, Griffith reverted to smaller, safer pictures, regained the confidence of exhibitors, and replenished his bankroll. Then he launched himself into another purely artistic endeavor that he really did not expect would succeed (though surprisingly, *Broken Blossoms* did succeed), followed up with another commercial group spearheaded by *Way Down East*, experiment again with *Dream Street*, and reverted back to box-office material, all leading ultimately to his most uncompromising and least commercial film, *Isn't Life Wonderful?* in 1924. Admittedly, Griffith's "artistic" ventures were not always as successful as he hoped, nor was he always right in his commercial judgments, but such a pattern enabled him to direct prolifically for almost a full decade following *The Birth of a Nation*.

Intolerance was of even greater world-wide and long-term influence than *The Birth of a Nation*, though that influence was less obvious. The narrative structure and melodramatic content of *The Birth of a Nation* made it an easy prototype for (among others) westerns and war films. Griffith's own *Hearts of the World* (1918) was virtually a remake of *The Birth of a Nation* transposed to World War I: the same family structure, the same separations and reunions, the same editing patterns. A brigade of French volunteers substituted for the Ku Klux Klan, and their leader again arrived in time to save Lillian Gish from rape at the hands of George Siegmann.

Intolerance on the other hand, excited the "intellectual" directors—George Pearson in England, Maurice Tourneur in America, Carl Dreyer in Denmark, Eisenstein in Russia, Raymond Bernard in France. With the war in progress, that influence was delayed in many cases for several years, and then (as in the case of Dreyer's *Leaves From Satan's Book*) not seen by a large "popular" audience. But in America, one had a concrete example of the film's impact on (if not influence on) routine commercial directors when Frank Lloyd's *A Tale of Two Cities* (1917) based its attack on the Bastille very closely on Cyrus the Persian's attack on Babylon, with many compositions and cuts duplicated completely.

Apart from the influence of *Intolerance* on the many directors who worked on it as actors and assistant directors—W. S. Van Dyke, Elmer Clifton, Tod Browning, Lloyd Ingraham, and others—one may perhaps assume a certain *input* from Erich von Stroheim, who played a small role in the film and also acted as an assistant and a tenuous, non-defined kind of art director as well. The use of sexual symbolism in the modern sequence, and especially in the decor of the room occupied by the Musketeer of the Slums (Walter Long), was not typical of Griffith, though it was in a sense an offshoot of the animal symbolism he had used in *The Birth of a Nation.* Yet such symbolism was to remain a permanent adjunct to Stroheim's films, both in those he directed and those in which he merely acted, but under the guidance of directors who respected him and would frequently give him leeway to write and/or design his own material. Much of the sexual symbolism in *Intolerance* reappears more than twenty years later as decor in Stroheim's military apartment in Renoir's *Le Grande Illusion,* as does the motif of "The Hopeful Geranium," used in the same poignant and symbolic way in both the Griffith and Renoir films. It's possible that Griffith thought of these things and rejected them for later use. It's far more likely, however, that they were devised by Stroheim, approved by Griffith (who would not *instinctively* re-use something not his), and re-utilized in later years by Stroheim. The actual source is unimportant. What *is* important is that they appeared in *Intolerance,* further underscoring its status as a "source" film.

Within three years, Griffith had made two of the most important and influential films of all time, establishing himself as both the foremost commercial film-maker and the foremost artistic innovator, even though the second film could not support both titles. With these two films, America had also established itself beyond question as the leading film-making country in the world. With much of Europe at war, and most European film production at both an artistic and economic standstill because of it, America—and Hollywood, in particular—was in a unique position to take that leadership and march ahead to a position of complete supremacy in the film-making hierarchy.

7

Stabilization

If *The Birth of a Nation*'s commercial success justified the investment of time, money, and creative energy in ambitious projects, then the failure of *Intolerance* sounded a warning note. The industry at large tended to move with more caution than usual, if only because there was no need for haste or daring.

With the countries of Europe either involved in or affected by World War I, film-making there posed no threat to American supremacy. While it would be absurd to deny that worthwhile and intelligent films were still being made in Europe, it would also be realistic to admit that the initiative and drive of prewar days were largely absent. Countries deeply involved in the conflict, such as Great Britain, Germany, and France, could obviously not afford to risk large sums of money on projects that, theoretically, could be bombed out of existence at any moment. They concentrated instead on simple, inexpensive films that met immediate entertainment needs and no more. (A British version of Dickens's *Dombey and Son*, made in 1917, was economically canny enough to eschew costumes and period setting and was given a contemporary framework, although it has since taken on an appropriate sense of period, being closer in time to Dickens's period than it now is to our own.) Even Sweden and Denmark, not directly involved in the war, had lost most of their outside markets due to it, and thus were turning out films for essentially domestic consumption.

America, sensing that European competition would be virtually non-existent at least until the end of the war, and undoubtedly for several years thereafter, felt no need to lengthen its already considerable lead. Instead, it spent the next few years consolidating its position, building and establishing new stars, giving directors time to learn and experiment, building new theatres, and enlarging studios. Finally, during this period, it pulled off a series of mergers that had the effect of gradually shrinking the number of producers and distributors, never quite achieving the kind of monopoly that J. Arthur Rank (a British producer-distributor-exhibitor) would enjoy in Great Britain in the 1940's but often threatening to come close.

The big money in movies has obviously come from exhibition, although thanks to Hollywood's publicity machine and its constant attention to production costs, grosses, and star salaries, one could be forgiven for assuming that Hollywood itself was the center of glamor and the theatres merely its servants. Obviously each depended on the other for both profits and existence, yet in theory, exhibitors *could* have managed without Hollywood. Theatre owners *could* have brought in foreign films, financed independent production, or gone into production themselves—and indeed did, and still do, in varying degrees. Hollywood, on the other hand, would have been helpless without exhibition. Its product was useless unless shown, and Hollywood could not maintain production without payments in advance from exhibition interests. To lessen this dependency, Hollywood in time began to acquire its own theatres.

The first step, however, was the acquisition of branch offices, or "exchanges," throughout the country. The merchandising of motion pictures in earlier days had gone through two stages. In the days of the one-reelers, when movies were unlikely to be exploited on individual merits and did not have the built-in appeal of star value, they were literally sold by the foot. This gave the exhibitor what amounted to rights for perpetuity—except that programs were short, each film was handled (or manhandled) considerably, and there was little reason to reissue a film or to assume a life expectancy in excess of the normal mortality rate of a thousand feet of 35mm nitrate film. In many ways, it was quite a reasonable system. Companies had incentives to make good films, knowing that buyers were attracted to the reputation of a trademark rather than to an individual film, despite the growing field of film reviewing, which was often surprisingly astute. The overall quality that Griffith had brought to the Biograph films made the Biograph trademark the sales angle, rather than the story or the star. Moreover, Biograph knew that their one-reelers could be made for approximately $500 each, and by estimating how many prints would be sold at so much per foot, they could thus calculate the profit fairly reliably. (In essence, it was the same mathematics later employed by companies like Republic and Monogram in the thirties, in estimating cost and profit factors in the making of "B" pictures.)

However, while this merchandising system was safe, it both minimized potential income from unusually good films, leaving the greater profits in the hands of the exhibitor and offered the producer very little legal protection. There was nothing to prevent an exhibitor (with perhaps distribution ambitions) from making a duplicate negative of a film that he had bought, and selling copies himself. Not only would this divert further income from the producing company, but the often poor quality of the duplicated prints could reflect on the original producer. This frequently happened, and since many of the films being offered for sale had not been copyrighted, there was little legal recourse. Even if a film had been copyrighted, proof of illegal duping was hard to find. Biograph, Edison, Vitagraph, and other producers tried to overcome this problem by incorporating their trademark into the decor of their sets, usually as a rather obtrusive wall decoration. The rationale was that the trademark offered proof of manufacture, and any person buying a print from a source other than an official one would recognize right away that he was being offered an illegal print. The infringements of copyright in this period were many, but basically the industry was still too small for the losses or profits involved to be worthy of lawsuits. The greatest losers were the writers, whose work was pillaged, "borrowed," altered, or literally stolen, with no payment to them. If their work was of commercial value, obviously they were being cheated not only of their immediate just rewards but of the chance to sell their material elsewhere. Some writers, like Peter B. Kyne, took this plagiarism in stride; others, like Lew Wallace, whose *Ben Hur* was filmed totally without authority, sucd—and won.

Once the industry grew out of the one-reel stage, there was obviously need for a distribution system that was not only more sophisticated

but also offered more control and more potential. While Hollywood*
was still small and exhibition beginning to expand, the middlemen—
the distributors—moved in. The situation was somewhat akin to that
of Great Britain's Industrial Revolution in the 19th century. Direct
contact between artisan and consumer was interrupted, and an intermediary was injected to demand products the manufacturer might normally not care to make, and then persuade the consumer—via advertising and other means—to buy something he might not need or want. Of
course, the parallel is not completely accurate. At the beginning of the
Industrial Revolution, craftsmanship was of a high and individualized
nature—something that cannot be said of the average film in 1912—and
its exploitation and mechanization represented an aesthetic loss. The
film distributor, in contrast, while eliminating much of the personal
contact and often exerting too much influence, was a necessity if the
industry was to grow.

Initially, the independent distributor was a type of goldminer. He'd
stake out the richest claim in his territory—or the richest *available*
claim—and then try to persuade the best producers to entrust him with
their product. For the most part, he'd represent a state—hence the
phrase "states' rights"—although occasionally two or more adjacent
states, with similar audiences and overlapping marketing problems,
would be linked to form a "territory." There was no limit to how many
distributors could work a given territory—the number would fluctuate,
depending on their own initiative and success and the number of products available—but once a producer had assigned his product to a distributor, that distributor had it exclusively for his territory. On the
whole, products were sold for a flat fee. The producing company would
try to estimate the product's potential in a given area, allow for the
distributor's expenses, and come up with a figure satisfactory to both
parties, but especially to the company. If the distributor was inept or
had misjudged his market, he could be out of business very quickly—
leaving the producers with their guaranteed flat fee and the chance to
find a second distributor.

---

* Throughout this chapter, "Hollywood" is used to both symbolize and unify all
American film production. However, it should be stressed that for many years, New
York and East Coast production would continue to be important, and in a geographical sense, Hollywood by no means held a monopoly on production, though
it was rapidly assuming leadership.

On the other hand, an enterprising state distributor, prepared to work hard, cooperate with exhibitors, conduct exploitation campaigns, and spend money to make money, could make a small fortune very quickly. The influence of the states' rights distributor on the producer was, in the early stages, fairly small, though. He might know his market thoroughly and be able to prove exactly what would make money in that territory, but the producers in New York or Hollywood, trying to turn out a mass product for a mass American (and eventually international) market, would pay him little heed. The distributor needed Hollywood much more than it needed him. If he got out of line or demanded too much, there were a dozen other distributors waiting to take his place—and his product. Smart independent distributors, who felt that they knew their audiences better than the head offices did, usually proved it by getting into production themselves. A perfect illustration is Louis B. Mayer, who made his initial fortune as a distributor for *The Birth of a Nation,* plunged into production in 1920 with some cheap features (including a modern-dress *Dr. Jekyll and Mr. Hyde,* using New York as a background, avoiding costume and set bills, and even turning the plot into a dream to retain a happy ending!), and then, by 1924, having achieved sufficient stature (and success), was invited to head up the big new MGM company!

The film industry's willingness to sell to distributors on a flat-fee basis perhaps indicated a lack of faith in their own product. More logically, it reflected the need to get back *immediately* enough money to plough into new pictures at a time when bank loans for the fledgling industry were not yet so easy to come by. But it was a short-sighted policy. D. W. Griffith, for example, saw only a fraction of the profits from *The Birth of a Nation.* Had the film been leased on a *percentage* basis, the continuous flow of payments would have far exceeded that one flat down-payment. However, especially at that period, and with so much time and space between them, Hollywood distrusted distributors. In time, the percentage deals were instituted, and long-standing relationships established between producers and distributors. Particularly with newcomers to the field, though, the distrust proved to have some foundation. Books could be "cooked," profits could be siphoned off into "print and advertising" costs, and many a producer would find that his costs in supplying prints would never be recouped, profits would be non-existent, and his distributor would emerge, untouched and untouchable, from a bankruptcy act. Nevertheless, the institution of states' rights distribution has been maintained throughout the industry's entire history, asserting itself quite prominently in the 1930's and 1940's, when independent production was at its height, and ironically, in the 1970's, coming full circle to encompass major company product again. Many of the major companies, producing very little themselves and unable to support their own studios and exchanges throughout the country, first cut down on their own branch offices throughout the country and then merged them. In Great Britain and Europe, one finds *several* major companies releasing through *one* quite separate company, while in the United States we have the distressing spectacle of the onetime leader of them all, MGM, releasing its product through United Artists. However, despite its longevity, states' rights distribution was at first seen as only a temporary system. Subsequently, it became the only feasible distribution method for either the smaller independent companies or big independent companies that didn't make enough films to support permanent offices of their own.

For companies to open their own branch offices throughout the country was the obvious next step. Such offices would take over the functions of states' rights distributors and would also ensure that the bulk of the profits stayed within the parent company. (Distributors who had proven loyal and efficient were frequently given the opportunity to come into the parent company via these branch offices, some remaining in those positions through virtually a lifetime, others, more ambitious, eventually trekking out to Hollywood to become producers themselves, frequently for the same companies. The "family" sense within the producer-distributor structure was strong; it was often quite *literally* a family organization too.) The advantages of maintaining one's own branches were obvious—ranging from a reduced (theoretically, eliminated) distrust and policing of book-keeping to overall advertising campaigns designed so that they could be adjusted to meet specific local needs. Relationships between distributors and exhibitors, and between exhibitors and patrons, were close. Recommendations for types of product coming in to the head office from the company's own man carried far more weight than those of an independent distributor, who might have reasons of his own, entirely divorced from the welfare of the supplying company, for recommending a change in the product flow. Ownership of one's own exchanges promoted not only cooperation but competition. The sales drive in honor of this or that executive quickly became a staple and oft-repeated distribution occasion, though not without its own inherent corruptions. (Theatres which cooperated by mass bookings that helped to boost the local sales manager's stock and increase his commissions were usually rewarded by being given the pick of the next season's product over the bids of other local exhibitors.)

Exchanges were strategically located in the key cities, often selected as much for their convenience as shipping or transfer points as for their value as exhibition towns. Each of these cities soon developed its own "film row," with the distribution offices clustered next to one another, providing exhibitors with the opportunity to screen and book new product and to examine advertising material. For movie-struck youngsters, these offices, with their gaudy, colorful posters of current releases, were their first contact with the world of film. More than a few such youngsters started life as office-boys in these institutions, graduated to salesmen, learned what audiences wanted and how movies were put together, and went on to become directors. William K. Howard was one of several who followed this route. The Triangle Company (run by Griffith, Ince, and Sennett under the overall supervision of the Aitken Brothers) was typical of the early, small company that expanded by setting up its own branch offices. In 1916, its headquarters was in New York at 1457 Broadway, and it established its own offices in Los Angeles and San Francisco, covering California; Denver, Colorado; Atlanta, Georgia; Chicago, Illinois; New Orleans, Louisiana; Boston, Massachusetts; Minneapolis, Minnesota; Kansas City and St. Louis, for Missouri; Buffalo, to cover Upper New York State; Cincinnati and Cleveland, for Ohio; Philadelphia and Pittsburgh, for Pennsylvania; and Seattle for Washington.

While producers expanded by consolidating the exchange system, exhibition was expanding, too, although the really big push would not come until 1919. In 1916, an estimated 21,000 theatres were operating in the United States, with an average of 500 seats per theatre and an admission price of only eight cents. However, a great number of small rural theatres with low admission prices obviously are responsible for those figures. In the metropolitan areas, theatres tended to be substantially larger, with admission prices ranging from ten to fifty cents, and with the two-dollar maximum being reserved for the still infrequent "specials" pioneered by *The Birth of a Nation*. Many of the metropolitan movie houses had been converted from stage houses, as had the Park Theatre in Columbus Circle—a huge, 3,000-seat theatre in the area now occupied by office buildings adjacent to the New York Coliseum. New movie theatres that were being built were almost as elaborate. Barely ten years after the word "Nickelodeon" had been coined in Pittsburgh, the 2,000-seat Rialto, billing itself as "The Temple of the Motion Picture," opened in Times Square, New York, in April 1916. It didn't need a "road show" attraction to mark the event. Douglas Fairbanks' *The Good Bad Man* and a Fatty Arbuckle comedy short, *The Other Man*, were deemed more than adequate, and certainly received good reviews. But it is the theatre itself that, for the opening program, got most of the press attention. The gaudy, garish movie theatres, designed like palaces, were still in the future; the aim at this point was for dignity and elegance, coupled with seating capacity. One of the "reviews" of the theatre itself said, in part:

> The theatre, both in atmosphere and tone, is simple and dignified. It is not jarring with effete splendor of garish design, calculated to fill the eye to satiation. From foyer to the screen, the impressive dignity of the Greek notes in architecture and general decorations engender a feeling of refinement and intellectuality. The atmosphere is a stimulating tonic and psychologically awakens the senses of perception without over-exercising one's mental energy. In other words, the mind is rested in an atmosphere of action. Which is indeed perfect recreation.

The last two lines so aptly sum up the aims of movies of the period that one suspects the review may well have been written and planted by production interests!

While production, distribution, and exhibition expanded, the merchandisers and the scavengers, creating their own sub-industries, feeding off exhibition, multiplied like moths around a nitrate flame. In 1908, the *Chicago Tribune* had vigorously denounced Nickelodeons and their shoddy wares. By 1913, however, it found it expedient to boost its own sagging business by collaborating with the Selig Company in promoting a serial, which its readers could enjoy in print one day and see on the screen the next. The trade papers carried ads for every conceivable artifact that a theatre could use—including ads for *The Kinematograph Weekly*, a first-rate *British* trade paper, but one of little practical value to the American exhibitor. The "Orpheum Collection of Music" was offered to exhibitors "tired of playing the same old waltzes" as accompaniment to their films. Stationary manufacturers offered all kinds of admission tickets to exhibitors and laboratory-report forms to labs and cameramen. By using one manufacturer's Gold-Fibre screen, the exhibitor was assured that *all* his films would reflect "The Golden Glow of the Sunlight." At the same time, he could order a set of nine anticensorship slides ("Keep the Pictures Clean and Keep Them Out of Politics"), to remind audiences of exhibitors' stand *for* morality and *against* potential government censorship. Advertisements were even aimed at the moviegoer himself. For $50, he could buy a Bing's Home Entertainer—a safe, easily operated home projector that could accommodate single 35mm reels, thus making every distribution exchange a potential source for home movie entertainment. Obviously, the industry wasn't yet worried about piracy or filmic bootlegging!

On the surface, the picture-making industry of 1916–19 was a placid, innocent one. Film was big business, and becoming more so. And because it was virtually the only mass entertainment business—radio was still a decade away, television undreamed of—it could afford to relax. A successful movie would obviously be imitated, but it didn't necessarily have to be topped. There was no need to try to outdo one success by making the follow-up bigger, longer, or more shocking. A good story and a good star were all that the fans demanded. With centuries of literature to draw upon, plus contemporary plays and novels, original screenplays, and the war in Europe to provide an up-to-date background for films of action, melodrama, and espionage, there was no shortage of material. Movies were relatively brief, and their sole desire was to entertain. Even the bad movies seemed to communicate that desire, to indicate friendly intent regardless of the result. It was a charming, leisurely period which may have lacked cinematic milestones but which served a useful purpose. Stars were consolidating their appeal, making a lot of movies every year while they were still young, fresh, and bursting with ideas, and when the economy of the industry was such that a star *could* make from five to ten films in a single year and *not* wear out his welcome. And writers, directors, and cameramen were learning and experimenting, although the seemingly unimportant program films they made in the process frequently later proved to have a spontaneity and a kind of raw poetry that made them (in the case of directors like John Ford and Henry King) very personal and a valuable key to their evolving styles.

If there seemed to be little competition for the moviegoer's time and money, since he had time to see a *lot* of movies, there was much competition and jockeying for position behind the scenes by both stars and studio heads. Major stars such as Chaplin, aware of their importance, would sign a short-term contract only, and as soon as it was up, demand—and get—far more money elsewhere. And studios strove constantly to steal a march on their competitors in acquiring material, or in trying to persuade stars to break existing contracts and sign with them instead. The incredible power of the star system led to another system hated by exhibitors, universally condemned, eventually outlawed, and yet not without its compensatory merits—the "block-booking" system.

This was a system by which the distributor sold an exhibitor an entire season's product en masse, often sight unseen, since when the contract was signed, many of the films had not yet been made. In order to get the films he wanted, the exhibitor also had to take many he did not want—in his eyes, the "bad" films. While the exhibitor's resentment of his lack of freedom of choice was understandable, so was the distributor's position. As a group, exhibitors have always tended to prefer the safe and the tried-and-true over the off-beat and experimental. Given total freedom of choice, most exhibitors would obviously book only the kinds of films and the star vehicles that they knew were box office. The distributor, admittedly, used the block-booking system to salvage the mistakes and the bad films. On the other hand, many of a distributor's best films might wind up on an exhibitor's "reject" list, and would have had sparse showings indeed, had they not been forced into exhibition via the block-booking system. For example, exhibitors dealing with Paramount in 1918 and 1919 would have been clamoring for the latest releases of Douglas Fairbanks, William S. Hart, and Mary Pickford but, left to their own devices, would probably have by-passed *The Grim Game* (an unusually well-done melodrama starring Harry Houdini and directed by Irving Willat) or Cecil B. deMille's rather grim psychological study, *The Whispering Chorus*, which, with Raymond Hatton as its star, was somewhat short on box-office allure. Forcing such unwanted pictures onto a contract in a sense by-passed the exhibitor, bringing to the public a kind of film that the distributor thought it would buy if only it had the chance.

In many cases, of course, the exhibitor's commercial instincts had been right. *The Whispering Chorus was* a flop, and indeed marked a turning point in deMille's career, causing him to abandon his interesting path of "artistic" pictures and concentrate on films of proven appeal instead. But in other cases, the public was delighted with product that the exhibitor had been forced to show, especially since the method of catering to pre-sold box-office values often led to stagnation. In the early twenties, for example, Paramount's Wallace Reid vehicles were enormously popular, mainly because of Reid's unique appeal. Knowing this, Paramount literally ground them out, economically, quickly, and with so little imagination that they all seemed cut from an identical mold. Had they not had the Reid name to sell them, they would certainly have been on an exhibitor's reject list. Films like *The Grim Game* might not have attracted audiences on the same scale as the Reid films; but once in the theatre, it satisfied and surprised them, and told them that the movies were still capable of something fresh.

Major stars, however, who were fast becoming entrepreneurs, guiding their own careers and heading their own production units, had more cause to be dissatisfied with the block-booking system. They saw their films, which *were* in demand, being used as bait to sell those which were not, and having no share of the ultimate profits—or having those profits "flattened out" and minimized when they were calculated on the basis of an entire season's product—they resented the system. Mary Pickford and Douglas Fairbanks, the leaders in this situation, demanded, and got, a new arrangement in which their films were packaged separately. But in a sense, this turned out to be merely a refinement of the block-booking system. Paramount set up a separate corporation to handle the production and distribution of such major stars as Pickford. Exhibitors had to deal for an entire block of Pickford films. Pickford at least could be sure that the returns were for her films alone, and that two of her films were not being used to sell eight lesser ones. On the other hand, while the finances were separated, the exhibitor's problems were not removed. In order to get the block of Pickfords, he still had to take another block that he didn't want—and he had to pay more for those Pickfords. In time, the stars realized that they were still being used, and that there was a growing resentment against them by exhibitors.

Already in 1916, Adolph Zukor of Paramount was planning to expand his power to near-monopolistic proportions. In 1917, his merger with Triangle became a virtual takeover of that company, with Griffith, Ince, and Sennett all signing with Paramount. Along with them went most of their major stars—William S. Hart, Charles Ray, Douglas Fairbanks, Dorothy Dalton, Ford Sterling, Dorothy Gish, and Fatty Arbuckle—and many directors, headed by Allan Dwan and John Emerson. This coup accomplished, Zukor planned to expand even further, and by 1919 was issuing press stories concerning the imminent "ultimate" merger with other companies. Alarmed, Griffith, Pickford, Fairbanks, and Chaplin (who was then allied with First National, a company that was rumored to be a part of the planned merger) announced that *they* would form their own company. (William S. Hart would have joined them, but was too cautious a businessman to risk investing his own money in the venture.) Initially their announcement was merely a strategic tactic designed to forestall the Zukor plans. Once under way, however, exhibitor response indicated to them that their idea was sound. In 1919, they formed United Artists and plunged into the business of making their own films the way *they* wanted to and selling directly to the exhibitor, thus eliminating both the middle-man and the block-booking system.

There were problems, however. Pickford and Griffith still had to supply pictures to First National under another contract and couldn't devote their efforts exclusively to the new company. And the inability to sell a large group of films, as under the block-booking system, meant that money was slow coming in. A second Fairbanks or Pickford film had to be made and financed long before the first one had recouped its cost, let alone shown a profit. Nevertheless, exhibitors welcomed United Artists, and, despite its business travails, it became a major force in the supplying of first-rate product throughout the twenties and thirties. Ironically, the company was once (in the very early 1940's) virtually put out of business by the very methods that made it such an attraction to exhibitors. With virtually no product to sell, it had to buy a whole group of completed films (mainly second-rate programmers and westerns) from Paramount. In the 1950's, it barely survived by hooking its infrequent prestige films to a lack-lustre group of "B's" in a thinly-veiled continuance of the block-booking system.

Throughout the twenties, the block-booking system was to survive, but with increasing resentment from exhibitors. The trade publications, designed to represent exhibition interests rather than production/distribution (although, of course, it carried all the latter's news and advertisements), backed up exhibitors in their fight against the system and were vigilant in watching for loopholes. Contracts signed long before many of the films were made listed either the titles of the agreed-to pictures or a given number of "specials" or vehicles with a given star. A distributor's failure to live up to the letter of the contract entitled the exhibitor to partially cancel and refuse to accept any substitution.

The attempts by distributors to counteract this system were often extremely ingenious. At one point in the late twenties, Warner Brothers had agreed to provide a Rin Tin Tin vehicle entitled *Tracked By the Police*. When the vehicle was completed (and it was a good one, one of Rinty's best), it turned out to be a rousing melodrama complete with an old train, a sabotaged dam, and any number of elements to delight an audience—but nary a policeman in sight, and certainly no justification for that title. Obviously a title change was needed, and the picture was so good that no exhibitor in his right mind could have complained. Yet, wary of providing even a wedge by which some of the foundations of the system could be whittled away, Warners chose another solution. After all the outdoor mayhem was over and Rinty had rescued the heroine from a watery grave, a final title card was inserted just before the "End" title. It stated that for his herculean efforts in defeating the damwreckers, Rinty had been made an honorary policeman—and that the case records read "Tracked by the Police." This somewhat unlikely information was accompanied by art-work of Rinty sitting on his haunches, policeman's hat on his head and night-stick clutched between his paws, while his happy canine grin seemed to suggest a personal satisfaction at having outwitted the exhibitors!

So careful were distributors not to give exhibitors cause to break a contract that they occasionally were forced to throw them an unintended bonus. A 1927 Warner contract promised delivery of a Dolores Costello vehicle titled *A Million Bid*. When delivery time arrived, the Costello vehicle offered was a spectacular melodrama entitled *Old San*

Francisco. Since the film climaxed with the heroine being auctioned off in the white slavery market of Chinatown,† it would have been a simple matter to use that sale as the justification for the original title. But *Old San Francisco* was a big production which would have been hurt by so prosaic and uninformative a title as *A Million Bid*. Exhibition journals pointed out that this was not the film contracted for, but that exhibitors, though entitled to reject it, should be happy that such a plum had unexpectedly been thrown their way merely to round out a contractual obligation. (*A Million Bid* was clearly not quite ready in time to meet that obligation; it was copyrighted a mere ten days after *Old San Francisco*, and wasn't nearly as good or elaborate a production.)

The block-booking system was constantly and bitterly opposed and finally, in the sound period, legally abolished. However, it continued to thrive undercover, and astute salesmen found numerous ways of coercion, threats, and bribes to ensure its maintenance as a fact of life.

As to the films of the late teens—those bounded by Griffith's *The Birth of a Nation* at one end and his *Broken Blossoms* at the other—it is possible to generalize about them in a decidedly positive way. It is true that the most important and influential films, and some of the slickest in a purely entertainment sense—Griffith's *Broken Blossoms* and *True Heart Susie*, Stroheim's *Blind Husbands*, Fairbanks' *His Majesty the American*—are all clustered together in 1919, a year that introduced the twenties rather than bade farewell to the teens. But prior to that, one has much to be thankful for: Chaplin's funniest comedy shorts (the Mutual group, the initial First National entries); the best, most varied and least pretentious films of deMille, Fairbanks, Pickford, and Hart; the charm of the various Charles Ray, Bessie Love, and Lillian Gish romances, with their natural and unforced link with the Victorian era; and the pleasing naïveté of a film like *20,000 Leagues Under the Sea*, which isn't content with some of the best underwater photography to date but has to improve on Jules Verne by adding a spectacular climax more reminiscent of Rudyard Kipling!

† Miss Costello avoided the fate worse than death at the hands of the Yellow Peril by prayer, which promptly, and right on cue, in the middle of Willie Fung's lecherous chuckle, brought on the San Francisco earthquake. This was a stock plot element in silent melodramas climaxing with the quake, and the heroine of 1923's *The Shock* likewise saved her virtue at the expense of quake victims. If Hollywood is to be believed, the Diety had much to answer for.

Even the lesser films offered their little surprises: a minor Ince romantic drama, *Happiness*, surely one of the most placid and uneventful films ever, distinguished by John Gilbert's charisma showing through what was meant to be a comic-cad role; or a Texas Guinan western, *The Gun Girl*, developed along lines of emotion and warmth rather than action, its director Frank Borzage already showing a humanistic side to his nature, and his filmic methods, which would later stamp him as Hollywood's closet parallel to France's Jean Renoir. Ince's *D'Artagnan*, was a rather tame version of Dumas, but in terms of selecting the best and most filmic ingredients from Dumas' crowded canvas of incidents and character, was so skilfully done that, when Fairbanks made his spectacular version in 1921, he followed the Ince structure and continuity exactly—to such a degree that Ince sued for plagiarism!

If Griffith's *Hearts of the World*, his big wartime spectacle, was a lesser film than *The Birth of a Nation* or *Intolerance*, it still contained elements that rendered it an advance in certain respects. Its lighting and pictorial composition were the most sophisticated of any Griffith film to date, and many of the close-ups of Lillian Gish were stunningly beautiful. It also showed a more relaxed Griffith than had been apparent in his two earlier spectacles, and Dorothy Gish was allowed to develop her comedic sense and timing far beyond the normal requirements of her role. The result was to divert audience interest away from Lillian Gish's more traditional Griffith heroine, but its effect on the picture was salutary. So was Griffith's willingness to present both sides of the picture, to admit the possibility of Germans being human, too—an attitude not often encountered in the fanatic anti-Hun melodramas of the period. And much of the film—particularly the incredible episode in which the nearly-mad Lillian Gish wanders through the rubble of the battle-field, still wearing her bridal veil, and literally "tuning out" reality as she looks for the body of her lover—achieved a remarkable blending of poetry and near-surrealism.

But much, far too much, is missing from these years—in a proportionate sense, much more than is missing from the twenties. We have only one of the many hugely successful historical and "vamp" films made by Theda Bara, and that one early and relatively primitive. None of the monumental Herbert Brenon-Annette Kellerman vehicles survive; in size they were said to rival Griffith, and stills bear this out. The Blanche Sweet and Dorothy Gish starring vehicles seem to have disappeared *in toto,* as have whole blocks of films made by such directors as Raoul Walsh and J. Gordon Edwards. While some survive, the bulk of the really interesting (or potentially interesting) screen vehicles for stage stars—Herbert Tree's *Macbeth,* William Gillette's *Sherlock Holmes*— have likewise been lost. The impossibility of brushing aside these films (and others of no reputation at all) has been proven in recent years by the rediscovery of Barker's *The Italian* and Tourneur's *The Wishing Ring,* and perhaps most of all by the belated rediscovery, in 1975, of a totally forgotten director, John Collins. Despite extremely perceptive and laudatory reviews for his films of 1914–18, he is an ignored and unknown figure to most American historians. The reasons are not hard to understand, however. For one thing, he was a director for the Edison company—and we all know that no directorial talent of note ever came out of Edison. Or we *did* know it until now. Collins's films show that not only were we wrong about him, but that it is quite possible that other directors of his caliber lie buried with the unseen Edison films. Collins married an Edison star, Viola Dana, and they worked together as a star-director team. Cameraman John Arnold was another key member of the team, as was star Robert Walker—another forgotten name, whose lethargic acting (in roles which demanded no more) in grade-Z westerns, serials, and quickies of the thirties gave no indication at all that here was an acting talent once akin to Robert Harron's.

When Collins and Viola Dana moved from Edison to Metro in 1916, they took Walker and Arnold with them. Arnold was accepted by Metro reluctantly and only at Collins's insistence—and went on to become head of their camera department. Collins's films for Metro maintained the high standard of his Edisons, but, while several were preserved (or perhaps, it would be more accurate to say, they were lucky enough not to deteriorate, since there was no determined preservation effort on their behalf), they never again saw the light of day. Once the Metro-Goldwyn-Mayer merger was consummated in 1924, all films before that date were considered ancient history, stored perhaps, but totally forgotten, awaiting the Lazarus-like resurection brought about by James Card, film curator-archivist for Rochester's George Eastman House. One factor in the virtual obliteration of John Collins's name is his tragic death in the great influenza epidemic of 1918. Had he lived, he would undoubtedly have become a major director (in the commercial sense of the word; he was that already in the aesthetic sense), and in light of later works, his earlier ones would have been remembered, reappraised, and reshown. But by the twenties, the teens were already ancient history. By the mid-thirties, where film study began, somewhat tenuously, it was taken for granted that if a name wasn't known, there was a reason. The incentive to dig and explore was small, even had the facilities been available.

Thanks to Eastman House, within two years four of the Collins-Dana films were rescued—one of them from Czechoslovakia, where the job of retranslating already translated colloquial titles presented a major problem in itself. The four films (hopefully to be supplemented by others) are *Children of Eve* (1915), *The Cossack Whip* (1916), *The Girl Without a Soul* (1917), and *Blue Jeans* (1917). *Children of Eve* is in some ways the most remarkable of all, a grim study of appalling labor conditions that is clearly based on the infamous Triangle Shirtwaist fire of March 25, 1911. In that disaster just off New York's Washington Square, on a site now covered by New York University, 146 workers, mainly women, lost their lives. Collins's treatment, austere, documentary-flavored, even had the courage—or audacity—to snare the audience's interest by the involvement of the heroine (a spunky lass who, in retrospect, seems a curiously prophetic combination of the Mae Marsh and Miriam Cooper roles in the modern story of *Intolerance*) and then to have the tragedy really hit home via the heroine's totally unexpected death in the final realistically-staged conflagration.

All of Collins's films were splendidly cut and photographed, with a mobility, pace, and sense of pictorial beauty perhaps found only in the films of Tourneur and Griffith. *Blue Jeans* is an especially stunning film since it invades Griffith's *Way Down East* territory of rural melodrama several years before Griffith did. Despite some decidedly unlikely plot machinations, complications, and coincidences—and that old perennial thrill of the stage melodrama, the man strapped to the log in a sawmill (a sequence usually avoided by the movies, except for purposes of parody)—*Blue Jeans* can still be taken quite seriously, and needs neither apologies nor weak suggestions that it be regarded as "camp" or unintended lampoon. Collins's unerring sense of place and people, the perfectly selected rural locations, and the absolutely "right" faces was quite remarkable. (Russell Simpson appears as a stern matriarch in *Blue Jeans,* some two decades before he was typed in such roles in the *remake* of *Way Down East,* and innumerable John Ford films.)

Viola Dana's contributions to these films is an important one. An unusual actress, she resembled Eleanor Boardman in looking attractive but somehow "plain" (by Hollywood standards). At her first introduction, often chewing gum or dowdily dressed, it was difficult to believe that we could interest ourselves in this kind of a heroine for the ensuing six reels. And yet within a very short time, a kind of inner beauty began to radiate through (in the dramas) or an inner vivacity (in the comedies), so that we were completely won over by her, well able to understand the devotion and love she inspired in her hero. Few actresses were able to pull off this trick, or would have wanted to try. Eleanor Boardman managed it with perhaps the definitive performance in King Vidor's *The Crowd*. But that was in 1928; Viola Dana was working the same magic a decade earlier, perhaps most notably of all in *The Girl Without a Soul*. Not only was Dana's dual role characterization helped by some astonishingly skillful split-screen camera trickery, but it was one of the few such characterizations (Frederic March's in *Dr. Jekyll and Mr. Hyde* was another) where one wasn't aware of one person playing two roles, but genuinely felt a sense of separation, of two individuals.

Viola Dana, today a sprightly, no-nonsense lady of eighty with clear recall, made several appearances with her films in 1976/77 (at the Telluride Film Festival, at the Pacific Film Archives in Berkeley, and at Eastman House in Rochester) and must have been gratified indeed to find not only her husband's talents rediscovered and applauded but her films—and her performances—still valid and still working, not by kindly nostalgic values imposed on them today, but by the power of their still unimpaired original qualities.

As long as films like *Blue Jeans* and *Children of Eve* continue to be rediscovered, we can never quite close the door on the pre-1920 period. True, we cannot expect a constant need to re-assess film history. Collins's immense talent probably did not extend to *influence* in his shortlived career. But the rediscovery of films such as his can only enrich our knowledge of the teen years.

The product of the Triangle Company is particularly useful in assessing the manner of making—and selling—movies in the teen years. Few of their films could be considered classics, but it must be remembered that the handful of films from the 1914–20 period that *can* be so considered represent a very small proportion of their studios' output. Tourneur's *The Wishing Ring* (1914) is certainly a classic of sorts, but it would be virtually lost in the shuffle if *all* the films from World Pictures—the tedious Alice Brady romances and the dull historical dramas like *Betsy Ross* (1917)—were placed side by side. Probably more of Triangle's product from this period is available than that of any other single company. Moreover, their company records and exhibitor manuals still exist, so that one can see how these films were sold to the public. In addition, many of their biggest names—directors and stars like Griffith, Hart, and Fairbanks—had long careers (after the cessation of Triangle activities) that are likewise well preserved, so one can form an accurate impression of the value of the Triangle films as related to their later work.

The most prolific years of Triangle activity date from 1916—the year in which Griffith not only directed *Intolerance* but also ran his wing of the studio and was responsible for the production of some fifty features. Undoubtedly each of those features—the acrobatic comedies of Fairbanks, the simple dramas, melodramas, and romances with Lillian Gish and Mae Marsh—was economically more viable than the costly and unprofitable *Intolerance*. These solid, satisfying "little" pictures had no ambitions other than to entertain—to be "friendly" to the growing movie audience by giving it just what it wanted. Undoubtedly, there *was* competition, but it was largely unrelated to the pictures on the screen: competition for power within the studio structures, competition to steal away from other studios the stars that had obvious box-office drawing value. But there was little competition in the sense of outbidding a rival for rights to a theatrical or literary property, or in copying and embellishing another studio's product, thus creating the ascending spiral of higher costs and plot or shock "gimmicks" to conceal the imitation, which so soon became (and still is, more than ever) the curse of commercial production.

However, *aggressive* competition by the studios for the public's time and dollar (actually, much less than a dollar) was virtually unnecessary. The movie was the unchallenged mass entertainment form. Radio had not yet entered the picture; television was even further away. The relatively new phonograph record industry was important, but hardly as an *adjunct* to the entertainment industry. The phonograph was an important home fixture, but not as yet associated with either the collecting mania or with fan followings. Its stars were few, since the mechanics and the media for creating vocal stars, and for publicizing them—radio and television—did not yet exist. Its stars were created by talent, reputation, and sometimes international renown, a means of selection which gravitated more to classes higher in the social strata than those who embraced the movies. Caruso undoubtedly sold far fewer records in his day than an Elvis Presley, backed by high-pressure promotion (including, of course, the movies) in *his.*

Not only were radio and television absent from the scene, but even comic books had not yet replaced the dime novel. This left sports, the theater, the opera or concert-hall, and vaudeville—all of them restrictive in terms of being seasonal or essentially big-city attractions. The movies not only had no real competition, but they were increasing their dominance of the entertainment field as they expanded. New, plushier theaters were built, producer-distributors erected their own theaters to house their own product, and the star system grew.

To be a star *meant* something; stars couldn't be artificially made by the brain-washing techniques of mass appearances and over-exposure in television series. (Even in later years, though stars were "made" that way, they couldn't be *sustained* artificially unless the public really wanted them.) Stardom—and the genuine *love* that went with it—had to be earned by sheer hard work and a demonstrable ability to perform and/or entertain. Stars—the best of them—became mystical, god-like creatures because the lack of mass media prevented them from becoming over-exposed, over-familiar, interviewed, and humanized. Apart from the rare public appearance at a premiere (or, during the war, at bond-selling drives), the only contact between star and public was on screen. The star took care to deserve the love that came to him or her from the audience and to live up to his on-screen image. In some ways, the magnetic aura of a star personality was especially important in these years, not only for his or her own survival and growth, but also for the economic health of his parent company. For many companies still deliberately kept a low profile, as if entertaining a tacit acknowledgment that the film was still a poor relation to the theater, and that to advertise its wares too strongly would be both in poor taste and a tactical mistake. The Triangle Company is typical, and its failure to add any sense of showmanship to its advertising was undoubtedly at least partially responsible for its ultimate failure, and the transference of most of its major directorial and performing talents to Paramount.

On the fact of it, Triangle should have been one of the soundest of
all movie-producing companies. The three supervisory producers—
D. W. Griffith, Thomas Ince, and Mack Sennett—between them represented prestige, reliable "bread-and-butter" product, and that staple,
comedy. The roster of stars included some of the biggest names in the
business at that time: Douglas Fairbanks, William S. Hart, Charles
Ray, Lillian and Dorothy Gish, Bessie Love, Norma and Constance Talmadge, Mae Marsh and Robert Harron, a number of stars considered
of almost equal stature, though somewhat forgotten today—Bessie Bar-
riscale, Enid Markey, Frank Keenan, H. B. Warner—and the periodic
prestige imports from the stage: Billie Burke, Sir Herbert Tree, and
DeWolf Hopper. Certainly it was a roster of directorial and star talent
that could challenge that offered by Famous-Players (Paramount);
yet the latter's product has a glossier, far more elaborate "look" to it
and was far more aggressively advertised. Triangle's down-playing of
adjectives ("delightful" or "pleasing" were among their most typical
and oft-used superlatives) may have been commendably honest, but it
did impart a low-key sameness to their product. One phrase that was
pressed into service as a company slogan and hung on banners from
the marquees of their theaters was "Clean Pictures for Clean People"—
a catchphrase which may have been admirable in its intentions but
somehow seemed to translate as "Dull Pictures for Dull People." Cogni-
zant of the fact that the movies were still considered not quite respectable, Triangle lost no opportunity to stress their concern to *earn* that
respect by citing, wherever possible, the endorsements of ministers and
teachers concerning the spiritual or educational values of their films.
Famous Players may have hastened Hollywood's gradual descent into
bad taste by stressing sex and sensation in its advertising for *The
Cheat*, but in essence, it was *honest* advertising. Many Triangle films
dealt in equally strong meat, but the public would never know it from
the advertising. The William S. Hart films ran an astonishing gamut in
their plot material, but the advertising was always keyed to the same
level, with the stress on the perennially unchanging Hart image. Likewise, Louise Glaum's vamp films, obviously hoping to tap the Theda
Bara market, so downplayed their exotic quality in the publicity that
Fox and Miss Bara had no trouble whatsoever in maintaining their
dominance of that particular field.

In the spring of 1916, the 3,000-seat Park Theatre at Broadway and

Columbus Circle in New York, the theater that had recently housed the premiere of George Bernard Shaw's *Pygmalion* with Mrs. Patrick Campbell, went over to movies and launched its new series with *The Flying Torpedo*, a topical melodrama with Bessie Love, guardedly advertised as a "preparedness subject." This surely was an event of both prestige and pride. Yet, as if afraid of being taken to task for crowing, Triangle's publicity seemed more intent on considering the honor bestowed on the company than in suggesting that movies *were* finally being accepted on the same level as the theater.

Triangle is unique in that, although it controlled a large percentage of the industry's most popular stars, it found itself floundering into dissolution within a very few years. One reason undoubtedly was that its creative talent could not match its star value. D. W. Griffith was clearly limited by the company's lack of ambition and was merely marking time. While there were some excellent directors working under his supervision, most of them were relative newcomers, using Triangle essentially as a training ground. Thomas Ince's major contribution to film was in an executive and organizational function, and Sennett, though commercially important, was limited by his own formulas and the restriction of his output to two- and three-reelers. The major asset of Triangle was its stars. Many of its films do survive today, and those that are most valid are first, the Douglas Fairbanks and William S. Hart vehicles, and second, the films of Lillian Gish and Mae Marsh. These were four artists of remarkable talent and appeal who could fashion their films into popular hits by sheer force of personality. Many of the other Triangle films that survive today—*The Social Secretary*, with Norma Talmadge; *The Beggar of Cawnpore*, with H. B. Warner; *The Clod Hopper*, with Charles Ray; *Happiness*, with Enid Bennett—are typical of the standards—and *standardized* elements—of films of the day. They satisfy, but never aim at more than that. Even their rigidly controlled running times—each film was five or six reels in length—was calculated to give the customers their money's worth (with a short or two thrown in) but not to send them out of the theater with the happy glow of having received far *more* than they expected.

There *were* exceptions to this standardization, of course. DeMille and Griffith films gradually became both longer and more ambitious, and certain other directors—Frank Lloyd and Allen J. Holubar in particular, two directors who tried hard to copy the Griffith methods—likewise aimed at larger and longer films. But this movement was very much a part of the end of the teen years, starting in 1918 and consolidating its expansion in 1919. The immediate post-*Intolerance* years of 1916 through early 1918 seemed content to remain relatively unambitious. And the stars were in no great hurry to establish themselves as impressarios, even though many already had virtual control of their careers. They realized that their first duty was to the audiences that had *made* them stars, and they carefully kept their experimental films to a minimum. Although there was a tremendous range and variety to the films of Mary Pickford—from comedy to pathos to action melodrama—most of them contained built-in, sure-fire elements of mass audience appeal. When she tried to give her audiences something stronger and more personal—as with *Less than the Dust*, a decidedly downbeat story set amid the poverty of India—the results at the box office were usually disappointing. But one failure surrounded by audience-pleasing successes could and did have little effect on her overall career. Douglas Fairbanks, on the other hand, having found a successful formula, stuck to it without variation. His energy and good humor, and the inventiveness of his writers, made the same basic ideas work time and time again.

While it is true that the years between *Intolerance* and *Broken Blossoms* (1919) were not particularly productive, they did far more than just settle back comfortably to purvey simple mass entertainment. Those years represent an interim period in which many of the industry's best directors either served an apprenticeship with Griffith or cut themselves off from an earlier apprenticeship in order to strike out on their own. Even those who had never physically worked with or for Griffith had usually been under his influence, and used these years either to consolidate that influence (as in the case of Henry King) or to put it aside and find entirely new styles of their own. John Ford and Erich von Stroheim both directed their first features in these years, and Raoul Walsh, Chester and Sidney Franklin, Tod Browning, King Vidor, and many others began to establish themselves firmly.

Nor should one minimize the films that were made in this period and dismiss them purely as transitory entertainment films. Many artists actually reached their creative peak in this period. Griffith, deMille, and Tourneur certainly did. Regardless of the greater scope and sophistication of his later features. William S. Hart's westerns of these years were his leanest and best. The variety and relative brevity of deMille's films gave them a vitality usually denied by the sluggish pace of his much longer and more elaborate films of the 1920's. Many artists may have been *major* artists, but they were also limited or specialized ones. Tourneur's films were fragile and simple, depending on such emotions as joy or wistfulness, water-colored by a painter rather than a director; he, too, was at his best in this period. Fairbanks and Pickford made so many films—Fairbanks at one point a dozen in one year—that they automatically evolved a brisk narrative style entirely adequate to their needs. Pickford's films had charm, and Fairbanks' incredible ebullience and gusto. Those very qualities were what made the stars so popular and their films so durable, and it is those qualities that were so largely

lost in the twenties, when both stars slowed down their pace first to
one or two bigger films per year and then, ultimately, to one "special"
per year.

Impressive as the deluxe productions were in terms of decor, magnificent camerawork, and impressive sets, there isn't one of them that
wouldn't have benefitted from the less pretentious, easy-going manner
of the pre-1920 films. Many of them cry out for ruthless wielding of the
editorial scissors. Mary Pickford's 1925 *Sparrows*, though an excellent
film and one of her best, is so aware of its status as a "special" that
when its completely satisfying climax comes at the end of reel seven, it
was thought necessary to add a second climax and a prolonged semi-
comic wrap-up, to extend the film to an appropriately impressive
length; it all but destroys itself in the process. Douglas Fairbanks' pictorially magnificent but dramatically rather dull *The Thief of Bagdad*
(1924) ran for thirteen reels, yet a television series of the 1960's, specializing in condensations of silent features, found it no problem at all
to edit it down to two and a half reels and still retain its splendor, its
plot, and all of its action highlights. Conversely, Fairbanks' 1917 *Wild
and Woolly*, a western spoof told in only five reels, was so fast, so complex, and so full of fun and episodes that just couldn't be sacrificed,
that it was found impossible to do it justice by editing it down to the
same format (of *half* its original length, as opposed to the one-*sixth* of
original length that sufficed for *The Thief of Bagdad*). As a result, it
was not used in the series.

The films of the late teens were, in film-making parlance, rather like
the "establishing shots" used functionally to get movies under way.
They established the art and industry that took off in the twenties. Yet,
one tends to forget both how essential and how pleasing the establishing shot can be. Not only would the body of the film fail to work with-
out it, but the shot itself is often both aesthetically pleasing and
crammed with information. Because the teen years have always been
regarded as a prelude to the greatness of the 1920's, and because the
films of these pre-1920's years seem to be shown (even archivally) far
less frequently than the glossier later silents, they have been unfairly
relegated to a simplistic plateau, as though, Griffith apart, they are all
frenetic Sennett slapstick and rural Charles Ray romances. The word
"Victorian" crops up frequently to put down the rather charming
naïveté of these years. Yet they are vital years in the development of

the motion picture, and in many ways, one would like to have seen them—and their spirit—prolonged just a few years longer. Obviously one could not achieve that without totally reshaping world history. The First World War, and the sophistication that followed it, would have to be somehow delayed, for the film—far more so than any other art/industry—cannot exist in a vacuum. But if Ford, Chaplin, and Stroheim *had* had time to achieve total mastery of their medium without having immediately to harness it to the more ambitious demands of the 1920's, what films we *might* have had!

8

The Art of the Sub-title

Although by the early 1920's the movies had made remarkable artistic and technological strides, the development of really good screen-writers had been somewhat slower. The best thus far had been the specialists who tailored their work to the requirements of an individual star. John Emerson (also a director) and Anita Loos had created a generous number of scenarios for Douglas Fairbanks—scenarios that were witty, pithy, modern, and yet at the same time allowed for the easy introduction of stunt acrobatic action sequences. C. Gardner Sullivan wrote vivid, gutsy, yet also human and sentimental stories for the western star William S. Hart, with the actor's final screen image very much in mind. His meticulous attention to descriptive detail was almost as visually oriented as the long passages of "stage-setting" description that punctuated the detective novels of Raymond Chandler in the 1940's.

But screen-writing as such, even from such professionals as Emerson, Loos, and Sullivan, was not yet regarded as a major factor of American film production. True, it was held in far less repute in other film-producing countries. England, for example, considered the screen-writer so unimportant and paid him so badly that, understandably, no worthwhile writer was interested in writing for the movies at all, and prestige authors of the day, such as H. G. Wells, remained unapproached and largely untapped. It wasn't until much later in the 1920's, when a new generation of British film-makers began to write and direct their own screenplays—men like Alfred Hitchcock and Anthony

126

Asquith—that British cinema achieved any real stature and took immediate steps to catch up with the competition.

The comparative unimportance of the scenarist, at least up to the early 1920's, is not hard to understand. A large percentage of the total movie output was eaten up by star vehicles, many of which were shaped to a pre-determined pattern, with variations on story lines often being decided at conferences between star, director, and scenarist. There was a certain skill in assembling a number of story components, but it was as much a mechanical as a creative skill. Further, in view of the continuing "image" that the star maintained, regardless of the writer employed, it was apparent that the star's creative personality usually dominated. This was especially true in the cases of Mary Pickford, Douglas Fairbanks, and William S. Hart. Then, too, at this comparatively early stage in the movies' development, all the literary works of the world—especially those that were old enough to have fallen into the public domain—were virgin territory. Various versions of such classics as *A Tale of Two Cities, Romeo and Juliet, Dr. Jekyll and Mr. Hyde,* and *Oliver Twist* were made. All of them were designed to exploit romantic stars or to emphasize size and action, so that the writing contribution was often no more than a careful selection and re-arrangement of pre-written scenes. Further serving to minimize the importance of the scenarist was the fact that many of the top directors—Erich von Stroheim being a typical case in point—worked solely from their own original material. D. W. Griffith dispensed with scenarios entirely, carrying all of the plot and construction details in his head, and conducting rehearsals by releasing details on the spot.

Finally, the cinema had not yet reached that point of sophistication when a script itself could be so powerful or poetic as to literally dictate the mood and form of the final film. That would come—Carl Mayer's evocative, almost stream-of-consciousness script for *Sunrise* being a classic example—but it was still a few years away. Obviously it would be wrong to make the bald statement that the screen-writer was unimportant in this period. But it would be accurate to say that because of these factors, he had been thrust into the background and was *regarded* as being of lesser importance.

Because of this, great stress was laid on the titles within a film to tell the story. In many cases, of course, these titles were written by the scenarists themselves. But there were those who specialized solely in titles, and even within that limited field, certain writers restricted themselves to titles for one kind of film—two-reel comedies, for example. The literary style of a title—its content, its purpose, the framing, the use of art backgrounds—all these factors were important in determining its effectiveness, and all of them were developed and refined as the movies themselves matured. Title-writing and title-designing rapidly became an art, and an important one. Bad titling could mar or ruin a good picture, while good titling could often salvage a mediocre one, even at times transforming it into a hit by totally changing the mood and intent of a story-line.

The importance of titles as an integral part of the silent film transcends their purely informational function. As their value came to be understood, they were incorporated into the actual structure of the film, contributing to its pace and its rhythm. Their value can readily be appreciated by viewing a silent movie from which the titles have been removed. For preservation purposes, it was fairly common procedure to remove all but two or three frames of each title from the negative or print held in the vaults for future copying and printing. Titles, requiring less attention in timing from the laboratories, were usually carelessly processed and inadequately "washed" for removal of the chemicals that could ultimately hasten decay. At the time, the mortality rate of nitrate film was not so well known. Nor did it seem that the average film could have commercial or artistic values beyond those of the immediate present. But it was found that, because of this inadequate laboratory treatment, the titles invariably began to decay first— and the decay, once started, would spread rapidly to the rest of the film. Accordingly, the titles—all but one or two frames—were removed from each preservation negative or print, on the theory that if fresh prints were ever needed, new titles could be reconstructed from the "guide" frames remaining.

In many ways, removing the titles was an extremely wise course. The films thus pruned have survived in far better condition than the majority of prints that were not so treated. In the bulk of rediscovered decaying prints or negatives, the rotting sections can be traced directly back to the titles, the worst of the decomposition occurring *within* the title footage. On the other hand, apart from the occasional specialized theatrical reissue, commercial demand for silent films in later years was slight. The bulk of the requests came from archives—and with no commercial stake in the properties and no profit motive involved, the studios had no economically justifiable reason for restoring the lost titles. Thus, many major silents were made up, at the request of museums and archives, from the negatives just as they stood—which meant that the film was interrupted periodically by quick flashes of unreadable wording. (The restoring, by freeze-frame or other processes, was usually beyond the financial ability of the average museum.) Obviously, where a story-line was complex and not told wholly in visual terms, the withholding of essential information was frustrating. However, even in films of action—westerns or sight-gag comedies—the lack of carefully spaced titles destroyed the rhythm of the film, accelerated reaction shots, eliminated all-important time lapses, and made frenzied jump-cuts out of what had been carefully planned and meticulously edited sequences.

The title, in the pre-1906 period, had been both a necessary informational device and a useful "out" for "directors" who were really that in name only. The titles told the audience what was happening, usually before it happened, thus robbing these simple films of even their limited dramatic and surprise potential. They also served to explain what had happened in an inexplicable long shot, which *should* have been broken up into medium and close shots, but rarely was. Moreover, they bridged jumps in location or time lapses before such photographic devices as the dissolve or the fade came into common usage. They were creative only when they became an end in themselves, as in some of the early Edison films, in which, by the process of stop-motion photography, the titles were sometimes amusingly animated. But their use was purely informational; direct dialogue was not used, other than in the "He is told that . . ." format. Physically, all titles looked much alike: white lettering on a black background, surrounded by a white border which, in some form, incorporated the name or trademark of the producing company.

The first major changes began to appear around 1911, when direct dialogue was included in the titles. At Biograph, under Griffith, the films were so expertly cut that audiences never had any doubts as to which character was delivering the line that they had read in title form. Other companies, with less astute editors, were more concerned with the possibility of confusing their audiences. They attempted to avoid this problem by listing the character, along with his line of dialogue, and sometimes—within the same title—the name of the opposing character and *his* reply. This gave titles the look of a play script. The Selig Company, with its quite ambitious full-length feature output, was one of the worst offenders. Further, it robbed the succeeding scenes of spontaneity, giving them instead a tableau-like quality, since often all the dialogue of a scene was given before it was played out, or only after it was finished. Fortunately, this method was not widely adopted, nor did it last long.

As the production of full-length features of five reels and more increased, from 1912 on, so did the literary standards of the titling improve. The bald informational statements of a one-reeler simply would not suffice with the more complex story-lines and multitudinous characters of the longer films. Although it has been hailed for so many other innovations, scant attention has been paid to the sophisticated use of titling in D. W. Griffith's *Intolerance* of 1916. Not only were titles used brilliantly to link sequences (the incident of Christ and the woman taken in adultery cuts directly to the film's modern story of bigots and reformers, joined thematically by the title, "Now let us see how this Christly example is followed in our story of today . . ."), but the titles themselves took on visual identity. In the later sequences of the film, where Griffith does not want to interrupt his flow of visual images, he superimposes his titles *over* his leit-motif shot of the woman rocking the cradle. Direct dialogue titles throughout the film tend to be in straightforward lettering against blank backgrounds, while informational titles are shot against tapestry-like backgrounds, imparting the dignity of history to what Griffith tells us. Each separate story has a distinctive visual title design. The harsh modern story retains the stark white-on-black motif; the Biblical story places its titles against a facsimile of the tablets inscribed with the Ten Commandments; the French story of the Catherine de Medici period stresses the soft woven tapestry background; and the Babylonian story presents its titles against a background suggestive of a rock temple wall, decorated at the top with Babylonian figures.

Griffith, in 1916, was several years ahead of his time in using his titles as an important part of the overall design to create atmosphere, mood, and period with visual symbols. As a former actor and playwright, Griffith was perhaps a trifle over-fond of florid prose and poetic flights of fancy, and found an outlet for this tendency in his titles, which were sometimes too long and too frequent. Many of his titles did have a genuine poetic flow to them, and even out of context, they impress. On the other hand, when confronted with a plot situation which required pure information and no poetry, Griffith often seemed to lose interest, flinging together a sentence that might be devoid of logic, grammar, and even basic punctuation. However, the overall quality of his titles was remarkable, and far superior to that of his contemporaries. He possessed an interesting penchant for reinforcing his screen images by both corroborative information (as, for example, by quoting the historical sources for his stagings or reconstructions) and by personal asides, drawing political and other parallels between his on-screen history and current events. While this latter personal foible may have seemed something of an intrusion at the time, it has given added perspective and depth to later analysis of his work. It has even made the films' viewpoints seem remarkably fresh, since history has a habit of repeating itself.

While Griffith was experimenting with the visuals of titles, two of the biggest male stars of the day—William S. Hart and Douglas Fairbanks—concentrated solely on the written word as a means of amplifying both their screen images and the content of their films.

Fairbanks' bubbling good humor spilled over into his titles, which were long and deliberately over-loaded with a kind of small talk. Even when the titles utilized a small type-face, they often covered every square inch of the frame, so that they were quite difficult to read. A rule of thumb was to allow a reading time of one second per word and then to add an additional five seconds to accommodate the slow readers. So, quite often, Fairbanks' titles occupied as much screen time as many individual scenes. However, the titles were an important adjunct to his on-screen action. He literally took the audience into his confidence, joked with them, and made them feel that he was out to entertain them to the best of his ability. Sometimes the informational point of a Fairbanks title appeared only at the last minute, at the very foot of a title which had been jollying the audience into a state of receptivity.

Although Fairbanks used words rather than visuals in the titles throughout his films, he often employed a novel visual style in the actual main credit. One of the early ones presented Doug as a chef, cheerfully mixing into his cooking pot generous ingredients from cans marked "comedy," "excitement," "drama," and other categories. In

When the Clouds Roll By (1920), he used the charming ploy, never repeated, of accompanying the credits for cameramen, scenarist, and others with scenes of those craftsmen at their trade—the scenarist typing out his story, and the photographers grinding their cameras. Perhaps most striking of all was his introduction to *His Majesty the American,* a 1919 release, and the first of his big new specials for United Artists. The film opens with a straightforward main-title design of black lettering on a white background. Suddenly Doug leaps *through* the title itself and, bouncing up and down with excitement, tells the audience (via, for once, quite short titles) that this is his first film for United Artists and that he's tried hard to make it his best, winding up with, "Gee, folks, I hope you like it!" Fairbanks, however, always liked words too much to leave any room in his title frames for visual design. His sole concession was to try to have the words match the spirit of the film. Thus, later in the twenties, the tongue-in-cheek titles for *The Black Pirate* emulated the jovial quality supposedly employed even by the most sinister of buccaneers, while the style of lettering suggested the decorative, florid style of quill pen and old parchment.

William S. Hart, who wrote many of his own stories (and, indeed, was an accomplished novelist and somewhat less accomplished poet), either by himself or in collaboration with C. Gardner Sullivan, one of the finest of early scenarists, likewise luxuriated in the unrestrained use of prose in his titles. He combined elaborate poetic flourishes with hard-bitten dialogue couched in the colorful, semi-literate style which he genuinely believed to be the honest, unvarnished way in which Westerners spoke, but which was as faithful to the dime novel as to actuality. (Hart loved and knew the West, and had grown up in it, but he was also an incurable romantic. The West that he put on the screen was initially raw and honest, but it was only a point of departure for him. He constantly embellished it, and his own screen character, until sentimentality and idealized visions tended to overbalance the more sober documentary aspects of his films.) His and Sullivan's titles were vivid and often pithy. Particularly effective was his terse and all-encompassing summing up of the qualities of an outlaw gang in *The Testing Block* (1920) as having been "collected by the broom that swept out hell!"

Admittedly, Hart's title prose tends to date rather badly out of the context of the films themselves, and seems to confirm the erroneous impression that "old-time movies" were florid and naïve. Hart introduced one of his western frontier towns with the title:

> A gun-fighting, man-killing devil's den of iniquity that scorched even the sun-parched soil on which it stood

and the town's principal villain with an equally expressive (if, by contemporary standards, somewhat intolerant) title:

> Silk Miller: mingling the oily craftiness of a Mexican with the deadly treachery of a rattlesnake, no man's open enemy, and no man's friend.

In *Hell's Hinges* (1916), Hart's inevitable instant reformation by the influence of a good woman—in this case, the sister of a minister—took place in a makeshift church and was accompanied by the title:

> I reckon God ain't wantin' me much, Ma'am, but when I look at you I feel I've been ridin' the wrong trail.

That same film's final fade-out was prefaced by a flight of poetry that was florid even by Hart's standards:

> And then from the mothering sky came the baby dawn, singing as it wreathed the gray horns of the mountains with ribbons of rose and gold.

Oddly enough, within the films themselves, where Hart's obvious sincerity and almost evangelical fervor are quite apparent, such titles work quite well and do not seem unduly old-fashioned, except possibly to those encountering Hart for the very first time a half-century after the event.

Hart and Fairbanks used and manipulated words to the fullest; Griffith, and an occasional director like Maurice Tourneur, used words in association with visuals. But the basic changeover in format to a visual title-style did not come until 1919. To be dogmatic about a "first" or an individual innovator would be futile, especially in view of the earlier examples provided by *Intolerance*. Robert Brunton is merely one of several film-makers who claimed to have been the first to practice the new art. But quite certainly 1919 was the year in which the development was noted to the extent that titles officially became known as "art-titles," and their creators were given screen credit. The early twenties was to be the heyday of this very specialized kind of art, a welding of still-florid prose to painted art backgrounds that could be explicit (clutching hands or lonely houses for "terror" scenes, a symbolic rat or spider to back up the verbal description of a villain), naturalistic, impressionistic, or stylistic. Sometimes live-action film (a seascape, for example) or a frozen frame of action would be used, photographed through gauze or cheese-cloth, or given a unique color tint, so that it would not clash with the photographic action of the film proper. Animation was used occasionally, but was unpopular as well as expensive. Another variety of title created a three-dimensional effect by using a clay model figure in the foreground, with a title card behind. All of this was quite compatible with an industry that was selling glamor and larger-than-life romance and drama, yet was taking itself more seriously than ever as an art form and was determined to display that artistry in every frame of film. Incorporation of live-action footage into a title card was a unique and often time-saving device in the opening portions of a film, though it was a device that disappeared after the early twenties. Lois Weber was a director especially fond of this method of introducing her characters in such films as *A Chapter in Her Life* and *The Blot*. If the title card informed us that the character introduced was dissolute, a drunkard, or a hard-working professor, then accompanying close-up footage of that character would confirm the description—and possibly save an additional establishing scene within the narrative itself.

Some of the most creative writing of the early 1920's came from the gag-writers for comedies, many of whom, like Al Boasberg, soon developed into full-scale comedy scenarists. From the pun-titles of the Sennett comedies ("They were glad to see her back again," a title that preceded a shot of Phyllis Haver, back to the camera, twinkling a smile at the audience over her shoulder), a whole new school of comedy title-writing emerged. One-liners, almost surrealist in their absurdity, were used both to start the film off with a bang and, at the same time, to introduce a leading character. A Mack Swain two-reeler, *Cowboy Ambrose*, started off by introducing its villain as one who was "arrested for shop-lifting in a plow-store." Inserts of letters often used a wrap-up line to devastating effect. Sennett's *Down on the Farm* opens with a long, and apparently deadly serious, letter informing the heroine that her uncle has died and that she has inherited his circus. The final line:

"P.S. We warned him not to tease the elephants." In Hal Roach's *Should Tall Men Marry?*, the heroine writes her father a shattering letter telling him that she cannot stay on the farm, will not marry the husband he has picked out for her, and is running away from home to marry the man *she* loves. It is signed: "Your obedient daughter." In time, the isolated one-line gags were extended to include two-title repartee. "I hope I'm not depriving you," says Charley Chase in *Bad Boy*, accepting a sandwich from a hulking manual laborer who has pretensions to culture and etiquette. "No depravity, I assure you!" is the reply. These isolated titles are certainly not offered as outstanding examples of sophistication, but they do share the virtue of brevity, wit, and an easy-going grace. And as comedy progressed from two-reelers to full features, the sophistication of the gag-writing improved tremendously. *Love 'Em and Leave 'Em* (1926) contains a delightful title introducing the seedy villain, played by Osgood Perkins, which tells us, "He spent six months curing himself of halitosis, only to find he was unpopular anyway"—which not only puts his villainy-to-come in its proper perspective but also establishes a light mood right away. The following year's *Orchids and Ermine,* one of the very best of the jazz-age Cinderella comedies that Colleen Moore did so well, perhaps represents the zenith of rapid-fire gag-titling in the silent comedy. Since the titles are so bound up with the period flavor of the story and the characters themselves, and use a great deal of contemporary vernacular, it would be unfair to take them out of context. Suffice to say that the various gold digger-millionaire exchanges have pungency, pep, and extreme brevity, and tumble over themselves so fast that the film has all the pace of a fast-talking *sound* comedy with Carole Lombard or Lee Tracy.

There is, needless to say, another side to the coin. Bad gags seem doubly bad when they are presented on the screen in type, without the saving grace of audible delivery. Syd Chaplin at one point revived and re-wrote many of brother Charlie's earlier comedies, afflicting them with the heaviest puns and the most tasteless vulgarity imaginable. His work rendered them doubly painful to watch, since they not only cheapened Chaplin's original work but also took away from Syd Chaplin's own considerable reputation as a creative comedian. In a like manner, excessively long titles with banal content were a curse of the increasing production of "B" pictures and cheap independent films, and were designed only to lengthen the running times of the films and cut down on the amount of pictorial footage that had to be shot.

The independents also had no qualms about picking up great titles from competitors' movies and using them, without alteration, in their own. In the early 1920's, a titler introduced a pompous office supervisor by explaining that "he was muscle-bound from patting himself on the back." That line came to be the cliché of silent comedies, as "Let's get outta here!" was to the sound western. It was used and re-used ad nauseum, to the extent that a New York film society, playing three 1920's comedies without having pre-screened them, recently found that same line turning up in identical circumstances in both of the features *and* in the short!

Considering its effectiveness at the right moment, one form of titling that was surprisingly disliked was the form now used for sub-titling foreign films—lettering superimposed over the picture at the bottom of the screen. Admittedly, in the 1920's, it was a new device and one that had not yet been made mechanically easy. Too, its wholesale use would have meant the total re-structuring of silent movies. With its acceptance, titles could no longer be used for punctuation, or as cutaways to cover up the lack of important shots that might have been ruined or, by oversight, not filmed at all. Finally, the need to compress text to a bare-bones minimum would have put all of the grandiose title-writers out of business, and would have thrown William S. Hart and Douglas Fairbanks into paroxysms of frustration. Nevertheless, there *were* moments when such a sub-title was the only answer—when there was important information to convey but when cutting away to a title card would destroy the carefully built-up rhythm of a sequence. Thus, sub-titles over film were used in such key suspense or action sequences as the cutting of the chandelier in *The Phantom of the Opera* or, more extensively, during the chariot race in *Ben Hur*. Had the device not suggested so many potential threats to the status quo of film-making in the 1920's, it might well have been investigated further and developed as an important occasional adjunct to the standard title.

The glorious years of the full-blown art title were 1919 to 1925, when there began a gradual but steady decline in its application. Films by the mid-1920's had achieved such visual sophistication that they no longer needed atmospheric titles to underline their moods. Moreover, that sophistication extended to the story-telling, too, so that fewer informational titles were needed. *Are Parents People?*, a comedy of manners of 1925, starts with an important establishing sequence telling us that a middle-aged couple is rich, sophisticated, and divorcing, but still basically very much in love. All of this information is conveyed visually, and it is not until the plot itself is well under way—some five minutes into the film—that we get the first title. Some American films, emulating and indeed pre-dating the most famous example, Germany's *The Last Laugh*, actually did away with titles entirely and told the story solely through the visuals. They were interesting experiments but didn't really work. The title was such an essential part of the grammar of the silent film that these experiments, laudable though they were, literally lacked a language, just as the attempt to make a sound film devoid of dialogue—*The Thief* (1952)—failed because it was impossible to accept as realistic a world full of every kind of normal sound *except* that of the human voice.

By the late twenties, the art title had all but disappeared, regarded, like multi-toning and tinting, as an unnecessary and artificial trapping. (Apart from the experimentation with Technicolor, even the bigger films were tending to revert to a simple amber tone, and even to ordinary black-and-white printing.) Russia had adopted the interesting device of absorbing the titles into its own rapidly-paced montage style of film-making. Titles would be broken up into single words, each word intercut with a relevant scene or fragment of a scene, and then at the end of the sequence, the whole title triumphantly produced *in toto*. Great Britain imitated this device in a small way—rather creatively in its own sub-titling of the climactic sequence of the German *Metropolis*—but in America the idea was little noted. Directors who needed the cumulative effect of a gradually revealed title preferred to do it within a single frame, starting their title at the top of the screen and revealing it only gradually, line by line. There was also some minor use made of perspective and movement within the frame. A whisper or a far-off cry might be indicated by the dialogue phrase being printed in hard-to-read small type in the dead center of the screen. For sudden excitement, as with Laura La Plante's scream for help in *The Cat and the Canary*, when clutching hands encircle her neck as she lies in bed,

the title (in this case, a simple "Help!") might zoom forward from infinity into a sudden full-screen close-up, the letters trembling and
quivering with fright.

Less spectacular but more stylized were the simple and sparse titles
of Murnau's *Sunrise*. They were brief, almost terse, but with a classic
rather than a purely functional brevity. The actual style of the lettering
was rough-hewn, almost like a woodcut. Tremendously effective and
appropriate at the time, it unfortunately seems less so today, since that
style of lettering has become the prototype to suggest terror in the
main titles and advertising materials for horror movies. At one key
point in *Sunrise*, the temptress suggests to the hero that he murder his
wife, making it look like an accident. "Couldn't she get drowned?" the
title reads—the final word "drowned" gradually elongating downward,
seeming to melt and dissolve into the blackness of an unseen lake.

But these were the stunts of highly individual films. For the most
part, the art of titling was being abandoned as part of the "old" Hollywood and beneath the sophisticated standards of the new. Raoul
Walsh's *The Red Dance*, a colorful melodrama of the Russian Revolution and a major Fox release of 1928, even reverted to the methods employed by Griffith in *Intolerance* twelve years earlier, though with so
little stress on the device that it was probably done at the instigation
of the director (Walsh was a former Griffith apprentice and protégé)
rather than to impress audiences. Dialogue titles spoken by, or informational titles relating to, the aristocracy or military of old Russia
were placed on a tapesty-like card imprinted with a black Tsarist symbol. Trotsky and other leaders of the Revolution were given titles
printed against a rough, rock-like surface. The poor, ignorant peasants,
with little to say or do, had to be satisfied with the old, nondescript
white lettering against a plain black background.

With the arrival of sound, the title was by no means abandoned but
instead reverted to its original status in the earliest days of the silents—
a lazy way of conveying information. Early talkies are full of titles
establishing locale, period, motivation, and even such theater-program
shortcuts as "Two hours later." With the astonishing visual techniques
that the movies had amassed in the late twenties, when titles were
often unnecessary, it is amazing that—given the added dimensions of
sound and speech—many directors, in those early days of sound, could
not invent visual symbols for transitional scenes and had to fall back

on the printed word. As late as 1936, in *Modern Times*—technically a silent, since it was devoid of dialogue—one finds even as great an artist as Chaplin using such a totally unnecessary title as "Dawn."

Of course, in a limited way, the title has retained its value even into the sound era. The satiric foreword, especially in the comedies of Preston Sturges, is a direct modern parallel to the chatty introductions of Douglas Fairbanks. Films that court an old-fashioned or non-realistic flavor find that a strategically placed title can often achieve that end without also achieving the undesired effect of self-ridicule. James Cagney's vigorously old-fashioned *The Oklahoma Kid* (1939) made effective use of such time-transitional titles as, "Meanwhile, the Kid continued to play his cards as he saw them." Reissues of silent films— *The Birth of a Nation* being a case in point—strengthened the power of individual titles by highlighting them and superimposing them over frame blow-ups of action sequences (battle scenes, mobs). This almost had the effect of likening them to chapter titles in a book, as opposed to the more placid original titles.

Narrative language in titles also served to enlarge the importance of the action or characters and turn them into symbols. The humble word "The" was never used so grandiosely as in the silent film. Sometimes whole casts of characters were given no names at all, but merely referred to (and this applied to drama as well as, more obviously, comedy) as The Boy, The Girl, The Girl's Father, and so on, to such variations as The Friendless One, The Kindly Heart, The Faithful Soul, The Musketeer of the Slums, The Great Heart (referring to Lincoln), and The Dear One—all of them, as it happens, Griffith characters who, with the exception of Lincoln, were known and identified *only* by those appellations in their respective films. (Griffith was also not above using titles to plant suspense falsely where none legitimately existed. Fairly early in *Isn't Life Wonderful?*, Griffith's 1924 film about inflation in post-war Germany, he has an unkempt, animalistic potential villain eye the heroine somewhat lecherously. A title informs us that he is "one who will rob Inge of her most prized possession." Knowing Griffith, we naturally assume that the title refers to the lady's virtue; only some eight reels later do we realize that food is somewhat more highly prized than virginity, and what he does in fact steal is Inge's carefully cultivated crop of potatoes!)

The word "The" crops up with striking regularity too, affixed to storms and sundry holocausts, to turn them into symbolic or cathartic events. Thus, when Lillian Gish staggers out into the elements, she is drawn to "The River," which is also "frenzied" and "tortured." The key title of the sequence reads, "And then The Storm"—not just any old storm, or the expected storm, or even the Biggest Storm Within Living Memory, but plainly and simply *The* Storm—a symbolic climax to the seasonal structure of the film and to all the emotional crises that have been built up.

Repetition of words was a device that, again, was more dramatic than truly life-like. In *Ben Hur*, one of the galley slaves has dropped dead at his oars, and his companion, who barely has the strength to do his share of the work, suddenly finds the energy to roar (to no one in particular, and to no purpose, other than to confirm to the audience that the man is dead), "He is dead—yet still they lash—and lash—and lash. . . ." The unfinished sentence, trailing off into infinity, was a frequently utilized device. The short sentence, ending with "and . . .", merely planted the seeds of an idea and let the audience, with its knowledge of movie plotting, fill in the details. Of course, talkies used an equivalent device. FBI men or outlaw leaders, giving instructions to their men, would start with, "Now this is what I want you to do . . .", the scene fading out before the specifics could be outlined.

Titles could also cunningly impart an aura of size and importance where absolutely none existed. William K. Howard's early (1922) Zorro-like melodrama, *Captain Fly By Night*, is typical. The titles try hard to make an epic out of a quickie. A gang of moth-eaten Mexicans are constantly referred to as "conspirators," and the villain's plans—which seem limited to straightforward banditry and personal lechery, and could hardly be more ambitious, anyway, with no more than twenty "conspirators" to back him up—are *said* to be those of a revolutionary plotting to overthrow the government. The rest of the titles do their best to impart a grandiose Dumas-like flavor.

Every so often, of course, even in the most original of sound films—one might almost say *especially* in them—one comes across a line of dialogue that immediately suggests a rephrasing of a great silent title that a director or writer never forgot. Preston Sturges was a great admirer of silent films and employed a great deal of silent technique in his comedies. In his 1941 *The Lady Eve*, Charles Coburn as a crooked card-sharp is faced with the reformation of his equally crooked daughter (Barbara Stanwyck) and remarks: "The trouble with people who reform is that they want to rain on everybody else's parade too!" What is this but a reshaping of, and tribute to, one of Griffith's greatest subtitles in *Intolerance:* "Women who cease to attract men often turn to reform as a second choice." Quite incidentally, that one title—entirely sober and appropriate in its context within the film—has proven to be one of the movies' permanent show-stoppers. Nearly three-quarters of a century later, that one great early example of the titler's art never fails to elicit long and enthusiastic applause from every kind of audience.

9

The Directors

The sheer number of directors at work in the American silent cinema was prodigious. The percentage of them that is remembered, however, or considered to have played a vital or innovative role in the development of the art of film, is remarkably small. Any survey work on the American sound film will produce frequent and often laudatory references to such lesser directors as Samuel Fuller, Edgar Ulmer, John Brahm, or Charles Vidor, yet parallel works on the silent film usually ignore totally such opposite numbers as William Seiter, Irvin Willat, Harry Pollard, or Emory Johnson. Even so undistinguished a silent director as Donald Crisp is afforded *more* recognition, purely on the basis of having "directed" Buster Keaton and Douglas Fairbanks, although direction of those two personalities was purely academic.

One reason perhaps is that the silent cinema, far more than the sound, tended to divide its directors into two camps—the innovators (Griffith, Stroheim, King Vidor, Murnau, Flaherty) and the non-innovators. This latter and very large group included the craftsmen as well as the mediocrities. Thus, a solid and incredibly versatile but admittedly uninventive director such as William Seiter was doomed to the same kind of critical obscurity as an outright hack like John Waters, even though his material rewards might have been substantially and deservedly larger. Moreover, while *directorial* styles were developed and perhaps recognized by the more discerning—there was certainly no mistaking a Griffith, Ford, or Tourneur film—there was virtually no place in the silent cinema for personal *thematic* styles. Almost all American-employed directors, regardless of their personal integrity and artistic ambitions, recognized that the motion picture was essentially a medium of popular mass entertainment, and worked within those limits. To suggest artistic compromise thereby is perhaps unfair. All too often, directors (or stars of sufficient power to control their own vehicles) over-estimated public interest in serious, provocative, or artistic themes. Nazimova's highly stylized and near-surreal version of *Salome* (1922), Rex Ingram's sincerely felt but painfully slow adaptation of Ibañez' *Mare Nostrum* (1926), or Griffith's calling attention to the plight of post-war, inflation-plagued Germany in *Isn't Life Wonderful?* (1924) were all films that had something to say. But their makers still hoped that they said it in a sufficiently entertaining manner for them to be commercially successful, too. The failure of films like these, even though backed by directorial or star names of some prestige, did little to stimulate the production of other films along similar lines.

Film, as a vehicle for a "personal statement," was as yet, and perhaps happily, unknown. Certainly "personal statement" films ran riot in the American cinema of the 1960's and 1970's. Too many of them were self-indulgent displays by immature artists who had more ego than message to impart. (A film such as 1976's *Stay Hungry* managed to get the author-director's name, and an obscure name at that, into the ads some five or six times!) In any event, the commercial set-up of the industry and the physical construction of silent films made "personal statement" films largely unworkable. They needed both the subtlety and the dialogue that only the sound film could bring. The humanistic traits that run through all of Jean Renoir's sound films, both French and American, would have been virtually impossible in the silent film. Moreover, the added importance of the scenarist in the sound film meant that he might be able to insert a personal viewpoint or statement of which the director might be unaware. Well before the era of such undeniably personal directors as Elia Kazan and Robert Rossen, quite routine and thoroughly commercial films were full of mild agitation and slanted viewpoints. Warner Brothers films conducted an undisguised and hero-worshipping love affair with President Franklin D. Roosevelt from the beginning of his term of office until its end. Even a pleasant little romantic programmer like Fox's *Coming Out Party* (1934) contains both optimistic and sarcastic comments on the New

Deal, comments probably quite unnoticed by its straightforward and uncomplicated director, John Blystone.

And, of course, one finds the most blatant examples in the work of screen-writers known (usually after the fact) for their Communist leanings. Lester Cole's screenplay for Nathaniel Hawthorne's *The House of Seven Gables* (1940), if not pro-Communist, certainly managed to inject anti-American elements. Vincent Price's harangue at the portraits of his ancestors was also a harangue at the capitalist structure of American society, and a sub-plot managed to call attention to America's involvement in the slave trade. Neither of these elements is present in Hawthorne's original novel, but so skillfully are they interpolated that anyone not familiar with that work would logically assume that they represented Hawthorne's thoughts. Certainly Joe May, a German director presumably not too familiar with Americana, would have been unaware that the film he was directing was being used as a vehicle for subtle propaganda. That subtlety would have been impossible in the silent film; and if retained in an obvious form, it would have been with the director's full knowledge.

Such use of the screen in the silent American cinema was largely limited to safe platitudes. The screen could afford to recommend equality for women, to advise against smoking, or to editorialize against the evils of liquor, since these were basically unarguable propositions. But the blatant propagandist content of *Potemkin* and other Russian imports made Hollywood shy away from any preachments that might imply political affiliations. Even the anti-Communist films of the 1920's—surely a safe enough issue—were cheap melodramas, usually independently made outside the basic Hollywood structure, and often revealing a surprising lack of knowledge of what Communism was all about. More serious issues—birth control or the causes of underpaid white-collar workers—were invariably dealt with, again on the level of independent non-Hollywood production, by such directors as Lois Weber, who tried to compensate for budget and star deficiencies with stronger-than-usual subject matter. Major issues—racial intolerance, drug addiction, the treatment of the aged or the insane, alcoholism—were studiously avoided on a serious level as being totally unfit subjects for an entertainment industry.

If nothing else, this lack of personal involvement in film, the reluctance or inability to use the screen as a personal forum, makes it easier to assess the achievements of silent directors. They all had the same tools, and they were all aiming at the same market. One would be hard-pressed, in the early 1950's, to compare the success of the work of John Ford, Orson Welles, Elia Kazan, and Preston Sturges, since their working methods, distribution arrangements, and intended audiences were so totally different. Yet a late-1920's comparison of similar talents—D. W. Griffith, Rex Ingram, F. W. Murnau, and Buster Keaton—would find all of those artists working under roughly the same conditions and aiming at exactly the same market.

A very few of the silent directors seemed almost restricted to that era, despite their later work in sound films. The pictorial splendor of Maurice Tourneur's films was complete in itself; sound and dialogue merely got in the way of the images. Although Herbert Brenon dealt mainly in adaptations of stage plays and novels—and therefore, presumably, would have needed and used sound well—there was such a gentility to his work (*Peter Pan, A Kiss for Cinderella, Sorrell and Son,* even the adventure classic *Beau Geste*) that the contact with reality brought about by sound seemed to throw him off-stride. Significantly, his best sound film was also his most gentle and humane: the underrated British-made *The House Master* (1938). George Fitzmaurice (*Son of the Sheik,* 1926) and Alan Crosland (*Don Juan,* 1926) were both specialists in the ornate, lushly-mounted, swashbuckling romance, played partially tongue-in-cheek and for larger-than-life fun. Both of these films—the former a Rudolph Valentino vehicle, the latter one of John Barrymore's best—are superb examples of the finest in escapist Hollywood romanticism. Both contain many moments of laughter—and yet, contemporary audiences tend to regard these laughs as signs of dating. They seem unable to realize that, just as the outstanding craftsmanship in set design, photography, and action was intentional, so were the moments of laughter. Audiences laughed then, as now. This kind of romp—not quite a spoof, yet not meant to be taken entirely seriously—disappeared with the coming of sound, not to return (and then only tentatively) until 1939's *Gunga Din.* Both Fitzmaurice and Crosland made interesting sound films, but neither had the opportunity to return to the kind of film that was his real forte.

William Seiter is a director to whom little critical attention has been paid. Yet commercially he was one of the most reliable directors of the 1920's, and if not an artistic giant, then certainly a consummate craftsman. Seiter worked primarily for Universal and Warner Brothers, and made films, for the most part, about the contemporary scene, designed for the average contemporary audience (insofar as anybody has ever been able to define just what that audience was). Seiter's work had taste and charm, and he had the happy knack of being able to present contemporary life and human foibles in dramatic or amusing ways, without distorting them or blowing them up to typically Hollywoodian proportions. His *The Mad Whirl* (1925) is usually represented (when represented at all) by a typical still of a wild orgy. Although the scene does appear in the film, in its proper context it is neither wild nor an orgy. The film is about the jazz age and flappers, but as they surfaced in a small rural town. A sub-plot involves the hero's eventually success-ful battle with alcoholism, played with all the earnestness that such a battle would have in life, but without the spectacular dramatics and torments that Hollywood adds as embellishment. *The Mad Whirl* still exists, but it is little remembered and hardly ever shown. Yet it is a far more honest representation of the jazz-age milieu than MGM's much glossier, star-laden *Our Dancing Daughters* (1928), usually ac-cepted as the "definitive" jazz-age film. Certainly Seiter's direction is far subtler than Harry Beaumont's heavy-handed, straightforward di-rection of the MGM film. Seiter's *Skinner's Dress Suit*, also of 1925, and also for Universal, likewise holds its own very well today as a charm-ing, funny, and realistic comedy about a young married couple, the problems of commuting, installment-plan purchases, that all-important raise, and keeping up with the current status symbols. For Warner Brothers, Seiter made a particularly pleasing film called *The Little Church Around the Corner* (1923), unusually adroit in harnessing its *Miracle Man* religious theatrics to a realistic rural milieu, and incor-porating some fairly strong capital-labor commentary as well. Seiter's films all had a great deal of warmth, and he seemed to care about, and believe in, his characters. His films invariably made money—sometimes big profits, as in the Reginald Denny comedies for Universal—and he, of course, was well paid for his work. Seiter was equally prolific in the sound period, but the kinds of films he did best were declining in box-office favor. Also, like all contract directors, he had to take what he was given—assignments ranging from hard-boiled comedy and Shirley Tem-ple vehicles to musicals and war films. Nevertheless, his best talkies re-tained much of the warmth and down-to-earth charm of his silents, particularly *Hot Saturday* (1932) and *The Lady Wants Mink* (1953). Seiter can also claim the distinction of having worked more felicitously with Laurel and Hardy than any other director, and of achieving a minor classic with them in the 1934 film *Sons of the Desert.*

If William Seiter was ideally suited to the silent film by temperament, then James Cruze fitted in almost by default, his artistic shortcomings transforming themselves into virtues. Cruze, initially an actor (and, like Griffith, not a very good one) and later a director (who owed a great deal to Karl Brown, the cameraman with whom he most frequently worked), hit his real stride as a director with *The Covered Wagon* in 1923. Its epic sweep was largely the result of Brown's stunning camerawork. Dramatically it was dull, and in terms of editing and the handling of actors, quite primitive. Yet it was in a sense the first real western epic, certainly the first western to shift the emphasis from a star personality like Hart or Mix to a quasi-documentary concentration on reconstructed events. The film was a huge hit, and Cruze's reputation was made. The simplistic approach of the film, and its over-long and rather dull successor, *The Pony Express* (1925), came along at just the right time to establish Cruze in a unique position. Artistic acclaim for European film imports was bringing with it a certain resentment and suspicion from hinterland audiences and critics. A lot of the European "tricks" were just that, and new ideas in set design and camera angles were being picked up and copied by the American directors. Many applauded this progress, the willingness to learn from others. On the other hand, Cruze's films of historical Americana needed to be simple and rough-hewn. They avoided editorial finesse, and Cruze's plodding 1-2-3 method of direction seemed at the time almost a defiant flaunting of old, uncomplicated virtues in the face of the new. Cruze's films were so popular that at one point he found himself the highest-paid director in Hollywood. To his credit, Cruze didn't limit himself to one formula. He attempted the bizarre (and unsuccessful) *Beggar on Horseback* (1925), and he made, in *Hollywood* (1923), a uniquely honest and less sensational forerunner of Billy Wilder's *Sunset Boulevard* (1950). Unfortunately, not a single print survives to show whether it lives up to the mouth-watering potential of its synopsis, cast list, and reviews. The lack of subtlety and the purely surface appeal in most of Cruze's silent films suggest that he was an ideal, if limited, director for that medium. Actually, he made some of his best films in the sound era, handling his actors with distinction, and instilling a real sense of pace and pep into such movies as *I Cover The Waterfront* (1933). Cruze's sound career seems to have been as widely ignored as his silent one was inflated.

A mere recital of directorial names parallel to Cruze, Seiter, and Crosland, even a summing up of their careers, would be fruitless. They are legion: Ray Enright, Lewis Seiler, John Blystone, Lambert Hillyer, Clifford Smith, George Seitz, Lyn Reynolds—all of them experts in the action genres; William deMille, Monta Bell, and Malcolm St. Clair for sophistication and wit; and Frank Lloyd, John S. Robertson, Fred Niblo, and Raoul Walsh for the bigger star vehicles and costume specials. These names, only a small scratch on the surface, underscore one important fact: that there are really *three* histories of Hollywood to be told.

Hollywood is unique in that it has always created and sustained a distinct division between art and commerce. In the history of almost any other national cinema, one does not find this division. In some cases, the countries are smaller and their filmic output is but a minute percentage of Hollywood's. In most instances, too, these cultures are older and more sophisticated, so that even a popular art like the cinema does not have to "play down" to its audience. In Scandinavia, for example, the great and innovative films that shaped their art were also the most popular and commercially successful movies.

In Hollywood, however, the dynamic progression of technical and artistic innovations came to us through Griffith, Stroheim, Flaherty, Murnau, and Welles. Only occasionally, as with the work of Chaplin, or an individual film like *The Birth of a Nation* or *The Big Parade,* did artistry and commercial success overlap. On the other hand, a list of the biggest box-office successes—the spectacles, the comedies, the star vehicles for Valentino, Pickford, Colleen Moore, Clara Bow, and Douglas Fairbanks—might not contain a single title that had prominently furthered the art of the motion picture. Yet these films are also important. Not only are they the cumulative by-products of experimentation and innovation, but their commercial success itself pays for more experimentation. Without Tom Mix, William Fox might not have been able to afford Murnau and *Sunrise;* without the profits from Rin Tin Tin, the Warner Brothers probably would not have been able to finance their foray into sound.

Yet if *Intolerance, Greed,* and *Sunrise* represent the innovative side of the industry, and *Blood and Sand, Robin Hood,* and *Little Annie Rooney* its money-making provinces, both aspects represent incomplete extremes. One can relate a perfectly valid history of Hollywood from either viewpoint. But not all innovative films, despite their brilliance, were widely influential; nor were all potential "blockbuster" films as successful as planned. There is a third history: the Hollywood of William Seiter (perhaps more than any other single director), which is neither particularly creative nor particularly lucrative, but is essentially *reliable*. It reflects the taste and the entertainment needs of perhaps the largest single percentage of the movie-going public. A "popular" history of Hollywood—ranging from Seiter and Reginal Denny through Rin Tin Tin, Shirley Temple, The Dionne Quintuplets, Sonja Henie, The Dead End Kids, and Ma and Pa Kettle—needs to be told, too. Until it is—and it clearly needs a specialized study that is not merely an adjunct to an overall history—the talented journeymen-directors such as Seiter will probably never really get their due.

Without in any way denigrating the achievements of the silent film, and admitting D. W. Griffith and such pictorialists as Maurice Tourneur and Rex Ingram to be notable exceptions, one can claim that the best of the silent directors—Ford, Vidor, Walsh, Borzage, Howard, King, Hitchcock, Hawks, Lubitsch, and even (though his case is more arguable) Lang—produced their best *bodies of work* in the sound period, even though in certain cases (Vidor's *The Crowd*) the finest individual film was from the silent era. It is a strange irony that, while the silent cinema itself was a complete entity, the artists who made it so were often not as fully realized.

10

The Early Twenties

The year that officially launched the 1920's was curiously lack-luster. Hollywood seemed reluctant to take advantage of the economic and artistic gains it had made in 1919. (By contrast, 1940 was to show a much more aggressive and intelligent utilization of the freedoms gained—or re-won—in 1939.) Griffith, Fairbanks, Chaplin, and Pickford had formed United Artists, to give themselves both greater freedom and control, and, not just incidentally, greater profits for their labors. Yet Griffith, having wrought a genuinely poetic film in the sensitive *Broken Blossoms,* devoted 1920 to a brace of romantic rural melodramas and a couple of exotic South Seas films. The 1920 output of Fairbanks, Pickford, and Chaplin was likewise somewhat below their 1919 standard.

There were signs that neither Hollywood nor the exhibitors were ready for too much progress. The bulk of the product remained—thematically, at least—unsophisticated, derived from novels, plays, and entertainment styles well established in earlier days. Griffith's own *Way Down East,* of course, headed the list. Other typical 1920 releases were Jack Pickford's *The Little Shepherd of Kingdom Come,* Will Rogers' *Jes' Call Me Jim,* a bizarre Barrymore thriller, *Dr. Jekyll and Mr. Hyde,* William Farnum's *If I Were King,* a superb version of *Huckleberry Finn,* directed by William Desmond Taylor, and a couple of rousing schoolboy adventures directed by Maurice Tourneur—*Treasure Island* and *The Last of the Mohicans.* No criticism of these individual films is implied; indeed, as isolated films, some of them are quite outstanding. Taylor's *Huckleberry Finn* is possibly still the best screen adaptation of Mark Twain, but it was undoubtedly hurt by Paramount's unadventurous policy. Taylor had made *Tom Sawyer* for the same studio earlier. It had been a rather stodgy, unimaginative film, saved only by some quite pleasing locations. Taylor, probably unsatisfied with it, must have leaped at the chance to do *Huckleberry Finn* as a follow-up, since it offers much more scope and is hardly an innocuous schoolboy's story, as *Tom Sawyer* had been. With a much better script, stronger players, and an extended use of location shooting, *Huckleberry Finn* was an infinitely superior picture in every way, and visually quite breath-taking. But, inferior or not, *Tom Sawyer* had been a huge hit, and Paramount was obviously unwilling to tamper with a successful formula. There was growing exhibitor resentment about longer pictures, and there are signs that *Huckleberry Finn* was drastically edited. Scenes do not run long enough for their full dramatic impact to be felt. Superbly selected and composed location shots flash on and off as quick establishing scenes, gone before one has had a chance to drink in their beauty. But even in its abbreviated version, *Huckleberry Finn* is a superb piece of Americana. If allowed to retain the leisurely tempo its locale and period require, it might well have been something of a masterpiece. Tourneur's *The Last of the Mohicans was* a masterpiece.

Tourneur's films did not just use pleasing locations or impressive panoramic exteriors. They were beautifully designed and lit, with a penchant for silhouette shots or for shots from framed dark interiors out into the light. Even Tourneur's more routine American silents, such as *Lorna Doone,* made for Thomas Ince in 1924, have the saving grace of a mystical visual beauty. But the beauty of his *Last of the Mohicans* was not achieved at the expense of story values. It is still a rugged adventure tale, faithful to the spirit of the Fenimore Cooper original, with a starkly tragic ending and some of the most savage Indian massacre scenes ever filmed. Whether exhibitors appreciated the sophistication of its camerawork is a moot point, but they certainly appreciated its pace and brevity; it told the whole story, without appearing to hurry, in a mere six reels.

The length of a film, and whether or not such lengths should be standardized, was one of the most pressing industry concerns in 1920.

On the one hand, it had been proved that the occasional "road show" attraction of extended length could bring both prestige and box-office benefits. *The Birth of a Nation*, three hours long, had been an absolute blockbuster; so had *Way Down East*, at almost the same length. Yet exhibitors, on the whole, were wary of longer pictures, possibly because they cut down on the number of shows that could be scheduled in a day. Early in 1920, exhibitor groups proposed that a standard 4,800 feet be adopted as an average length for a feature. This was an astonishingly short and conservative length, since even at the rate of silent speed projection, this would mean a running time of only seventy minutes. However, exhibitors were clearly thinking in terms of the pre-1920 features with Mary Pickford, Charles Ray, Louise Glaum, Douglas Fairbanks, William S. Hart, Sessue Hayakawa, and other major stars—all of which had been profitable and most of which had stayed rigidly within that seventy-minute framework. And in a sense, the exhibitors may well have been right. Apart from bigger sets and sheer physical size, these stars did nothing in their later and longer films that they hadn't done as well—or better—in their earlier and shorter works.

Another problem constantly confronting Hollywood in the early 1920's was that of retaining its respectable image. Earlier, the theatrical world had coined the phrase "the legitimate theater" as both an insult to, and a defense against, the upstart movie industry. Gradually, if none too subtly, the industry had fought back and gained for itself at least a modicum of respectability. It had discouraged scandal within its own ranks; it had limited vice to those films which (as in the Theda Bara vehicles) ultimately showed the terrible price that inevitably had to be paid for any moral shortcomings; and it certainly loaded the scales in favor of Victorian virtue. Although this would change very rapidly in the early 1920's, in 1920 itself, even the vamp careers of Theda Bara and Louise Glaum were at an end, while the rewards that came to the virtuous—Lillian Gish, Mae Marsh, Bessie Love, Dorothy Gish, Jewel Carmen, Carol Dempster—were more attractive than ever. The bigger producers (and stars) preferred not to rock the boat, to play it safe with their never-never-land morality, and to avoid controversial issues.

It comes as somewhat of a shock to realize that some films of 1920 *did* tackle important social and political issues in a forthright fashion.

However, none of them were made by major producers. Ince's *Dangerous Hours,* directed by Fred Niblo, was at first a rather hysterical account of Tsarist and then Communist tyranny (both shared the common denominator of putting rape at the head of the list of political offenses!), but then turned into a rather sober and interesting account of Communist tactics in fermenting unrest and strikes among labor unions. *Uncle Sam of Freedom Ridge* was a fervent propaganda piece in favor of the League of Nations, a courageous film to make, in view of general American sentiments against that body. *The Face at Your Window* pulled off the rather all-encompassing trick of being anti-Communist, anti-capitalist, *and* anti-labor! *Empty Arms* even came out in favor of birth control. But these were all relatively minor films. There was a lot of red meat in the melodramas of the period, too. Drug addiction came in for a good deal of condemnation because the dope fiend was a conveniently clichéd villain. But by the same token, attitudes toward racial questions were presented in terms of clichés. A recurring theme in the melodramas of the period is of the "yellow" man who schemes to marry the "white" girl. The "impossibility" of such a union is taken for granted, and the villain's mere thinking of it is proof in itself that a) he *is* a villain, and b) his race is inferior. Although white-black marriages seemed too controversial to attract Hollywood's attention, the casually accepted inferiority of the Negro is again a built-in factor in many of the lesser melodramas of the period.

Because they were not major productions, and were unconcerned about the prestige of star or director, many of these lesser films tended to be both much stronger and more realistic in their dramatic construction, and much more explicit in matters of violence and sex. As such, they drew a great deal of criticism from pressure groups and critics, many of the exhibitor-oriented reviewers even going so far as to advise exhibitors which sequences to cut from their prints in order to avoid offending audiences. One critic, for example, felt that Fox films on the whole—perhaps influenced by their Theda Bara vehicles—tended to be coarser and more brutal than those of any other company, and should be examined carefully so that the offending sequences could be removed.

Whether critics had the right to assume responsibility for suggesting the cutting of films—and whether exhibitors should have had the right to make those cuts—is rather beside the point. Clearly, in a legalistic sense, they did not. But in a practical sense, they frequently assumed that right—and with silent films, it was fairly easy to make such cuts without seriously damaging the film. (In talkies, of course, cuts are much more evident because of the inevitable removal of syllables of speech, or notes of music, from the sound track.) But because of this cavalier attitude on the part of exhibitors, the major companies were more prone to play it safe, leave controversial issues out of their pictures, and thus avoid local censorship and snipping of costly prints.

The role of film critics in the 1920's is an important and interesting one. Despite their arrogance in imposing their own set of moral values, they often offered astute analytic criticism, too. Even on relatively unimportant pictures, the skill and artistry of John Ford, for example, was recognized quite early. But any serious consideration of the function of the critic in the 1920's is better withheld until the films of 1925 and later have been discussed. For it was in the latter part of the 1920's that the reviewers wielded their greatest power, in some cases being literally bought by Hollywood interests to mold or change public opinion, and in other cases forming a curious but seemingly spontaneous front against the inroads of foreign films.

Although, in the pre-war years, there had been a flurry of interest in the Italian historical and Biblical spectaculars, the European film was just beginning to put in a business-like appearance on the American movie front. Servicemen, returning from the war in Europe, were glad at first to re-embrace the still somewhat Victorian values and morals that dominated American films; only gradually did their boredom and new "sophistication" manifest themselves. The year 1920 saw the beginning of a trend toward new maturity in the American cinema, and a recognition that themes dealing with sex did not have to be limited to the clear-cut good-and-bad issues of the vamp films. Cecil B. deMille began his highly successful marital romances and farces, films which seem heavy-handed and obvious today but which at the time were considered to be mature and skillful maneuvers on very thin ice. *Madame X* helped establish the florid "confession" genre, and Tod Browning's *The Virgin of Stamboul*, released very early in 1920, was one of several Priscilla Dean vehicles that showed how a "good girl" could be the catalyst in an exotic story promising steamy sex. *The Woman and the Puppet* (later filmed rather more successfully as a Dietrich-Von Sternberg talkie titled *The Devil is a Woman*, and turning up again still later as a Brigitte Bardot vehicle) proved to be a handsome but rather turgid showcase for Geraldine Farrar and Lou Tellegen.

Individually, none of these films were exactly breakthroughs, and they made less of an impression than two imports from Germany, *Passion* and *Sumurun*, which starred Pola Negri and were directed by Ernst Lubitsch. Lubitsch's direction was still somewhat stolid (though subtler by far than that of more representative German directors of the period, such as Richard Oswald), and *Passion*, a spectacle of the French Revolution, lacked the sweep and inventiveness of Griffith's American films. *Sumurun* was an Arabian Nights fantasy, again rather heavy-handed—mawkish in the self-pity of its drama, clumsy in its comedy—but, in terms of pictorial design, both advanced and fascinating. However, the major factor contributing to the success of these two films in the United States was not Lubitsch but Pola Negri. Her vitality and earthy passion—an Anna Magnani in an age of Pickfords and Gishes—brought a much-needed note of honesty and reality into the star system. Negri and Lubitsch, and such infrequent American films as *The Woman and the Puppet*, provided the opening wedge in an onslaught designed to upset many of the old values at precisely the time that America at large, with Prohibition as the catalyst, was turning its back on established moral, political, patriotic, and other values. Within a year, such films as Valentino's *The Sheik* and Stroheim's *Foolish Wives* would help to reinforce and accelerate this onslaught. But for the time being, this opening wedge was still suspect, and was opposed with vigor by most of the established critics and other public-opinion shapers. Thus, *Pollyanna*—one of the most unrelievedly sentimental (and so, one of the least typical) of all the Mary Pickford vehicles—was praised to the skies as "ideal family fare," in contrast to the "plethora of rot" which was being offered on all sides.

However menacing the "rot" may have seemed in 1920, it was either relative or limited to the independent films and "exploitation" features—for little of it is apparent in the representative 1920 films that have survived. The overall trend was toward melodrama and action, with themes of Americana forming a prolific back-up group. Comedy was curiously scarce, but this may have been because 1920 was, for many major film-makers, a year of transition. It was the year in which, for example, Fairbanks made *The Mark of Zorro*, the enormous success

of which caused him to abandon his popular modern acrobatic comedies and concentrate fully on elaborate swashbucklers. Chaplin, too,
was not seen in *any* new film in 1920. *A Day's Pleasure,* an enjoyable
slapstick two-reeler that was, however, somewhat of a throwback to
the lesser standards of Chaplin's earlier Mutual series, was released
very late in 1919 and was in circulation in 1920. But his production
energies were all devoted to his first full-length feature (excepting
Sennett's *Tillie's Punctured Romance,* of 1914, which was not a Chaplin
vehicle and had not been directed by Chaplin), *The Kid,* which would
not be released until early 1921. Harold Lloyd was still working only in
shorts. So was Buster Keaton, although one of Keaton's 1920 two-
reelers, *One Week,* was possibly the single funniest film of that year,
and by any standards was one of Keaton's best.

Dominating the film scene was still the mighty D. W. Griffith. Even
if his greatest achievement, *Intolerance,* was four years behind him,
there was still plenty of innovative showmanship left in the old maestro. In 1920 Griffith's affairs were complicated. He was much in debt
to the banks. He had moved from Hollywood to the East, building his
studios at Mamaroneck, New York, on a peninsula jutting out into Long
Island Sound. It was a photogenic area that could be pressed into
service as the Old South or rural France. As a founder-partner in
United Artists, he had to supply prestige pictures to the new company,
but under an older contract with First National he also had to provide
films to a rival distributor. Using his headquarters in Mamaroneck,
taking lengthy location jaunts to Bermuda, and pushing his players
into epics and pot-boilers alike, he turned out film after film. It was
perhaps no coincidence that his own company, United Artists, got the
prestige films, while a somewhat irked First National had to accept the
programmers. (Still, in fairness to Griffith, it must be admitted that one
of his programmers was usually as good as someone else's "special.")

One of Griffith's 1920 First National releases, *The Greatest Question,*
was in many ways one of his best "lesser" movies. One of a group of
rural romances and melodramas made right after his bigger war films
(such of *Hearts of the World*), it illustrated Griffith's wish to get back
to films about "the sun and the wind on the corn." Set in Kentucky, *The
Greatest Question*—perhaps more than any he ever made—showed just
how much the people and places of Griffith's childhood meant to him,
and how he tried to express that love in his films. The opening shots of

a little white wooden church, nestled atop a gently-sloping hill, from which the camera pans to shots of the stacked wheat sheaves in the valley below, could almost have been shot at Mount Tabor, the little churchyard near Crestwood, Kentucky, which was Griffith's church as a child and where he is now buried. Pictorially *The Greatest Question* is superb, with some of Griffith's best use of landscape for lyrical and dramatic symbolism. Melodramatic, perhaps, it is a bit rambling and tries to cover too much ground. There is a "suspense" plot, covering many years (Lillian Gish, as a child, witnesses a murder; years later, she is confronted by the same group of murderers, prompting the expected last-minute cross-cut race to the rescue); a romantic sub-plot; and a secondary theme (from which the title derives), built around the then-newsworthy and fashionable topic of spiritualism. However, like so many 1920 films, it is a kind of transition film from Victorianism to the coming sophistication. At the end, after close association with death, grinding poverty, and attempted rape and murder, Lillian and her boyfriend (Robert Harron) decide that they "don't know enough to get married," and will wait a while. But that same year, in *Way Down East*, Lillian was mature enough to play a country girl betrayed into a mock marriage, to have an illegitimate child, and thus to feel herself unworthy of genuine love when it finally appears in the person of Richard Barthelmess.

Everybody thought Griffith somewhat out of touch with reality when he paid an enormous sum for the rights to *Way Down East*—more than twice as much as the total budget for *The Birth of a Nation*. It was already considered an out-of-date barnstormer, suitable for summer stock perhaps, but well beneath the dignity of the most prominent film director. Griffith thought otherwise, and was soon proven right. *Way Down East* turned out to be a blockbuster at the box office; next to *The Birth of a Nation*, it was the biggest success that Griffith ever had. The profits helped to pay his large studio overhead, and to sustain him through a number of lean years when even apparently sure-fire successes like *Orphans of the Storm* weren't doing as well as they should have. Its great commercial success, coupled with its thematic antiquity, often causes *Way Down East* to be dismissed as of little interest artistically. The film itself answers this absurdity; so does its recognizable influence on other directors. For example, Russia's Pudovkin (arbitrarily and with less thematic logic) borrowed the ice-floe sequence as the climax to his own *Mother,* and copied it so carefully that it is impossible to determine whether certain scenes might have been duped from a print of *Way Down East.* Another, less spectacular, example of Griffith's virtuosity is found in the charming performance of Mary Hay (later Richard Barthelmess' wife) as Kate. It is full of little bits of "business" which give the straightforward role life and individuality, such as the hesitant, comic little half-slide as she leaves the room. Touches like this, which round out a stock character, can be traced back to Blanche Sweet in *The Lonedale Operator* (1911) and to other early Griffith one-reelers.

Way Down East, with its melodrama, rural comedy, and plot of the innocent maiden betrayed, is the film most often selected by Griffith's detractors as exhibiting all of his so-called "old-fashioned" and "Victorian" traits. In some *positive* ways, he was old-fashioned. He believed in old standards and traditions of behavior; he admired and utilized classic styles of dramatic construction. He especially admired Dickens, and emulated that writer's literary cross-cutting and dramatic use of coincidence in his own films. *True Heart Susie* (1919) had been, despite its setting in contemporary rural America, an amalgamation of themes from *David Copperfield* and *Great Expectations,* while the upcoming *Orphans of the Storm* (1921) would be the most Dickensian of all his films. But for all its superficially melodramatic trimmings, *Way Down East* is very much an anti-Victorian film. The reformers and the self-righteous are condemned. The God-fearing but bigoted New Englanders are forced to admit that they are wrong. And the callous seducer turns out to be a rather likeable villain after all, despite his zealous exploitation of the double moral standards of the day. Indeed, except for a mild trouncing, he gets away scot-free to practice his moral turpitude elsewhere.

It is true, however, that *Way Down East* betrays its period more than other Griffith films. *Intolerance, The Birth of a Nation, Orphans of the Storm,* and *Isn't Life Wonderful?* do not date either as film or as drama. It is only our knowledge of film history and film mechanics that enables us to pinpoint their age. But a stranger to film could look at *Way Down East* and, backed by a reasonable knowledge of Americana, could only identify it as having been made somewhere between 1915 and 1923. Perhaps what dates it is not theme or individual situations— all of which are elevated from the hackneyed by superb playing, direction, and photography—but its comedy interludes and stereotyped comic characters. Griffith had a good sense of humor and such a developed sense of drama that he knew exactly when a *single* gag would work best, as a safety valve, allowing audiences at a pitch of excitement to relax momentarily so that a new climax could be built. But he was never strong on prolonged comedy, and he was on unsure ground in transferring stage comedy to the screen. It had to be there; of that he was sure. *Way Down East* was an old standby, not to be tampered with too much. It was all right to expand—to transform a simple storm into a hair-raising chase across ice-floes cascading toward the brink of the falls—but he wouldn't delete. The public expected cornball comedy from this property; it would be there for them. However, it is not there just for its own sake. Overdone or not, it does relieve the dramatic pressure and brings about the necessary delays and changes of pace. The rhythm thus acquired more than pays off in the closing sequences, just as the bantering byplay in the first half of King Vidor's *The Big Parade* (1925) exists in order to be ripped away for the contrasting stark realities of the second half.

In any event, there is so much that is good in *Way Down East* that one can easily overlook its comic shortcomings and Griffith's occasionally irritating editing quirks. Griffith was unduly fond, for example, of fading out—and back in again—*within* scenes. Presumably this was his way of showing that life didn't move in well-ordered theatrical scenes, that there were hesitations, delays, confusions. Occasionally this way of suggesting a time-lapse did work well, but more often it led to a sense of jerkiness; a scene that seemed finished suddenly sprang to life again. More seriously, the device was picked up by Griffith disciples who didn't fully understand its purpose. *Helen of Four Gates,* a 1920 British film very much in the Griffith mold, directed by Cecil Hepworth, uses the fade-out/fade-in trick so much, often sevtral times within a single scene, that it becomes not only unnecessary but decidedly irritating. Another recurring Griffith flaw, certainly well exemplified by *Way Down East,* although the later *The Love Flower* is a more spectacular illustration, was his reluctance to leave a film alone once shot and a passion for inserting close-ups at a later date. Many charming location sequences have been spoiled by his insistence on intercutting later studio-shot close-ups of the heroine—regardless of the fact that hair-style and make-up may have been quite different, and that the black backdrops and careful mood lighting of the studio scenes don't and can't match the relaxed naturalism of the location scenes.

In *Way Down East*, these shortcomings are relatively few. In vast, sweeping panoramic shots and in vignetted detail close-ups, Griffith captures the New England countryside magnificently. G. W. Bitzer and his more imaginative successor, Hendrik Sartov (who specialized in photographing the Gish close-ups and who remained her cameraman when she moved to MGM), between them produced some magnificent images: the scenes of a snowbound New England village; the static yet lyric love scenes by the river at dusk; the long Chaplinesque shot of Miss Gish wandering aimlessly down a long country lane; and most of all, the magnificent climax, which is a tour-de-force of camerawork, editing, juxtaposition of the real and the staged, and endurance, for Miss Gish spent many hours on the freezing ice of the Connecticut River while this sequence was shot. Even recognizing that much of this sequence is, and has to be, faked, the sheer excitement that it generates has been undimmed by time, and audiences of the seventies react to it with the same spontaneous thrill and enthusiasm as did audiences of the twenties. (The intercut waterfall is, of course, Niagara, which rather gives the game away—but after all, how could a Griffith use a falls of lesser stature?)

Way Down East was remade in the mid 1930's by Henry King. It didn't work, and seemed far more outdated than the original. Ironically, King's classic *Tol'able David*, made originally in 1921, was also remade as a talkie by another director. It didn't work either. In the 1930's, the periods and behaviors that both films sought to evoke had already begun to disappear, and the new versions lacked the ring of truth of their originals.

Griffith never again made a purely romantic story that succeeded quite as well as *Way Down East*, although he approached it in *The White Rose* (1923). Somehow in that film, Mae Marsh's predicament as the unwed mother, thrown out alone into the world, was even more touching than Lillian Gish's. No matter how helpless she looks, or how quickly those lovely big eyes fill with tears, we can never *really* worry about the future of a Gish heroine. There is a set of the chin, a firm look of determination that tells us she has an unconquerable inner strength which will allow her to survive. In *The White Rose*, however, Mae Marsh *looked* helpless and showed no signs of possessing inner fortitude. Despite the banality of much of *The White Rose,* it had some magnificent moments. An unforgettable one is the brief but almost unbearably poignant episode in which Mae is about to jump into a swirling river to drown herself and her baby, and is stayed only by the more immediate need to breast-feed the child. This reminder of the essence of life causes her to change her mind. Miss Gish's obviously dynamic strength-of-will apart, however, her performance in *Way Down East* was superb, and contained at least one classic sequence (her vigil with, and baptism of, her dying child) rare in Griffith films, in which the emphasis was usually on plot and not on character. It remained her finest work on the screen until her Hester Prynne in 1926's *The Scarlet Letter.*

Perhaps one might best round out the picture of 1920 by focusing attention on a typical programmer of the day, in direct contrast to *Way Down East.* A good case in point would be the films of Louise Glaum. Miss Glaum, a former vamp in the tradition of Theda Bara, was in the midst of trying to establish herself as a romantic but more mature and sympathetic figure, a forerunner of the Bette Davis and Kay Francis screen characters of the mid-1930's. Yet the producers of her films, hoping to cash in on her prior reputation, still tried to sell her films via exotic titles and come-on advertising. *Sex* was a blatantly raw title for a 1920 release, and was probably permitted only because the film itself—in which Miss Bara was a woman with a shady past and a virtuous present—stressed the sacrifice and sadness which inevitably were the lot of those who followed the primrose path. Miss Glaum's *The Leopard Woman* was a less serious essay, a slightly later 1920 release and one of the early films directed by Wesley Ruggles. It is a mélange of vampery, espionage, regeneration, and jungle adventure which really has to be seen to be disbelieved. It is exactly the kind of silent film that is so often and so cruelly parodied (in such movies about silent movies as *Dreamboat*) by people who really know nothing about silent movies. In desperation and indignation we cry, "But silent movies were *never* like that!" *The Leopard Woman,* however, provides the occasionally needed reminder that some silent movies *were* like that. It also shows why such parodies always fail. The unintended humor at the original often reaches such heights that deliberate attempts to re-create it could only be heavy-handed and lugubrious. Nor is *The Leopard Woman* exactly a bad movie. Even if it doesn't make much sense, it is decently put together, extremely well photographed (by Charles Stumar), and as a star vehicle presumably satisfied the fans. It is, however, such a bizarre and pointless movie that one wonders how it ever came to be made. The most logical explanation is that the producers wanted to get some extra benefit from the extremely handsome and elaborate sets created for some other film, and whipped up a flimsy story to hang on them. Like so many films of that type (which have to be sold to exhibitors via trade shows that frequently display only the opening reels of a film), it shoots its bolt in the first half of the film. The second half, a prolonged safari, is all wrap-up, and none of the many possibilities for action or plot twists (Is the hero really blind, or is he just testing the heroine's loyalty?) are explored at all.

However, whenever the plot palls, there are always the sub-titles to fall back on. They were written by a German trio—Carl Schneider, F. J. Van Halle, and Leo Braun—who seem to be waging a campaign to eclipse even the florid title-writing of the Griffith and William S. Hart films. No simple "Dawn" or "Sunset" here; each event warrants Tolstoyan flights of prose. Fate is always "Fate—The Jester." Most amusing of all are some of the accidental understatements. After the hero has been subjected to full-blooded titles referring to patriotism, love of empire and the true meaning of love, and exposed to plot problems that run the gamut from Edgar Rice Burroughs to Sigmund Freud, a charmingly simple title tells us, 'There are many things he wanted to know!" Equally diverting is the grim sentence he metes out to a native—"Two hundred lashes, followed by hanging"—*not* for having murdered a native porter (which is apparently socially acceptable) but for *intending* to kill *him*, the white bwana! And for the benefit of any illiterates in the audience, every time Miss Glaum invites guests to her soiree, a follow-up title emphasizes that the soiree will take place "this evening" and that it will also be "a party!" With all their literary flourishes, the writers still somehow forget to include a single title to explain why the film is called *The Leopard Woman!*

The unsophisticated fun of *The Leopard Woman* was very much a part of 1920, too, but, fortunately, a small part. This genre would never disappear, but it would be increasingly recognized for what it was, and handled far more subtly and with tongue firmly in cheek. Meanwhile, 1920 was also the year in which John Ford joined Fox and with *Just Pals* launched his long and prolific association with that company. It was the year, too, of *Kismet,* one of the most tasteful examples yet of filmed theater and an invaluable record of the acting style of Otis Skinner at his prime. Reluctantly but unavoidably, 1920 bid farewell to the "innocent" age of the teens as Rudolph Valentino and Erich von Stroheim, each in his own way to contribute so much—either commercially or artistically—to the movies' new sophistication, waited in the wings.

Despite the industry's gradual and somewhat self-conscious awareness of film as an art and the increasing prestige of the director's name as a box-office component, 1921 was primarily a year noted for stars. Most well-established stars, to whom moviegoers in those days were fanatically loyal, continued in their largely predictable formula vehicles. And at least one major new star appeared—Rudolph Valentino, who seemed so out of step with alleged current box-office tastes that even his studio, ostrich-like, refused to believe that it was his own magnetism that was attracting crowds to the box office. There were few outstanding films in 1921. Arguably the best film of the year was Henry King's *Tol'able David,* and even that, initially at least, was boosted to popularity primarily because of its star, Richard Barthelmess. The other two really big hits of the year—*The Four Horsemen of the Apocalypse* and *The Three Musketeers*—likewise owed their commercial success largely to their stars, Rudolph Valentino and Douglas Fairbanks, respectively.

Valentino apart, most of the prominent male stars had enjoyed their popularity for a good part of the preceding decade. The comedy stars (Chaplin, Lloyd, Keaton) and the action stars (Fairbanks, Mix, Hart) apart, the leading men of the day still remained firmly attached to the values of the teen years. They reflected boyish charm (Wallace Reid, Charles Ray) and stolid, respectable reliability (Eugene O'Brien, Thomas Meighan). The appeal of some stars, then as now, defies analysis. The bumbling, youthful ineptness of Harrison Ford—with more than a trace of effeminacy in his screen image—today seems singularly unattractive, and suggests that he might have been better employed in comic "other man" roles, the kind of part that Ralph Bellamy made very much his own in the later 1930's. Yet Harrison Ford was an enormously popular leading man and appeared in productions of major commercial importance—Marion Davies' *Little Old New York,* for example. It is possible that the humility of his screen character linked him, at least superficially, with Richard Barthelmess and Charles Ray. The brash, dynamic go-getter (exemplified in the later 1920's by William Haines and in the 1930's by James Cagney and Pat O'Brien) was still, curiously, regarded as an unsympathetic character. He was used mainly as a counterpoint in domestic and "getting ahead in business" comedies to stress that slick business acumen was less desirable than steady, plodding hard work and a wife and family. Quite possibly, Harold Lloyd's get-up-and-go character of the early 1920's, when material success began to assume much greater importance anyway, had a great deal to do with reversing this attitude.

It is easy to understand Richard Barthelmess' huge popularity in the early 1920's. While he embodied all of these earlier traditional values of humility, integrity, and honesty, and at the same time had the required boyish charm and good looks, he had a virile and subdued rugged quality that one could respect. Popular as the Charles Ray character was, it's easy to see why the more unique Richard Barthelmess, with both sensitivity and an unstressed he-man quality, was infinitely more popular. It's easy to see, too, why his 1921 *Tol'able David* was not only a great personal success for him but one of the best films of that year. If one were foolhardy enough to try to assemble a "Best Ten" list of Americana on the screen (assuming, of course, that one could pinpoint what the casually used term "Americana" really means), a choice handful of titles would be indisputable: Vidor's *The Crowd*, Ford's *The Wagonmaster*, and *Pilgrimage;* Griffith's *Way Down East* and *True Heart Susie;* Tourneur's *Last of the Mohicans;* and *Tol'able David, Stella Dallas*, and to a lesser degree, the first of the three versions of *State Fair*. The last three titles were all directed by Henry King and represent something of an unofficial trilogy which, hopefully, may one day be accorded the acclaim that has been heaped—justifiably, but somewhat over-generously—on Satyajit Ray's Indian trilogy.

Despite some outstanding successes—due in some cases to a rapport with his material, in others to good basic script material, and in the sound period to a particularly successful working relationship with cinematographer Leon Shamroy—King could not be termed an "outstanding" or "innovative" director in the same way that one can apply those terms to Griffith or Vidor. In one sense, it seems grossly unfair to refer to him as a traffic-cop type of director, and yet essentially that is what he was—though, like John Ford, a brilliant traffic cop, and a warm and humane one, too. For directors of the past to be re-discovered by contemporary critics, they usually have to have been off-beat, ahead of their time, or even abysmally bad but at the same time interesting in a bizarre way (a category that certainly encompassed the French enthusiasm for Edgar Ulmer).

But King fits into none of these categories. Far from being ahead of his time, he was exactly *of* his time. *Tol'able David, Stella Dallas,* and *State Fair* were all about environments that he knew, the kind of people that he grew up with, and places that he loved. All three films were remade about ten years after the originals, but already the period that they attempted to evoke had begun to disappear, and the new films lacked the ring of truth of the originals.

King, as we have said, is a traffic cop. He has kept the traffic flowing smoothly, with reasonable success for both traffic (the films) and the pedestrians (the box office). A certain amount of order and routine is necessary in a complex community and industry like Hollywood. Just as too much routine would cause stagnation, an exclusive monopoly giving all control to the Stroheims and the Welleses would result in chaos and collapse—a glorious, wonderful collapse perhaps, but a very definite one. But, like Buster Keaton's bus-driver in *San Diega, I Love You,* King tosses routine aside every once in a while. His field is—quote—"Americana," and when he returns to that field (*The Gunfighter, I'll Climb the Highest Mountain, Wait Till the Sun Shines, Nellie,* and parts of *Margie* and *Jesse James*), his suddenly renewed vigor and his honest nostalgia make one wonder all over again why he has seemingly tried so hard (from *Romola* on through *David and Bathsheba*) to turn himself into a second Cecil B. deMille. Certainly his spectacles have been dull and uninspired. Being an original deMille is a debatable honor, and being a duplicate one, without even deMille's flair for showmanship, seems even more pointless. *Tol'able David* is a simple tale, told with unspectacular but solid technique and real style. Well scripted (by Edmund Goulding), leisurely without being slow, unfolding against quietly lovely rural backgrounds and with fine photography (by Henry Cronjager) of sweeping panoramic and pastoral scenes, it is not only King's best picture but also Barthelmess's. Making himself look and behave a good deal younger than he in fact was, Barthelmess creates a remarkable portrait as young David Kinnemon—and was shrewd enough not to emulate Charles

Ray and become a type by following through with a whole string of imitation Davids.

Eisenstein and Pudovkin were reportedly much influenced by *Tol'able David,* although it's less easy to pinpoint that influence in their films than is the influence of Griffith on it. However, the film certainly influenced many American directors, not least among them John Ford, who seems to have based the ending of his street-duel in *Stagecoach* (1939) on the climax of King's cabin-fight here. If there are flaws in *Tol'able David,* they are minor ones. In an atmosphere of realism and restraint, Ernest Torrence's slobbering and camera-hogging—even as a psychopathic heavy—seem a trifle overdone. But dear old Ernest, with that same slobbering and hogging, livened up many a dull picture on other occasions, and he really had no way of knowing (especially so early in his career) that this time he was appearing in a classic. Originally *Tol'able David* (along with *Java Head,* another Joseph Hergesheimer novel) was owned by Griffith. But Griffith was not anxious to film it right away; certainly not so soon after the similar *Way Down East,* which had also starred Barthelmess. Nor could he really afford to keep Barthelmess on his payroll at that economic low point in his (Griffith's) career. So when Barthelmess, anxious to set up his own company, offered to buy the property from Griffith, the director acquiesced willingly. Perhaps the highest compliment one can pay *Tol'able David* is that, even had Griffith ultimately made it, it could hardly have been quite as good as the version that Henry King gave us.

At exactly the opposite pole from Barthelmess in terms of audience appeal was the most dynamic new star of 1921, Rudolph Valentino, who, together with Clark Gable of the 1930's, was the most clear-cut romantic idol that the movies ever created. Although there has never been any dispute about his tremendous appeal to women, Valentino has always been somewhat underrated as an actor. Admittedly never a *great* actor, he could be and sometimes was a very good one, with a capacity for sensitive underplaying and gentle humor that too few of his films exploited. Unfortunately, once his appeal was established, he was rushed quickly from one picture to another in order to cash in on his vogue while it was at its peak, and before too many competitors came along. Moreover, Valentino had a useful but sometimes disastrous method of pacing the tempo of his performance to match that of his leading lady, and since he was frequently cast opposite such tempestuous stars as Nazimova, Nita Naldi, and Gloria Swanson, none of them noted for underplaying, he did tend to succumb to the temptations of over-acting. (It is interesting to watch his fluctuating acting styles in films where he had *two* leading ladies. In 1922's *Blood and Sand,* for example, his scenes with Lila Lee, playing the quiet, long-suffering sweetheart and wife, have tenderness and restraint; while the exotic love scenes with the siren-temptress Nita Naldi are so flamboyant and full of nostril-flaring passion that they seem almost like parodies today.) Too, he was rarely given the opportunity to work with a really good director. Garbo at least worked under Mamoulian, Feyder, Lubitsch, Cukor, and Clarence Brown, whereas Valentino was restricted to such directors of varying talents and specialities as Sam Wood, George Melford, George Fitzmaurice, Fred Niblo, Sidney Olcott and—on a much higher level—Rex Ingram and Clarence Brown. In his one film for Brown—1925's *The Eagle*—Valentino delivered such a polished and charming performance that one can only conjecture as to whether a stronger role with the same director could have done for him what King Vidor did with another romantic idol, John Gilbert, in *The Big Parade.*

After some years of negligible activity in minor films, in which his Latin looks constantly prevented his ever being given a role of real importance (he once almost landed the Mexican bandit-hero role in Griffith's *Scarlet Days,* but at the last minute Griffith decided that Valentino's "type" wouldn't go, and replaced him with a heavily made-up Richard Barthelmess!), Valentino achieved overnight fame and popularity in the leading role (though without star billing) of *The Four Horsemen of the Apocalypse.* A handsome production by Rex Ingram, it was not a star vehicle in any sense of the word, but with its romantic Argentinian locale, war scenes, love scenes, elements of mysticism and tragedy, and an attention-getting tango sequence that exploited Valentino's grace and animal magnetism, it was inadvertently a perfect showcase for the new star. It was the first of a group of adaptations from Vicente Blasco Ibañez novels that enjoyed a brief but spectacular vogue in the early and mid-1920's. The underlying tone of disillusionment and defeatism that pervaded Ibañez' works matched the general feeling of vague discontent that pervaded America following the end of World War I, just as—on a much larger and more influential scale—the literary fatalism of Jean Paul Sartre and his existentialist philosophy dominated so much of the French cinema in the immediate post-World War II period. Ibañez' novels had literary prestige and, with their colorful locales and larger-than-life dramatics, fitted in perfectly with Hollywood's desire to weld culture and box office. Significantly, two of the most successful Valentino films, *The Four Horsemen of the Apocalypse* and *Blood and Sand,* and the first two American Garbo vehicles. *The Torrent* and *The Temptress,* were from Ibañez novels. Equally significantly perhaps, when Rex Ingram returned to Ibañez again with *Mare Nostrum* (but *without* a star of Valentino's power to both rivet attention on the film and draw the public to the box office, it failed. Antonio Moreno, one of the many Latin lovers to follow in Valentino's footsteps (although as an actor he preceded Valentino into movies by many years), starred in the film, together with Ingram's incredibly beautiful actress-wife, Alice Terry. But its slow pace and somewhat unexciting mysticism made it—apart from a poetic and visually exciting opening and closing—heavy going.

The Four Horsemen of the Apocalypse, like all Rex Ingram films, needs to be seen in its original prints. Ingram's art was essentially that of the painter. His films were rather stiff, formal, and unexciting dramatically, but photographically they were superbly lit and composed, and used color tones to breath-taking pictorial effect. Audiences seeing *The Four Horsemen of the Apocalypse* today, even with good (but not "original") prints, just can't envision the stunning effect that it had originally, and not surprisingly, they feel that its impact has been overrated through the years. But even with this disadvantage, the magnetism of Valentino's personality still comes through. The incredible thing is that Metro attributed the astonishing commercial success of the film to Rex Ingram's prestige, to Alice Terry's popularity, to the offbeat quality of the story itself—to anything but the obvious appeal of Valentino. Clearly this attitude was not just a shrewd move to prevent Valentino from getting delusions of grandeur with attendant salary increases. Valentino was not yet an official star, and throughout the rest of his Metro films, his name was carried below the title of the film with only featured billing. Had they been genuinely aware of his enormous value, Metro (as Paramount did later) would certainly have rushed him into a series of exotic romances. As it was, his career marked time while Metro—acknowledging that he had *some* value, but displaying no faith in his solo drawing power—put him into films where (in their view) the prime drawing cards lay elsewhere: with director Rex Ingram in *The Conquering Power* and with star Nazimova in *Camille*.

Casting Valentino in *Camille* would seem to indicate a certain showmanship, but the film itself suggests that it was either accidental or aborted. There are two major surprises in this curious and static version of the Dumas romance. The first is that the most interesting contribution is made by the much maligned Natacha Rambova,* whose bizarre, expressionistic sets and decor are both eye-popping and dramatic. The second surprise is that Metro would allow Valentino to be cast in a role that was subsidiary even by average leading-man standards, but insanely so for a man who had made such an unprecedented impact on feminine moviegoers. Nominally, he *does* have the male lead, but Nazimova (who, from an earthy Pola Negri type, suddenly transformed herself into a kind of cultural goddess in films like *Camille* and *Salome*) contrives to keep him off-screen as much as possible, and in their big scenes together consist mainly of many (much gauzed and filtered) close-ups of her, a stress on medium two and three shots for Valentino, and only rarely a reaction close-up of him. No wonder that Valentino was increasingly dissatisfied at Metro and quickly moved over to Paramount! Although a "modern" adaptation of Dumas, *Camille* is set in such a wild, jazz-age never-never-land that it now seems an authentic (if rather strange) period piece—as, probably, Radley Metzger's nudie-erotica version of 1970 will also seem a few generations hence. This Armand and Camille are a strangely cold and passionless pair of lovers who seem to come to life only remotely when they transport themselves into a curious vision of the parallel *Manon Lescaut* story. There is no acting to speak of. It is all a matter of stolid tableaux posed against those incredible sets—no performance anywhere, for example, to match Henry Daniell's marvelous De Varville in the sound version by Cukor and Garbo. But tedious dramatically and romantically though the film is, there are other aspects to hold attention. The florid titles are a literary gourmet's delight; the camerawork is

---

* Mme. Rambova, later Valentino's wife, is best remembered for the destructive effect she had on his career, making such impossible demands on studios and warping his personal judgment to such a degree that she was later—by contract—barred from interference. The colorful nature of their relationships has always made such good copy that it has been largely forgotten that she had real talent as an art director and designer.

interestingly inconsistent, supplying Nazimova with an endless range and variety of softening filters which are ruthlessly yanked away when anyone else comes within camera range. And then there are those sets and props, full of obligatory German symmetry, a fireplace that looks like a Christmas pudding, and a bedroom window like a goldfish bowl. Ray Smallwood was obviously a man who could be totally controlled and dominated by his star, and was never allowed to make any suggestion that could turn this film into anything remotely resembling a movie.

Metro's refusal to recognize Valentino's appeal—or their inability at that time to exploit it—must rank as one of the potential filmic tragedies of the 1920's. Had he stayed with the company, the kind of artificial dream-vehicle that was to be his forte would have found a perfect outlet in the exaggerated lushness of the Metro (and later MGM) production system. Moreover, he could have been directed by talents as diverse as King Vidor, Clarence Brown, Victor Seastrom, and Sidney Franklin, and photographed by Sartov and Daniels. The filmic appetite is stimulated by the mere thought of a Valentino vehicle directed by Tod Browning and designed by Natacha Rambova—and ultimately, of course, the teaming of Valentino and Garbo.

Valentino's business judgment in leaving Metro and going to Paramount was at least superficially sound. Paramount was interested in profits rather than prestige. They took Valentino from the literary drawing rooms of Ibañez, Dumas, and Balzac and thrust him into the desert sands of E. M. Hull's currently sensational (and notorious) romance/sex novel, *The Sheik*. Paramount was astute, yet cautious. Although it was clearly Valentino's film, it was ostensibly an Agnes Ayres vehicle. *She* received the sole star billing; he was still merely featured. Moreover, the film cunningly seemed to provide all the exotica of the novel, yet actually pulled its punches at the appropriate moment. "Why have you brought me here?" asks the trembling heroine to her sheik-abductor, who replies, "Are you not woman enough to know?" Yet torrid titles like this were as close as the film got to real erotic content. Melodramatic action dominated more than sex, and in any case, all was made quite respectable by the last-reel revelation that the sheik was not only a white man, but an Englishman into the bargain. Nevertheless, 1921 being a comparatively early year in Hollywood's emancipation, the film was considered strong enough to rouse the protest of pressure groups, to become a huge box-office success, to boost Valentino's following enormously, and quite incidentally, to introduce the word "sheik" into the modern romantic slang of the twenties. Valentino's later sequel (and his last and best film), 1926's *Son of the Sheik* was everything that the rather crude *The Sheik* should have been and wasn't. It was lush, exciting, genuinely erotic, and direct in the key confrontations—but by 1926, there had been such a change in movie morals that nobody was offended by it, and in any event, its tasteful tongue-in-cheek approach disarmed any serious criticism.

With the homespun, traditional values of Richard Barthelmess at one extreme and the new exoticism and pseudo-sophistication of Valentino at the other, *Tol'able David* and *Camille* somehow sum up the direction of film, with the star rather than the director as the dominant factor in 1921. D. W. Griffith, in one of his commercial retrenching periods, offered only lesser pictures in 1921, although perhaps this judgment is unfair. *The Love Flower*, though a melodramatic film with a rambling and loosely connected story-line and a "safe" vehicle for Carol Dempster and Richard Barthelmess, still had a great deal of lyricism and pictorial beauty, and was "lesser" only in relation to Griffith's other films. *Dream Street* admittedly was a sad disappointment—one of the few consciously pretentious Griffith films, an attempt to outdo the poetic quality of *Broken Blossoms* and yet keep it within the framework of romantic melodrama. Even its sentiment seems forced, and it is one of the least durable of all Griffith films, perhaps notable only as one of the early attempts to experiment with sound sequences. However, most of Griffith's energy in 1921 was devoted to one of the best of his massive historical epics, *Orphans of the Storm*, which, while certainly one of the year's finest films, is technically a 1922 production, since it was not released until early in the next year. Similarly, Erich von Stroheim's *Foolish Wives*, produced—and highly publicized—in 1921, was not released until early 1922. In fact, both the Stroheim and Griffith films were premiered in New York during the same week, and since they represent such totally different sets of values, they are extremely useful in establishing the changing tenor of the film scene in that year.

Griffith's influence continued to make itself felt in another 1921 film, however—Douglas Fairbanks' *The Three Musketeers*. Fairbanks, having now abandoned (though only temporarily) the carefree spirit of his modern comedies, was almost slavish in his imitation of Griffith in his big, swashbuckling extravaganzas. With its plethora of sub-titles, and interweaving of sub-plots, *The Three Musketeers* was almost reminiscent of the much more austere *Intolerance,* and respect and awe for Griffith's methods almost proved its undoing. Like Griffith, Fairbanks devoted a great deal of time—too much time for what was basically a "fun" picture—to establishing his period and his characters. For almost four reels nothing happened, and then, untidily, everything happened at once; at one point, two duel sequences almost overlapped. Nonetheless, with its carefully written story, its production mountings, and the Fairbanks acrobatics and personality, it was still one of the best of the earlier and somewhat over-produced Fairbanks specials. Interestingly enough—and not without point—Fairbanks was sued for plagiarism by Thomas Ince, who had made his own version of the Dumas classic much earlier under the title *D'Artagnan.* Ince's version had been economical and lacking in dash—yet from the wealth of incident, adventure, and characters that peopled the Dumas novel, Ince had come up with a selection of highlights and cohesion of plot line that was so paralleled by Fairbanks' later version that the accusations of plagiarism were not without foundation. Ince's own record for ruthlessness, however, and his occasionally dubious business ethics worked against him, and his suit fizzled out.

Light escapist entertainment was still the backbone of 1921's film output: the westerns of Tom Mix and William S. Hart; the sprightly romances and comedies of Dorothy Gish, Constance Talmadge, and the delightful Mary Miles Minter; the polished sex dramas of deMille (*The Affairs of Anatol*); the gradually increasing number of feature comedies (Sennett's *Small Town Idol,* still one of the best spoofs of the movies and the star system, as well as excellent, fast-action slapstick, and *Doubling for Romeo,* curiously another satire of the movies, this time with Will Rogers, subtler, gentler than the Sennett film, but no less biting); and, of course, the Mary Pickford films, increasing in popularity despite Mary's decision to emulate Fairbanks and make fewer but longer—and bigger—pictures. Actually, her 1921 output was a rather unsatisfactory compromise. She made three films—too many for all of them to be ultra-carefully conceived specials, yet too few to retain the casual artlessness and spontaneous quality of the days when she was turning out half-a-dozen a year. Nevertheless, they decreased in entertainment value in direct ratio to their size and "importance." Best of all was *Through the Back Door*, a delightful mixture of pathos and visual comedy, with Mary as an orphan in wartime Belgium. Unusually careful scaling of sets and furniture, and the utilization of an enormous hound in many scenes with Mary, were exceptionally effective in maintaining the illusion of a diminutive (if overly-healthy and well-fed, for a wartime orphan!) child waif.

The Love Light was one of Mary's few forays into serious romantic tragedy, with the young leading man, Fred Thomson (soon to be one of the best western stars of the 1920's), somewhat curiously cast as a hero who ultimately turns out to be an enemy spy. Constructed in formula fashion—leading one to expect a traditional happy ending—it deviated from that formula to no particular point for its climax, satisfying neither the Pickford fans nor those who took their movies more seriously.

Little Lord Fauntleroy, the biggest Pickford vehicle of 1921, was a triumph of art direction and smooth trick photography, with Mary playing both the title role and that of Dearest, the mother, in multiple-exposure scenes which couldn't be faulted today. Through the years *Little Lord Fauntleroy* has had more exposure than most of the Pickford vehicles. It is the one that she has endorsed the most and permitted to be shown most freely, since it avoids what she for so long considered to be the "dated" and "old-fashioned" curly-headed-girl stereotype, offering her instead in the off-beat pantomimic role of a young boy and also as a charming, mature woman. Unfortunately, apart from its pictorial elegance—although it cannot be stressed enough that that elegance was always enough to give distinction to *any* Pickford vehicle —it was slow-moving and tended to the maudlin, so that it does not rank very high in the overall context of her work.

John Barrymore, in films since 1915, was only now beginning to cultivate a deliberate classic-romantic image with *The Lotus Eater*. Another stage player, George Arliss (like Barrymore, a superb pantomimist but, theater-trained, at his best when luxuriating in dialogue), made an interesting movie debut with *Disraeli* and *The Devil*.

Pola Negri's increasing popularity in German imports made it easier for other German films to make some slight headway in the American market, and the famous 1920 expressionist film *The Cabinet of Dr.*

Caligari, belatedly released in the United States by Sam Goldwyn, while of only slight commercial and critical interest at the time, proved to be a film that would have lasting influence on American directors. Although its influence has been curiously minimized by many writers on film—perhaps because they didn't see many of the lesser films, ranging from 1925's *The Bells* to 1932's *Murders in the Rue Morgue,* where that influence was displayed most prominently—*Caligari* in the long run probably had as much effect on the more thoughtful Hollywood directors as *Potemkin.*

But Valentino was the major catalyst of 1921, not just as a star of considerable box-office importance, but also for the immediate and lasting effect he had on the rapidly changing movie scene.

As 1922 began, Hollywood assumed unquestioned leadership of world cinema, both artistic and commercial. The great heyday of the Scandinavian silent film was already almost over; its true greatness and its widespread influence would not even be recognized until much later. Italy's "golden age" had been in the teens, and there would be no renaissance until the years following World War II. France had one giant of a film-maker in Abel Gance and a developing avant-garde movement, hardly enough to make a great impression on world cinema. And while Germany had developed major stars and directors, it was still only on the threshold of its great period. While its films were photographically striking and thematically sophisticated, they were too turgid and ponderous to achieve widespread support abroad. And Great Britain, having abandoned the austere, inexpensive stage derivations and adaptations of novels that had been its hallmark since the beginning of the First World War, was moving profitably into the open air, using rural England for its backgrounds, but slavishly copying the more obvious Hollywood methods and stories.

Hollywood was financially secure; its films had size, dash, style, and beauty, and its stars and directors were popular box-office names the world over. Hollywood now ceased to be a mere geographic location; it became synonymous with all American film production. Film-making in the East, primarily in New York and Fort Lee, was still considerable. Not only did many stories demand a big-city milieu, but the three-thousand-mile gap proved to be a useful barrier between temperamental stars or executives who worked better when kept apart. But D. W.

Griffith was the only major director working exclusively on the East Coast. Hollywood was more and more becoming a mecca for proven or potential talent, with its own publicity machine grinding out a picture of magic, glamor, and illusion that was to last, implemented by and reflected in the fan magazines, for more than three full decades before dry rot set in.

The deliberate catering to the fans—and especially to the sweethearts, wives, and mothers who are supposed to exert a dominant influence in deciding what films their menfolk will take them to—is certainly reflected in the product of 1922. Above all, it was a romantic year. The westerns and the comedies were present as usual, but it was a year in which greater stress was on vehicles for the women stars, dynamic (or so they seemed then) love stories, such as Valentino's *Blood and Sand,* and swashbucklers in which action and history took a second place to the sweep of romance: *The Prisoner of Zenda, The Count of Monte Cristo, When Knighthood Was in Flower,* and even Douglas Fairbanks' *Robin Hood.* An extraordinarily handsome production, *Robin Hood* was also one of the slowest of all Fairbanks extravaganzas. Despite all the pageantry, huge sets, and crowd scenes, literally no action took place until about two reels from the end. And even then, Fairbanks disposed of his basic action—the race to the rescue, the assault on the castle—in one reel, leaving a full reel to return to and wrap up his love story. On the fan magazine covers, women outnumbered men by a substantial margin, as they did in the portrait sections inside. The style of still photography was changing, too. Gone were the stylized daguerreotype photographs with their halo lighting. In their place were much glossier and more carefully lit portraits, stressing poise, elegance, and glamor, turning the stars from apparently friendly and fun-loving individuals into aloof goddesses.

The two best, most influential, and most contrasting (thematically and stylistically) films of 1922 appeared at the very beginning of the year; D. W. Griffith's *Orphans of the Storm* (discussed more fully elsewhere) and Erich von Stroheim's *Foolish Wives.* The latter seemed to espouse a new, self-conscious sophistication and to be essentially modern, whereas the Griffith film resolutely stood by all the old virtues —personal, moral, and filmic.

Orphans of the Storm collected a crop of rave reviews but was only mildly successful. *Foolish Wives,* on the other hand, despite some reviews that recognized Stroheim's brilliance, was generally attacked, described as ugly, degrading, an insult to American womanhood, and the product of a man who should either be prevented from making films or at least carefully controlled when he did so. Thanks to an astute publicity campaign while the film was in progress, however, and its admittedly sensational nature, it went on to become a spectacular money-maker for Universal, though in a severely censored and truncated form that was to establish a precedent and pattern for all of Stroheim's subsequent films. For all its cinematic skill, *Foolish Wives*—a typically extravagant Stroheim concoction of depravity-amid-glamor—in this case, Monte Carlo—did leave a sour taste in the mouth. Nor could that be wholly explained away by the massive cutting; in the early 1970's, Arthur Lennig, a meticulous scholar and historian, painstakingly reconstructed the film from a number of disparate prints, including some of European origin. The much longer and now nearly-complete film had fewer loose ends and mystifying motivations were now explained, but it was neither a better film nor a better-tasting one.

The late spring of 1922 also saw the release of Robert Flaherty's *Nanook of the North*. This was neither the first feature-length documentary nor perhaps completely documentary anyway, since a good deal of it was staged, but it was certainly the first film of its type to enjoy a reasonable commercial success. Its built-in sense of urgency and excitement, and the dignity of the Eskimo hunter, gave it more showmanship than most documentaries were ever able to muster, and it remained Flaherty's best (and least pretentious) work. Its ability to turn real life and hardship into adventure may also have had some influence in the decision to make *The Covered Wagon* a near-documentary western the following year.

The year 1922 marked the end of the beginning of the twenties. Griffith was ushered out, Stroheim and Lubitsch ushered in. The star system was about to undergo a radical change, with a stronger stress on the female star than ever before or since. And the greatest years of the silent era were just around the corner.

11

Griffith in the Twenties

The Twenties began with D. W. Griffith apparently firmly in command of his position as both master innovator and master showman. *Broken Blossoms* and *Way Down East* had both been highly profitable, and he had moved from Hollywood to the East Coast, where in his new Mamaroneck Studios he was presumed to have both artistic and economic freedom.

Unfortunately, Griffith made his move—an expensive one—at a time when the film industry was undergoing radical changes and when audience demands were making a great shift because of the new sophistication of the post-war years. Griffith had no sympathy with this change. He doubtless felt that it was of a transient nature, and that audiences would swing back again to the kinds of films he had always made and intended to go on making. It was a major error in gauging audience taste—which made it an equally major business error. Griffith had never been a good businessman, nor had he any real interest in amassing profits—except to pour them back into making more films. Moreover, with some justification, he had a certain amount of vanity in his make-up. He knew what he had done for the movies; his name was always used in the advertisements as the major guarantee of quality and prestige. His optimism, based on faith in his own ability and the power of his name, caused him to continue operations and to pay for his new studio with a series of bank loans. By the early twenties, he was so heavily in debt to the banks that only an unbroken string of successes could have rescued him. The amount of indebtedness was so great that total ownership and control of his films virtually slipped through his fingers. If he defaulted on payments or failed to finish a film by a given time, the banks had the right to take over, and to change or finish the film in any way they saw fit in order to salvage their investments. The only positive aspect of all of these complicated financial dealings was that the negatives of the Griffith films became tangible physical assets and were protected far more carefully than they might have been had Griffith been in better financial health or working as a contract director for a major studio. Through the care given them for purely financial reasons, all but four of the Griffith films did survive.

It was against this background, and needing a solid commercial hit to sustain the success of *Way Down East*, that Griffith in 1921 launched *Orphans of the Storm*. Like *Way Down East*, it was based on an old barnstormer of a play, *The Two Orphans*. Griffith liked the basic theme but thought it was too mild to stand unsupported. So he plunged it wholesale into a story of the French Revolution, weaving its fictional characters into actual events and bringing them into contact with Danton, Robespierre, and other historical figures. When the film opened with a grand-scale premiere at the Apollo Theatre in New York, Arthur James, editor-in-chief of *The Moving Picture World*, wrote an unprecedented full-page editorial rave (quite separate from the publication's equally enthusiastic regular review), which was headed "Mr. Griffith Rises to a Dizzy Height" and said, in part:

> It is a triumph for D. W. Griffith to eclipse his own great productions which led the screen into new and finer realms, but with this picture he has succeeded in doing it. No more gorgeous thing has ever been offered on the screen. It has motion within motion, action upon action, and it builds up to crashing climaxes with all that superb definition which makes Mr. Griffith first and always the showman. No man of the stage or screen understands so well the art of exquisite torture for his spectators. He takes their heartstrings, one by one, then stretches them out until they are about to snap, ties little bowknots in them, and finally seizes them by handfuls and twists them until they quiver in agony. Then he applies myrrh and aloes and sweet inguents and sends the spectators away happy in the memory of attractive sufferings that they can never forget. His detail is perfection, and its grandeur is the sum

total of many perfections. Its massed scenes surpass the greater of
the European spectacles thus far of record.

The rest of the press responded with like enthusiasm. *The Motion
Picture News* stated: "The standard bearer of the celluloid drama has
again demonstrated that he has no superior as a painter of rich and
panoramic canvasses," while the *Exhibitors Trade Review* remarked, "A
great work of art. It has the sweep of *The Birth of a Nation,* the remarkable tragic drive of *Broken Blossoms,* the terrific melodramatic
appeal of *Way Down East,* and a warning written in fire and spoken in
thunder for all Americans to heed."*

While time and perspective must convince us that *Orphans of the
Storm* is a lesser film than *The Birth of a Nation* and *Intolerance,* the
reviews at the time were quite genuine in feeling that it was Griffith's
finest work. The *lay* press was equally enthusiastic, and the above reviews from the *trade* press are cited only because they definitely represent trade opinion. Exhibitors looked to Griffith for certain profits; producers regarded him as a prestigious figure-head for their industry;
directors either learned from him or stole from him. Within just a few
years, however, the trade would reverse these accolades, and their
criticism of Griffith would be equally unrestrained.

Griffith appeared at the premiere and spoke at some length to the
audience. Stars Lillian and Dorothy Gish, seated in a proscenium box,
also greeted the audience, and Lillian made a speech following the
screening. It was a gala affair, but a good deal of its thunder was stolen
by Universal's ballyhoo for Von Stroheim's *Foolish Wives.* This film
had received so much exploitation during the preceding months, and
had already earned a great deal of word-of-mouth notoriety even before the preview, so that it was very much *the* film event of January
1922. Its premiere, attended by scores of notables, was set for a week
after that of *Orphans of the Storm,* and it stole most of the limelight.

Coincident with Griffith's premiere, First National suddenly released
an Italian version of *The Two Orphans.* With brazen effrontery, they
pointed out to exhibitors that audiences were clamoring for this kind
of film, and they even billed it as "The production with a million dollars' worth of publicity behind it."

---

* The warning referred to is the film's pronounced and oft-repeated preachment
against Communism.

While it did well, *Orphans of the Storm* was not the box-office block-buster that Griffith expected, and needed badly. Because it was neither a financial landmark nor an aesthetic advance over his previous films, it is usually dismissed far too casually by most historians (even the few responsible ones) as representing "Griffith in decline"—a most unfair and inaccurate generalization. The "decline" of Griffith has been dated from any number of periods, depending on the "historian," his knowl-edge of film, and most influential of all, his dislike of Griffith. Some his-torians would even have us believe that the decline began with *A Cor-ner in Wheat* (1909). Decline inevitably occurred, but much later, and not necessarily for the reasons usually cited. Of course, all film-makers tend to decline in their later years. Even Charles Chaplin and Carl Dreyer, who were never forced to surrender their freedom and adapt to studio contractual requirements (as Griffith was), were unable to keep their later films from representing a decline from their creative peaks. At worst, *Orphans of the Storm* can be said to represent Griffith the artist-showman rather than Griffith the artist-innovator. Here the old maestro was out primarily to make a good picture that was also a "money" picture. To this end, he studied audience reaction carefully in its initial New York run and made several changes—deleting some of the more physically harrowing scenes (close-ups of rats crawling over Dorothy Gish, detail shots in the execution scenes), reviving Frank Puglia from an apparent death scene to take part in an happy ending tableau, and, more ill-advisedly, building up the comedy footage of Creighton Hale.

However, such commercial considerations in *Orphans of the Storm* were backed by all the technical mastery that Griffith had achieved in the preceding years. If there were no new innovations, the old ones were re-employed, polished, and developed. The detail shots in the battle scenes (troops moving into formation, close-ups of pistols being loaded and fired) gave them a documentary quality which made them explicable as well as exciting. The notable lack of such shots (or even of many close-ups) in the similar battle scenes in Rex Ingram's *Scara-mouche* a year later was one of the major factors contributing to the surprising dullness of those otherwise spectacular scenes. Griffith's fre-quent habit of "pulling back" from the action—to view a battle as framed through the draperies of a window—literally made the audience a spectator through a window on history. The fast, rhythmic editing in the bacchanal sequence, as the prisoners were released from the Bastille, smoothly intercutting brief and increasingly large shots with moving camera shots that always cut off just *before* one had time to absorb them fully, was one of the finest episodes ever created by Griffith. It was a tremendously exciting sequence, quite superior to the more famous machine-gun sequence in Eisenstein's much-later *October*—a dazzling sequence certainly, but a mechanical and contrived one. Its fast cutting was functionally creative in that it intensified the emotions of the spectator, but it was dramatically far less honest than the cutting of Griffith's bachannal. And if the climatic mob scenes and the race of Danton's troops through the streets seem to be a repetition of the climax of *The Birth of a Nation,* what wonderful repetition it is—especially since it had to be shot entirely in the studio at Mamaroneck, with a greater stress on low-angled shots and a tighter cutting pattern to create the illusion of a mad dash through all of Paris instead of past the relatively few street sets that Griffith had constructed. Next to *Intolerance, Orphans of the Storm* is Griffith's biggest spectacle, though its large sets are not always generously served by the fickle sunshine. Some of the biggest scenes of the film's climax were shot on a weekend, the only time when Griffith could enlist all the locals as extras. On those occasions the sun resolutely refused to shine, resulting in a downcast atmosphere from which it was impossible to extract the brightly-lit clarity that Griffith wanted. An MGM unit would merely have scrapped the day's work and reassembled the unit when the sun *was* shining. Griffith, however, without outside backing and faced with the enormous upkeep of his studio, could not afford such a luxury. In any case, the excitement of these climactic episodes is such that nature's uncooperative attitude was probably not even that apparent.

Having made the decision to fuse the old Italian stage (and screen) perennial with the new blood of the French Revolution, Griffith as usual went whole hog, re-creating many actual events and characters, and utilizing his beloved "historical facsimilies" based on old paintings or engravings. Authorities in both this country and France were called upon for advice, and the works of such noted historians as Paine, Guizot, and Abbott were consulted. Thomas Carlyle's *History of the French Revolution* was, however, the Bible of the whole venture. Lillian Gish has remarked that every leading member of the cast had a copy of it and read it from cover to cover until they were thoroughly imbued with the proper sense of period. Another book that Griffith turned to often was Dickens' *A Tale of Two Cities*. Several reviews of the time added an erroneous credit by listing the film as being "based on the novel by Dickens." Dickens was a great personal friend of Carlyle and drew most of *his* research material from him, including the incident of the Marquis' carriage killing the child and his inquiry after the welfare of the horses. This incident, used both by Dickens in *A Tale of Two Cities* and by Griffith in his film, was later picked up by MGM in their sound version of *A Tale of Two Cities* and was obviously modeled on Griffith's staging of it. Dickens' peculiarly cinematic style, with parallel plots and a form of cross-cutting, and a rich bravura that excused the excesses of coincidence, had always fascinated Griffith, who admitted Dickens' influence quite openly. This influence affected not only the dramatic structure of Griffith's films but also the content.

It may have been the strong flavor of Dickens in so many of the Griffith films that caused him to be widely dismissed as Victorian and old-fashioned. It may, admittedly, make moments of *Orphans of the Storm* seem a little quaint. For example, Griffith seems less worried about Lillian Gish's being unjustly thrown into prison on a trumped-up charge by the aristocrats than he is by *"the greater injustice"* that has her sent to the prison for fallen women. There is a delightful moment later in the film when Robespierre reminds her of this prison sentence; as Sartov catches her in a lovely and innocent close-up, Lillian admits it and says, in title, "Yes, monsieur—but I was not guilty." However, there is a major difference between injecting a Victorian flavor (which Griffith did well) and propagating Victorian morality (which he decidedly did not). It's odd that *Orphans of the Storm* should often be called "old-fashioned," while such accusations were never leveled against Wallace Worsley's *The Hunchback of Notre Dame* or Henry King's *Romola*. *The Hunchback of Notre Dame* was a good if stilted and over-measured film, while *Romola* was visually superb but dramatically mediocre. Both had Dickensian plots, and structures that would have delighted Griffith—parallel plots, class conflicts, dramatic separations, and personal stories set against turbulent historical backgrounds. What both films lacked, in addition to keeping these diverse elements closely woven, was sweep, passion, the surge of history, and (Chaney's performance excepted in the *Hunchback*) life-size emotion. Griffith could

have worked wonders with both films; *Romola,* especially, needed
him badly.

Griffith's detractors who assail *Orphans of the Storm* for being out of
date are baffled when confronted with the film's political content and
usually choose to ignore it completely. Griffith had never made any
secret of his opposition to "kingly tyrannies," and *Orphans of the Storm*
not only afforded him the luxury of dramatizing his views but also gave
him the chance to attack something he felt even more strongly about—
Bolshevism. His original synopsis for the film read, in part:

> . . . scenes are shown of the exaggerated luxury of those last days
> of the tottering omnipotence of the monarchy. The orgies and
> tyrannies of a section of the old French aristocracy is shown as it
> affects the common people. . . . Then comes the rolling of the
> 'Ca Ira,' the crashing of the Marseillaise, and the madness which
> we now call Bolshevism. *Orphans of the Storm* shows more vividly
> than any book of history can tell that the tyranny of kings and
> nobles is hard to bear, but that the tyranny of the mob under
> blood-lusting rulers is intolerable.

The opening titles of *Orphans of the Storm* were climaxed by this
still very timely line: "We in the United States with a democratic government should beware lest we mistake traitors and fanatics for patri-
ots, and replace law and order with anarchy and bolshevism." Later
in 1922, Griffith, referring to Robespierre's Committee of Public Safety,
stated: "Robespierre uses it as a weapon for destroying all who do not
think as he does. This condition was not unlike that in Russia today.
Some may see in it a lesson for our own people. . . .

As with all of Griffith's historical epics, in *Orphan of the Storm,*
every effort was made to document the facts and episodes presented.
Thus, any errors were usually deliberate errors of omission, committed
in the name of showmanship or dramatic license. For instance, one gets
the impression at the end of the film that the French Revolution is all
but over, and since Danton is one of the heroes of the film, no mention
is made of his own subsequent execution. When Lillian Gish is rescued
from the guillotine, the scores of other poor aristocrats denied a last-
minute rescue are conveniently irised-out, and the fact that the Reign
of Terror is still very much in progress is somehow lost. But for the
most part, the film remains remarkably factual, even to details. During
the carmagnole orgy scene, the original musical score for the film

featured "Ca Ira," the frenzied tune sung by the Paris hoodlums of the time. (The score was arranged by Albert Pesce.) Griffith also made a point of stressing Robespierre's effeminate, mincing walk. (Griffith's titles term him "the original pussy-footer!") Like all of the big Griffith films, *Orphans of the Storm* was shot without any scenario, but was rehearsed carefully in advance. Lillian Gish has mentioned that most of the rehearsals took place in the New York theater still housing the successful run of *Way Down East*—and that the only written word referred to was Carlyle's history. Much of the dialogue that was improvised in the course of these rehearsals was remembered, and later incorporated into the titles of the film.

Way Down East, made in 1920, had been a life-saver for Griffith—and still was. The overhead of the new Mamaroneck studios was enormous, especially for an individual producer-director making as few films as Griffith. The popular Richard Barthelmess had been on salary for a long time after his last completed film for Griffith, and finally left to form his own company. *Dream Street*, a very pretentious pseudo-*Broken Blossoms*, was doing poorly, and receipts were negligible. (Strangely, despite its "arty" flavor, it was well-liked by exhibitors—but not by audiences.) The receipts from *Way Down East* had to support Griffith, maintain his studio, pay his salaries, and help pay for *Orphans of the Storm* too. Because of this, and because it was such a popular film, Griffith raised the rental rates on *Way Down East*, thereby losing good will among exhibitors, which, in turn, at least, partially accounted for the disappointing returns on *Orphans of the Storm*.

Other factors were involved, too. Audiences of the early 1920's were turning cynical and jaded; they were getting caught up in the jazzy and increasingly superficial tempo of the times. And they wanted films that reflected those times. Films like *Orphans of the Storm*, which dramatized what are loosely termed "the old values," were considered far more out-of-date then than they would be even today. By 1922 this attitude was only beginning to develop. But by 1924 it was in full bloom, and thus audiences had no time for Griffith's sincere patriotism in *America*, which dealt with the Revolutionary War. They turned instead to the slick, jazz-oriented films of the day—the kinds of films that Griffith himself had no interest in, but was finally compelled to make, merely to keep active—but not before one last grand, disastrous, and wonderful essay in *real* film-making: *Isn't Life Wonderful?*

Pollyanna (1920) with Mary Pickford

The Whistle (1920) with William S. Hart (here battling old nemesis Robert Kortman); not a Western, but a strong emotional drama with a capital-vs-labor subplot.

William Farnum continued to make an occasional Western in the Hart tradition, but was fast being overtaken by Tom Mix.

Dr. Jekyll & Mr. Hyde (1920)—made in Paramount's Long Island Studio; with John Barrymore.

Huckleberry Finn (1920)—directed by William Desmond Taylor

Tol'able David (1921)—Richard Barthelmess and Ernest Torrence

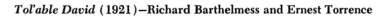

Oliver Twist (1922) with Lon Chaney as Fagin, Jackie Coogan as Oliver, Edouard Trebaol as the Artful Dodger, George Siegmann as Bill Sikes, and Gladys Brockwell (Nancy Sikes).

Isle of Lost Ships (1923), directed by Maurice Tourneur, with Milton Sills and Anna Q. Nilsson.

Location shooting in London's Trafalgar Square for Tourneur's *The Christian* (1923)

The Hunchback of Notre Dame (1923) with Lon Chaney

Shooting *The Covered Wagon*, 1923.

The changing face of the movie theatre:
The Rialto in Omaha, Nebraska, 1923.

Crowds lined up for a Mary Pickford movie in a small 1917 theatre

Douglas Fairbanks' first for United Artists:
His Majesty the American (1919)

Robin Hood (1922)—Fairbanks with
Charles Stevens

The Mark of Zorro (1920) with Fairbanks

Greed (1924)—directed by Erich von Stroheim, with
Zasu Pitts

Greed—on location in San Francisco; Gibson
Gowland and Zasu Pitts

Greed—on location in Death Valley; Jean Hersholt
and Gibson Gowland

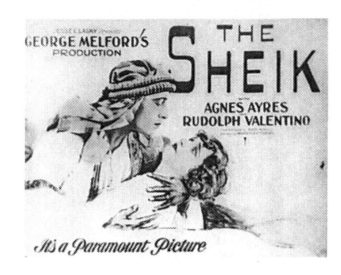

Advertisement for *The Sheik* (1921); despite fame and popularity, Valentino has still not acquired star billing

Typical example of fan and romantic magazine exotica surrounding Valentino in the early 20's

Moran of the Lady Letty (1922)—Valentino with Walter Long in a good if little-remembered melodrama.

Monsieur Beaucaire (1924)

Crowds assembled for Valentino's New York funeral procession (1926)

DIRECTORS

Raoul Walsh directs Dmitri Alexius (as Rasputin) in *The Red Dance*

Sidney Olcott with Betty Bronson (*Not So Long Ago*)

Herbert Brenon

Edward Sutherland

Frank Borzage

Malcolm St. Clair

Charles Chaplin

James Cruze

Mack Sennett

Erich von Stroheim

Rex Ingram (holding megaphone)
with Rudolph Valentino

John Ford with actor Jay Hunt
(*Lightnin'*, 1925)

Josef von Sternberg

William K. Howard (right) with cameraman James Wong Howe

F. W. Murnau

Another factor contributing to the disappointing performance of *Orphans of the Storm* was probably its lack of a strong, popular male star. Initially Griffith had planned to use Barthelmess, who, though unsuited to the role of the aristocratic Chevalier, would certainly have been valuable box-office insurance. While Joseph Schildkraut was fine in his first American film role, he lacked the virility and sincerity that Barthelmess would have provided. Dorothy Gish, a shrewd and witty observer, pointed out that, especially with the French period make-up, Schildkraut bore an uncanny resemblance to Priscilla Dean throughout the film, "and in the love scenes with Lillian, looked prettier than she did!" However, if there is one serious criticism that can be leveled against the film, it is the obtrusive comedy of Creighton Hale. Griffith, who never regarded one of his films as finished, and continued to tamper with them for revival showings years thereafter, added much of the Hale foolishness after the film was premiered, in the belief that it was needed to lighten the tension. Unfortunately, it became more than a device to pause and relieve tension. It was comedy relief for its own sake, foolish and unfunny, and injected right where it was least needed—in the middle of the escape from the Bastille!

Orphans of the Storm had a pronounced influence on the European spectacles that followed it, notably the French and German, but also, to a lesser degree, the Russian cinema. The famous use of what Seymour Stern has termed "symbolic space" when Griffith, to show omnipotent power, shows the Committee of Public Safety (photographed from above) in the center of a huge, cold, otherwise empty room, was copied intact by Eisenstein in *October* to show Kerensky installing himself in the Winter Palace. (This symbolic shot was actually first devised by Griffith for use in a similar context in *Intolerance*.) Pudovkin, too, appears to have borrowed from *Orphans of the Storm* just as he had earlier borrowed from *Way Down East*.

It is a matter of some interest (and surprise) that *Orphans of the Storm* was the only Griffith historical spectacle *without* a villain. Robespierre, and the peasant-turned-judge, Jacques Forget-Not, fulfill all the functions of villainy, but because their transgressions have political and emotional rather than personal roots, Griffith tends to play down their melodramatics and lets them go unpunished at the end—save for a title referring to Robespierre's own eventual execution. The lecherous Marquis, who, "inflamed by Henriette's virginal beauty," kidnaps her and thus separates her from the blind Louise, is a good heavy in the grand manner, but he acts mainly as a plot motivator and vanishes after the first third of the film. The same is true of Sheldon Lewis and the wonderful Lucille LaVerne, who give a couple of grand barnstorming performances, but whose unspeakable evil is unproductive of any real tragedy; they, too, escape without harm.

If most of these comments have focused on the film rather than on its stars, it is because *Orphans of the Storm* is more notable as a Griffith than as a Gish film. This is not to minimize the lovely and sensitive performances of Lillian and Dorothy Gish, or the incredible compositions and lightings of cameraman Sartov, whose close-ups of Lillian have a radiance and beauty unsurpassed in any of her other films. As opposed to *Way Down East* and even *Hearts of the World*, acting opportunities in *Orphans of the Storm* are somewhat subordinated to the surge of melodrama. Sheer "trouping," the maintenance of astonishing physical stamina, and the ability to look both fragile and lovely at all times are the main requirement of the roles of the orphans. When a chance arises for sensitivity, or for high-powered acting, it is seized avidly by both sisters. Especially memorable are the gracefully played scenes of the orphans' departure for Paris, a charming little episode with touching pantomime and some especially lovely close-ups; and the still-poignant scenes in the climactic episodes, when the girls meet again at Henriette's trial and are separated on the way to the guillotine. One bravura sequence is the mid-picture reunion that doesn't come off, with Lillian—hearing her blind sister singing in the street below and being led away—and being arrested, despite her protestations of innocence, before she has a chance to effect a rescue. Griffith never milked a non-action sequence for suspense quite as much as he did this one; indeed, both of the Gishes were of the opinion that it was much overdone. In normal context, it certainly would have been. Since it came immediately before the intermission, however, it must have provided an overpoweringly effective climax to the first half of the film.

Considering the enthusiastic reviews that it had garnered, the disappointing box-office performance of *Orphans of the Storm* must have been especially galling to Griffith. Even though not the box-office blockbuster he'd hoped for, it was not a failure, however. Thus it became somewhat of a landmark: it was the last Griffith film to be successful both artistically and commercially.

Also, coincidentally, and not because of any inherent traits in the film itself, it marked a turning point in Griffith's influence on his fellow film-makers. Up to that time, virtually all of his films had been studied and copied in one way or another, stylistically and thematically. *The Birth of a Nation* and *Intolerance* had not only affected the editing pattern and structure of films up to 1920 but had provided plot and sequential material to be copied wholesale by others. *Way Down East,* considered out-dated until it began making money hand over fist, prompted a resurgence of similar romantic melodramas, of which William Seiter's *The White Sin* (as late as 1924) was quite typical. *Hearts of the World* had been blatantly copied by director Allen Holobar for a 1918 war film for Universal, *Hearts of Humanity*. Not only was the plot remarkably similar, but so were individual episodes based on essentially Griffithian cross-cutting. Further, the most famous sequence in Griffith's film—Lillian Gish descending into madness—was duplicated by Holobar's leading lady, Dorothy Phillips, who made the most of her slight resemblance to Gish, even copying body movements and facial gestures. There is strong evidence within the film to suggest that Erich von Stroheim wrote and/or directed much of it. His large role as the villainous Hun was an extension of the smaller role he had played in the Griffith film, and the whole film is full of touches and methods re-employed and developed further by von Stroheim in his later films but totally alien to the straightforward, uncomplicated style of Holobar. The conclusion to which one is reluctantly drawn is that von Stroheim, having worked on *Hearts of the World*, offered (somewhat unethically) to put that experience to work for Laemmle in making what was essentially a plagiarization, and that the opportunity to write and direct his own film, *Blind Husbands*, the following year may have been the incentive and the reward. Actually, *Hearts of Humanity* is a remarkable film in many ways, full of spectacular, well-staged action scenes and with a savagery that goes far beyond anything in Griffith. (Stroheim attempts to rape the heroine by tearing off her clothes *with his teeth*, taking time out to toss a troublesome baby out of the window to its death!) Whether the term is "plagiarism" or "influence," certainly *Hearts of Humanity* offers a prime example of Griffith's methods being adopted by others.

But after 1922 such influence waned. American films were slowing down their pace, concentrating far more on showcasing stars and on creating opulent set designs. Ironically, as Griffith's influence was waning at home, it was increasing abroad, where familiarity with many Griffith films had been delayed by the war. The Soviet cinema admittedly borrowed a tremendous amount from Griffith, Australian and British cinema likewise. Raymond Bernard's French *The Miracle of the Wolves* (1923) was virtually an homage to Griffith, containing (among other things) re-stagings of the death of Brown Eyes from *Intolerance*, Lillian Gish's flight through the storm in *Way Down East*, and a prolonged climax of battle, siege, and cross-cut ride to the rescue that seemed to be as long as many ordinary features! Most notably of all, one can point to Mauritz Stiller's 1924 Swedish classic, *The Atonement of Gösta Berling*, which is structured and edited exactly like a Griffith film, including a chase across a frozen lake with wolves in pursuit as a melodramatic highlight. Griffith's use of animal symbolism—introducing each character, as in *The Birth of a Nation*, by associating him or her with an animal that is a key to the character and giving the audience instant but subliminal information about each one—is developed on a more sophisticated and naturalistic level in the Stiller film, but the source is obviously Griffith.

A combination of desperation, integrity, and sheer bravado shows through in the films that Griffith made following *Orphans of the Storm*. Clearly out to use his name to salvage his reputation, Griffith made no more pot-boilers like *The Idol Dancer*. Each production was a "big" one, sometimes too big for its own good, and the advertising for them stressed Griffith's genius with an unconvincing false modesty.

One Exciting Night, released late in 1922, was a twelve-reel "old house" melodramatic farce, burdened by too much plot, too many characters, and too much crude Negro stereotype comedy, and only partially redeemed by a well-staged storm climax. As a stage play it might have been fun; as a six-reel programmer it might have been lively. But as a "special," supported by the limited talents of Carol Dempster and the mannered Henry Hull, it was tedious, and watching it is often genuinely painful for staunch Griffith supporters. Critics, aware of Griffith's financial problems, seemed kindly disposed toward the film and gave it better reviews than it deserved. Griffith himself professed to like it. Its one value in 1922 was its novelty. If nothing else, its original story (by Griffith) introduced the old-dark-house comedy-thriller to the screen,† and elements in it clearly influenced such later silents (and, indirectly, their sound remakes) as *The Bat, The Cat and the Canary,* and *The Gorilla.*

The White Rose (1923) was clearly an attempt to recapture the mood, style, and hopefully, the success of *Way Down East.* It was set largely in the Louisiana bayou country, beautifully played by Mae Marsh but hindered by a plot which intercut two vaguely parallel stories and then edited one of them down to a severely subordinate position. Its sub-titling tended to be excessively florid, even for Griffith, but it had a great deal of poignancy—due largely to the superb performance of Mae Marsh—and striking visual beauty. Unfortunately, as with *Broken Blossoms,* it really *has* to be seen in its original form, with its superb photography (by Bitzer, Sartov, and Sintzenich) enhanced by some unusually meticulous tinting, toning, and hand-coloring. The last known extant original 35mm print, a thing of real beauty, deteriorated in the 1960's. A duplicate negative was made from it first, but it was of poor quality—and the faded, washed-out black-and-white prints that have been made from it to represent the film to posterity are but a pale shadow of what this quite lovely film once was.

America (1924) was Griffith's attempt to do for the American Revolution what *The Birth of a Nation* had done for the Civil War and Reconstruction. He had been urged to make it by the Daughters of the American Revolution and other groups, which then failed to support the film. Griffith had massive cooperation from the U.S. Army, and in many ways it is one of his best films, showing that he had lost none of his cunning in staging and sustaining mass action sequences. Paul Revere's ride and the cumulative battle scenes are tremendously exciting still. There are a number of serious weaknesses in the film that could have been corrected without too much trouble, and one can only assume that the streak of vanity in Griffith's nature made him believe that audiences would accept the film as it was because he, Griffith, was presenting it that way. Some of the sub-titling is ungrammatical, to say the least, and the editing sometimes a bit ragged. In order to build suspense, some sequences drag on too long, creating exasperation rather than anticipation for the major action sequences to follow.

† One possible forerunner of this genre might be Cecil B. deMille's 1914 version of the ultimately four-times-filmed *The Ghost Breaker.*

A charming balcony love-scene is placed at just the wrong moment. The war is getting under way, the nation is being called to arms, and the Neil Hamilton-Carol Dempster flirtation suddenly seems trivial indeed. Dempster's performance is both poor and inconsistent—but in this case it is almost wholly Griffith's fault, since she is clearly being instructed to model certain scenes on Lillian Gish, others on Mae Marsh. Some intelligent re-cutting and limited re-shooting could have corrected these flaws, although even with them, it is one of Griffith's most impressive and handsomely mounted spectacles.

It is hard to understand why *America* was not a success. Even if mid-1920's America did find its patriotic values old-fashioned, as a rousing adventure yarn it should have matched the success of the same year's *The Iron Horse*. Nor are complaints about Griffith's old-fashioned attitudes very convincing. True, he does use the love between the "high-born" aristocrat (Carol Dempster) and the "low-born" patriot (Neil Hamilton) as a kind of running theme, symbolically resolved at the end, when a new, democratic nation is born. But Griffith's use of such a linking theme is far less pronounced than that of Cecil B. de-Mille, who seemed far more concerned with confirming the desirability of class consciousness than with dissolving it. His *Male and Female* (1919) constantly emphasizes that love and marriage can work only on a "kind-to-kind" basis, a phrase he re-uses in other films—most notably in *Saturday Night* (1922), where two marriages of aristocrat-to-commoner are doomed, and salvaged only by a last-reel reshuffling of divorce and remarriage. (One of the husbands is told that he can't hope to hold his lower-class wife with mink, mansions, and automobiles, when all she wants is hot dogs and jazz!) Thus, most of the deMille films of this period seem incredibly quaint today, whereas *America,* with its unorthodox yet near-documentary approach to history, its stirring action scenes, and its good cast (Neil Hamilton was an ideal Griffith hero, and Lionel Barrymore was fine as the nominal villain, the unspeakable Captain Walter Butler of the Cherry Valley massacres) is still valid.

Considering the commercial failure of *America,* Griffith showed rare courage and integrity, if poor business judgment, in rushing right into *Isn't Life Wonderful?* for late 1924 release. It is one of his finest and most important movies, but even today is a harrowing and exhausting work. So, one can readily understand its apathethic rejection by American audiences in 1924. One of the screen's first major works of social comment, it deals with the plight of the everyday man—refugee, war veteran, unemployed academician—in the inflation of post-World War I Germany. It is a grim, unrelenting film, its occasional romanticism and mildly optimistic climax justified by Griffith's own positive but unavoidably detached approach to the material. Beautifully, lyrically photographed, and with the one truly outstanding performance of her career from Carol Dempster, it is in many ways one of the major film works of the 1920's, and was of profound influence on German director G. W. Pabst's more pessimistic approach to the same problem in his own 1925 film, *The Joyless Street.*

Isn't Life Wonderful? was a gallant gesture, but it was also the final nail in the coffin of Griffith's independence. He knew that he could no longer hope to maintain his autonomy or his studio at Mamaroneck. He rushed through his final picture for United Artists release, *Sally of the Sawdust* (1925), with a great deal of help from Paramount, which provided production facilities to help get this film out of the way quickly, so that he could begin to work for them as a contract director.

Sally of the Sawdust was based on W. C. Field's stage success *Poppy,* and was to serve as the major introduction of that unique comedian to the screen. [He had starred in two early shorts and had played a comedy cameo in *Janice Meredith* (1924).] In many ways *Sally* was, and is, an amusing and entertaining film. Fields' pantomime and unsentimental comedy is often very funny, and Carol Dempster, especially in the final reels, adopts a hoydenish Fairbanksian style which is rather engaging. Unfortunately, Griffith re-structured *Poppy* to make it a Dempster rather than a Fields vehicle. Evidently much more Fields footage was shot than was actually used, and his material—especially carefully polished routines—suffers from being edited and cross-cut to suit the purposes of a film that threatens to become related to *Way Down East.* Alfred Lunt's hero is particularly ineffective (and largely inactive), and the non-matching cuts and lighting are unusually careless even for this stage in Griffith's career. Nevertheless, the film has some charming Connecticut exteriors and contains a good deal of enjoyable fun. It *could* have been a major Griffith work and a novel departure into comedy. It is, at least, one of the most entertaining of the lesser Griffiths.

Sally of the Sawdust was certainly superior to the first of Griffith's

Paramount films, *That Royle Girl* (1925), which repeated the folly of downgrading Fields' material and screen time even more, at the expense of Dempster. It was poorly received, and Griffith tried to rationalize (perhaps with some accuracy) his sudden fall from grace by explaining that he was now having to make films purely for the box office, and just didn't know how.

Griffith's next—and, as it happened, final—film for Paramount was a major step up. *The Sorrows of Satan* (1926) was a potentially exotic property originally intended for deMille. Based on a novel by Marie Corelli, it had been brought to the screen twice earlier, in a 1917 British version and in a very free adaptation by Denmark's Carl Dreyer (1919's *Leaves from Satan's Book*, actually inspired more by *Intolerance* than by the original novel). With its jazz-age background and elements of subdued sex and horror, it seemed commercially well-suited to the entertainment demands of the mid-1920's. Again, it failed to click. Reviews and box-office returns were disappointing, and because of contractual obligations to the Corelli estate, was withdrawn from even archival availability after seven years. Writers, unable to see it during the thirties, forties, and fifties, merely parroted the old phrases about its being a poor film, illustrative of Griffith in extreme decline. Re-discovered in the 1960's, it turned out to be quite a remarkable film, pre-dating much of Josef von Sternberg's exoticism and resurrecting some of the best of the old Griffith. Too, it shows that Griffith *could* work—perhaps, in some ways, to his advantage—as a studio director under supervision. In the sense of pure craftsmanship, *The Sorrows of Satan* is one of Griffith's best films. There is none of the untidy, ragged cutting that marked so many of his 1920's films, and the lighting and photography, backed by the superior equipment and large stages of Paramount's Long Island Studios, are first rate. Far from representing Griffith in decline, *The Sorrows of Satan* stresses that the talent is still very much there. It also marked Carol Dempster's farewell to the screen with a performance that, if not quite up to the brilliance of *Isn't Life Wonderful?*, was quite certainly her next best.

Griffith's final silents were made for United Artists, but again on a contractual, assignment basis. *Drums of Love* (1928) rather curiously reversed his usual formula—a spectacular action sequence at the beginning, and mere plot and intrigue thereafter. It was an interesting film, not least for Griffith's ability to turn winsome and rather dull Mary

Philbin into a sexually provocative actress. *The Battle of the Sexes* of the same year, a remake of Griffith's much earlier film of the same name, did seem rather like a talkie without sound, but was considered fairly safe, contemporary, jazz-age material. It had quite a bit of sparkle and life, and while perhaps beneath Griffith's dignity, was a vivacious film that audiences seemed to enjoy.

Griffith's final silent, *Lady of the Pavements* (1929), did in fact have music and dialogue sequences, though only the silent version has survived. It was an old-fashioned costume romance, and its script had many holes in it, but it did seem to fit into that pattern of self-indulgent last-stand silents, discussed in Chapter 19. Visually, with William Cameron Menzies' sets and Karl Struss' photography, it was a stunner: opulent, mobile, full of dazzling camera tricks. Many a silent director had a far less imposing swan-song to his credit.‡

‡ Griffith did make a brace of talkies. *Abraham Lincoln* (1930), sincerely felt but rather stiff, was extremely well received at the time and was considered to be a comeback for Griffith. Unfortunately, he followed it with *The Struggle* (1931), an anti-liquor preachment which at the time—with the crusade for the abolition of Prohibition reaching a climax—was both unpopular and outdated. The film was considered a disaster and was withdrawn almost immediately. Ironically, it survives rather better than *Abraham Lincoln*, with a dramatic intensity and unwitting neo-realist elements which have turned it into a rather modern film. In 1931, however, it spelled an ignominious finis to Griffith's career.

12

The Mid 1920's:

The New Dominance of the Female Star

With the withdrawal of D. W. Griffith from the limelight—or to be more exact, with the withdrawal of the limelight from D. W. Griffith—no one director took over as the standard by which the progress of screen art or entertainment could be measured. Perhaps no one director could. Griffith had always been unique, towering above the others, and with the language of film now stabilized and its art in many very capable hands, there was really no need for an innovator—not, at least, until the next major breakthrough, the coming of sound.

Griffith had been regarded as both an artistic standard bearer and a reliable purveyor of superior entertainment, at least until 1920, and to a much lesser degree until 1924. Then the dual role was split, with Stroheim, Ingram, Lubitsch, Vidor, Brenon, and Seastrom assuming the mantle of "artistic" directors and deMille, Ford, Borzage, Brown, and Niblo that of the reliable "commercial" ones. Such a separation is, of course, arbitrary, but it seems reasonable in assessing the trends of the time. Today, in the light of fuller knowledge of these directors' careers, one might well reverse some of those categories. Certain producers and producer/directors were well publicized by their studios and assumed a kind of box-office value in themselves, even though audiences knew little about what a director actually did, or how his work made his pictures good or bad. But their very names were usually a guarantee of prestige and quality. Rex Ingram's films were, for a while, big money-makers—not because there was a cult for his rather stilted but handsome pictorialism, but because his name on a film was a guarantee that it was elaborate, romantic, and usually a vehicle for a sensuous star, from Valentino and Moreno to Novarro. Similarly, deMille's films were known to be modern, sophisticated, and daring, Brenon's to be tasteful and oriented to the theater or the novel. The type-casting of directors was far more prominent in the silent period than in any other, and depended in part on the studio system. Type-casting of directors is now as extinct as the type-casting of free-lance, non-contract players. The director's name on a film is no longer any kind of guide as to theme or style. (An audience attracted to Sidney Lumet's *Murder on the Orient Express* might well be repelled by the same director's *Dog Day Afternoon,* to cite two typical mid-1970's examples.)

In the mid-1920's, the stars assumed a far greater importance for the public—not only for talent but also for the assumption that they were largely responsible for the artistic qualities of their films. To a degree this was true, and to another degree, understandable. Many of the top stars—Pickford, Fairbanks, Chaplin, Hart, Barthelmess, Gish, Lloyd— were their own producers or close to it, and through their selection of material, directors, and cameramen they did shape the style of their films. Too, with the declining influence of Griffith, the *look* of film had changed. Technique, if not abandoned, had been camouflaged; the editing tempos had relaxed, and films had drifted into a pattern of slower development and longer scenes. While this was a boon to both the cameramen and the art directors, whose visual effects could be on screen longer and available for greater manipulation, the audience saw this greater visual sophistication as merely a background to the star, and in its end result such an assumption is perhaps justified. Obviously, the greater speed and tempo of pre-1920 films did not preclude good acting; the outstanding performances of Mae Marsh in *Intolerance* and Henry B. Walthall in *The Birth of a Nation* prove that. But the slower tempo and longer scenes of mid-1920's films—plus, perhaps, the added help and participation of the director, more concerned now with telling his story through *people* rather than *action,* and thus giving more guidance to his cast—did mean that it was easier to create a good performance, especially for those who were stars before they were actors. Betty Compson's very moving performance in *Docks of New York* (1928), Betty Bronson's poignant mixture of pantomime and emotion in *A Kiss for Cinderella* (1926), or Eleanor Boardman's incredibly subtle acting in *The Crowd* (1928) would have been impossible in the faster-moving and often jaggedly structured pre-1920 films.

The early twenties saw the gradual disappearance of those stars solidly locked into the innocent, almost Victorian simplicities of the pre-1920's—or if not their disappearance, their reduction in importance. Charles Ray was a typical example. Little more than a teen-ager in his earliest films for Thomas Ince, he soon specialized in the gangling, rural, all-American boy—something of a hayseed, though with enough virtues and stated (though not always demonstrated) talents to reach success in the big city or on his home ground. Ray did have a winning charm, and in his early days was undoubtedly helped by his youth, since the majority of the early male stars, many of them coming from the stage, were much more mature. However, the Ray films, made under Thomas H. Ince, were somewhat standardized and the small-town travails repetitious. Too, Ray's screen character had very little backbone. He could be bullied, cheated, and exploited until the final reel, when he usually asserted himself and put the villain in his place. This self-effacing quality was sometimes carried to rather ludicrous extremes, as in *The Girl I Loved*, where he loves the girl and she loves him, and his failure to speak out—even as she enters the church to marry another man—condemns both of them to lives of unhappiness and compromise. *The Girl I Loved* and *Sweet Adeline* were both Ray films of the early 1920's that tried to perpetuate his earlier image. But too many signs of maturity were creeping into his face, and these leisurely-paced rural romances were losing their appeal in the more sophisticated 1920's.

To his credit, Ray, his own producer in the early 1920's, tried to add stature to his films, without rocking the boat too much, by trying an occasional change of pace. *The Old Swimmin' Hole* (1921), based on poems of James Whitcomb Riley that were published in 1883, tried to tell its story *entirely* visually, without any sub-titles whatever—a dubious device at best, but one that came closest to being effective in F. W. Murnau's German *The Last Laugh* of 1924. *The Old Swimmin' Hole* is in some ways the definitive filmic country idyl. And because it is, the titles are sorely needed, not just because we are robbed of the colloquialisms of country language, but because, with nothing at all happening, country people *do* communicate. They have all the time in

the world to talk to each other, and even assuming that city stereotypes of country folk are accurate, and that they talk in laconic terms,
conveying only what is necessary, that limited dialogue exchange is
all the more important. One has no real trouble following the plot of
the title-less film, yet so much of the activity is fascinating—money is
used hardly at all, and business is conducted on a barter system—that
the accompanying dialogue would be far more intriguing than the
cleverness of pantomiming it all. Nevertheless, the film, downplaying
the Ray character, is a sociologically if not filmically valuable record
of a way of life that was virtually disappearing, but was still familiar
enough to be captured on film. Little of the film stays in the mind for
long, but one recollects with hazy pleasure the sense of warm after-
noons by the river-bank, or of a boring afternoon in the school-room,
and the difficulty of keeping awake for the teacher's lesson, while the
sun streams through the window. Although only a six-reel film, *The
Old Swimmin' Hole* is paced so slowly that one feels one is living
through the entire time span covered by the non-story. In that sense,
it almost pre-dates the marathon-length non-story films introduced by
Andy Warhol in the underground/experimental films of the 1960's.

A further Ray experiment—a foray into historical romance with an
expensive version of Longfellow's *The Courtship of Miles Standish*
(1923)—proved disastrous. After an almost decade-long career in
which he had ambled effortlessly through close to thirty features with
homespun titles like *Nine O'Clock Town, String Beans, Egg Crate
Wallop, Alarm Clock Andy, Homer Comes Home, An Old-Fashioned
Boy, Nineteen and Phyllis* and *Peaceful Valley,* Ray found both his
audience and his personal fortune gone with the failure of *The Courtship of Miles Standish.* Throughout the rest of the silent period, he
made an unsuccessful attempt to re-establish himself as a ranking star
in both action and sophisticated playboy roles. But his earlier image,
and his own awkwardness in unfamiliar surroundings, worked against
him, although some of the late 1920's films in which he appeared—the
elaborate actioner *The Fire Brigade* at MGM, or the very gutsy little
sex melodrama, *Vanity,* made for the deMille Corporation—were very
good.

In direct contrast to Ray, another equally spectacular casualty of
the new sophistication of the 1920's was Theda Bara. Not the first
screen vamp but certainly the biggest and most successful, Bara existed

as a deliberate antidote to the virtuous good girls of the teens. If Lillian
Gish, Mae Marsh, and Bessie Love had not existed as virginal screen
heroines, then there would have been no need to create Theda Bara.
From 1914's *A Fool There Was* on, Bara took screen sex seriously and
aggressively. (She made historical spectacles and non-vamp films, too,
but it was the vamp films that were the most successful.) Far too little
Bara footage has survived to allow us to make concrete, reliable observations on the merits of her work. In fact, of all the major Hollywood
stars from any period, she is the most poorly represented in terms of
surviving films. Nevertheless, from what does survive, one can certainly draw the conclusion that her films, intended both as moral
preachments, on a sensationalist level, and as titillating entertainment,
were exaggerated only for dramatic effect, and not because of a
tongue-in-cheek approach. Bara was a dynamic personality, and even
in *A Fool There Was,* one of her earliest and (presumably) more primitive films, one has no urge to laugh at its lack of restraint. But by the
1920's, sex was no longer such a moral sin. It still called for on-screen
punishment, but the atonements were less drastic. By the mid-1920's,
many of the "nice" girls—Clara Bow, Colleen Moore, Marion Davies—
were entering vamp territory, seldom to do more than tease, and
usually for comic purposes—but nevertheless, the dividing line between
good girl and bad was down. Even the orthodox, no-nonsense vamps—
Carmel Myers, Greta Nissen, and especially Nita Naldi—plied their
trade with sleek sophistication and good humor. Nita Naldi, so much
less a visual parallel to the blood-sucking vampire bat than the sometimes nightmarish Theda Bara had been, made Valentino's seduction
in *Blood and Sand* (1921) look so enjoyable that moral punishment
seemed both unfair and also well worth it. One could muster up very
little sympathy for the virtuous but somewhat dull little wife (Lila
Lee) left by the wayside.

One of the most surprising—and surprisingly little noted—aspects
of the American cinema of the twenties is the dominance, in contemporary themes, by women. Feminist writers, out to decry the exploitation
and role-standardization of women by a Hollywood ruled by male
executives, might have a point if they limited themselves to the thirties.
In *Arrowsmith* (1931), Ronald Colman, the idealistic doctor-hero, is
about to rush off to a fever-ridden island and tells his wife (Helen
Hayes) that it's "no place for a woman." She retorts that in addition to

looking after him and washing his socks, she wants to be with him. "*Darn* being a woman!" she concludes, but moments later, she apologizes for having "cracked up" and submits to the position allocated to her. Colman pats her paternally on the head, calls her "my sweet," and dashes off to adventure, and incidentally, an extra-marital affair with Myrna Loy. In *Female* (1933), Ruth Chatterton plays the all-powerful executive who owns and runs a vast corporation, using men—both in a business and sexual sense—until she meets the one man (George Brent) who won't be bossed by a woman. After going to pieces as a result of this emotional encounter, she decides to be "a woman," and both marries him and turns the business over to him. At the very end of the thirties, in *Dodge City,* one finds Errol Flynn remonstrating with Olivia de Haviland's decision to work in a frontier newspaper office, pointing out that she should be home, in a kitchen or having babies. These are by no means isolated examples. The major roles for women in the thirties were usually well out of the mainstream of contemporary feminine experience: *Queen Christina, Mary of Scotland, The Scarlet Empress* (about Catherine of Russia), and *Marie Antoinette* all focused on royalty—and the roles were played by Hollywood royalty: Garbo, Hepburn, Dietrich, and Shearer.

In the twenties, however, this position was totally reversed. The male exotics were relatively few. In differing ways, Fairbanks, Valentino, and John Gilbert headed the field, and they rarely (with the exception of Gilbert's role in *The Big Parade*) played Americans. Their runners-up—Ramon Novarro, Ricardo Cortez, Antonio Moreno—lived up to their star names by specializing in romantic Latin roles. The American male hero was forced into an inferior position in which the most desired characteristics were precisely those forced on *women* in the thirties: he was there to back up, and provide for, his mate. Even Harold Lloyd, whose determination to get ahead certainly fitted the materialistic tempo of the twenties, was essentially an extension of the pre-twenties Fairbanks, and his basic motive was to prove himself worthy of his girl—who often remained quite aloof, unaware of (and uncaring about) his tremendous exertions on her behalf and concerned only with the end product. Dependability, linked with a certain dullness, were the most typical qualities in the male heroes of the twenties. Even Richard Barthelmess, a much more virile carry-over into the twenties of the old Charles Ray image, did not entirely escape this image, and it is significant that his most popular films were made at the beginning of the 1920's (*Tol'able David*, 1921) and at the end (*The Patent Leather Kid*, 1927). Today it is sometimes a little hard to understand the tremendous popularity in the 1920's of stars like Milton Sills and Thomas Meighan, who tend to seem stolid and wooden, as did many stars of lesser box-office stature but similar personality: Lewis Stone, Conrad Nagel, Tom Moore, and Percy Marmont. Reliability was their common denominator. They were the bread-winners—the husbands or the ambitious boyfriends—whom the heroines could respect, or in many cases mother, but whose prosaic lives offered little competition to the color and adventure claimed by women, now that they had gained the vote and were out to kick up their heels.

Although Greta Garbo played an American woman in only two of her ten American silents (*Wild Orchids* and *The Single Standard*, both 1929), her romantic attachments in most of these films followed a re-markably similar pattern. She was frequently married to much older men: Marc McDermott (twice), Lewis Stone, Anders Randolf, Bran-don Hurst. What passions prompted a woman like Garbo to marry men like these is never explained, nor is her continued devotion to them in the face of their apathy or contempt for her. In *Wild Orchids*, attempt-ing to re-kindle Lewis Stone's long dormant libido, she dresses in exotic Javanese pajamas, but his only response is to say, "You look silly, dear; take those things off and get to bed." In these films, husbandly indiffer-ence enabled Garbo to have flings (very often innocent and non-sexual) with other men, sometimes princes or other exotics, and to re-turn either to a chastened husband, or on his convenient death or suicide, to find final happiness with a younger man. But even these younger men—Conrad Nagel or John Mack Brown—tended to be as colorless as the husbands they were replacing, promising perhaps a more successful physical married life but not much more, and in no way suggesting that they could possibly dominate or even be an equal partner.

While Garbo's films were made from 1926 on, this feminine domi-nance is apparent from the very beginning of the 1920's. It was perhaps given new impetus in 1923 by the importation of Pola Negri from Germany. One of the few European players to have achieved star status in the United States via her German films that had been released here, Negri seemed to symbolize the European sophistication that was being absorbed into the American film. As a screen type, she was earthy and tempestuous, a rather remarkable forerunner of Italy's Anna Magnani, following World War II. Many of her earlier roles (such as 1923's *Bella Donna*) were those of a *femme fatale* who ultimately sacrifices herself in atonement. Her later films suggested more strongly that it was time America learned from Europe and brought its manners and mores up to date. *A Woman of the World* of 1926 (based on a 1924 story, *The Tattooed Countess*) cast Negri as a European countess who, after romantic disillusionment, comes to stay in a small American town. There her smoking in public seems an affront, her use of an elaborate cigarette holder almost a calculated insult. Her exotic dress and behavior, and unspecified but broadly suggested shady background, cause her to become a local scandal, and the crusading district attorney orders her out of town. In the climactic episode, she takes a bullwhip to the attorney and publicly humiliates him by lashing him at a church bazaar. His acceptance of the beating is an admission that he was wrong, and that he in fact loves her. The district attorney, too, is played by a rather colorless character actor, Holmes Herbert, and in the subsequent marital relationship, even if his facial scars heal sufficiently to conceal the treatment received from his wife-to-be, there is little doubt that the countess will dominate him and continue to set the little town by its heels.

Mary Pickford, while continuing the mixture of sentiment, romance, and melodrama that had characterized her pre-1920's films, strengthened her screen role considerably. In the earlier films, while the stories revolved around her and she dominated the screen, still, in films like *Daddy Long Legs* she had to win her man. In later films, the men were relatively unimportant and had to win *her*. In *The Love Light* (1921), she falls in love with and marries a man (Fred Thomson) who ultimately proves to be a German spy. He is killed, leaving her with their child. In *Little Annie Rooney* (1926), William Haines is a ne'er-do-well ultimately reformed by love of Mary. In some of her films, her character is so strong that there is no need either for a male star or a romantic interest. In *Sparrows* (1925), a marvelously atmospheric thriller, as close to a horror film as Pickford ever came, her male viz-a-viz is the *villain*, played by the magnificent Gustav von Seyffertitz.

In comedies such as *The Primitive Lover* (1920), where the theme is of a *Taming of the Shrew* variety, the heroine's role is so charmingly played by Constance Talmadge that one almost hopes that the pip-squeak hero (Harrison Ford) will fail in his attempts to win her back. He doesn't, but one is at least left with the feeling that the ultimate choice is entirely and voluntarily the heroine's, and that the hero is indeed lucky to have won her.

Clarence Brown's *Smouldering Fires* (1924), vaguely a forerunner of the afore-mentioned talkie *Female,* casts Pauline Frederick as the female executive who falls in love with one of her employees. But she gives up neither her efficiency nor her control when she marries him. In *Dancing Mothers* (1926), a remarkably sophisticated film directed by Herbert Brenon (and not particularly popular or well-known today, probably because it does not live up to the jazz-age-frolics implied by its title), Alice Joyce plays a wife who resents the double standard that allows her husband (Norman Trevor) and her teen-age daughter (Clara Bow) to have affairs but condemns her to the role of respectable wife and mother. In a quite unexpected climax, she castigates husband and daughter for their selfishness and walks out on them. *Mantrap* (1927), one of the best of the Clara Bow vehicles, presents Clara as a big-city girl who marries a Northern trader (Ernest Torrence) for security and goes back to the wilderness with him. There, out of sheer boredom, she flirts with a vacationing big-city lawyer (Percy Marmont), tries to seduce him, and does indeed run away with him, at her instigation. She declares her right to live her own life, and while she does finally return to her husband, it is on her own terms.

In *Love 'Em and Leave 'Em,* a 1926 Paramount comedy directed by Frank Tuttle, the hero (Lawrence Gray) is not only uncertain which of the two sisters ("good" girl Evelyn Brent or mildly "bad" girl Louise Brooks) he really loves but is also dominated by both of them. The less sympathetic sister easily twists him around her little finger—not at all hard to understand, since the role is played by the bewitching Louise Brooks. And the "good" girl is not only far more talented than he, offering advertising ideas to the department store for which he gets all the credit, but doesn't even need the aid of a man in that most elementary of situations, the attempted rape. In the film's climax, Brent is fighting off the lecherous and vengeful attacks of semi-comic villain Osgood Perkins, while hero Gray rushes to the rescue. When he arrives, he finds Brent totally in command of the situation, standing over a battered, beaten, and nearly insensible Perkins. Gray is further made to look unnecessary and ridiculous by his attire; he has come from a fancy dress ball, and is wearing tights and a plumed hat. Brent looks at him somewhat contemptuously and says, "Pull up your pants, and let's go." On a more serious level, in 1927's *White Gold*, Jetta Goudal—condemned to a boring life on a sheep-ranch with a husband who loves her but is under the dominance of his father—shoots and kills a would-be rapist (George Bancroft) and chooses not to refute the evil though untrue insinuations of the father. The husband *wants* to believe in her, but cannot without her explanation. Unwilling to accept a husband who has so little faith in her, she leaves him for an uncertain future: "Perhaps back to where I came from—perhaps to prison—but at least I'll be *free*."

These are not just random selections, but are wholly representative of the role women played in movies in the twenties. Even straightforward gold-digging comedies, such as Colleen Moore's delightful and spirited *Orchids and Ermine* (directed in 1927 by Alfred Santell), which may start out as a typical Cinderella fable, with the good girl sticking to her ideals but still trying to land a rich husband, has reversed the role by the end of the film. The heroine has established both her integrity and her independence, and it is the millionaire who has to pursue *her*. The women dominated these films not only *emotionally* but also *physically*. Paramount stressed Clara Bow's youth, vitality and sexiness by giving her co-stars who were older, stolid, virtually devoid of sex-appeal, and often thin! Although it's a good film on its own, it may well be that *Mantrap* sets off Clara's bounce and vivacity by pairing her with two mature and far from robust leading men—the much older character actor Ernest Torrence and the emaciated Percy Marmont. Clara was forever tossing her curls, pulling up her stockings, and flashing a gleaming smile, frequently stressing her sexiness (in *Wings* and *Hula*, in particular) in scenes of tasteful nudity. Clive Brook, her leading man in *Hula* (1927), gets no closer to a laugh than an occasional wry grin, disrobes only to the point of removing a jacket, and maintains that stiff, aloof quality that was both his trademark and the antithesis of Bow's abandoned, devil-may-care allure.

Gloria Swanson was another star who was always stronger than her men. The ubiquitous Lawrence Gray was with her in *Stage Struck* (1925) and in the previous year's *Manhandled*, her romantic partner was the likeable but far from dynamic Tom Moore, who had considerable competition from the more sophisticated Ian Keith and Frank Morgan. A further method to elevate the female and suppress the male was the episodic or fragmented story. Another Swanson vehicle, *The Loves of Sunya* (1927), was typical: Gloria featured in a series of exotic romantic/dramatic stories (actually all visions of the future, projected to her by an Indian mystic), while her true love, John Boles, remained on the fringe of all the activity, to be claimed only at the climax.

Having achieved legal equality in the twenties, the woman of Hollywood aimed at, and largely achieved, a kind of goddess-like stature as well. She lost it when the talkies and the Depression came along at virtually the same time. Not only did she have to speak, instead of merely receive adulation, but she had to compete with men, on an equal footing, in a battle for survival.

13

Genres

Genre: A kind, sort or species; category, especially as applied to works of literature or art as falling into distinctive groups with respect to style, form, purpose, etc.

The definition of the word "genre" extends further. In painting, for instance, it refers to a specific kind of work in which objects of everyday life are depicted realistically. As yet, dictionaries do not deal with the term as it applies to motion pictures, even though writers on the motion picture use the term far more than do writers on literature (which is surprising, since books have always outnumbered films, and always will). Film has tended to subvert somewhat the meaning of the term. For example, the term "western genre" *is* a *categorical* phrase: it indicates the type and content of a story, plus a geographical location and a historical time-span. But it also indicates a certain standardization. Repetition of situations, stock characters, and plot motivations are *expected* in the western film. The more they are present, the more firmly entrenched a particular film is within the genre. Thus, a typical John Ford silent western such as *The Iron Horse* (1924) would be considered far more of a genre film than *The Man Who Shot Liberty Valance* (1962), which, with its underlying sadness, was relatively free of cliché and repetition.

Curiously, although the silent film as an entity is complete, with a beginning, an end, and—now—a perspective as well, few of the genres *within* it are complete. One of the complexities of the silent film is that,

205

while one can discuss it as a total and fully realized art form, discussion of individual films involves hesitations and reservations, and an enforced comparison with what came later, a critical stance almost unique to film. Certainly a genre novel or a genre painting is more easily assessed on its own merits. On the other hand, the arts of painting and literature are centuries old, and doubtless, if there had been critical appraisal of those arts when they were only thirty years old, even greater problems would have been presented.

Satiric Comedy

In terms of film genres, obviously some *were* completed within the approximately thirty-year span of the silent film. Comedy is too huge a field to be termed a genre in itself, and must be split up into subgenres, some of which—such as satire—so depended on both an accurate depiction of reality and on the use of sound and speech ("reality" and "speech" are, of course, inter-related) that they could not reach full fruition until movies could talk. Despite valiant and often subtle attempts at satire on the silent screen, one can always point to a similar talkie that did the job much better. Even though made by a man (King Vidor) who was both a good director and who knew and loved movies, *Show People* (1928), a silent satire on the movie industry, seemed clumsy and blunted, much less effective than Victor Fleming's *Bombshell* (1933), a talkie of only a few years later. Another late silent, *Chicago* (1928), a satire on the morality of the Roaring Twenties, was served much better in the hard-bitten 1942 William Wellman sound remake, *Roxie Hart*. Satire, to be effective, depends largely on a recognizable reality and on casual, underplayed lines of dialogue. Satirical content in the silent film depended far more on the skill of the actor and the director than that of the writer, and since it had to be sufficiently visual to be appreciated by a mass audience, it was invariably broadened. Broadened satire too easily slides into burlesque or lampoon, the fate of many an intended silent satire.

Sight-Gag Comedy

But if satiric comedy needs a realistic framework, then sight-gag comedy demands just the opposite: if not a world of fantasy, then at least a world that is not completely real. The sight-gag comedy, bounded by Mack Sennett at one extreme and Buster Keaton at the other, was a *total* and fully realized genre of the silent screen. Sound did not destroy it, but it certainly diminished it. Even the best of the talkie Laurel and Hardy comedies (and they were often subtle and creative in their use of both speech and sound) paled beside the silents that had been their inspiration, as a quick comparison of their silent *Big Business* and their sound *Tit For Tat* readily shows.

The Love Story

One might also make a good case for the love story as representing a sub-genre that achieved a total fulfillment and unity within the silent film. True, sound brought a new dimension which allowed certain love stories to be played in juxtaposition with realistic surroundings and periods: World War I (*A Farewell to Arms, Waterloo Bridge*), the rise of militarism in Germany (*Three Comrades, The Mortal Storm*), or the Depression of the early thirties (*Man's Castle*). But the silent love story was often deliberately non-realistic, using elements of fantasy and mysticism that were far less common (and less successful when employed) in the sound cinema. Often larger than life in character and incident, they compensated by withholding explicit emotion and letting the audience supply that quality itself. Without spoken dialogue and attendant speech patterns, which automatically linked them to a period and a locale, silent screen lovers were partially blank figures for the audience to fill in from their own experiences, wishes, or dreams. Thus, despite the occasional silliness of its story (and admitting the mastery of director Frank Borzage in this genre), *Seventh Heaven* (1927) works so well because the audience is able to control the emotionalism and thus create a satisfying level on a purely personal basis. In an almost exact reversal of Alfred Hitchcock's use of the screen to manipulate the emotions of the audience, the silent screen director, especially in the love story, could use the audience to manipulate the emotions of the screen characters. The sound remake of *Seventh Heaven* (in 1936 by Henry King) replaced Janet Gaynor and Charles Farrell with the clearly French Simone Simon and the equally clearly non-French James Stewart. The maudlin and often cloying dialogue gave audiences no opportunity to increase or decrease the intensity of emotion according to individual temperament, and the film just did not work. King also directed a remake of D. W. Griffith's *Way Down East* as a talkie; here, the writers, aware of the emotional pitfalls, overcame them by simply ignoring them. The remake began about a third of the way through the original plot-line, thus totally eliminating the strong emotionalism of the country girl's betrayal by a callous seducer and the birth and death of her child. It played instead for rural comedy, leading to a much more artificial (and studio-bound) melodramatic climax than that of the original. The love story is a large and often ambiguous field, and one certainly cannot discount the success and poignancy of many such films in the sound era. Still, it is significant that many of the best of them—Max Ophuls' *Letter From an Unknown Woman*, John Ford's *Pilgrimage*, Henry Hathaway's *Peter Ibbetson*—rely far more on visuals than on dialogue, and often veer away from realism into mysticism, linking them with the great romanticist genre of the silent period: *Sunrise*, *Forever*, *Street Angel*, *Seventh Heaven*, *La Boheme*, *Broken Blossoms*, *The Four Horsemen of the Apocalypse*, and *Flesh and the Devil*.

Animated Cartoons

But if the love story and the sight-gag comedy can be accepted as fully realized genres within the silent period, all other categories cannot. Typical is the animated cartoon, which, more than any other genre, was marking time until the arrival of sound and color, and the accompanying quickening of pace that was so essential to its success.

Animation of one sort or another was present in the early filmmaking endeavors of most countries. Its consistent use in the United States dates back to 1909, when Winsor McKay's *Gertie the Dinosaur* cartoons set an astonishingly high standard for smooth movement and graceful (if simple) line drawing. But even though, in 1909, there was as yet no clear-cut comic tradition in American film, Gertie was regarded as being novel rather than funny. She was designed to be seen in tandem with an on-stage performer, who talked to her, gave her instructions, and sometimes joined her on screen. This involved careful timing, with the on-stage performer disappearing behind the curtains to reappear in animated form on screen; or a red ball, bounced up and down on stage, reappearing on screen as a red-painted blob. Despite the animation skill, *Gertie* was almost as much vaudeville as film, and surviving *Gertie* prints, with but little indication of the live collaboration from the stage, seem rather pointless to the uninitiated. McKay's animation is still impressive, however, especially in his occasional "dramatic" works, such as *The Sinking of the Lusitania,* a wartime film that was both anti-German propaganda and an attempt to provide a documentary reconstruction of a major news event not covered by regular newsreel cameramen. The incredibly detailed drawings of the *Lusitania,* intercut with inserts of newspaper headlines relative to the notable victims, and strongly-worded editorializing sub-titles concerning the bestiality of the Hun, make this a fascinating and seldom-repeated experiment. The build-up is particularly cinematic, with careful compositions and even a use of the moving camera (as the submarine changes course and moves in for the kill) anticipating the much more dramatic "direction" of animation, which would reach full fruition with the use of the multi-plane camera in the late 1930's. At the same time, *The Sinking of the Lusitania* uses the language of the cartoon film to minimize the horror and slightly blunt such grim images as that of a mother and child sinking beneath the waves. Fish with large Disneyesque eyes swim away in fright as the U-boat glides into the scene. Throughout the World War I years, animation was used quite extensively, both for propaganda in theaters and for training purposes in the armed forces.

Typical wariness of audience response to the cartoon film can be seen in Raoul Barré's *Grouch Chaser* cartoons, made for the Edison Company in 1915. In each case, three or four cartoon segments are inserted in a simple one-reel story of linking dramatic or comedic content. The titles—*Cartoons in a Hotel, Cartoons in a Seminary, Cartoons on Tour, Cartoons in the Country*—tell virtually all. *Cartoons in a Seminary* deals with a group of teen-age girls who sneak a boyfriend and his comic book over the walls of their school, and have to hide him—and the comics—from their stern, old-maidish teacher. More than half of the footage is devoted to the animated sequences—black line drawings on a white background—some of which feature (human) characters who achieved minor animated stardom and reappeared in others in the series. The result is a hybrid. The animation is not sufficiently interesting (or funny) to make the cartoons notable on that score alone, and the sometimes pleasing framing stories (well-photographed, and with mildly popular players, such as Johnnie Walker) are too unsubstantial to have appeal on their own.

The main problem with silent animation is its own self-imposed limitation. Always it restricts itself to being a novelty, content to be amusing or diverting, never competing with the two-reel comedy in trying to be really funny. In a way, this is understandable. From 1915 on, the two-reel comedy, initially slapstick but increasingly more sophisticated, made rapid strides. Chaplin, Lloyd, Keaton, Larry Semon, Laurel and Hardy, Harry Langdon, Will Rogers, and Charlie Chase, to name only the top-liners, were all at their creative and prolific peaks at one period or another (some of them overlapping, and for extended periods) during the years 1915–1930, when the animated film was still struggling to find both an identity and an audience. It would have been futile to attempt to compete with their laughter-creating capabilities, and so the cartoon did not try. It retreated instead into a shell, notable (if at all) for skill in drawing and for technical expertise rather than for humor.

For the most part, screen cartoons aped the newspaper cartoons both in drawing style and in content. They concentrated on brief stories rather than on a flow of gags, and because of the expense of animation, each gag tended to be prolonged and milked, rather than used quickly and sharply, as Lloyd did, and then thrown away to make way for the next one. Even dialogue was usually supplied not by inter-titles but by the "balloon" borrowed from the newspapers. Apparently unaware of the freedom inherent in the cartoon medium, the animators tried to keep their action relatively realistic. Apart from the age-old cliché of the character who is able to walk on air because he is unaware that he has left firm ground behind him, there was comparatively little that was "impossible" in the silent cartoons until the free-wheeling imagination of Max Fleischer in the late 1920's. Felix the Cat would remove his tail and turn it into a car-crank or a flight of stairs, or might pull an exclamation point from the skies and use it as a club, but these devices were limited and blunted through repetition. Oddly enough, animation often came to the rescue of Mack Sennett, who devised live-action situations with impossible solutions in his comedies, and needed animation to complete the gags. (In such cases, animation was invariably a letdown, and the more skilled comic craftsmen rarely used it.)

Despite the earlier success of Gertie the Dinosaur, it was human characters like Mutt and Jeff that dominated the silent cartoon, thus depriving it of the charm of exaggeration and contrast that was to be a major asset of animation when the trend turned to animal characters who behaved with incongruous human traits. (Only Betty Boop, with her Clara Bow sexpot image, was really successful as a human animated figure, and then not until the sound era, when she had a voice— and catchy songs—to assist her.) But what the silent cartoon *really* lacked was speed and pace, deficiencies all the more apparent when the cartoons were compared with the two-reel comedies, so abundant in those qualities. Oddly enough, it is only in the illicitly filmed pornographic cartoons of the twenties that one finds this sense of speed and exhilaration. Perhaps its application was one of taste rather than comedy, a means of speeding the audience away from a gross sexual gag before its impact had had time to become offensive. One of the few pornographic cartoons of the 1920's that has survived—*Buried Treasure*—is a case in point. Even by the explicit and permissive standards of the 1970's, it is a rough, crude, and often embarrassing work, certainly worthy of an "X" rating. But it hops, skips, and jumps from one gag to another with a surrealistic frenzy which is an almost exact counterpart of the dizzy and frenetic Warner Brothers cartoons of the 1950's. Further, it is a *violent* cartoon, full of gags of pain and sadism. Again, the average cartoon of the 1920's was gentle; chase and threatened danger were common denominators, but pain and destruction were not. Since those characteristics *were* common to two-reel comedies (especially those of Laurel and Hardy), their absence again tended to give the silent cartoon a bland, innocuous flavor.

Toward the end of the 1920's, there was a greater stress on experimentation with animation. Disney's early *Alice* cartoons, though without much individuality, were exceptionally skillful in their combination of a live-action Alice with drawn figures and animals. Best of all were Max Fleischer's *Out of the Inkwell* shorts, with their astonishingly adept mixture of live action and animation figures (in much more complicated involvement than in the Disney films) and a wild, surrealistic flavor in which everyday objects—furniture, automobiles, houses—took on life and sprouted hands, feet, and facial features. Even when compared with the technical accomplishments of the animated film in its peak period—the 1940's—the achievements of Fleischer's *Out of the Inkwell* series are remarkable.

With the coming of sound, and particularly the use of music, the animated cartoon became less of a novelty and more of a sophisticated form of entertainment. Initially black and surrealistic, then veering more to charm when color was added, absorbing directorial techniques from dramatic live-action films when simulated stereoscopic values were introduced via the multi-plane camera, the cartoons eventually moved into feature-length production. When rising costs (and declining talents) eased the two-reel comedy out of production, the animated cartoon took over totally as the most uninhibited outlet for screen comedy, duplicating many of the gags and routines from silent slapstick but adding an entirely new and surreal quality of its own. The peak was reached by the late 1950's, when rising production costs forced the animated film to economize and to retrench by returning to the *first* structural formats: simple stories, few of individual gags, and limited animation movement. The decline of the cartoon from that point on was rapid and tragic. But until the end of the 1950's, one can point to the animated cartoon as perhaps the *only* genre that desperately needed what only sound could give it—noise, pace, rhythm, color—and that progressed, consistently and steadily, until it reached its zenith some fifty years after its inception.

Spectacle

Although spectacles, particularly historical and Biblical spectacles in the Cecil B. deMille manner, have long been casually accepted as representing "old-time Hollywood," the facts are otherwise. They, too, represent a genre that, while in some ways at a peak in the 1920's, did not at that time reach its fullest potential. In fact, the spectacle has *never* really fulfilled all its possibilities, since there has never been a time when conditions were right—in terms of available talent, technical expertise, and audience popularity—for the genre to enjoy maximum artistic and commercial success.

In the 1914–16 period, when D. W. Griffith made *The Birth of a Nation* and *Intolerance,* and when his apparent* rival, Herbert Brenon,

---

* The limiting term "apparent" is used only because none of Brenon's films prior to 1917 appear to have survived, and one can judge his spectacles only by some extremely imposing stills, and by cursory accounts of his lavish methods—which in one case involved changing the landscape and geography of Bermuda! But Brenon's strength as a director in his post-1917 films, many of which do survive,

was making spectaculars for Fox starring Annette Kellerman, only some of the conditions were present. The spectacle was new, and thus free of cliché and standardization. Griffith himself was still experimenting with film, and thus ideas and technique were as important as size. Production costs were still low, salaries reasonable, and crews non-unionized and kept to a hand-picked minimum. Even the cost of constructing those mammoth Babylonian sets was not inordinately large, although it exploded the largest budget allocation made for any set up to that time. But certain key professions had not yet developed within the industry. For example, despite the cowboys, who were a rough-and-tumble lot and could provide realistic scraps and falls from a horse, the art of the stuntman had not yet been born. Nor had the allied art of the second-unit director, who specialized in the handling of mass action, often involving horses and vehicles, devoting his time to organizing, staging, and shooting key action sequences while the main director concentrated on the narrative and dramatic elements of the film.

While camerawork and tricks *within* the camera had made amazing strides in film's short history, there were still many things that couldn't be done. The expertise required for glass and matte shots and for convincing miniatures was still being developed. One either had to stage spectacular sequences on a full, life-size scale or fall back on a kind of symbolic imagery, such as Griffith's burning of Atlanta in *The Birth of a Nation,* in which realistic action was juxtaposed with miniatures which weren't meant to convince but to convey an *impression* of the chaos of war. Finally, despite the richness created by toning and color-tinting, film was still not panchromatic. Sky scenes had a tendency to look flat and washed out, with virtually no reproduction of clouds. When a director wanted a skyline or silhouette shot—a city, marching armies—he had to settle for drabness rather than majesty, or to superimpose contrasting clouds.

By the 1920's, all of these problems had been largely overcome. Panchromatic film had been introduced, making possible far greater nuances and subtleties of lighting, and paving the way for the eventual demise of the dramatic but often unrealistic color-toned stock. The

---

was primarily an emotional one. His best films were faithful adaptations of literary works. His spectacles may have rivaled Griffith's in size, but it's doubtful that they rivaled them in imagination.

professions of stuntmen and second-unit directors had been well established, and technical expertise involving camera trickery and the
realistic simulation of huge sets by skillful glass shots, or by the in-
perspective placing of miniatures or silhouettes in front of the camera
lens, had attained such perfection that the deception was impossible to
detect. In fact, backed by all this expertise, the use of spectacle had
become easy, economical, and commonplace. Bursting dams, floods,
fires, and earthquakes soon became no longer novelty highlights but
basic melodramatic ingredients in relatively unimportant films. And
when the films were of major importance, gimmicks were needed to
stress that the film had something more to sell than just size. Thus, religious spectacles, such as deMille's *The Ten Commandments* (1924)
and *The Road to Yesterday* (1925), or Michael Curtiz' *Noah's Ark*
(1929) offered religious episodes as counterpoint, and in some cases
prelude, to a modern story with parallel characters and problems. Both
The Road to Yesterday and *Noah's Ark* offered train wrecks as well!
Even the gimmick of combining historical and contemporary themes
lost its novelty very quickly, since from the beginning the cheaper
films picked it up, too: *Madonnas and Men,* an independent film made
very early in the 1920's, paralleled the debaucheries of ancient Rome
with those of New York somewhat before deMille picked up the theme.

So glutted were audiences by spectacle in the 1920's that after the
initial ones, like *Orphans of the Storm* (Griffith, 1921), they were
taken for granted and quickly became a staple commodity. The expertise now existed to make first-class spectacles, but the audience for
them was blasé. Hollywood saw them only as useful and reliable fodder, not as vehicles to challenge the imagination of a director. Seeing
the incredible action and mob scenes of films like *Ben Hur* and *Noah's
Ark* today, one is impressed, for they represent a standard that has
never been surpassed in terms of conviction and visual excitement. It
is perhaps hard to realize how standardized such a genre had become,
especially with the Europeans also turning to spectacle and the best
of them being imported for U.S. release. Germany and France, in particular, had the advantages of still-standing castles and fortresses, still-
extant battlefields, and a legacy of history denied to the United States.
Their spectacles compared more than favorably with Hollywood's in
sheer size and often approached a near-documentary level. But many
of them, such as Germany's *Lucrezia Borgia,* had nothing to offer but

size and cinematically were quite primitive. Even the best of them lacked a sense of showmanship and certainly the Hollywood level of technical ingenuity, while many showed all too plainly that they were borrowing from Griffith in their construction, in their characters, and in their staging and editing of action sequences. Nevertheless, the biggest and best from Germany, France, Hungary, and other European countries—some made by directors such as Ernst Lubitsch, Alexander Korda, Michael Curtiz, and Fritz Lang, who would eventually migrate to Hollywood—did receive U.S. distribution, adding to the quantity and thus the standardization of the spectacle as a genre.

One can only conjecture as to what kind of a film Griffith's 1916 *Intolerance* would have been had he made it with all the technical resources available to *Ben Hur* a mere eight years later. Undoubtedly he'd have made a slicker film, a bigger film, and a more economical film. (He wouldn't have had to build a whole Babylonian set, any more than MGM had to build a whole Roman arena set.) On the other hand, one hardly hears *Ben Hur* discussed as a major or serious work, only as a landmark film for its legal and financial hassles, and its production logistics. In contrast, *The Birth of a Nation* and *Intolerance*, made with no advantages other than imagination, are still the leaders of their genre and the yardsticks by which all subsequent spectacles, even much bigger ones, are judged.

In many ways, the thirties *should* have been the peak period for the spectacle film. Costs were higher but still not inordinately so, and technical progress had been nothing short of incredible. The matte, process, and other trick work that went into the making of such disaster spectacles as *San Francisco* (1936), *The Hurricane* (1937), and *Suez, In Old Chicago*, and *The Rains Came* (the latter trio released by Twentieth Century Fox from 1937 to 1939) was both technically fascinating and, more important, totally convincing. It's worth noting that these films were directed, respectively, by W. S. Van Dyke, John Ford, Allan Dwan, Henry King, and Clarence Brown, all firmly rooted in the silent film and the traditions of D. W. Griffith.

In the thirties, however, Hollywood seemed strangely ashamed of the spectacle, as though it was an echo from an old-fashioned past. Most of the spectacles were basically vehicles for the studios' romantic idols. Tyrone Power, at Fox, went blithely from desert sirocco (*Suez*) to Chicago fire (*In Old Chicago*) and thence to flood and earthquake in *The Rains Came*. Nor were all of these films essentially spectacles. *Suez* was a lavish but somewhat ponderous re-write of history, a fictionalization of the life (and love-life) of Ferdinand de Lesseps, builder of the Suez Canal. The two big action sequences in the film were there primarily as punctuation, to bring the stock figures and courtroom intrigues to life. Only John Ford's *The Hurricane* was really designed as a spectacle, building steadily to its climactic holocaust and then devoting the last third of the film to it, making it an emotional climax as well as a physical one, much as Griffith had done with his storm in *Way Down East*.

Nevertheless, the expertise in these films reached a new peak and has never been surpassed. In the disaster and spectacle films of the 1970's, the earthquakes and floods were the whole show, on screen for virtually the entire running time, and with all-star casts playing second fiddle to the effects. They were grand *shows*, fascinating exhibitions of mass special effects, but they remained essentially stunt panoramas. For all the skill lavished on *Earthquake* (1976), none of it achieved the sense of utter realism and sheer terror that were created by the few minutes of earthquake in *The Rains Came*.

So the spectacle has never really been utilized to its best advantage. With steadily rising production costs, and the absence of directors with the imagination of Griffith and Ford, perhaps it never will be. But the spirit of the spectacle, and the joy taken in its own magic, was unique to the silent film. There have certainly been bigger and trickier spectacles since *The Birth of a Nation, Orphans of the Storm,* and *Noah's Ark*—but (allowing *The Hurricane* equal status) never better ones.

The Detective Story

Some genres clearly had little chance of making much headway in the silent era. Although the golden age of detective story fiction did not really begin until the end of the 1920's, this genre in one form or another dates back to the Victorian era. But it is an art—or an entertainment—that needs extremely subtle handling if it is to remain faithful to the traditions of its source and, at the same time, translate them into cinematic terms. Despite the plethora of detective stories that have been brought to the screen since the coming of sound, only a handful can be considered genuine classics.

Since the detective story is, by its very nature, more talkative than visual, with the need for clues to be discussed and suspects interrogated, it was obviously not well suited to the silent film. Cheap independent producers would often fall back on the detective story, since it gave them a perfect excuse for a static and inexpensive format: endless dialogue titles told the story in a narrative that rarely moved outside of a few standard interior sets. These dull and unimportant films were made by the smaller companies and sold on a states' rights basis; they made little impact and were soon (and rightly) forgotten.

On a more ambitious level, such popular fictional detectives as Sherlock Holmes and Bulldog Drummond were utilized, but their characters were removed from their original context and placed in tales of action and adventure rather than deduction. Even so, the results were so disappointing that there was little evidence of the establishment of even a minor genre. Typical was John Barrymore's *Sherlock Holmes* of 1922. Every attempt to "open up" the famous William Gillette play merely compounded the mistakes, and the effective theatricality of the original was lost without anything cinematic replacing it. Admittedly, John Barrymore was then readying himself for *Hamlet* on the stage, and his loyalties were obviously more to Shakespeare than to Doyle. Albert Parker, the director, was a rather stolid film-maker who had been galvanized into energy when associated with Douglas Fairbanks but seemed to have no instinctive energy or joie-de-vivre on his own. *Sherlock Holmes* was partially shot on location in London, but the authentic backgrounds were rarely used as more than cutaways or transitional devices. The play's already measured pace was slowed still further by a thirty-minute prologue. Once into the plot, the original play's most successful theatrical ploy—a deliberate build-up to one encounter between Holmes and his arch-enemy Moriarty—was weakened by the addition of an earlier and quite casual meeting. Some of the photographic compositions and lighting effects in Moriarty's lair were impressive, pre-dating the pictorial richness of some of Fritz Lang's German melodramas, but there was no consistency to the photographic style, flat images following rich ones with depressing constancy. Most of all, the film astonishes with its determination to be, for the most part, a photographed play. Rarely has potential been so mis-used or a major silent film been so filled with lengthy sub-titled conversations. Since the play was not essentially one of deduction but stressed instead the cat-and-mouse maneuvers between detective and opponent, it would have been easy to expand on the few action episodes (the famous encounter at Moriarty's Gas Chamber in Stepney, or his final arrest). Instead, these scenes are treated with far less sense of melodramatic excitement than in the play, while the Holmes-Watson conversations are repeated at inordinate length, without the benefit of voices to give them body and nuance. Although *Sherlock Holmes* is a disappointing film, it is not bad enough to be singled out for such a long, sustained bout of criticism. But it does, rather conveniently, typify the problems of the detective genre within the limitations of the silent film, problems which existed in many of the early Edison one-reelers (such as *An Unpaid Ransom*) and merely increased as the silent film grew more visual and further and further removed from the traditions of the stage.

The Horror Film

Because of its inherently visual qualities, the horror film would seem to be an eminently suitable vehicle for genre exploitation by the silent film. Yet it, too, was restricted, and limited to rather specific sub-genres. One of the reasons for this was doubtless critical response to material deemed "unsuitable" for screen fare. Reviewers and exhibitors were constantly mindful of their self-imposed "responsibility" to their audience. Frequently they took it upon themselves to attack films purely on content and to suggest (and sometimes implement) the cutting of "unsuitable" material. Films which even approached horrific content were often condemned as being tasteless, sickening, or the adjective most frequently used, "repulsive." Even D. W. Griffith's 1926 *The Sorrows of Satan*, a variation on the Faust legend, was criticized for the "gruesome" quality of its climactic episode, in which the hero is menaced by the Devil in bat form. Actually, the restraint of this sequence—carefully avoiding special effects and handling the Devil's transformation purely through shadows, cutaways, and suggestion—weakens the impact of what should have been the film's climax and

makes it seem tame stuff indeed, coming as it did in the wake of so
many German fantasies and semi-horror films which were visually
much more explicit and powerful. Another 1926 film, Rex Ingram's
The Magician (based on a novel by Somerset Maugham, and suggested
by the notorious career of black-magic practitioner Aleister Crowley),
was probably Hollywood's† first full-blooded essay in the "mad doctor" school and contained the ingredients of many a later horror film,
including, most specifically, James Whale's 1935 *The Bride of Frankenstein*. Certainly, by 1926 standards, it was strong material. It aroused
equally strong critical antagonism, with most reviews suggesting that
no story with such horrific content could remotely be termed "entertainment." The film was a commercial failure, not least because Ingram
by now had a considerable reputation as a sensitive, romanticist film-
maker, and his audience was specifically *not* the audience for *The
Magician*.

But leaving aside the question of whether movie-makers in general
shied away from the horror film because of fear of critical opposition,
one must also accept the fact that the genuine horror film—i.e., one
that succeeds in scaring its audience—worked under severe handicaps
without the benefits of sound. Since logic is never a strong point of the
horror film, but audience emotion is, the director is free to use all of
the techniques of film grammar to *involve* his audience: color, shock
cuts, use of the subjective camera, sound, music, and so forth. Actually, the less he shows and the more he leaves to their imagination,
the more effective his horror is likely to be. And suggestion and audience involvement in the silent film were difficult, since they required a
great deal of subtlety. Most of the really effective moments of screen
horror have occurred in sound films (Dreyer's *Vampyr*, Robert Wise's
The Body Snatchers, Mark Robson's *Isle of the Dead*) where the audience has been effectively led up the garden path by the director and
its resistance either weakened or relaxed. This has rarely been achieved
without a total (if only temporary) belief in what is going on, and has
usually been implemented by the use (including the *withholding*) of

---

† *The Magician* can be loosely termed a "Hollywood" film in that it was made for
and distributed by a Hollywood company, MGM, but director Ingram had by that
time abandoned Hollywood, and made *The Magician* and several other films at his
French Riviera studios in Nice.

sound. When the audience is straining to hear sound, or expects to hear one thing and unexpectedly hears another, they are instruments in the hands of the director.

This manipulation was no more possible for a director of silent horror films than it was for a director of straight thrillers, such as Alfred Hitchcock. The basic unreality of the silent film deprived it (except in the case of the emotional love story) of total audience participation. Things couldn't be merely suggested, and allowed to grow in the mind of the audience; they had to be spelled out. The sophisticated early Danish cinema *tried* to manipulate audience emotions in a number of near-horror films, a surprising number of which seemed to be influenced by Edgar Allan Poe's theme of premature burial, and a number of astute critics (this was circa 1910!) recognized and applauded the intent. But for the most part, the silent horror film—if one may even term it that—aimed far more at excitement than at terror. Early versions of *Frankenstein, Murders in the Rue Morgue,* and the often filmed *Dr. Jekyll and Mr. Hyde* were joined in the mid-1920's by even more tableau-like visual thrillers, such as *The Phantom of the Opera* (owing as much to the old serials as it did to the gothic novel from which it originated) and *The Lost World,* both of 1925. Only *The Phantom of the Opera,* with its classic unmasking scene, a masterpiece of manipulative editing, really succeeded (and still does!) in actually *scaring* the audience—and that because the revelation had to be a purely visual one. Moreover, Lon Chaney's make-up was so grotesque as to equal if not surpass anything that the audience might have anticipated or imagined. This is something that cannot be said for the two sound remakes, where the finally unmasked Phantom's face was a decided letdown from audience expectations.

The classic "old house" thrillers—most notably 1927's *The Cat and the Canary,* but also including *The Bat, The Gorilla, One Exciting Night,* and *Seven Footprints to Satan*—certainly formed a sub-genre of their own, admirably suited to the decorative style and slow pace of the mid to late twenties. But they were all deliberately artificial, usually stage-derived, and aiming as much at comedy as thrill, despite the occasional genuine shock. Again, the high point of this particular genre comes with sound—in James Whale's *The Old Dark House* of 1932.

The enormous commercial success of the Lon Chaney vehicles for MGM cannot be discounted, but their critical success is largely a myth, created by the curious latter-day adulation of Tod Browning, who directed most of them. They are so formularized, so interchangeable in plot and characters, that their popular success is hard to explain. One can only attribute it to the incredible pantomimic performances of Lon Chaney, who certainly salvaged them all from their mediocrity, and to the fact that they were all so short and inexpensive that they could hardly help but make money. For the most part, they were cruel, perverse, excessively morbid tales. One alone might seem strong meat, with Browning's penchant for ironical climaxes quite striking; but seen collectively, they are a clichéd group. The plot of *The Unknown* (1927) is typical. Chaney is a murderer who, in order to affect a disguise (a distinctive marking on one arm had been recognized), poses as an armless wonder with a circus. His arms painfully strapped out of sight, he eats, drinks, and lights cigarettes with his toes. His self-torture seems justified when the girl he loves (Joan Crawford) warms to him because she has a psychopathic phobia against being handled by men and feels safe in his armless presence. Overjoyed that his unstated love for her is apparently returned, Chaney blackmails a doctor into amputating his arms and returns to the circus to claim his bride—only to find that she has now overcome her fears in the arms of the strong man (Norman Kerry) and is about to marry him. Kerry has an act in which his great strength holds at bay two stallions, roped to his arms. Chaney tries to sabotage the act so that Kerry is torn asunder, but his scheme goes awry, and it is he who is killed. With equally morbid variations, Chaney went through the same paces in a dozen other MGM films. Curiously enough, his best and most satisfying films are those made for Samuel Goldwyn much earlier in the 1920's (*The Penalty*, in particular), films which have no reputation either on their own merits or as Chaney vehicles but which as rich and colorful melodramas are far superior to his later works.

Chaney's kind of screen horror, based largely on physical and mental deformity, made tolerable only because of his unique artistry, was neither needed nor (until the desperation of the 1960's) wanted in the sound era. It is interesting to note that the one or two horror films that did tread that path—such as 1932's *Island of Lost Souls*—were promptly recognized as being tasteless and were commercial failures, despite the great popularity of the horror genre at that time.

The Western and Gangster Films

These two genres are interwoven in their rise, in their achievements, and in their (during the silent period) limitations. To talk of the "limitations" of the western (which is discussed more fully elsewhere) in the silent period—which, after all, offered the realism of Hart, the poetry of Ford, the sheer excitement of the idealized cowboy hero (Tom Mix, Ken Maynard), and the spectacle of the epic—seems an unfairly negative approach, and one must qualify it. Just as the silent film is a totally different, separate and stylized art, distinct from the sound film and not just its precursor, so is the western a totally separate entity in that period.

The opening-up of the West preceded the development of the motion picture by only a few years. Its own genuine heroes were immortalized first by dime novels and picture postcards, and then by movies themselves. Both "good guys" (Buffalo Bill Cody) and "bad guys" (train robber Al Jennings) cashed in on and exploited public interest in their own colorful images by starring in early movies. At the turn of the century, kids playing cowboys vied for the honor of "being" Kit Carson or Bill Hickok. Within a very few years, as the movies were creating their own myths and pushing the real ones into the background, the younger brothers—or sons—of those same kids would be rivals for the honor of "being" Fred Thomson or Bill Hart, the western stars who played those characters on screen.

The West was dying as the movies were coming to life, but for a while, at least, they overlapped. The Arizona Territory didn't become a state until 1913; there was still something of an untamed frontier quality to much of the West. In Hollywood, the cowboys' lifestyle was prolonged by the arrival of the film-makers. The cowboy, the wrangler, and the rough-rider were all indispensable to the early movie-makers. Films (and not just westerns) couldn't have been made without the equipment and know-how of the cowboy, whose horses and wagons moved film crews and equipment to distant locations and helped stage much of the action. The still-popular Wild West shows, with their livestock, wagons, and genuine Indians, became a vital and integral part of the Hollywood studio scene. The Westerners, sad to see their way of life giving way to progress, must have been overjoyed at the new lease on that life provided by Hollywood, and whooped it up in style, embellishing Hollywood westerns with their own anecdotes and recollections.

Hollywood never seemed to realize, until the legendary West had all but vanished, that they had a marvelous chance to catch it all on film while it was still *there*. A semi-documentary account of the Daltons' depredations was made, with the one surviving member of the Dalton clan making an appearance and telling the audience, "Crime does not pay." One of the great cavalry massacres of the Indians was rather tactlessly re-staged on its original battleground, literally on the graves of the decimated Indians, but reshaped to Army specifications, with tactical errors corrected and the Indians made to appear far more of an equal match than they had in fact been. The noted British filmmaker and historian Kevin Brownlow has related how, in the mid-1920's, Hollywood had a unique opportunity to record on film one of the last great overland drives of a herd of longhorn cattle. Paramount, apparently aware of that opportunity, so arranged the shooting schedule of *North of '36*, a 1924 epic planned as a sequel to *The Covered Wagon*, that it could be made while the cattle drive was in progress. But, alas, the real thing did not measure up to Hollywood standards. The wagons were drawn by bullocks, not by horses. The costumes of the cowhands didn't seem colorful enough. The cattle herd itself was left alone, but horses replaced bullocks for key scenes, and Hollywood extras replaced the riders. Fortunately, the film's leading lady, Lois Wilson, was a camera afficionado. She photographed the whole expedition from beginning to end—the *real* West, and Hollywood's revamping of it. Quite fortuitously, *North of '36* still survives, so that her camera record is all the more valuable.

Just as, during the two World Wars, Hollywood was too close *emotionally* to the war and too far removed from it *actually* to see it in any kind of perspective, so also was it too close to the emotional qualities of the West in the silent period. Despite the initial success of *The Covered Wagon* and *The Iron Horse*, the epic qualities of the western remained relatively untapped by the silent screen. The epic western is an invaluable propagandist tool in times of stress and national emergency. But, conversely, it needs to be able to feed off feelings of patriotism, pride in accomplishment, and a sense of national progress and unity. These feelings were present during the early stages of the Depression, and especially at the beginning of World War II, and it is significant that these were the two periods that produced Hollywood's best and most prolific cycles of epic westerns. The twenties, with their satisfied sense of well-being, and with their apparent repudiation of traditional values (anyone who took a drink was a lawbreaker and in rebellion against governmental strictures), offered the antithesis of attitudes of national pride. Thus, the move to the epic western was aborted. Instead, westerns became merely a grand "show"—full of action and excitement, re-created but often jingoistic and distorted history. Their scale was impressive, their entertainment values undeniable, but for the most part, they were one-dimensional. Elements of social criticism were rare (even the well-intentioned *The Vanishing American*, dealing with the history and contemporary exploitation of the American Indian, sold out to sentiment and melodrama), and no film of the 1920's had that sense of sadness and melancholy, of a way of life coming to an end, that was so typical of *Ride The High Country*, *The Man Who Shot Liberty Valance*, and so many other westerns of the 1960's.

Even though the appeal of the western has always seemed to rest on such essentially visual ingredients as splendid horses in motion, grand vistas of plain and mountain, and fast action, it is still rather jarring to realize how much the western also depended on technical developments that in the silent era had not yet taken place. Even though the dialogue of the western is traditionally simplistic, in sub-title form it often appears false and stilted, owing too much to the style of the dime novels. C. Gardner Sullivan's and William S. Hart's dialogue titles strove so hard to preserve the idiom of Western speech that they often became an artificial *concentration*. The deliberately phonetic spelling created labored phrases that would have had an easy and unpretentious grace when translated into speech by a Will Rogers, a Buck Jones, or a John Wayne. Moreover, the mere *sounds* of the West—not just galloping hooves and gunfire, but the natural sounds of cattle, wind, water, creaking harnesses, the animated conversation and piano music of a bar-room, Western music itself—created a documentary-like background that frequently brought (especially to the better westerns) a quality of realism to balance out the pantomimic recital of tradition-shaped action sequences. Despite the patterns of violence within the western, it was never a very *realistic* violence. In the 1930's, when the gangster cycle was at its height, and when gang victims *did* bleed (though not to the excesses shown in the 1960's and 1970's), the western still remained essentially bloodless. Even so outstanding a western as 1932's *Law and Order,* one of the few sound westerns to retain the austere style of Hart and Ince, still asked audiences to believe in a man being shot point-blank in the back, several times (with his back to the camera) without bullet-holes or blood showing. This charade element of the western was even more pronounced without sound effects to help create an illusion of reality.

Even photographically, the western was somewhat hindered in the silent years. William S. Hart's approach to the West was far more realistic (at least on his terms) than John Ford's more romantic view. Whereas Ford, especially in his sound westerns, liked to show man's relationship to the land and his domination by it by stressing panoramic long-shots, or low-angled shots with the horizon low in the frame, as a rider or a troop of cavalry rode across the frame, dwarfed by sun and space, Hart took the opposite tack. His chase and riding scenes invariably placed the horizon high up in the frame; or the camera itself would be high up, looking down on riders picking their way through the rocks or along narrow trails. The opening chase scenes of Hart's 1917 *The Return of Draw Egan* are a perfect example. Hart certainly wanted the Western landscape to be shown as it was. To this end, he didn't follow the normal practice of western film-makers of wetting down the ground before shooting riding scenes, to prevent the dust from rising. When Hart's horsemen rode, they created clouds of dust, and when the action stopped, horses and riders were often caked with it. Did Hart's penchant for shooting *down,* for avoiding the romantic skyline shots, indicate a conscious attempt to show his Westerner not being dwarfed by landscape, but in a sense being as one *with* it? (Frequently in Hart's exteriors, it is difficult at first to pick out his individuals, so completely do they melt into their backgrounds.) Hart was such a dedicated film-maker that one would like to be able to accept this apparently symbolic use of landscape as being entirely conscious on his part. On the other hand, there is an equally rational technical explanation: Hart's cameraman (usually Joseph August) realized that cloud formations would not be picked up by the non-panchromatic film, and that to include low-horizon landscape scenes would leave the composition dominated by uninteresting expanses of blank sky. Hart's most exciting use of sky within the frame occurs in

1925's *Tumbleweeds,* which *did* have the benefit of panchromatic film stock.

Color, too, is an enormously important asset, whether it be the muted pastel colors used to create the romanticist image of Delmer Daves' *Broken Arrow* or the bold, stylized colors in Ford's *She Wore a Yellow Ribbon* or Vidor's *Duel in the Sun,* with their flaming red sunsets and use of color for mood as much as for the picturesque application to landscape. But these three films were all from the sound era, and relatively well into that era—the second half of the 1940's. The silent western could and did use tinted stock effectively, and in the late 1920's, when two-color Technicolor was introduced, it was utilized for *Wanderer of the Wasteland* and *Redskin.* But while extremely pleasing in effect, two-color Technicolor always had an artificial look to it. Since the Western landscapes were so obviously real (and since the trend at the beginning of the 1930's was to such essentially realistic and even near-documentary films as *The Big Trail*), the application of that early color to the western was probably considered a liability rather than an asset. Instead, more attention was paid to exploiting the grandeur of the West via new wide-screen processes, which failed to attract much exhibitor support primarily because the industry was already undergoing sufficient technical upheaval for the transition to sound film. It's interesting that with the spectacular rush to color in that early sound period (1929–1933), it was almost always used in an essentially artificial manner: for horror films, operettas, and musicals. Only on rare occasions when the musical happened to involve a Western location—*Whoopee, Rio Rita*—were the Technicolor cameras turned (sparsely, since the films used essentially interior sets) on the great outdoors. Only in the mid-1930's, when a more naturalistic three-color Technicolor system was introduced, did the western begin to embrace color wholeheartedly. It was to prove not only an artistic but also a financial boon, for color, especially in the days when it was still a novelty, added tremendously to the apparent production values of any western. One only has to look at *Dodge City* in color and in black-and-white, side by side, to see how the use of Technicolor hid many economies and magnified the effect of those scenes on which money *had* been spent.

It is rather sad that by the time the West itself could be seen in its proper historical and emotional perspective, and by the time, too, that film was able to harness sound and color effectively, many of the men who could have taken advantages of those conditions to make first-class westerns—William S. Hart, writer C. Gardner Sullivan, star personalities such as Tom Mix and Tim McCoy—were all well past their creative and physical prime. One must be grateful, however, that John Ford grew up and matured with the movies, so that some of his finest work in the western genre came in the latter part of his career.

The gangster film, inevitably, arrived on the scene much later than the western and had far fewer historical, traditional, and literary roots. Actually, the first gangster films were not gangster films at all, but more accurately underworld films, dealing with petty crime and small-time hoodlums. Nevertheless, there is an odd obsession with the word "gangster" in the films themselves, not only in their narrative intertitles, but also in at least one case, in the title of the film itself.

Big-city crime—in the form of robbery, murder, or arson—had been a staple ingredient of movies from the very beginning, but mainly because, as in little films like Edison's 1905 *A Desperate Encounter Between Burglars and Police*, the initial crime paved the way for a film of pursuit and action. It seems fairly safe to assume, however, that *Musketeers of Pig Alley*, made in New York for the Biograph Company by Griffith in 1912, was the first genre-oriented gangster film. It was followed by a number of others, most notably Selig's *The Making of Crooks* (1914) and Thomas Ince's *The Gangsters and the Girl* (1914). In differing ways, these are all exceptionally good little films, but more importantly, they establish certain basic behavioral patterns common to all subsequent gangster films. *Musketeers of Pig Alley* establishes the now-familiar (and much used by Fritz Lang) device of girl and sensitive boy caught up in the web of crime, and also introduces the unlikely tradition of the "Gangsters' Ball," in which the underworld declares a temporary truce and displays itself in its comparative finery. In Elmer Booth,‡ the film also offers a forerunner of the James Cagney anti-hero. Not only did Booth look a little like Cagney facially, but he was also short, lithe, and possessed of the same nervous energy and quick gestures. Unconcerned as yet with censorship, *Musketeers of Pig Alley* allowed this likeable bad-guy to escape punishment. Returning

‡ Booth was the brother of Margaret Booth, ultimately MGM's foremost film-cutter. An excellent and naturalistic actor, unique in his early day, he was killed in an automobile accident before his career had a chance to get under way.

a favor, the heroine (Lillian Gish) lies to give him an alibi—and a later scene seems to imply his continued immunity through a payoff to an on-the-take cop. The Selig film, *The Making of Crooks,* is a remarkably uncompromising essay on juvenile delinquency, with the pool-hall shown (as in the later Dead End Kids era) as the initial breeding-ground of crime. The film comes to its conclusion with the heroine dead and all of its young hoodlums in jail.

The most typical and prophetic of them all, *The Gangsters and the Girl,* anticipates the basic story-line of not only hundreds of westerns but of key 1930's and 1940's gangster films (*Bullets or Ballots, The Street With No Name, White Heat*) as well—that of having the detective hero masquerade as a gangster and work from the inside to bring about the downfall of the gang, collecting evidence and alerting the police for the final showdown. The film is quite cunning in its use of the back alleys and rooftops of Los Angeles to simulate New York. Producer Thomas Ince obviously took a personal interest in this one, since he also appears as one of the detectives. Although essentially an action film, *The Gangsters and the Girl* does deal in realistic grays rather than blacks-and-whites, and gives some of the gangsters sympathetic qualities. Its least successful aspect is an attempt to provide colorful underworld dialogue—slang, mixed with illiteracies and racial flavor—via the sub-titles. It works even less than the transposed dime-novel dialogue used for the westerns.

Likewise an underworld film rather than a gangster film, the remarkable 1913 feature *Traffic In Souls* does indicate some of the power and far-reaching influences of organized crime. So expert is this film, and the three discussed above, that it is difficult to believe that they existed in a vacuum. Others, now lost, may well have influenced them, or copied them. On the other hand, it is understandable that the gangster film found infertile soil for its roots in 1912–14. The western and the Civil War film had proud and recent traditions to draw upon. There was no sense of pride in the gangster film, and the only form of *really* organized crime—the Mafia—was both shrouded in secrecy and too powerful for Hollywood to want to offend. (References to it were usually ambiguous in comedy films; Harold Lloyd's encounter with a "Black Hand" group is never identified as anything other than a sinister secret society.) In addition, audiences were still too close to the virtuous and clearly defined heroes of Victorian literature to accept the anti-hero offered by Elmer Booth or Jack Pickford (in *The Making of Crooks*).

The gangster film, as a genre, clearly had to await the rise of gangsterism itself, in the Prohibition era of the 1920's. In the meantime, crime remained small-scale, and usually merely the background for films of social comment (*The Mother and the Law* and its derivation, *Intolerance*) or pure action: Douglas Fairbanks rescuing his girl from underworld hoodlums, or William S. Hart coming East and outwitting the big-city bandits by Western brawn and know-how. Nevertheless, such films not only sustained existing clichés but introduced new ones. One was the gangster's fastidious attention to clothing, his rise to power inevitably punctuated by better clothes, more clothes, and the ultimate ritual, being fitted for made-to-measure tuxedos. Clothing was a way of establishing instant social status, too. In *Reggie Mixes In*, a Douglas Fairbanks comedy-melodrama of 1916, the leader of the gang, William Lowery, is the only one allowed the luxury of a hat, bow-tie, and pin-striped suit, his gang having to content themselves with caps and sweaters. Here, and in such later (and better) films as *Scarface*, clothing serves the dual purpose of separating the leader from his minions and of reminding the audience that the criminal basically has no taste and, by implication, no intelligence, either.

Crime films of the pre-1920's also helped build the cliché that most gangsters were aliens, primarily of Italian or Greek extraction, a generalization strengthened by some of the criminal/gigolo performances of the pre-stardom Rudolph Valentino.

With the 1920's, Prohibition, and the rise to notoriety of men like Al Capone, gangsterism made the headlines, and provided hot, topical fodder for the movies. But as yet, Hollywood really knew nothing about the gangster or the social forces that created and sustained him. As a result, the new gangster films, spearheaded by Josef von Sternberg's *Underworld* (1927), written by Ben Hecht, merely transplanted William S. Hart's good badman to a big-city milieu. *Underworld* and its many imitators and successors all introduced us to the gangster full-grown, already at his peak. None of these films acknowledged the frustration and unemployment of the post-World War I period that drove many to crime, or the systematic rise to power from small-time hoodlum to big-time czar that characterized the careers of so many men like Capone. Hollywood's underworld was a world unto itself, a world in which the criminal elements battled more among themselves than with the forces of law and order, in which few innocent bystanders were hurt, and in which the public seemed neither menaced, exploited, nor cheated.

It was also a glamorous and sentimental world. Most of the underworld seemed governed by a rigid code of ethics, and crime and violence usually took place off-screen. Above all, it was a stylized and unrealistic world, somehow reminiscent of the Dickensian underworld of *Oliver Twist*. The gangster hero, with George Bancroft as the prototype, invariably died at the end, but it was usually a tragic and noble death rather than a mean and petty one. In keeping with the good-badman image transposed from the West, he was a man of honor whose death was brought about in a self-sacrificing manner, usually to unite the unspoiled young lovers who sought to escape the underworld environment.

These initial gangster films built on and expanded the already extant clichés and established others, usually drawn from the western. *Underworld* is full of such clichés, ranging from gang-leader Fred Kohler's humiliation of the hero (Clive Brook) in a saloon, a situation one finds still treated as though it were fresh in westerns as recent as John Ford's 1962 *The Man Who Shot Liberty Valance,* to the ultimate showdown and street shoot-out between the lone badman and virtually the city's entire and fully mechanized police force.

The predictability of actions by the good-badman hero, the deliberate avoidance of physical action, and the slowing-down of pace by attempts to impart gangster flavor via colorful sub-titles, more literate but no more effective than those in *The Gangsters and the Girl,* turned most of the late 1920's gangster films into pedestrian, sentimental films. Exceptions were few: Frank Capra's *The Way of the Strong* (1928) did have far more physical action than most, with a vigorously staged jail-break (with the use of an armored car as a battering ram) as a splendid highlight. But Capra was a new director, fresh from sight-gag comedy, and for the time being more interested in visual action than stylized dramatics. And even *The Way of the Strong* had a story-line clearly patterned on that of *Underworld,* complete with a noble self-sacrifice in the final reel.

The morality of the gangster films was often more than a little confused. The gangster had to pay the extreme penalty, in one form or another, merely because he *was* a gangster. Yet the acts that resulted in his death (either in his performance of them or through later execution by the law) were often nobly motivated and quite unrelated to gangsterism per se. Lesser characters in the films often committed these same acts and got away scot-free because in that era of more lax censorship they were considered morally justified. The secondary heroine (Evelyn Brent) of the 1929 *Broadway* cold-bloodedly murders the gangster who has been responsible for her lover's death, and the law, though aware of it, turns a blind eye. In such early talkies as *Corsair* and *City Streets* (both 1931), not only do a number of cold-blooded murders go unpunished, but the heroes (Chester Morris and Gary Cooper, respectively) are allowed to retire from the rackets, settling down to happy and luxurious married life with their ill-gotten gains.

The gangster film badly needed sound to give it at least a superficial realism, and above all, to give it pace. Dialogue encounters in the silent gangster film could be stiff, ponderous, and painfully pretentious, as witness a scene in *Walking Back* (1929), which is essentially a jazz-age delinquency movie but brings gangster elements into its closing reel. Visually it is quite powerful, especially in a bank hold-up scene, due partly to the striking art direction and set design of Anton Grot, who would control the "look" of so many later Warner Brothers gangster movies. But in one scene, the two debonair gangsters (George E. Stone and Ivan Lebedeff) confront the young hero (Richard Walling) and engage in a prolonged bantering dialogue scene that is plainly plagiarized from Ernest Hemingway's short story *The Killers*. The constant repetition of one gangster's line by his companion, the derisive use of the phrase "Bright boy!", lines magnificently effective as spoken by William Conrad and Charles McGraw in the 1946 version of *The Killers*, fall totally and irritatingly flat when dragged out in sub-title form. And the succeeding car-chase sequence, though quite effectively shot, largely from a subjective viewpoint, needs the sound track to enhance its effect and camouflage its occasionally faked effects.

Little Caesar (1930) is frequently cited as the first of the gangster films. This is, of course, both an oversimplification and a gross distortion, but it was undeniably the first gangster film that really caught on with the public. It opened up a whole new market, spectacularly exploited, for a gangster cycle. Though a dated and heavy-handed film today, one can understand its impact at the time, not least in that it focused on two dynamic "new" personalities—Edward G. Robinson and, in a sense, Al Capone. This was the first gangster film built around a recognizable personality from contemporary headlines. It created a new kind of screen gangster—neither hero nor villain, but an in-between figure with the kind of magnetism that a real gangster presumably *had* to have to achieve and sustain his position.

Obviously a detailed examination of the gangster film, which underwent many changes in emphasis during the sound period, is outside the scope of a book devoted to the silent years. But in order to fully appreciate the limitations under which the silent gangster film existed, it *is* necessary perhaps to at least summarize some of those changes.

Sound—and there were *many* sound gangster films, by such notable directors as John Ford, John Cromwell, and Raoul Walsh *before Little Caesar*—brought with it many changes and developments. First of all, the *sound* of the gangster's world—the chattering of machine guns, the explosion of grenades, the scream of tires, the jazz music of the speakeasy, the staccato delivery of dialogue, both menacing and humorous—brought tremendous pace to the genre. The sound cinema's insistence on realism, or what was considered realism at that time, jettisoned the sentimentality of the silent gangster film and supplanted it by a vicious, dog-eat-dog quality. Oddly enough, although the gangster was now far less noble (Cagney in *Public Enemy*) and often depicted almost casually, as a kind of specialized businessman (Spencer Tracy in *Quick Millions*), he still retained a surprising amount of sympathy. Audiences saw in him echoes of the Westerner. In the Depression era, they could readily sympathize with a man who took what he wanted by force. The Production Code clean-up of 1933 did away with films that dwelt on the magnetism and neo-glamor of the gangster himself (*Scarface* of 1932 was one of the last and best of these) and concentrated instead on the efficiency of the law. Robinson and Cagney merely switched sides, often retaining exactly the same codes of ethics and supplying the same kind of physical violence, but now sanctified by legality. In the post-Production Code era, the poor gangster had but little chance. The "thinking," charismatic gangster was gone, replaced by the moron and the hoodlum, who stood no chance of survival against an FBI filled by clean-cut, idealistic young men backed by the latest scientific equipment. From that point on, the gangster film quickly became a standardized action-show format again approximating the western, although there continued to be interesting tangential developments: a return to the traditional gangster film at the end of the 1930's; a wartime veering to a Damon Runyon approach (gangsters were now funny and likeable, redeemed by patriotism); and cycles of satire, of *film noir*, of psychologically motivated gangsters, and of nostalgic reconstructions of the 1920's.

But most of the interesting developments took place in the 1929–33 period, and it is here, too, that one finds most of the parallels with the western. Films like John Ford's *Born Reckless* more and more introduced scenes that were exact parallels of western incident, the climactic saloon confrontation in that film being almost a blueprint for the climactic shootout in Ford's much later *Stagecoach* (1939). The villains of the western—Fred Kohler, Robert McKim, William Boyd—were easily accepted by audiences as the villains of the gangster films. From an initial restriction to the big city (and a nightmarish, dark, studio-created city at that), the gangster films moved into more rural surroundings, the bank hold-up and succeeding chase differing only in that the western used horses and the gangster films high-powered autos. The shootouts in hideout cabins were likewise interchangeable. A curious phenomenon of the early 1930's—a kind of Fascist-oriented gangster film, advocating police-state methods to rid the United States of crime (though largely forgotten now, it was a startlingly prolific cycle)—has another immediate parallel in the many pro-vigilante westerns. In 1932, one has the rather odd coincidence of Walter Huston starring as a vigilante lawman in *two* films scripted by W. R. Burnette: *Law and Order* (with Huston playing a character patterned on Wyatt Earp and cleaning out the badmen in the famous O.K. Corral gunfight) and *Beast of the City* (with Huston as a police chief who leads his men into a bloody massacre of the gangsters who have just been exonerated by due process of law, and who cannot be touched legally). Burnette wrote scripts in both western and gangster genres, frequently overlapping and repeating themes and characters. In a sense, he might be considered the chronicler of the gangster in the same way that Zane Grey was the chronicler of the Westerner.

The similarity and interchangeability of the western and gangster genres is proven by the number of gangster films that have been remade as westerns—among them *High Sierra, Show Them No Mercy, Kiss of Death, The Asphalt Jungle*, and *The Last Parade*—and by the number of directors who have alternated regularly between the genres. Raoul Walsh's 1939 *The Roaring Twenties* was the first film to look back on the gangster era, to re-create it as a past event rather than to reflect it as a current event. In so doing, it became warm, nostalgic, more legend than fact—although it was a definitive wrap-up of the genre, going back to World War I and following through to the repeal of Prohibition. In a like manner, the same director's *They Died With Their Boots On,* made just two years later, was a definitive (if historically questionable) wrap-up of the West, encompassing the Civil War, its aftermath, and the Indian wars in one elaborate if clumsy package.

The western undoubtedly has far more unity within the silent film than the gangster genre, which can only offer tentative beginnings prior to the coming of sound. As genres, neither can be satisfactorily studied solely within the context of the silent film, and *both* can profitably be studied as interrelated genres.

The Documentary

The documentary has deliberately been left as a kind of post-script, since to a large degree that was the position it occupied in the American silent film. Since it is a style of film-making, it is not, in a purist sense, a genre. Even if it were, it would be the least utilized genre in the American film. During the silent period, the documentary had not, in any case, been defined. When it was, primarily by the British documentarians of the 1930's, the definition was an arguable one—to the extent that a lyrical, poetic film-maker like Humphrey Jennings was virtually ostracized by the "orthodox" documentarians, who saw their purpose as re-creating actuality objectively, and calling attention to social or other problems without editorializing to the extent of suggesting solutions. This is, of course, an oversimplification, and filmically worthwhile documentaries *were* made within that seemingly rigid framework. However, given those guidelines of what the documentary was supposed to be, it is not surprising that the American silent cinema —ever suspicious of "messages" and films not designed solely as entertainment—tended to avoid involvement with the documentary field. Even when the documentary was accepted into the mainstream of American film-making in the 1930's and especially during the war years, it evolved largely through government, private, and essentially non-Hollywood auspices.

The one conclusion one can draw about the documentary in the 1920's is that Hollywood did try to harness it to its own entertainment needs, and if one accepts Robert Flaherty's 1922 *Nanook of the North* (a sponsored, non-Hollywood film, though ultimately a commercial success) as the basic beginning of the feature-documentary in America, then the path from that point on leads more and more to the entertainment-feature and away from truthful reportage. Even *Nanook of the North* was not free of charges of falsification for the purposes of color and melodrama. Nanook's igloo was often a mock-up to facilitate camerawork, and the Eskimos featured in the film were reported to be highly amused at Nanook's dramatic use of the harpoon when they themselves found a high-powered rifle much more practical. When Hollywood (and to be specific, Paramount) suggested that Flaherty make a film for them, the result was *Moana* (1926), a lyrical work that might well have captured the essence and dignity of the islanders of the South Seas but was no more an honest reportage of their way of life than *Nanook* had been for the Eskimos. Flaherty also had the commercial foresight to include a minimum of bare-bosom footage, which received a maximum of attention in the advertising campaign.

A far more blatant example of the corruption of the documentary by Hollywood can be seen in the work of Ernest B. Schoedsack and Merian C. Cooper. "Corruption" is perhaps a harsh word to apply to work which was efficient, creative, and often absorbing, but it does illustrate Hollywood's conviction that documentaries were basically dull and of little appeal, and that in order to work they had to be sugar-coated or faked until they were entertaining. (The number of sincerely motivated but unutterably dull documentaries that were made in Great Britain in the thirties does lend some support to Hollywood's attitude!)

Schoedsack and Cooper, aviator/adventurers, initially made *Grass* (1925) for Paramount release. It was inexpensively made and turned a tidy profit. Dealing with the migration of the Lapland tribes, perpetually nomadic as they move with their reindeer herds, seeking new pastures, it was absorbing stuff, beautifully photographed and in need of little faking. Nevertheless, it was a somewhat austere film, and in their next, *Chang!* (1927), one already sees the Hollywood influence at work. *Chang!* was an exceptional film, but essentially an adventure film without stars, despite its on-location footage and a plethora of poetic man-versus-nature sub-titles. Shot in the jungles of Siam, it highlights—in its initial sections—encounters with a tiger, and then devotes its last half to a herd of marauding elephants—their destruction of a native village, the subsequent hunt and capture of the elephants, and then their taming and training to domestic tasks. On the face of it, little is really faked; but it is all very carefully "arranged" and even staged. Recognizing the comedy qualities of a monkey, the film-makers carefully worked into the narrative at strategic moments a good deal of footage that included him. A tiger chasing a native is clearly the real thing—but intercutting and point-of-view shots (the native looking down from his treetop refuge at the tiger) obviously are added to exploit and expand the situation. There are even odd instances of specific faking (although this has been denied by surviving members of the unit), one of the most ingenious occurring during the elephant herd's destruction of the native village. Presumably the elephants did their work so thoroughly and quickly that there wasn't enough footage to provide the lengthy highlight that was required, even with cutaways and alternate camera angles. Thus, a miniature set was apparently built, and destroyed by baby elephants! The scene is shot from above and used only briefly—perhaps to prevent the deception from becoming apparent—but its insertion does provide a useful cutaway which enables the sequence to be prolonged.

Perhaps the most intriguing aspect of *Chang!* today is in how much it serves as a kind of unofficial blueprint for Schoedsack and Cooper's *King Kong* of 1933. That later fantasy classic bases its whole structure, and the mystery element of its title, on the earlier film. Also, in *Chang!* one can see several *Kong* highlights at their root source: the natives on the high wall, the rescue of the child from the path of the onrushing monster, and others. *Chang!* is a notable film in many ways, certainly an entertaining one, and geographically and historically a valuable reference. But it is not a documentary. With *The Four Feathers* (1929), Schoedsack and Cooper moved into the fiction film. The best parts of it were the documentary scenes (especially of a hippo stampede), which they shot and arbitrarily inserted, but, still, documentary was now the servant of fiction. *King Kong,* as the climax of a (to that point) eight-year film career, represented the total abandonment of documentary to fiction and showmanship.

Hollywood's injecting of life and showmanship is, of course, not necessarily a bad thing. The most exciting and effective American documentaries ever made were Frank Capra's *Why We Fight* films of World War II—admittedly produced by and for the Armed Forces, but with the wholehearted participation of Hollywood names and resources. They were often heavy-handed, they were propagandistic, and they distorted footage—and even truth—quite arbitrarily. But they were dynamic pieces of film-making and effective informational tools, and were related to *Chang!* in their conviction that if information is to be conveyed and remembered, it has to be done with emotion, flair, entertainment values, and a little sensation. It may well be that Hollywood's influence on the documentary film is as important, in its own way, as the documentary influence on British fiction and narrative films from World War II on.

14

The Western

Even though some of the earliest film milestones were, in a limited sense, westerns—Edison's *Cripple Creek Bar Room* of 1898, because of its setting, even though it had neither plot nor incident, and the 1903 *The Great Train Robbery*, with its very basic western plot and structure—the western as a clearly defined form was slow in developing.

Two elements may be considered major factors in this delay. One was that westerns were produced on the East Coast until 1910, when film-making began its migration to the West Coast. Although some westerns were made in California prior to that date, they were certainly outnumbered by those produced in New York and New Jersey. Even though those regions had relatively wild areas, and some rugged cliff and river locations, there was nothing about them to suggest expanses of space, let alone the vast reaches of the plains country. Even with carefully chosen locations, there was the feeling of a well-tamed country, of the inevitable Main Street just outside camera range. Adding to the geographical shortcomings were those of costuming. Understandably, there weren't many geniune cowboys on hand in the New York area, and ideas of Western garb were usually drawn from the exaggerated cover illustrations of the dime novel and put into practice with the limited facilities of local costumers. The pointed-peak Mountie, or boy scout, hat was pressed into service to substitute for the more accurate stetson, and little thought was given to authenticity in breaking up the costumes into appropriate groups. Sheriffs and badmen, farmers and cattlemen all seemed to share whatever remotely Western garb could be found. The long leather wrist and lower arm cuffs, around which the cowboy could wrap and tighten the end of his lasso while roping cattle, more often than not turned up as part of the sheriff's garb, as did the woolly chaps, again essentially a cowman's accouterment—and for "show" rather than practical work, at that. However, the best of what was available seemed to be given to the sheriff as the most colorful of Western characters, and the others often had to make do by combining what was left with standard city clothing.

The second major flaw in the early westerns was the lack of a recognizable hero with specific characteristics. In a sense, *The Great Train Robbery* had been a kind of documentary—an overview of crime in the West, much as *The Life of an American Policeman* was an overview of police activity in a big city. Westerns that followed *The Great Train Robbery* were refined fairly quickly, with an individual "good guy" and "bad guy" substituted for the *groups* in that 1903 film. But individualizing was only a step. The western hero, above all American heroes, needed charisma, personality, an abundance of virtues, and an unrealistic lack of vices that could be offset by likeable weaknesses. Yet these qualities were a long time coming. Another Edison western, *A Race for Millions* (1906), was remarkably prophetic in its collection of clichés-to-be, including a traditional *High Noon* shoot-out for its climax. The plot, however, was an uneasy mixture of old and new. Its story of claim-jumping, and its (studio) background of saloons and street, belonged very much to the nineteenth century. Yet the final race to record the mining claim has the villain aboard a locomotive and the hero pursuing in an up-to-date automobile. The chase, through New Jersey landscapes, is quite effectively done, but the final shoot-out in the dusty streets is a cursory affair, a matter of brief skulking back and forth in a single small and largely painted set, and a quick exchange of shots. The hero, attired in the nattiest of 1906 motoring togs, strikes an incongruous note, as does his ability to outshoot the presumably far more experienced villain. Interestingly, though, the hero is clean-shaven and tidy, with his automobile outfit virtually a uniform, if not white at least a clean-cut gray. The villain, in contrast, sports a drooping black moustache and is attired from sombrero to boots in black—undoubtedly one of the first examples of western archetypes being designated by color. However, the camera keeps at long-shot distance from hero and villain at all times, and they are almost as impersonal as the two groups, outlaws and sheriff's posse, in *The Great Train Robbery.*

It was this kind of western—lacking in atmosphere, certainly lacking in realistic milieu and detail, deprived of attention-getting three-dimensional (or even two-dimensional) leading characters—that was the norm for many years, and that caused the genre to be regarded with such contempt by (among others) William S. Hart. Even after G. M. Anderson and Tom Mix had established the concept of the western hero (1907–09), the formless, characterless westerns continued to be made, some of them so badly that it's no wonder the quick death of the genre was predicted. *The Sheriff's Love* is a 1910 one-reeler that, conveniently for film history, seems to embody *all* of the weaknesses of the genre at that time. It is an East Coast-made film, and its exteriors suggest a fairly extensive park rather than the limitless space of the real West. Its costuming is a hodge-podge; there is no concentration on any one character, although ultimately the sheriff appears to be the one who should interest us most; and the narrative sense is dismal. One is totally lost for a sense of time period or motivations. Although it is a simple little film, one has to see it two or three times to deduce what is going on, when, and why. The director also keeps it so "busy"—with all of the "actors" in the saloon so constantly mobile that one never knows who or what to watch—that any attempt to concentrate on individuals is thwarted. Even as late as 1915, much better but still mediocre Edison westerns continued to suffer from unconvincing backgrounds and costuming, and the lack of a nominal hero.

Prior to 1912, the literary influence was James Fenimore Cooper rather than Zane Grey—for the very logical reason that Grey did not begin writing his western stories until 1913. The "noble Indian" preceded the cowboy as the first western screen hero—although the adjective "western" is perhaps arguable since, due to the Cooper influence, many of these little action stories, such as Griffith's 1909 *Leather Stocking,* dealt with Indian warfare on the Eastern seaboard.

Nor were action and violence necessarily the keynotes. Many of them were idyllic love stories or dramas, as their titles indicated: *Grey Cloud's Devotion, Silver Wing's Dream, Little Dove's Romance, A Squaw's Love.* Frequently, any white-redman conflict was totally absent, and the films dealt solely with Indian life and characters. Interestingly, during this period the Indian became accepted as a symbol of integrity, stoicism, and reliability, with the Indian figure and the Indian head used constantly as an advertising trademark on fruit, tobacco, and other goods. Not until much later was he replaced by the cowboy as a symbol—but one intended to suggest glamor, excitement, and virility to the city dweller who, it was hinted, might duplicate some of the rugged characteristics of the cowboy if he smoked the same kind of cigarette!

To G. M. ("Broncho Billy") Anderson belongs the credit for creating the screen image of the western hero—something that such genuine Western personalities as Buffalo Bill Cody and Al Jennings had been unable to do in their early flirting with movies. Anderson, a minor New York actor and model, had appeared in several roles in *The Great Train Robbery*, and from there developed further as an actor and director with Vitagraph. Then, as a partner with George Spoor in the Chicago-based Essanay Company, he chanced to star in (because no other actor was available at the moment) an unauthorized adaptation of a Peter B. Kyne story. Titled *Broncho Billy and the Baby* (1908), it turned out to be a primitive forerunner of the much-filmed (including twice by John Ford) *Three Godfathers*. It was a simple little film, with more plot and sentiment than action. An outlaw risks his chance of freedom by helping an injured child. Taken in by the child's parents, he is introduced to the Bible and finally leaves, a reformed man. In one short reel, the film established the knight-like character of the western hero, introduced the "good bad man," and also established the tradition of the hero as a wanderer, who puts things right but cannot stay around to enjoy the home—or the civilization—that he has helped to create. The success of the film was such that Anderson decided to stay with the Broncho Billy character. To the elements stumbled across so fortuitously in that first film, Anderson gradually added and polished others. The western hero had to be handy with a gun, but must not precipitate gunplay; where possible, he must defeat the badmen via trickery, cunning, or his fists. Fearless in combating evil, he should be awkward and shy with the ladies—often bursting into a scene in anger, and melting into clumsy bashfulness when confronted with the heroine. Anderson's trick of fumbling with his hat while trying to think of something to say to the heroine became a standby with all western heroes, especially William S. Hart and Ken Maynard. Lastly, he had to be a daring horseman, and colorfully nick-named. "Broncho Billy" was the first of a long line of western stars whose first names ranged from Tex to Hoot, Wild Bill, Sunset, Crash, Whip, Lash, Rocky, and Red.

Anderson was not exactly equipped to fulfill all of these requirements. He was not a polished actor (although that may have helped the rough-hewn sentiment of his shame-faced encounters with leading ladies), nor was he any kind of an equestrian. His face was craggy, and he was too bulky for athletic stunt work. Nevertheless, since he was setting precedents rather than following them, audiences were delighted. Moreover, Anderson worked hard to acquire riding skills, and his films improved rapidly. Most of them were shot in and around Niles, California, so that visually they had a tremendous edge over the Eastern-filmed westerns. Costuming, while far from being totally authentic, was good, and the plots were often quite neat and dramatic, with the Broncho Billy character to provide a focus. From 1908 on, Anderson made literally hundreds of short westerns, all tremendously popular and profitable. As a director he was hardly brilliant or innovative, but he was certainly workmanlike. Too, only a handful of the hundreds of shorts he made have survived, and it would certainly be unfair to attempt an analysis of his directorial capabilities on the inadequate evidence extant. While the Broncho Billy character was not exactly a *continuing* character (as, for example, the Hopalong Cassidy character was, with William Boyd playing Cassidy in sixty-six sound westerns, followed by another fifty-two half-hour television films), and would be a straightforward cowboy hero in one film, a good badman in the next, and even stray into nonwestern territory occasionally, his characteristics *were* constant throughout, and he built up a tremendous rapport with audiences.

In terms of individual films, Anderson's contribution to the western might be considered slight. By 1911, both Griffith and Ince were surpassing him in scope and in sophistication of technique. In attempting a comeback in 1918, Anderson was hopelessly outclassed by William S. Hart and Tom Mix. *Shooting Mad* (once considered a remarkable film, since for years it was erroneously dated as 1912) was a slickly-made, well-cut little film, but quite old-fashioned. Its final scene (of Anderson and his wife and baby going to church) seemed almost a parody of

Chaplin's climactic scene in *Easy Street*. Moreover, Anderson was now beefier, burlier, and craggier than ever, no match for the intensity of Hart or the slim folksiness of Mix. Anderson tried a full-length feature, realized that the western had passed him by, ventured into production with a series of Stan Laurel comedies, and retired in the early 1920's. He remained in obscurity for so long that many assumed he was dead until he came out of retirement in the late 1950's to make some television appearances and play a cameo role in a new western, *The Bounty Killer*. But in a very general sense, Anderson was of tremendous influence in the evolution of the western, establishing a format and a character some echo of which would be found in every western subsequently made.

If Anderson was a self-made Eastern cowboy, then his successor, Tom Mix, was the real thing—an adventurer, cowboy, and daredevil of the first order. True, his publicity machine exaggerated his pre-movie experience into a soldier-of-fortune scenario that no one man could ever cram into a single lifetime, but there was no doubt about his rugged courage, his horsemanship, or his ability to handle livestock. Mix joined the Selig Company shortly after Anderson had established the Broncho Billy character. To the traits that Anderson had devised, Mix added more of his own—a stress on daredevil stunting that was beyond Anderson's ability, and a semi-comic, folksy approach that emphasized the light-hearted camaraderie of ranch life and was close to the spirit of Will Rogers.

The Selig westerns—initially one-reelers, expanding eventually to two, then three, and finally four and five reels—were an uneven assortment. Many of them had the crude, off-the-cuff look of early Keystones, with the cowboys horsing around on the ranch much as the Keystone comedians ran and chased and fell in Los Angeles' MacArthur Park. Some of them were about *making* movies in the West, and such 1914 films as *Mr. Haywood Producer* and *Sagebrush Tom* had interesting glimpses of old cameras, Selig notepaper, dressing rooms, and the like. Mix himself directed a great many of the shorts and was clearly a much less efficient director than Anderson. However, when the films swung into action, they were often quite rugged and exciting, and they did improve appreciably through the years, with *Chip of the Flying U* and *In The Days of the Thundering Herd* standing out among the more ambitious features. Unlike William S. Hart, who was to follow him, Mix had no burning desire to put the "real West" on the screen, nor any conviction that his future lay with movies rather than with rodeos, ranching, or the Army, in which he had served earlier. Nevertheless, he was shrewd, an opportunist (in the favorable sense of the word), and a good businessman. It is odd that he should choose to stay with a minor company like Selig for almost a decade, especially when they did not see fit to cast him in their occasional "specials," such as the 1914 *The Spoilers*. It is equally odd that nobody recognized the tremendous potential in the man and tried to lure him away—perhaps to Universal, which would have been an ideal studio for him in the teen years, giving him a chance to work with both Harry Carey and John Ford. Mix's fame and influence had to wait until he joined Fox in 1917.

Following Mix in chronology, but preceding him in influence, was the first really outstanding western personality, William S. Hart. Hart came to Hollywood well into his middle age, with a long stage background behind him and a genuine love of the West. Although an Easterner by birth, he had spent much of his childhood in the West, knew it and respected it—so much that he frequently expressed disgust at the artificiality of the West depicted on screen. Hart's initial contact with Hollywood was ostensibly a transitory one. He was in California in mid-1914 with a touring company of *The Trail of the Lonesome Pine*, re-established contact with his old friend Thomas Ince, and persuaded him to give him a shot at acting in westerns. Ince didn't share Hart's zeal for the West, or for the possibilities of raising the prevailing standards of the western. On the contrary, he felt that the western was a dying genre. Nevertheless, his own business was flourishing, and dying or not, westerns did well for him because he had the studio space, the locations (primarily in the picturesque Santa Ynez Canyon), and the livestock and props to do them well. Initially Hart appeared as the villain in two two-reelers, both made by actor/director Tom Chatterton, and considered them disappointing. However, Hart was then given the opportunity to co-author, with C. Gardner Sullivan, a top scenarist, a five-reel feature western entitled *The Bargain* (1914). Reginald Barker, one of Ince's top talents, directed. Again in collaboration with Barker, and as soon as *The Bargain* was finished, Hart rushed into a subsequent feature, *On the Night Stage* (1915). As the good badman opposing the town minister (Robert Edeson) until ultimately reformed by the heroine, Hart had by far the most colorful role, even though he was not the nominal star. Moreover, Edeson, though a good actor, was a rather stolid one; it wasn't difficult for Hart to wrap up all the acting honors quite effortlessly. All four films, the two two-reelers and the two features, were shot quickly and efficiently in July and August of 1914. Hart was pleased with the two features, felt that he had at least made his point, and assumed that his association with movies was over. He returned to New York.

Unexpectedly, however, *The Bargain* proved to be a hit—so much so that Ince decided not to release it through his normal distributor, Mutual, but to sell it to the much more prestigious Famous Players. Anticipating that Hart would become a major star, Ince also decided to hold *On the Night Stage* out of release until that had been accomplished.

Ince contacted Hart and offered him a contract at $125 a week as an actor/director. The economy-conscious Ince was always somewhat miserly in paying salaries, but this offer was low even for him, especially since it involved a double function, either one of which should have paid far more. Certainly other stars and directors then working for Ince, and working in only one capacity, *were* earning far more. Hart, however, was unaware of Ince's methods and of the success of *The Bargain*. He accepted eagerly, anxious to throw himself into westerns. While he later achieved an improvement in his financial status under Ince, he was never given remuneration commensurate with the work he did or the tremendous profits his films made for Ince. Relationships between the two men were always strained, and sometimes even bitter.

Nevertheless, Ince *was* an astute and efficient producer. He virtually created the role of production supervisor, later taken on by Irving Thalberg and Dore Schary. He was the first to insist on fully-rounded scripts that gave every possible assistance to actors, directors, and cameramen. Even though the films were silent, dialogue was written in for the actors so that they would have maximum understanding of their roles. Ince himself doctored, worked on, and added to virtually all of his scripts. When expensive scenes were being shot, he arranged to have them covered by several cameras so that the same action, shot from different angles, could be incorporated into later films. If unusual locations were being utilized, he'd often send along actors from totally unrelated films to shoot scenes on that location for interpolation into their own movies.*

To the scripts, Ince added suggestions to the director on acting styles desired for certain scenes, or to the cameraman on choice of angle or use of color tints. Although he had been initially an actor, and subsequently a director, Ince's most important and creative function was in the role of production supervisor. He gave a personal stamp to every Ince production, and this, coupled with an enormous ego, made him feel justified in assuming directorial credit whenever he felt like it. Whenever an Ince film turned out especially well, he would either take the full directorial credit himself, sometimes generously "share" the credit, with the real director reduced to second billing, or on occasion release the film with no directorial credit, but with his own name appearing so prominently in the titles of the film that one could only assume that he was the sole author. Ince's mania for recognition extended not only to placing his name before the public as much as possible ("Thomas H. Ince presents A Thomas H. Ince production . . . supervised by Thomas H. Ince") but even to using his name subliminally. Even the leaders to the films, never projected, and intended only as a means of identifying the number of the reel for the projectionist, usually included his name—very often twice—in an elaborate logo-design that was seen by nobody but laboratory workers and projectionists! Ince's ego earned him the amused scorn of comedians like Buster Keaton, who more than once satirized Ince's credit-eccentricities, and the resentment of his corps of directors, the best of whom, seeing that their work was unlikely to gain outside recognition under his regime, left as soon as they could to work elsewhere.

Nevertheless, Ince was an important figure. He instituted many money-saving and product-improving procedures which became standard throughout the industry. And despite his ego, he *did* make valuable creative contributions to his films. Moreover, with a unique personality like William S. Hart, he had the wit to stand aside and not interfere with or dictate to him.

---

* For example, William S. Hart's *Hell's Hinges* used a dramatic sand-dune exterior for scenes of townspeople fleeing from the burning town. Apparently, immediately after those scenes were shot, and without even a change of camera angle, players from the H. B. Warner feature *The Beggar of Cawnpore*, set in India, were shot in a similar scene for insertion into that picture.

Hart's rapid development was not unlike Chaplin's. Both were from the stage, neither knew much about film, and both instinctively sought to change and improve the area in which they worked—Chaplin by slowing down and refining comedy, Hart by bringing maturity, poetry, and realism to the western. Both became major international stars in very short order. Hart directed beginning with his fifth film, and though he frequently brought in others to direct for him—such as Cliff Smith and Lambert Hillyer, whom he particularly trusted and with whom he had the strongest rapport—he remained the essential author of his films, controlling plot, acting styles, and action.

To contemporary audiences, Hart is not an easy talent to assess. So intense was he at times, bringing an almost evangelical fervor to his characterizations, that his best films (such as *Hell's Hinges*) often seem too extreme and his sincerity sometimes questionable. To the uninitiated, it is advisable to "ease" into Hart with a more restrained entry such as *The Return of Draw Egan* (1917) and work up to the stronger films after one has formed a less exacting relationship with him, and learned to accept his tremendous sincerity, his foibles, his tendency to repeat and enlarge on favorite plot situations, and above all, his sentimentality. Hart's very strong personality as an actor often overshadowed his directorial ability. But he understood film technique, when to use it, and when to withhold it. He resembled Chaplin and Von Stroheim in preferring a simple approach, telling much of his story through facial expressions. But when a cut or sudden mobility of the camera would underline a narrative point, he'd use it—all the more effectively for having withheld technique until that point.†

In fact, if Hart had not been such a dynamic personality on screen and had limited himself to direction, he might be far more respected by historians today. While Griffith stood alone as a directorial giant in 1915–16, Hart was certainly entitled to rank with deMille, Tourneur, Barker, and Collins as one of the most skillful of the second echelon.

It is probably a measure of Hart's impact that he was the first major star to be systematically satirized by screen comedians, who knew that Hart's traits were so well known that their barbs would hit home with any audience. Douglas Fairbanks, who worked alongside Hart at

† For additional comment on Hart's stylistics as a director, see the chapter on genres in this book and also the chapter on Hart and *Hell's Hinges* by this author in *The Rivals of Griffith* (Walker Art Centre, 1977).

both Triangle and later Paramount, often kidded Bill very genially in his own movies, which were often a direct reversal of the Hart formula. Bill frequently played the westerner who went East and outsmarted the big-city crooks. Doug responded by playing the New York dandy who loved the West to a point of absurdity, and went there to prove himself more than a match for the western badmen. These genial tiltings between the two major stars resulted in some memorable sequences, one of the best occurring in *Branding Broadway* (1918), where Hart pursues the badman into New York's Central Park on horseback, and ropes and hogties him! At least one of Mack Sennett's best comedies, *His Bitter Pill* (1916), was a merciless lampoon of Hart plotting and Hart character traits—with rotund Mack Swain playing the Hart role. Griffith's *Hoodoo Ann* (1916) included a charming sequence in which the young lovers (Mae Marsh and Robert Harron) go to a small-town movie theater to see a western. The actor playing the western hero, Carl Stockdale, pushes a slight physical resemblance to Hart into an amusing spoof, while the western itself pokes fun at the genre's carelessness with details. Even into the 1920's, when Hart's star has waned, Hal Roach and Will Rogers continued to satirize him.

There can be no doubt about Hart's enormous popularity. Admittedly, the competition was slim. Anderson and Mix had none of the production values or large-scale action sequences that distinguished Hart's films, and while Harry Carey was an up-and-coming western star at Universal, he himself was similar to Hart, and his films were much more modest. For a long time, Hart had the field pretty much to himself. He had restored public interest in and respect for the western. His plots were strong, gutsy, and adult, even by today's permissive standards. With his great cameraman, Joseph August (later to work so felicitously with John Ford in the thirties and forties), he brought the austere, dusty West of the Mathew Brady photographs to life. His success certainly increased the number of westerns being made, but in many cases they were one-shot affairs, like Griffith's *Martyrs of the Alamo,* and not star vehicles. Stars from the stage like Dustin Farnum and William Farnum made westerns—but not exclusively. Most of the new players who tried to set themselves up as western stars—William Russell, Roy Stewart—were too lacking in Hart's magnetic qualities to even approach his popularity, though their films tried to emulate and sometimes improve on the Hart formula. William Russell's *Six Feet*

G. W. Bitzer (left) with D. W. Griffith on location for *Way Down East* (1920)

Shooting the ice-floe climax for *Way Down East*

Griffith's Mamaroneck studios, jutting out into Long Island Sound

**Lillian and Dorothy Gish—
Orphans of the Storm (1922)**

America (1924)—the Cherry Valley massacres

That Royle Girl (1925)—Griffith directing W. C. Fields

WOMEN

Bebe Daniels

Bessie Love

Nazimova (with Valentino in *Camille*)

Pearl White (in her last serial, *Plunder*)

Mary Brian (with Betty Bronson in *Peter Pan*)

Gloria Swanson

Pola Negri

Mary Astor

Laura LaPlante

Betty Bronson

Janet Gaynor   Eleanor Boardman

Louise Brooks (with Lawrence Gray in *Love 'em and Leave 'em*)

Clara Bow

Greta Garbo (with Antonio Moreno in *The Temptress*)

Jetta Goudal (with Noah Beery in *The Coming of Amos*)

Joan Crawford (with John Mack Brown in *Our Dancing Daughters*)

ART DIRECTION

Fine example of a glass shot: only the immediate foreground is real, the huts in the background, hill, foliage, and castle are all painted on glass.

Co-director Clarence Brown poses in "natural" arch of rock set for Maurice Tourneur's *Last of the Mohicans* (1920)

The same set in position to frame the action

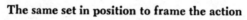

A fine set by Joseph Urban for *Yolando* (1924)

The Bowery at the turn of the century: a set for Universal's *Fool's Highway* (1924)

The set designed by William
Cameron Menzies for Fairbanks'
The Thief of Bagdad (1924)

A Ben Carre set for a Russian
prison in *The Red Dance* (1928)

A Germanic set from Borzage's
Street Angel (1928)

Exterior and interior sets for Michael Curtiz' *Noah's Ark* (1929)

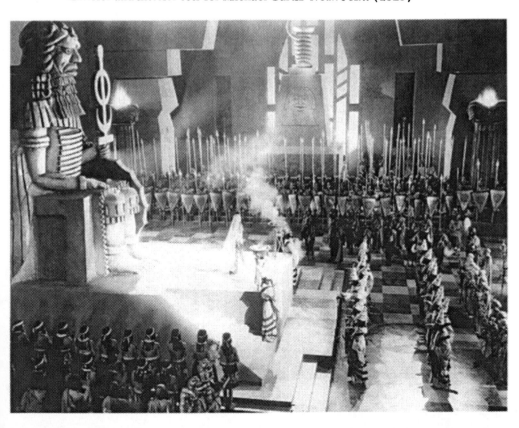

Simple flats, a couple of props, and ingenious lighting create a remarkable effect: a Ben Carre/William Cameron Menzies collaboration on *The Iron Mask* (1929)

Typical MGM/Cedric Gibbons art-deco: *Wonder of Women* (1929) with Lewis Stone, Leila Hyams

A Hans Dreier set for Sternberg's *The Case of Lena Smith* (1929)

Charles Hall's bizarre night-club set for *Broadway* (1929)

Cramped quarters at Paramount's Long Island studio, hemmed in by suburbia. An overhead shot of the space limitations; and the scene as it appeared on screen in *The Battle of Paris* (1929)

Sunrise (1927)

Four, directed by Henry King, was a particularly interesting "mood" western of 1919 that somewhat foreshadowed King's 1950 classic, *The Gunfighter.*

Bearing such colorful names as Blaze Tracey, Three Word Brand, Draw Egan, and Black Deering, Hart rode, fought, and reformed his way through *The Toll Gate, The Testing Block, The Narrow Trail, Breed of Men, The Aryan,* and a score of others (all 1916–1920)—with the occasional but infrequent non-western thrown in. While Hart interspersed his good badman with straightforward hero roles, his characters were never the grown-up Boy Scouts into which the western hero was so soon to evolve. Hart's screen character was basically chivalrous, but he could and did act tough with the ladies on occasion. He also smoked, drank, cussed, and as the expression goes, "caroused"— the latter by implication rather than explicit statement. Since the western so clearly separated good from evil, and since the movies were trying at that time to win public approval and prove that they could be an influence for good, the western was pressed into service. Many a Hart western established its boundaries by linking the villains with the saloon and the good guys with the church. Hart started on one side and wound up defending the other.

His plots were strong and initially quite tight, the telling accomplished in five reels. However, Hart downplayed action for its own sake, feeling it artificial. A superb athlete, he mixed it in without doubles in some really rugged brawls. He was also a fine rider, and even up to his last film, when he was nearly sixty, did all of his own riding. Feeling that the "riding close-up" or running insert was an unreal and egocentric device, he very rarely used it, and he downplayed stunts, often achieving horse falls and wagon crashes by editing—ironically, making them seem more stilted and unreal than if a stuntman had staged them. This austerity of action was hardly noticed in the early portion of his career, when Hart was at his peak—from 1916 through 1918. But Hart was not a young man, and inevitably began to slow down as he reached the age of fifty. His films got longer, the action content was reduced, and the sentimental sub-plots became more pronounced.

Audiences slowly began to lose their enthusiasm for Hart, especially when, in 1917, Tom Mix joined Fox and began a series of westerns that were the antithesis of Hart's. Hart's final films (for Paramount) were hardly failures. They were carefully made, and only one of them, *Singer Jim McKee* (1923), was really bad, and that due primarily to its absurdly rambling and sentimental plot, which was almost a self-parody. At least one of the Paramount Harts, *Travellin' On* (1922), was so successful that it was responsible for Paramount purchasing the novel *The Covered Wagon* (1923). Studio executives urged Hart to change his format, drop the austerity, and provide more comedy and streamlined action, but Hart still had autonomy and the conviction that he was right. He finished his Paramount contract, made one final farewell "special" *Tumbleweeds* (for United Artists release in 1926), and then retired. His last film was a good one; its only concession to popular taste was the addition of a comic sidekick, played by Lucien Littlefield. Otherwise it was a stark, poetic, historically accurate depiction of what was, in Hart's eyes, and as expressed by him in a subtitle, "the last of the West"—the opening-up of the Cherokee Strip to homesteading. The land-rush sequence, beautifully staged, almost mathematically precise in its editing, was less smooth than subsequent land-rush sequences (in Ford's *Three Bad Men* or Ruggles' *Cimarron*), but its rough-hewn quality was an asset, making it look almost like a newsreel coverage of the event. Although it was not the commercial success it deserved to be, and was mishandled by its distributor (who had little faith in it and wanted to cut it down by two reels), it was a noble swan song to Hart's twelve-year career.

When Tom Mix joined Fox in 1917, his initial westerns were much influenced by Hart. They had strong plots, were gray in tone, and relatively sparse on action. Their editing, however, was often extraordinarily rapid; from the very beginning, they *moved*. Within a short time, Mix evolved his own very different style. While the films could be and were enjoyed by adults—they were, after all, western parallels to the Fairbanks frolics—they were designed primarily for youngsters. There was plenty of juvenile appeal, often comedy with a dog, and plots that stressed circus-like action, stunts, and thrills for their own sake—but on a fantasy-like level, where people rarely got hurt. Even the villains, who certainly didn't pull their punches, were usually subdued by trickery, fancy roping, fist fights, or clever intervention by Tony the wonder horse, rather than being cut down by gunfire. But the incredible stunts and falls—from horseback, wagons, locomotives, cars, airplanes—were very much the real thing, packed a genuine punch, and were usually performed in close-up by Mix to eliminate any suspicion of doubling. Mix made first-rate use of picturesque locations (the Grand Canyon, the Colorado Gorge), which were splendidly photographed by Daniel Clark. Moreover, Fox never overplayed their hand with Mix. No matter how big a name he became, they stuck to the formula that had made him popular. Several attempts to transplant Mix into non-western territory failed (though the films were actually rather good, especially *Dick Turpin* (1925), with history totally re-written to give that British equivalent to Jesse James a happy ending and romantic retirement), and the experiment was not repeated. For the rest, they remained short, action-packed, and good to look at, with Mix's virility underscored by the comic device of giving an aura of effeminacy to lesser male characters. (Mix's romantic rival, and lesser villain, in *The Great K and A Train Robbery* (1926), is neatly put in his place by a sub-title that tells us that, if he had gone to college, it would have been Vassar!)

No pretention ever crept into the Mix films—a lesson that later western stars might well have profited by.‡ Mix lived up to his movie-star image off screen, delighting in show, publicity, and in flaunting his wealth. On screen, in a decade when Fox had more directorial than star talent, he was their biggest money-maker. Although considered lost for years, a dozen or more of his films do survive, and with their mixture of good humor and rugged action, it's easy to see why he, and such films as *Soft-Boiled,* (1923), *Sky High* (1921), *The Great K and A Train Robbery* (1926), and *The Last Trail* (1927), were so popular. Nor was his format totally inflexible. When Mix ventured into Zane Grey territory, as in *Riders of the Purple Sage* (1925) and its sequel *The Rainbow Trail* (1925), the bantering comic quality vanished temporarily, but the strong story values and the continued production care kept them well up to audience expectations.

The beginning of Mix's career coincided with the beginning of the end of Hart's. Inevitably, all of the newer western stars tended to follow one of their two images. Jack Holt, Neal Hart, Harry Carey, and

‡ In the thirties and forties, as soon as Roy Rogers, Gene Autry, and Bill Elliott achieved major popularity, they were promoted to "specials"—over-long films swamped in plot, decor, and songs, losing the very qualities that had made them so popular. All three stars finally reverted to their less imposing formats and regained lost ground.

Buck Jones followed essentially in the more realistic and restrained footsteps of Hart, while the greater majority of the newer western stars adopted the fancy costumes and stress on circus-style stunts made fashionable by Mix: Ken Maynard, Fred Thomson, Jack Hoxie, Bob Custer, Yakima Canutt, and Tom Tyler. One or two stars fell neatly between the two extremes. Tim McCoy's costumes were neat and flamboyant, à la Mix, but his western background (as an Indian agent) was authentic, and like Hart, he tried sincerely to put the truth of the West on screen. Hoot Gibson was essentially an entertainer, bringing a welcome comic touch to his westerns. In that, he resembled Mix. But his costuming was realistic, even to the extent of rarely using or even wearing a gun, and his films downplayed action, so that he was equally akin to Mix. Apart from these major western stars, all active at one period or another throughout the twenties, there were any number of hangers-on from previous glories (Francis Ford) and mediocre talents (Bill Patton, William Fairbanks, Al Hoxie) who never rose above the level of independent quickies.

The two major catalysts of the western film in the silent period were the advent of William S. Hart in 1914 and the release of *The Covered Wagon*, directed by James Cruze, in 1923. Coming roughly in the middle of this period was a new director, John Ford, whose first feature-length western, the five-reel *Straight Shooting*, was released in 1917. All that remains of Ford's prolific early career are this film (starring Harry Carey and Hoot Gibson) and a 1920 Buck Jones vehicle for Fox, *Just Pals*. The latter was more of a piece of rural Americana than a bona-fide western, though it did contain a traditional western fight and a chase finish, and Jones obviously thought highly enough of it to remake it reasonably faithfully along more orthodox western lines, as *The Cowboy and The Kid*, in 1936. Ford's early westerns all received extremely enthusiastic reviews, and one constantly finds the same elements being praised: rugged action, excellent photography of well-selected exteriors, and good human stories.

Straight Shooting, a cattleman-versus-farmer range-war story, similar to George Stevens' *Shane* in many respects, was remarkable for a first feature. Ford had been an extra in the climax of Griffith's *The Birth of a Nation* and carefully structured *his* climax after Griffith's, even to individual compositions and duplicating of specific incidents. The film as a whole had the editorial balance and structure of a Griffith film, too, with a slow build-up to a major action sequence in the middle, a relaxation of pace, and then a street shoot-out between Harry Carey and a lesser villain, leading to the gathering of two groups of riders, a besieged farmer's cabin, and an exciting race to the rescue. If the Griffith influence was dominant, there was nevertheless much of Hart in the film, too, particularly in the reformation of Carey's good badman character. In 1917, the film's impact was probably lessened by the fact that it overlapped the two schools. Hart was still at his peak, and Mix's first Fox release, coming out almost simultaneously with *Straight Shooting*, suggested a new style in the making. Possibly if Fox had not presented Mix at just that time, the Ford-Carey combination might have meant much more at the box office. Even as it was, though, the film was a resounding commercial success—a bonus for Universal, which had hired Ford to do only a two-reeler and found themselves unexpectedly with a successful five-reeler on their hands. It restored the then-faltering Harry Carey to popular favor and established Ford as an artistically and commercially innovative talent. However, Ford's major strides forward would have to wait until he, too, joined Fox. While today *Straight Shooting* is an eminently satisfying western on its own level, it is perhaps most interesting for originating at such an early date the many themes, individual compositions, and uses of landscape that were later to become Ford trademarks.

The Covered Wagon (1923) is a film perhaps far more impressive for what it achieved than for what it actually was. A modestly important film at its conception, it grew in scope and budget during production until, almost accidentally, it became the screen's first major epic western. Pictorially it is a stunning film. Karl Brown's superb photography, with its many fine panoramic vistas shot in breath-taking locations, gave the film both poetry and documentary values. Dramatically, it was more primitive. Such "highlights" as a prairie fire were unimpressively staged, and the picture was better off without them when they were pruned out of the release version, after the full-length edition had played road-show engagements. The big Indian attack sequence was certainly staged on a large scale, but was sadly lacking in excitement, and the arrival of the rescuing cavalry troop was accomplished with hardly more cross-cutting and other tension-building devices than had been present in Edison's *The Corporal's Daughter*. The normally fool-proof situation of the runaway horse was staged in a single long shot—even Porter's runaway in *The Life of an American Policeman* had had a *collection* of static takes—and served no purpose other than to establish the boy-girl relationship and show up the villain as a bluff and a coward. The plot itself had curious priorities, with the relatively humdrum personal problems of the hero frequently diverting attention away from the more important and interesting business of empire-building. Too many studio-shot inserts in the riding scenes lessened the realism, and the stiff performance of J. Warren Kerrigan as the wagon-boss undoubtedly seems far weaker today because of so many subsequent and more relaxed performances by John Wayne, Gary Cooper, Ben Johnson, and others in similar roles.

Today, *The Covered Wagon* has little excitement or showmanship, nor many of the near-documentary values that characterized its very early sound counterpart, *The Big Trail,* an undeservedly ignored film that was everything *The Covered Wagon* should have been and wasn't. Its most impressive elements today, apart from the overriding one of its pictorial grandeur, are those few sequences in which the inherent dramatic values of a situation take over in spite of the pedestrian directorial handling of them—as in the episode of the wagons fording the swollen river—and the naturalistic comic byplay between those two inveterate scene stealers, Ernest Torrence and Tully Marshall, as a couple of ragged frontier scouts. Disappointing though the film is today, however, it's easy to understand its tremendous impact at the time, when its grand scale and partially depersonalized approach (for all of his inadequacies, the hero is not the focal point of the film, as William S. Hart always was) did suggest something quite new—the mating of the Hollywood film with the on-location documentary, as pioneered by Robert Flaherty the year before in *Nanook of the North.*

Not only did *The Covered Wagon* become one of the biggest money-making films of the silent period, it commercially revitalized the western. The year of its production, about fifty westerns were made, including the Hart and Mix films. The following year that figure was more than tripled, including a number of epics designed to cash in on *The Covered Wagon,* and the instigation of new groups of smaller westerns built around individual western stars.

John Ford's *The Iron Horse* was one of the most beneficial results of *The Covered Wagon*'s popularity. Although James Cruze's simplistic directorial style hit a responsive note at that time, Ford was an infinitely superior director. Moreover he loved westerns, and although only twenty-nine at the time, had already made nearly fifty films, most of which had been westerns. One almost sensed that Cruze felt he was slumming in making *The Covered Wagon*. He did everything he could to play *down* the normal western characteristics and play *up* the qualities that might cause it to be regarded as something other than a genre film. Ford, on the other hand, threw himself into this prestige production with tremendous enthusiasm, and conversely, one senses that he occasionally disliked the "importance" of the theme and was happiest in the (to him) more familiar action sequences. Certainly the excessive footage devoted to Lincoln was imposed on him by Fox, frustrated at being beaten to the punch by another producer in doing a biography of Lincoln. Too, one suspects that the long and excessive number of titles that introduce the film and are interspersed throughout are there largely after the fact, to compensate for Ford's having gotten down to narrative development in a very businesslike manner.

Despite its great length and its slow opening third, *The Iron Horse* is one of the finest of western epics. Even its linking story—that old canard from the "B" movies of the hero searching since childhood for the man who killed his father—is rather neatly interpolated into the main thrust of the story, and while it is unnecessary, it never gets in the way of, or delays, the epic sweep of the theme. Like *The Covered Wagon*, it was filmed almost entirely on location, but with far more imaginative use of the landscape and none of those cyclorama-backed inserts to remind one of the omnipresence of the studio. The big Indian attack scenes are slammed over with tremendous gusto, with Ford's editing and camera mobility unstressed (as they would be in his later sound westerns, too) but present and utilized only when necessary. George O'Brien made a relaxed and likeable hero, and a most athletic one, clearly doing most of his own action scenes—a marked contrast to the pampered theatricality of J. Warren Kerrigan's performance in the Cruze film. *The Iron Horse* made a star of O'Brien and launched a liaison with Ford which was to last well into the sound era; their last collaboration came forty years later in *Cheyenne Autumn*.

The Iron Horse combined documentary-like qualities with showmanship, and moreover, created the sense of drive and national achievement that *The Covered Wagon* lacked. It was a big commercial success, but *not* for those qualities. Ford had so loaded it with action, romance, and comedy (it was perhaps a little overloaded with typical lowbrow Irish slapstick comedy, a permanent failing of Ford's, though an endearing one) that it could hardly miss. It was one of the best of the western epics and greatly influenced the railroad-building sagas made subsequently—especially the Russian *Turksib* and deMille's 1939 retelling of the same story in *Union Pacific*. But the American public in the early 1920's was not particularly interested in themes that sought to stimulate patriotic pride. They would buy the western epic for its action and spectacle, but not for its inspirational qualities. Most of the post-*Iron Horse* epics that offered too much of the latter, and not enough of the former, failed badly at the box office. Even Griffith's monumental *America,* which seemed to offer a plethora of both, and the last half of which was a veritable marathon of brilliantly staged Indian battles and cavalry charges, was sadly ignored at the box office. Irving Willatt's follow-up to *The Covered Wagon, North of '36* (from another Emerson Hough novel), and Cruze's own return to the western epic with *The Pony Express* were both commercial disappointments.

The market for big westerns *had* been established, however. Hollywood soon learned of the apathy to patriotism and pride in past achievement, and turned instead to big action shows. Universal's *The Flaming Frontier* was a spectacular star-studded reenactment of the Custer massacre, and while the film itself appears to have been lost, Universal used its highlight footage so frequently in later westerns (*Badlands of Dakota, The Indians Are Coming*) that we certainly have a good idea of its size and scope.

The star vehicles—those of Fred Thomson, Tom Mix, Tim McCoy, and Ken Maynard, in particular—were dedicated first, foremost, and essentially to action. Thomson's films were based largely on the Mix format. The star himself was ruggedly good-looking and a fine athlete; like Mix, he did most of his own stunts. His films had outstanding photographic quality and polished if not luxurious production mountings, and the riding, fighting, and acrobatic stunts took pride of place over plot. Ken Maynard's long-running series at First National in the late 1920's must surely be one of the most elaborate "series" westerns ever made, although their commercial value to the exhibitor in the 1920's was substantially higher than that of the average "series" western in the 1930's. Even up to the end of the series—when budgets usually fell off and enthusiasm waned—the Maynard films, of which *Red Raiders* (1927) is one of the best, maintained a large-scale production akin to that of Ford's later *Stagecoach*. Further, their major action sequences—Indian attacks, stagecoach races—were considered good enough to be re-used constantly throughout "B" westerns of the sound period. Maynard, whose dialogue delivery in the sound period was not good, and whose figure ran all too easily to portliness after the mid-1930's, was, in the late 1920's, at his peak: a fine physical specimen of a man who, deprived of the humanizing (and in his case, belittling) advantage of dialogue, cut a most impressive figure in the saddle, delighting in daredevil feats of horsemanship performed in full close-up view of the camera.

In their own way, the Tim McCoy westerns for MGM were almost as good, though concentrating far more on reasonably accurate historical reconstructions and, as was McCoy's bent, frequently crusading on behalf of the American Indian. The McCoy westerns were unique but also problematical. They contained too much history and romance and not quite enough continuous action to be juvenile-oriented, yet at the same time they were too short, snappy, and simplistic to have major adult appeal. MGM was never on very familiar ground with non-"A" pictures, and the carefully made McCoys were too expensive in relation to their earning power for the studio. Nevertheless, it was a thoughtful, well-made (the directors included W. S. Van Dyke and even a Russian, Tourjansky!), and still most impressive series.

Although action remained the keynote of the silent western, and none of them achieved the depth or psychological insights of such later sound westerns as *The Gunfighter* or *The Man Who Shot Liberty Valance,* neither were they just parades of meaningless action. One might perhaps level that criticism (or description) at the Mix, Thomson, and Maynard westerns, but only in the sense that one could term the Busby Berkeley musicals parades of "meaningless" music. Maynard and Berkeley both existed to exploit to the full the specific visual aspects of their chosen genre, and they fulfilled that aim admirably.

Many silent westerns, particularly those from the bigger studios, were as concerned with telling intelligently presented and well-acted stories as they were with slamming over the fights and chases. Zane Grey even formed his own production company at one early point to ensure that his stories reached the screen as he wrote them. It was a

practice followed by other popular American writers, among them
Edgar Rice Burroughs and Gene Stratton Porter, and it *never* worked—
either commercially or in the quality of the films thus produced. Grey,
in the early 1920's, dissolved his company and made a deal with Paramount, which filmed his novels (and many synopses or mere ideas,
credited to non-existent novels) for some twenty years. It's a pity that
this body of work cannot be studied in toto, for while the talkies became far less important commercially, they maintained a surprisingly
high and literate standard, while some of the silents were quite exceptional.

Wild Horse Mesa, directed by George B. Seitz in 1926, is possibly
the most faithful adaptation of any Grey novel. Grey was on location
with the film and expressed himself well satisfied with it—as indeed
he might be, since it summed up both his own attitude to the West§
and catered to many of his personal foibles, including some questionable racial attitudes. *Wild Horse Mesa* is a quiet, thoughtful western,
its possible anachronisms (it is set in the contemporary 1920's, with
jazz-age references) less apparent now than then. Jack Holt presents
such a manly and virile figure that there is no need to stress his heroics, and indeed these are rather surprisingly downplayed. Theme takes
such precedence over character that we are two reels into the seven-
reel film before we meet either hero (Holt) and villain (the magnificent Noah Beery), and its story of the need to protect the wild horse
preserves strikes such a modern ecological note that the film dates not
at all, and can (and does) play with surprising success to 1970's audiences.

Many of the Paramount Zane Greys—ranging from traditional actioners (*To The Last Man*) to films of social content (*The Vanishing
American,* which unfortunately weakened its plea for justice for the
American Indian by overdoing the melodramatics of the white villain,
Noah Beery)—were not only exceptional as westerns but served as valuable training grounds for upcoming players and directors of note. It is
a pity that the great bulk of the silent Greys are either lost or unavailable for study today.

---

§ Croy, an Easterner, went West for his health. He was not only restored to
health but found a new, more optimistic approach to life. This theme was to become an oft-repeated motif in many of his novels, perhaps most obviously in
Heritage of the Desert.

It is perhaps appropriate that the last classic silent western should come from John Ford, with his 1926 *Three Bad Men*. In many ways, it is superior to *The Iron Horse*. It is a shorter film, less pretentious, and a particularly neat blend of the austerity and authenticity of Hart and Ince with the gloss, pace, and showmanship of Ford. The story is a good one, something of a western variant on *The Three Musketeers* and not, as is commonly thought, an adaptation of Kyne's *Three God-fathers*, though it has its similarities to that, too. From its opening scene—a close iris of a man chopping at a tree, the iris then opening out to reveal the full panoramic grandeur of the West behind him—lake, mountains, sky—to its climactic land-rush sequence, it is exciting, human, rough-hewn poetry, one of Ford's finest films and, surprisingly, his last western until *Stagecoach*, thirteen years later.

The western seemed to be facing obsolescence at the end of the twenties. Not only did its visual and physical qualities seem threatened by the coming of sound, but Charles Lindbergh's triumphant transatlantic flight in 1927 promised to replace the cowboy with the aviator/explorer as America's traditional hero figure. In *Photoplay*, the leading and most intelligent of the fan magazines, an editorial predicted the total demise of the cowboy hero unless he took to the air, which seemed to suggest only the survival of Tom Mix, whose westerns had always stressed a modern-age approach and frequently utilized planes. The predicted cycle of aviation/exploration movies did indeed materialize. Oddly enough, these sometimes quite accurate and sincerely motivated films (Capra's *Dirigible* through Garnett's *SOS Iceberg*) are often greeted with laughter and disbelief by contemporary audiences, conditioned to reject *individual* heroics in place of the organized, *mass* explorations of space exemplified by the landing on the moon.

The defeat of the western hero was, however, only temporary. Although his return in the first big sound, wide-screen westerns (*The Virginian, Billy the Kid, The Big Trail, Cimarron*) would not be an unqualified commercial success, he would stake his claim and hang on tenaciously until he became both fashionable and profitable again in 1939.

15
Comedy

There can be no doubt that the comedy film, especially in the mid-1920's, formed one of the richest and most unique aspects of the American film. It is also one of the best documented: Mack Sennett, Charles Chaplin, Harold Lloyd, and Buster Keaton all issued autobiographies, and their careers and films have also been the subject of several books. Walter Kerr's book *The Silent Clowns* is a rich and near-flawless survey of the field, and such earlier books as Theodore Huff's *Charlie Chaplin*, Gerald McDonald's book on the Chaplin films, and Rudi Blesh's *Keaton, The Films of Laurel and Hardy, The Films of Hal Roach*, and *The Art of W. C. Fields* supplement it with even more concentrated coverage of the respective subjects. The improved status of film scholarship has resulted in far better approaches to film comedy than nostalgia; 1977 saw the publication of the best book yet on Harold Lloyd, *Harold Lloyd: The King of Daredevil Comedy*, edited by Adam Reilly and with contributions by a number of critics and historians, and the preparation of at least one very solid work on Harry Langdon. Moreover, the films themselves are in a good state of preservation and more than usually accessible via television, theatrical, and non-theatrical distribution. Not only that, their continued viability is proven by the enthusiastic audience reaction to them. The laughs they generate, particularly in contrast to the meager pickings from contemporary film comedy, are enormous, and it is not the laughter of nostalgia. They continue to work entirely on their own level—unlike, unfortunately, so many silent dramatic classics, where too many contemporary audiences consider it smart and sophisticated to laugh at them, and to go to them looking for an excuse to laugh.

In view of this happy state of documentation and availability, perhaps what is needed here is not another detailed reappraisal of the art of Keaton or Chaplin, but rather a succinct survey of the whole field of American comedy.

Of all the film arts, comedy is the hardest to do well. It it much easier to excite, scare, or emotionally move a person than it is to make him laugh. The emotions that provide terror or sadness are more universal, and easily manipulated by the filmmaker. A sense of humor is a much more personal attribute, however; what is funny to one can be in bad taste to another. In addition, much humor depends on both understatement and/or topicality, which can cause it to date very quickly or seem inexplicable in a later period, when the very subtlety that made it funny in the first place has become a liability. (Political humor is particularly prone to such dating. Many of Will Rogers' barbed thrusts of the 1920's are now merely bemusing, just as Bob Hope's jokes may become virtually meaningless in a decade or two.)

Considering the sophistication of very early French film comedy and its imitations by the Italians and the British, it is surprising how long it took for an American comedy tradition to get under way. American comedy up to 1909 was a matter of single jokes and mild slapstick. There was some indication of wit, to be sure. Edison's very early *Streetcar Chivalry* was an amusing commentary on the rules of conduct on a crowded streetcar, the seated male passengers pointedly ignoring the plight of a homely baggage-laden matron but rushing to their feet to offer a seat to a pretty girl. But it sought to be no more than amusing. Biograph's *Dream of a Racetrack Fiend* used its comedy structure only as an excuse to give the audience a tour of the New York City harbor in 1906. Even trick films using superimpositions, reverse-printing, and stop motion seemed to be keeping their magical qualities almost deliberately in check, reluctant to pursue laughter aggressively and with imagination.

The first major breakthrough came, as did so many others, with D. W. Griffith—although his interest in comedy was slight, and he relegated much of the writing and performing of comedy subjects to an assistant, Mack Sennett. So, it may well be that from the very beginning, Sennett was the catalyst of American screen comedy. The Griffith film (with Sennett in the lead) was *The Curtain Pole,* made in Fort Lee, New Jersey, in 1909. It is clearly a copy of the now well-established French farce/chase pattern, with the latter half of the film devoted to a cumulative chase through the streets. To the French must go the credit for most of the comic formulas that Sennett was to use, and admittedly, to develop far more than the French had done. Apart from instituting the comic chase, the French had also added glamor and spice via pretty female participants, and two of the most reliable formats of all, the deflation of pomposity and the defiance of authority. The Keystone Cops had their ancestors in a very early half-reeler entitled *French Police,* in which jovial gendarmes look on and laugh as robberies and other crimes are committed under their very noses.

There is a recognizable direct line of French influence in American comedy from 1909 on in the films of Mack Sennett, *The Curtain Pole* leading to 1912's *The Manicure Lady* (a surprisingly sophisticated sex farce, again nominally a Griffith Biograph film, but with Sennett in the lead and probably much in control), and thence to 1914's *Tillie's Punctured Romance,* the first American feature-length comedy. Although based on an American play, it was very much reshaped by Sennett to accommodate the Keystone Cops and other visual comic elements, and its plot structure—the tricking of a country girl into marriage by a fortune-hunting city slicker—had a decided European flavor to it. It was the kind of plot that Sennett was to adapt and re-use endlessly in such typical Keystone comedies as *Her Torpedoed Love* (1917). Prior to leaving Griffith and Biograph, Sennett had charge of an entire comedy unit, turning out many comedies, some of which were already satires of recent Griffith successes. These films are little known today and virtually unavailable outside of the archives of the Library of Congress in Washington, D.C., but they are important in establishing just *what* Sennett contributed to comedy at this time. For example, in his Biograph group, one finds Fred Mace playing exactly the kind of character that Ford Sterling was to play in the latter Keystone Comedies, complete with make-up, costuming, and pantomimic mannerisms. This tends to suggest that even with a successful comedian like Sterling, much of the groundwork for his screen character had been laid earlier by Sennett.

From 1913 on, Sennett was to devote himself exclusively to comedy:

one-reelers, two- and three-reelers, and the occasional feature. His role in film history is somewhat enigmatic. To him certainly goes the credit for creating comic formulas, establishing a comic screen tradition, and providing a training ground for some of the screen's finest comedy talents—from Chaplin and Arbuckle to Langdon and Capra. But his actual achievements were less notable. The French have always been ecstatic about the "surrealism" and the "poetry" of the early Sennetts, but one suspects that they are looking at them through the eyes of nostalgia, or via compilations of excerpts. Perhaps because his films offered little in the way of plots and concentrated on set-pieces of visual action, it has always been easy to lift a highlight from a Sennett comedy and allow it to perform out of context; and in excerpt form, the speed, imagination, and frenzy of the early Sennetts can be misleading.

Since there was no comedy tradition before Sennett, he was setting precedents rather than following them, and was entitled to make mistakes. Lack of subtlety was one of them, coupled with a tendency to rely on obvious slapstick rather than the more inspired sight-gag. The term "slapstick" derives from an old vaudeville prop—a goat bladder stretched on a stick. One comedian would hit another with it, and accompanied by a loud noise, and the other would fall. In essence, that was the formula of the early Sennetts. And if one fall was considered funny, then presumably ten falls would be ten times as funny—funnier still if it was a fat man or woman who fell. Early Sennetts had relatively little in the way of custard pies (a much exaggerated tradition anyway) and elaborate Keystone Cop chases, but they were full of people running in and out of rooms, or through gardens, or along city streets, constantly colliding with one another, falling in a heap, and getting to their feet, only to be knocked down again. Taste and subtlety were virtual strangers to Sennett at this time, although in many cases, shock value and a sense of outrage were funny in themselves and justified the lack of taste. Much of his humor involved crude racial stereotypes, particularly Negro and Jewish, but this was a hangover from the vaudeville stage and almost certainly unintentional on Sennett's part. Another irksome quality of the Sennetts at this time was the players' propensity to pantomime. Before going into a piece of action, they would pantomime it to the audience—as though working out an idea that had just struck them—and then perform it. In the case of a player

like Ford Sterling, this meant excessive gesticulating and facial grim-
acing; one exposure to it was usually more than enough.

In their favor, however, the Sennett films were often wild, unpredict-
able, and uninhibited; and reflecting Sennett's apprenticeship under
Griffith, their editing was often brilliant. What let them down most
often was their story weakness. It is significant that by far the best
Sennetts were those that satirized accepted movie (or stage) traditions,
such as *His Bitter Pill* (1916), Mack Swain's parody of the William S.
Hart westerns. These films were funny not just because they had a
great deal of exuberant action but because for once they had a solid
story to hang it on. (The general superiority of the Hal Roach comedies
to those of Sennett is likewise attributable to Roach's insistence on a
solid story basis. Also, Roach's comedians—Charlie Chase, Laurel and
Hardy, Will Rogers, and Our Gang—were normal people without the
baggy clothes and exaggerated make-up that made the Sennett comics
clowns rather than people.)

Once Sennett had established a tradition—and a market—for comedy,
others took advantage of it and in some cases bypassed him. Certainly
the early comedies from Vitagraph—those with John Bunny and Mr.
and Mrs. Sidney Drew—had a maturity and charm that Sennett's film's
lacked. Too, Sennett was locked into his formulas; once he had established them, he was reluctant to depart from them. In essence, the Sennett comedies of the 1920's are no different from those of the teens;
they are just slicker and more polished. The same gags and the same
plotless "stories" are merely re-told with other players. This had the
result of losing Sennett his very best names just as they were becoming really valuable to him. Chaplin, Fatty Arbuckle (a most endearing comedian, and a subtle director), and Harry Langdon all found
that they could get both more money and more freedom to develop
their own brand of comedy away from Sennett. They had no choice
but to leave him.

Chaplin's contribution to comedy in 1914–16 was perhaps even
greater than Sennett's. He came to Sennett in 1914 from vaudeville,
knowing literally nothing about the art of movie-making, and plunged
into the Sennett factory method, churning out often off-the-cuff slapstick material and making some thirty-five comedies in a single year.
None of them are outstanding, but there is a wide range between the
crude knockabout of the early ones and the relative sophistication of

the later ones. Graduating midway into directing himself, Chaplin reduced the number of gags, cut out the unnecessary pratfalls, and extended the time devoted to the gags that were used; the frenetic quality was gone, and a subtlety and humanity replaced it. In the process, Chaplin turned himself into the world's best-known and best-loved comedy performer.

At the end of his Sennett contract, Chaplin left to join Essanay, enjoying both more money and considerably more freedom. There he turned out another fourteen films, still essentially slapstick, but with more of a stress on occasional pathos. *The Tramp* (1915), generally considered Chaplin's first major work, is from this period. The incredibly thoughtless, even casual, cruelty that was always an ingredient in Chaplin's screen image (in *The Tramp* he is constantly treading on, or over, his own work-mates or jabbing a pitchfork into their nether regions to hurry them along) was gradually softened during the Essanay period; the abrasive qualities were reduced, the attractive ones extended. As a body of work, the Essanay films mark a tremendous stride forward from the Keystones. Chaplin's next move was to Mutual. He was working more slowly now, and only twelve Mutual comedies were made over the nearly two-year period from 1916 to 1917. In many ways, these are the best Chaplins. The weakest of them, the purely slapstick entries, such as *The Fireman,* are still superior to the best of the Keystones and Essanays; and the *best* of them (*The Immigrant, Easy Street, The Rink*) could stand with his best work from any period. In fact, they are far more confident and inventive than many of Chaplin's later features.

At the conclusion of the Mutual films, Chaplin moved on once again, but his new group—for First National (1918–23)—lacked the unity and near-perfection he had achieved at Mutual. The best of the group were the first ones, *A Dog's Life* and *Shoulder Arms,* which still seemed buttressed to the Mutuals. Thereafter, Chaplin tried too hard to live up to the artistic pretentions bestowed on him by the critics and, aware of his own commercial and artistic importance, tended to be far less generous with the comedy content of his films and notably economical in the way he staged it. He never let his audience down, but on the other hand, he never delivered *more* than was expected, as Lloyd and Keaton continually did. Too, he wavered uncertainly between shorts, extended shorts, and features, unable to make up his mind which way to go. It's a rather sobering thought that, despite his fame and popularity, Chaplin contributed only three full-length starring features throughout the twenties: *The Kid* (1921), *The Gold Rush* (1925), and *The Circus* (1928).

It was probably the same uncertainty, rather than a clear conviction that he belonged in silents, that caused him to retain the essentially silent structure throughout his first two films of the sound era, *City Lights* (1931) and *Modern Times* (1936). Neither, however, really qualify as bona-fide silents. Apart from music, they use sound effects and either simulated or actual dialogue. They merely withhold dialogue from the principal characters and retain the use of often unnecessary sub-titles. *City Lights,* often considered Chaplin's masterpiece, tends to fluctuate in its appeal, and is often affected by the tenor of contemporary movie-making and the emotional tempo of the times. When reissued in 1950, a more than usually uninspiring year cinematically, it seemed to hit a responsive chord. Yet today, its magic seems to have gone again, and its comedy material seems more like a series of sketches, ideas being tried out rather than actually executed. Even its highlight, the boxing match, seems inferior to similar material done on other occasions not only by Chaplin but also by lesser comedians. *Modern Times,* on the other hand, despite its compromises with silence, seems to get better with every viewing and may well be Chaplin's masterpiece. Part of its appeal may lie in the fact that for once Chaplin did not monopolize all of the narrative and comedy. Paulette Goddard's performance, a strange but wholly effective welding of Fairbanksian bravura and optimism with the wistful and defeatist pathos of Leni Reifenstahl's Junta from *The Blue Light* (1932), might well be listed along with Mae Marsh's performance in *Intolerance* and Eleanor Boardman's in *The Crowd* (though in a pantomimic rather than an acting sense) as one of the great performances of the silent cinema—and what matter that it was performed in 1936 and by an actress never a part of the silent film?

Chaplin was the most blatantly imitated of all movie comedians. Even Japan had its copy, while Hollywood was full of them. Billy West was so adept at imitating Chaplin's physical mannerisms and makeup that his comedies could easily have been sold as the real thing, were it not for the lack of warmth and the elements of pathos that West was unable to duplicate. Even Harold Lloyd started his career by stealing from Chaplin, copying his Mutuals with little attempt to disguise the source of inspiration. But apart from his enormous personal popularity, Chaplin's major contribution from 1914 to 1916 was in taking comedy out of the realm of crude knockabout, refining it, and bringing it sophistication and respectability. Certainly Chaplin's enormous success made it easier for other comedians—Arbuckle, Lloyd, and Keaton, in particular—to develop individually and at their own speed, and not be trapped within the pattern of violence and slapstick that seemed essential during the period of Sennett's leadership.

Despite the huge success of Chaplin and the growing success of Lloyd, Keaton, and Arbuckle, Hollywood adopted a rather curious and snobbish attitude toward comedy in the teen years. Sight-gag and slapstick comedy (as yet, nobody was taking comedy seriously enough to define the difference) were essentially a matter of violence. Sight-gags were often built on deception and did not have to involve violence or even action, a rigid requirement of slapstick. It was considered great stuff, as long as it kept its place—in the two-reeler. Once comedy was promoted to feature length, it was supposed to become "respectable." Douglas Fairbanks had the clout to ignore this unwritten law. His films of 1916–19 were primarily comedies, often of a witty and satiric nature, but they were merchandised for their action content and for Doug's breezy and peppy personality rather than for their comedy. But Fairbanks apart—and noting, too, the occasional charming feature-length comedies offered by Mabel Normand, Constance Talmadge, and Dorothy Gish—the feature-length comedy of 1915–20 was apt to be a "polite" situation comedy deriving from the *Saturday Evening Post* and featuring an essentially non-comedy star like Bryant Washburn.

When Fatty Arbuckle and Buster Keaton did get into feature comedies in this period, they were resolutely prevented from doing the very things they did best. When Keaton made *The Saphead* in 1920, an adaptation of a play that Fairbanks had once starred in, it was devoid of *any* sight-gag material until he forced the issue in the final reel. However, it was not until 1922 that the great sight-gag comedians began the transference from two-reelers to features. Harold Lloyd took the plunge first, and with all the confidence of his on-screen character made two features that year—*Grandma's Boy* and *Dr. Jack.*

(Chaplin had made *The Kid* a year earlier, but then had retreated to shorts again, indirectly implying that for him to make features was either a mistake or at least premature.) Keaton quickly followed in Lloyd's footsteps.

In late 1923 a new kind of comedy was added: Lubitsch's *The Marriage Circle*. With its European locale and its light-hearted treatment of marriage, divorce, and affairs, it was delightfully sophisticated *frou-frou* and caught on immediately with an audience that believed itself to be sophisticated but had been able to find little above the level of *Blood and Sand* to prove it. Almost single-handedly, *The Marriage Circle* seemed to unlock the flood-gates for a cycle of similar films. It wasn't that it was phenomenally successful. Rather, it proved that there was a market for this kind of film, and Hollywood was full of directors of wit and style who had longed to make it and had been forced into slapstick or farce instead. Mal St. Clair, Monta Bell, Paul Bern, and a little later Harry D'Arrast all persuaded their studios to give them a try at what was, thanks to *The Marriage Circle,* a sure thing, and they rose to the occasion beautifully. In fact, many of their initial films surpassed Lubitsch in silken elegance—if for no other reason than that they were on surer ground and were familiar with the mores and morals of the American public at that time. Their comedies were slick and glossy, usually dealing with the impact of a European *femme fatale* on respectable America, the avoidance—or repairing of— divorce, and even, in Paul Bern's *Open All Night* (1924), a theme as up-to-date as wife-swapping! Although not calling attention to their technique, many of these films—since they were, after all, essentially situation-comedies of a type that would be handled entirely by dialogue on television today—were remarkably sophisticated in dealing with primarily verbal situations in entirely visual terms.

Mal St. Clair's *Are Parents People?* (1925), which managed to be charming, wistful, and even joyous while dealing with the serious subject of divorce, was one of the most adept of all these films. We are almost a reel into the film before the first sub-title appears, yet the film has told us all we need to know about the relationship between the married couple (Adolph Menjou and Florence Vidor) and why it was deteriorating, and told us via images and editing. Later on, the decisions of the teen-age daughter (another charming performance from Betty Bronson) are conveyed by close-ups of her shoulders straightening or her ankles crossing, uncrossing, and then setting themselves determinedly as the decision is made. The camera itself does not move in *Are Parents People?*, but it records subtle nuances on the faces of the protagonists and doesn't underestimate the perception of the audience. Some of the funniest bits of pantomime are played in extreme long shot. When, after a wholly innocent night together, teenage daughter and prospective boyfriend are interrogated by the worried parents, the situation, the question, and the response are carried without either a title or a close-up—merely daughter and boyfriend successively shaking their heads vigorously in response to an anxious parental inquiry. The film also includes a devastating satire of the Barrymore of *Beau Brummel*, a superb piece of pantomime by Andre Beranger, cast as an egocentric movie actor.

Sophisticated comedies of the caliber of *Are Parents People?*, *Woman of the World*, *The King on Main Street*, and *Gentleman of Paris* continued unabated until the end of the silent era. Lubitsch was the leader, though not necessarily the master of the genre, since he took time out for romantic and dramatic films too: the lovely, lyrical *The Student Prince* and the dramatic *The Patriot*. However, with the coming of sound, many of the best directors of this kind of froth—Mal St. Clair and Monta Bell, in particular—faltered somewhat and lost ground. Lubitsch, on the other hand, found dialogue and music the additional weapons that he needed, and in films like *The Smiling Lieutenant* (1931) and especially *Trouble in Paradise* (1932), he established himself indisputably as the master of the genre.

Suddenly the mid-1920's movie theater became a very happy place. Comedy was everywhere, and in all forms. Between the sophisticated marital farces of Lubitsch and the comedy-thrill classics of Harold Lloyd lay the more down-to-earth (yet no less appealing) comedies of Reginald Denny, the vigorous slapstick actioners of Larry Semon (who never made a "classic," but whose stunts and high-powered dives into goo and mud created non-stop laughs, much to Keaton's chagrin, since he could never quite figure out how Semon achieved such results), and the sometimes (though not always) more sedate vehicles for the ladies: Gloria Swanson, Colleen Moore, Constance Talmadge, and even Mary Pickford, whose *My Best Girl* was a particularly relaxed and enjoyable romantic comedy of 1927.

Raymond Griffith managed to combine the urbane sophistication of a Menjou with the dry wit of Keaton and the comedy-thrill climaxes of Lloyd. His *Paths to Paradise* (1925) offered just such a combination.

Keaton and Lloyd were at their prime. Harry Langdon, a taste for whom had to be acquired (he was the Carl Dreyer of the clowns), rose to fame and fell to obscurity in the gap between the two Chaplin films, *The Gold Rush* and *The Circus*. Newcomer W. C. Fields never achieved the success in his many silent films that he did in sound, though not because he was deprived of his voice. Most of his silents were really dry-runs for his talkies, and like the vaudevillian that he was, he needed time to hone and polish his material. Too, the rough-hewn quality of his films and his deliberately abrasive screen character—the very qualities that made his films unique in the 1930's, when they were very much *of* their time—worked against them in the 1920's, when comedy was judged by the glossy, professional Hollywood standards that Fields' East Coast-manufactured films could not match. When stars from shorts left for features, they were replaced by others—Laurel and Hardy, Will Rogers, Charley Chase. Incredibly, they were all individual and unique; their styles and material occasionally overlapped, but that was all. The relatively censorship-free screen left them free to tackle as many sacred cows as they liked—religion, politics, race, public figures, homosexuality, drug addiction, disease and deformity, old age, and death. There were occasional appalling lapses of taste—but they were few, and in any case, largely confined to the films of dozens of lesser comics who worked for independent companies and who were rightly forgotten in a year or two. But that freedom gave bite, zest, and maturity to the films of Laurel and Hardy, Keaton, and Lloyd in particular—and with everyone and everything fair game, *nobody* was being discriminated against!

One of the most surprising things of all is not only that the great comedians of the 1920's rarely overlapped in their stories or gags, but that when they repeated or reworked their own material, they did so in a unique way. Virtually every Harold Lloyd film climaxed with a chase—yet so well integrated were those chases into the demands of the story that one has no trouble at all recalling which chase and which specific gags appeared in any one film. Keaton's *College* (1927) inevitably trespasses on the territory of Lloyd's *The Freshman* (1925), but there is no sense of duplication—not least because Lloyd's eternal optimist produces different motivations and gags than Keaton's permanent pessimist. Laurel and Hardy's *Liberty* (1929) spends most of its footage atop a high building, still under construction, and does so almost as amusingly as Harold Lloyd in *Never Weaken* (1922), yet the one gag that comes instantly to mind from that film is actually a more typical Laurel and Hardy gag on ground level. They have inadvertently donned each other's trousers—and their efforts to switch garments result in their constantly being discovered in taxis or behind garbage cans, at the crouch, an apologetic-embarrassed smile on their faces, in the act of removing their trousers!

There is no point in even exploring that oft-asked question of who was the best or the funniest of the silent comedians. If "success" is determined in terms of laugh reaction alone, then Laurel and Hardy and Larry Semon would undoubtedly head the list. If all-round artistry were taken into consideration, then Chaplin would undoubtedly occupy the first position. If box-office grosses provided the criterion, then Lloyd would be leading the parade—but one should not forget that Lloyd got into feature comedies *first*, and made more of them than Chaplin or Keaton. Perhaps the only safe generalization that can be made is that Keaton was the *least* appreciated in his time, and has survived the best. Keaton's dour comedy, his dry put-downs of women,* his resolute rejection of pathos, and his generally slower pacing took him well out of the mainstream of visual comedy in the twenties. Even the critics gave his films a kind of grudging praise, indicating that he was offering "more of the same," and then turning around to recommend some other film for "real laughs."

Keaton's films always demanded a great deal from the audience. While this is true to a degree of all silent films, in that audiences had to use their imaginations and emotions constantly, it was especially true of Keaton's work. Frequently he would spend a long time on elaborate build-ups to gags, the payoff of which might be nothing more than a facial expression which in itself could be interpreted in more than one way. If the audience failed to pay attention during that build-up, or worse, looked away from the screen during those few

* Laurel and Hardy, with their constant vendetta against women, and wives in particular, W. C. Fields, with his perennial battle against nagging wives and mothers-in-law, and Keaton, with his usually helpless and rather stupid heroines, undoubtedly aliented a large percentage of the female audience, whereas Lloyd, Chaplin, and Langdon attracted and embraced them by their attitudes toward women, which consisted of putting them on pedestals and worshipping them.

seconds of gag payoff, then minutes of screen time would have been wasted. That audience not only had to be prepared to think, but to think quickly. A typically ambiguous gag occurs in *Seven Chances* (1925). At the height of the climactic chase, Keaton rushes to the side of a cliff and jumps to the top of a tree, just as that tree is in the process of being felled by a woodcutter. The tree crashes to the ground, and Keaton disentangles himself from the wreckage and sprints off again. The woodcutter looks on in bemusement, though since the gag is shot in extreme long shot, as was Keaton's method, to show all of the action and its relationship to the locale, one first has to *imagine* the facial expression of the woodsman, which is suggested only by his bodily stance. There are at least three interpretations and questions to the gag: What on earth motivated Buster to jump to the treetop? (The woodcutter has no knowledge of his pursuers.) Was Buster in the tree-top as a matter of course, and if so, why? Was Buster standing on the ground, in the path of the tree, and if so, why didn't the woodcutter see him? One only has a second or two to ponder these ambiguities before the chase is underway again.

On other occasions, the audience has to *anticipate* in order to get the full impact of a gag, and unlike Laurel and Hardy, whose gags *depend* on anticipation, and who carefully planted clues for the audience, Keaton flatters his audience by assuming they will be astute enough to anticipate, and plants no clues at all. An illustrative gag appears in one of Keaton's most charming and funny comedies, *Our Hospitality* (1924). It is a story of Southern feuding, and at one point Keaton is being pursued through the mountains by a member of the enemy clan (played by Francis X. Bushman, Jr.). Many of the gags, involving heights and a waterfall, are spectacular and mechanically ingenious, but one of the best gags is constructed solely through cutting and involves a knowledge of editing structure for the audience to anticipate the gag. Keaton is marooned on a ledge, and his pursuer throws him a rope, the other end of which is tied to his own waist. Buster secures the loose end to his own midsection and waits to be hoisted to safety. But now that Bushman has Keaton a prisoner and can control his movements, he takes careful aim with his revolver. Keaton instinctively yanks on the rope, and there is a sigh of relief on his face as he sees the rope above him slacken and fall, an indication that his antagonist is on the way down. Seconds later the body hurtles past, and Keaton's expression is a subtle one of relief, yet *without* vindictive joy in the thought that Bushman is probably falling to his death. A split second later comes the realization that they are still roped together, and that Bushman's fate will rapidly be his own. The climax of the gag is really the expression of resigned desperation on Keaton's face. A second later he is yanked out of the frame, and the last shot of the gag is a miniature, from above, of the two bodies hurtling downward—but to water, and presumed safety. The whole gag takes far less time to play than it does to read, and depends entirely on anticipating and understanding that split-second facial change of Keaton's.

While many of Keaton's sight gags and chases are extraordinarily elaborate and even spectacular, they are also unusually well controlled and disciplined. Often, Keaton the director will partially nullify the laughs coming to Keaton the performer by throwing in a second-rate gag, deliberately designed to reduce laughter, give the audience a momentary breathing spell, and allow the tension of the chase to build all over again. Too, some of the gags (especially in *Sherlock Jr.* of 1924) are so complex that the audience's attention is split between a laugh reaction and figuring out how the gag was achieved. Keaton was always consistent with his gags; they had to be *possible,* and the audience had to see that no trick was involved. In *Sherlock Jr.* Keaton even dissolves the side of a house at one point, revealing it to be a set, letting the audience in on the mechanics of the gag involved, and *still* making it funny. Where Keaton gags *were* frankly impossible, they always took place within the framework of a dream, making them somehow logical again within that context. Most of Keaton's comedies *had* a dream-like quality which often extended into surrealism. Any one of the frames of a tuxedo-and-tails Keaton, pursued down real Los Angeles streets by hundreds of women dressed as brides seeking to claim him as a husband (a scene from *Seven Chances*), could be taken out of context and turned into a still of genuine Dada-ist proportions.

Keaton's surreal flair often extended to the grammar of the film itself. In *Seven Chances,* instead of compressing time in the traditional manner by fading out and fading in, his image remained constant on the screen, and only the backgrounds faded out and in. So when the new image arrived, he was already thrust into the action, as though impatient to get started and merely waiting for the mechanics of film to

catch up with him. Keaton is really one of the major victims and tragedies of the sound film. His whole screen persona depended on his
inability to communicate with the rest of the world. Like a man from
an alien world, quite unaccustomed to human logic and foibles, he
floundered around, overlooking the obvious, harnessing the equipment of the world to his own ends, pursuing his objective in a straight
line via methods that might seem absurd to normal humans, expecting
little because he really understands little, and yet somehow, and
usually quite accidentally, coming out on top—much to his own surprise. This unemotional, unspoken (Keaton used few dialogue titles
in his films, and moved his lips so little that even they seemed to be
thoughts rather than words), and of course, largely visual style was
rendered obsolete when sound arrived. Once the world around him
spoke, there was no logical reason for Keaton not to speak, and his
whole character had to change. Co-starring him with Jimmy Durante
merely meant that most of the dialogue went to that fast-talking
comedian, leaving Keaton in even more of a vacuum. Keaton's sound
films, over which he had no personal control, all had moments of inspiration, but on the whole were a sad end to a starring career. Although active in films until the end of his life (on Feb. 1, 1966), his
last thirty years were taken up with a sad succession of two-reel comedy quickies of varying quality (saddest of all were the cheap Columbia two-reelers, where his brilliant classic routines were re-shaped and
rushed through at the pace of hectic pratfalls and crude slapstick),
occasional leads in independent features, rewarding guest spots in
bigger features, and toward the very end, some interesting supporting
roles and appearances in documentaries.

Once, in 1934, it seemed that a solution toward salvaging the basic
Keaton character might have been found. He starred in a French
comedy titled *Le Roi des Champs Elysees.* Unreleased in the United
States, it was a rather charming little comedy that started out like a
René Clair farce and gradually turned into a traditional Keaton comedy as his role took over, and he assumed some control over the gags.
But the French seemed to have no conception of *building* gags. The
pace was too fast, and Keaton appeared to have had no time, on a
short shooting schedule, to do more than improve what was there, and
create a little out of virtually nothing. Moreover, Buster played a native
Frenchman, so the old dilemma of his inability to communicate with

the world around him was not resolved. While it wouldn't have been a permanent solution, the idea of Buster as an American turned loose in a country whose language he couldn't understand would at least have provided a logical excuse for the retention of his basic screen character in the world of sound. In any event, *Le Roi des Champs Elysees* was a more satisfying finale to his starring career than some of the more ambitious American talkies that immediately preceded it. Keaton himself, seeming to sense that this would be his last starring feature,† apparently decided to write Finis to his character on an optimistic note, and in the final scene embraces his girl friend and, before the final kiss, presents a beaming smile to the audience—the only time he had really smiled on screen except for one or two isolated examples in his earliest shorts, when the smile occasionally appeared by accident before the pessimistic Keaton image was fully fashioned.

Harold Lloyd's comedies have been underrated for years—perhaps because too few of them have been available for re-appraisal. Then, too, those that have been available have been studied by critics and historians in the isolation of private screenings, and Lloyd films, above all others, need an audience. In fact, Lloyd's uncanny knowledge of audience reaction was built into the films. He knew what would create a *universal* laugh, and his films were paced to that laughter and the subsequent development of gags constructed around the assumption of the initial response to that gag. Lloyd has been attacked as being "mechanical," as being unfunny in himself, as lacking the individual pantomimic genius of a Keaton or an Oliver Hardy. All of this is true. His films *are* mechanical; they are constructed by teams of gag-men, to the extent that a director on a Lloyd film is almost reduced to the status of a floorwalker. Some of the best Lloyd films were directed by virtual nonentities, the lesser ones sometimes by first-rate directors. Often the directorial credit seemed to be merely a matter of whose turn it was to get the title. Seeing a Lloyd film alone can be a depressing experience. Lloyd seems to be striving almost desperately to be funny at all times; the mechanics of setting up a gag and writing in all the coincidences and tangential incidents required to make it work seem

† There actually was one subsequent Keaton film, made in England in 1935, titled *The Invader* and known as *An Old Spanish Custom* in the United States. It re-used old Keaton gags and had moments of charm, but on the whole was far beneath the already unexacting standards of *Le Roi des Champs Elysses*.

extremely labored. Yet all of these things that seem unfunny and transparent when seen *without* an audience come magnificently to life
before an audience. What seemed unfunny and obvious now seems
amusing; what seemed merely amusing now becomes hilarious. Moreover, for the most part what worked in the twenties *still* works, so
shrewd and accurate was Lloyd's gauging of what is funny to a mass
audience. Lloyd's own charm, his innate optimism, and his aggressive
pursuit of success, elements so typical of the 1920's, all combine to give
his films a perennial freshness and zest, despite the mathematical way
in which they were made. One can only regret that theatrical revival of
Lloyd's films has been minimal. In the mid-1970's they were sold to
television, thus depriving them of that mass audience, and the joy of
shared laughter, that they need so badly.

Harry Langdon never had the mass appeal of Lloyd nor the wit of
Keaton. For a while, however, he did appear to be tapping the Chaplin
audience, probably because he was closest to Chaplin in spirit, and
also because his best films—*Tramp Tramp Tramp, The Strong Man,*
and *Long Pants,* all of 1926–27—came while Chaplin was off the screen.
Langdon's little man had the nobility of Chaplin and the passivity of
Keaton. He was an optimist, forever being flattened by fate, but with
such an innate (if unjustified) faith in humanity that he always
bounced back for more. His unique little wave of greeting—uncertain
yet hopeful, accompanied by a smile that was sincere yet at the same
time tentative—summed up most of his screen personality. But there
were other, more fragile characteristics, too. His character was that of
the grown man who is mentally almost a child, who knows about life—
including sex and marriage—but doesn't really want to accept it. Langdon's understanding of the child mentality caused his screen character
to behave in childish ways at times, consumed by petty jealousy and
vindictive spitefulness. It could be and usually was a most endearing
portrait, but unless rigorously controlled, it could slip into a kind of
infantilism that was tasteless. Directors Frank Capra and Harry Edwards understood both Langdon and his screen character, and did
keep him well under control in the three genuinely classic comedies
referred to above. Langdon, however, was more prone to listen to the
suggestions of gag-man and writer (and later director) Arthur Ripley,
an extremely talented man whose black outlook on life nevertheless
made him far more suitable for the anarchistic comedies of W. C.

Fields and, much later, the *film noir* thrillers of the 1940's. Even before Langdon took over total control of his films, writing and directing them himself—and losing his tenuous hold on both his character and his public—the writing was on the wall. The last of his three classics, *Long Pants,* was also the blackest and the most extreme. It was the closest that silent comedy ever came to a Luis Buñuel type of *noir* comedy, with much of the footage devoted to Langdon's attempts to murder his bride so that he can take up with a prostitute whom he feels compelled to "save." The film winds up with a savage underworld bloodbath, after which a chastened Harry returns home.

Langdon was the least demanding of all the major clowns, needing neither to make the sacrifices of Chaplin, to achieve the financial successes of Lloyd, or to "prove" himself, like Keaton. He was quite happy to emerge from each film as a relative failure, accepting contentment rather than success. In some ways, his was the most complex screen character of all the great clowns, with roots in both vaudeville and non-comedic films, and later echoes in unrelated fields. Much of his eloquent pantomime and his facial expressions seemed to derive directly from the Lillian Gish of the earlier Griffiths. One can place pantomimic sequences from Griffith's *True Heart Susie* (1919) side by side with similar sequences in *The Strong Man* (1927) and find Langdon mimicking Gish with as deadly an accuracy as she was also mimicked by Marion Davies in that delightful and much underrated 1928 comedy, *The Patsy.* Later on, in the post-World War II Italian cinema, especially *La Strada,* one finds Guilietta Massina playing Gish-like waif roles, but basing her pantomime more on Langdon than on Gish. And in the forties, animator Chuck Jones made a bizarre but quite brilliant little series of cartoons for Warners featuring a little black jungle boy, Inki, and his nemesis, a myna bird. Inki's naïve innocence and trust were clearly borrowed from the Langdon character, complete with the trusting hand salute. Although Langdon's decline in the sound period was as swift, sudden, and tragic as Keaton's, his influence was not inconsiderable—and, like Keaton, some of his better work in the thirties was as a writer and gag-man, contributing to the comedies of others.

The work of Langdon, Chaplin, Keaton, Lloyd, and, on a lesser plateau, W. C. Fields, was supplemented by an incredibly prolific volume of work from lesser clowns in the twenties. Undoubtedly the most consistently high-class body of comedic work came from the studios of Hal Roach, which produced the Laurel and Hardy, Charley Chase, Will Rogers, and Our Gang comedies, along with supplementary series. Roach's output on the whole was vastly superior to Sennett's. It encompassed the best of Sennett slapstick and sight-gag material, but added logical plot lines and a far less frenetic pace. The best of the Roach films were not only sophisticated and witty but often visually extremely subtle. Moreover, many of Roach's directors— F. Richard Jones, Leo McCarey, and later on, George Stevens—were meticulous craftsmen and men of great taste who later became key directors of sophisticated comedies of the thirties. The finest of the Roach silent two-reelers of the mid and late twenties—*Sundown Limited* with Our Gang, such satiric Will Rogers comedies as *Don't Park There* and *Uncensored Movies,* Charley Chase's‡ brilliant (and the word is not used loosely) *Mighty Like a Moose* or *Bad Boy,* Laurel and Hardy's often violent but always charming minor masterpieces (*Putting Pants on Philip, Two Tars*)—can and do rank with the best work of the major feature-comedy stars.

Because of the ready market for comedy in the twenties, supply far exceeded realistic demand. Many potentially major comics were just lost in the shuffle. The laconic duck-waddle, and off-hand brashness of Lloyd Hamilton was unique. He was a major and extremely popular star of two-reelers in the twenties, elevated by some to a near-Chaplin status. Yet few of his films have survived, and his appeal today is far from universal. The acrobatic Lupino Lane, from the British music-halls (and as big a star there, until the mid 1940's, as Danny Kaye or Al Jolson), apart from appearing in semi-straight roles for Lubitsch and Griffith, made a whole series of endearing and often lightning-paced two-reel comedies, many of which were built around vaudeville skits and trick sets of Lane's own conception. His best films, however, were satires which used his acrobatic skills logically: *At Sword's Point,* a brilliant if belated spoof of Fairbanks' *The Three Musketeers* (1921) and *Montie of the Mounted,* a rousing burlesque of the western genre.

But for all of the great comics—and the lesser but still deserving ones who have been forgotten—there were nonentities and mediocrities who deserved the obscurity that they earned. There is nothing sadder than

‡ Chase was also a very talented gag-man, writer and director as well as a player of debonair and meticulous timing.

watching a silent comedy without talent, in which the title-writers work overtime to inject humor via pun-titles because nothing on screen is very funny, and in which the comedians run around and fall down and mug because they have no material to work with. The Fox Company made a whole series of two-reel comedies in the twenties which were surprisingly elaborate and off-beat but which, because they had no comic star of individuality or flair, were (for the most part) dragged down to the level of the cheapest independents. Cheapness of production costs was the only incentive to make these abysmal comedies; low rental fees were the only incentives to book them. But they did find a place on rural middle-of-the-week bills, where an exhibitor needed a comedy to round out a program and couldn't afford to pay for a Keaton or a Laurel and Hardy. Ironically, because these poor comedies were played so little, many of the prints have survived in pristine condition. It is often much easier to find a mint-condition print of a Clyde Cook or a Bud Duncan comedy than it is of a Keaton or a Chaplin. The volume of these comedy mediocrities is so enormous that, statistically, they would provide invaluable ammunition for anyone wanting to demolish the myth of the Great Golden Age of American Screen Comedy. Fortunately, they are scattered, and the comedians who played in them—and stole so shamelessly from Keaton or Laurel and Hardy or Chaplin—disappeared so quickly that only a computer could compile damaging evidence from them. And mediocre and even horrendous as they are, they still deserve to be sifted and re-examined. Every so often out of a welter of tenth-rate material, one finds an obscure comedy with a Walter Hiers or a Billy Dooley or a Monty Banks that is really first-rate. Among them, too, one finds the interesting footnotes to history: a film titled by Charles MacArthur, a film photographed by Lee Garmes, or a comedy of surprising modernity in its theme, even if its conception is not matched by its execution. Above all, one cannot afford to judge a film purely by its label, to assume that an independent quickie is necessarily of inferior quality. Al Christie's independently made 1920 feature comedy *So Long Letty*, though based on a stage play, was infinitely superior to and much funnier than Warners' talkie remake of almost a decade later—and was distinguished by one of the most remarkable comedy performances seen on the silent screen. T. Roy Barnes, in a Bob Hope-type role seemingly crying out for fast-talking dialogue delivery, by sheer weight of personality made dialogue seem totally unnecessary. (Later, in W. C. Fields' sound classic *It's a Gift* (1934), Barnes, as the aggressive salesman looking for Karl LaFong early in the morning, while everyone was still trying to sleep, showed how well he could handle dialogue too.) The golden age of comedy ran unabated from 1922 until the end of the silent period. True, it slowed down a little, as did all Hollywood pacing, but that slowing-down process merely refined the comic art. Some of the best silent screen comedy is to be found at the end of the decade, well after sound had been established. Laurel and Hardy's *Big Business*, made in 1929, is possibly both the simplest and the funniest comedy ever made.

The coming of sound didn't kill the sight-gag. In fact, Laurel and Hardy (in particular) were able to harness exaggerated or stylized sound in a manner that actually enhanced it. But certainly sound wrought tremendous changes in visual comedy. Much was lost. Keaton's *Seven Chances* (1924) or Harold Lloyd's *The Kid Brother* (1926)—arguably those two comedians' finest works—would never have been possible in the sound film. Yet sound wrought beneficial change as much as it brought about regrettable loss; the comedy became far more than responsibility of the writer and director than that of the performer. If we lost *Seven Chances, The Kid Brother, The Strong Man,* and *Hands Up,* we also gained *20th Century, It's A Gift, Duck Soup, Blessed Event,* and *Love Me Tonight.*

16

The Peak Years

There can be little argument that, both as art and as entertainment, the American silent film began its peak years around 1923, climaxing in 1927–28. At that point, both the dominant influence of the German cinema and a slightly less commercial and more artistic outlook on the doomed silent film combined to make that last year or two prior to the advent of sound a kind of "buffer" period. In this period, Hollywood's creative artists were able to work with reduced opposition and supervision on projects that at any other time would have been considered uncommercial.

Paradoxically, while this was one of the American cinema's most dynamic periods, it is difficult to find truly representative films—that is, films that reflect both the skills and the arts of which Hollywood was then capable, and also the times in which they were made.

In the Depression years of the 1930's, many films did reflect the urgency of the country's plight, whether in terms of social criticism (*I Am a Fugitive From a Chain Gang*), comic satire (*Modern Times*), romanticism (*Man's Castle*), whimsy (*One More Spring*), screwball comedy (*My Man Godfrey*), or the musical (*42nd Street*). All of these films (and many more) produced between 1931 and 1936 spotlighted the Depression, discussed it seriously, offered solutions, or laughed at it when there seemed no other alternative. Toward the end of the 1930's, anti-war and then anti-Nazi films appeared. Films as diverse as *Blockade, Watch on the Rhine, Of Mice and Men,* and *Sullivan's*

Travels—all made between 1938 and 1943—were intended as essentially "entertainment" films. Yet all had something important to say, and any one of them, without necessarily being a great film, could be held up, out of context, as a mirror of its time.

Very few films of the 1920's could serve this purpose, except in the most superficial way. *Our Dancing Daughters* (1928), while often cited as the "definitive" jazz-age film, is really no more than the definitive record of what MGM—a glossy studio run by rich executives with very little contact with everyday life—*thought* the jazz age was all about. *Sullivan's Travels* (1941) deals with poverty (the Depression lingered, if on a less drastic level, until America's wartime economy abolished it), racial issues, a film director's responsibility to Hollywood, Hollywood's responsibility to its audience and the world, and other side issues—all within the framework of comedy. In a sense, it was Fellini's *8½* much earlier, and on a broader and certainly less self-centered level. Certainly *Sullivan's Travels* tells far more about America, and Hollywood's importance and relationship to it, in the 1940's, than almost any film of the 1920's told about the America of its period. (King Vidor's *The Crowd* (1928) is an exception worth noting.)

This is not solely the fault of Hollywood, which in the 1920's was admittedly more conscious of its role as purveyor of mass entertainment. It is certainly partially the fault of the times themselves, which chose not to be too dramatic. There were, to be sure, important issues, but they tended to be either abstract or localized. President Woodrow Wilson's failure to lead the United States into the League of Nations may well have had long-range effects, but in the 1920's it seemed to be more a matter for political debate than popular concern. After a long fight, women achieved the vote and at least nominal equality; their cause seemed to have been won. The resurgence of the Ku Klux Klan was disturbing, but not frightening. That one could not buy an alcoholic drink legally was perhaps a gross violation of basic rights; yet since one could buy that drink illegally, there was no reason to be up in arms about the suppression of freedom.

Basically, it was a happy and uneventful period in terms of issues. America, putting the war behind it, was relaxing and enjoying a new prosperity. The need to make good, and the many ways to do it, were the major issues of the day—and of course, the movies *did* reflect this basic urge, most notably and obviously in the comedies of Harold

Lloyd. In one sense, Lindbergh's historic flight to Paris was a real-life extension of and climax to the Harold Lloyd success drive. In *Cat People* (1942), the hero complains that he cannot deal with a complicated marital problem. He points out that he had "a grand time as a kid" and that his parents were great. He concludes somewhat lamely, "My problem is, I've just never been unhappy." In a rough sense, his predicament was paralleled by Hollywood in the 1920's. America "just wasn't unhappy," and Hollywood could deal with it only in positive or optimistic terms. Grim films were made, and tragic ones—but they were unrelated to the mainstream of life, as if Hollywood had to seek out the primitive and the sordid (via films like *Stark Love* or *Greed*) or reconstruct it, in the larger-than-life adaptations of plays or classic novels, which rarely seemed to be set on American soil.

After the impressive but somewhat top-heavy films of the early twenties—*Scaramouche*, *Robin Hood*, *Little Lord Fauntleroy*—there was a refreshing willingness (perhaps spurred by exhibitor complaints) to bring movies down to a more reasonable length. True, the pace of films continued to be slow, and prestige continued to be indivisible from length. The "big" pictures continued to be very long ones: *Seventh Heaven* was twelve reels, *Beau Geste* eleven, *What Price Glory?* twelve, *The Patent Leather Kid* twelve, and *The Big Parade* and *Wings* thirteen reels each. Even these were frequently trimmed down by a reel or more when they left their first-run and road-show engagements and went into general release. The well-crafted and unhurried Clarence Brown films for Universal in the mid-1920's—*Smouldering Fires* and *The Goose Woman*—managed to tell their stories well in seven or eight reels. And the stars, whose films were essentially light romantic or comic vehicles, often limited themselves to six reels, despite their box-office importance. Clara Bow's *Mantrap* and Colleen Moore's *Orchids and Ermine* (1926 and 1927, respectively) were both sprightly films that would certainly have suffered had they been prolonged beyond a six-reel length.

Even Douglas Fairbanks, so immovable an advocate of the long film, and so concerned with "stature" via interwoven sub-plots and excessive sub-titles in the Griffith manner, seemed convinced in the mid-1920's that comparative brevity, apart from being more economical, was an asset to his films. *The Thief of Bagdad* (1924) ran for fourteen reels—handsome, awe-inspiring, full of camera trickery and incredible production design, but with only occasional snatches of action, and those dependent more on novelty (Doug's fights with various monsters, the flying carpet scenes) and the spectacle of mass action (the conjuring up of the magical army in the climax) than on Doug's specialty: physical prowess combined with a sense of humor. *Don Q, Son of Zorro* (1925) was reduced in length, but only by a reel. And it was even more drastically reduced in action; virtually nothing happened except for a leap or two until the reasonably exciting but too-long-withheld climax. However, *The Black Pirate* (1926) was down to a much more reasonable nine reels, and the picture, apart from having the novelty of the new two-color Technicolor, benefited tremendously. The old sense of fun crept back; it wasn't a spoof, but it was much larger than life, and action and derring-do dominated. The titles lost the portentiousness of the prior Fairbanks films and became part of the fun. The basic unreality of the silent film enabled *The Black Pirate* to be violent, and to kid its own violence at the same time, as in a sequence where the hapless captives of a merchant ship are shepherded together and surrounded by a circular trail of gunpowder (leading to the ammunition supply in the hold), while one of the pirates jovially pantomimes the explosion that will seal their doom in a moment or two. One of the prisoners swallows a valuable ring to keep it out of the pirates' hands, but his act is observed, and a swarthy pirate leads him out of camera range, cutlass at the ready. Moments later he returns alone, nonchalantly wiping the blood off the retrieved ring.

Even better than *The Black Pirate* was Fairbanks' next film, *The Gaucho* (1927). This film, too, maintained a relatively short running time, though the footage had begun to creep up again slightly, due no doubt to a more serious and involved plot than usual. At the time, *The Gaucho* was not considered one of Fairbanks' best films. Doubtless his tiltings with religion had much to do with this assessment. Fairbanks threw himself into everything wholeheartedly, and if the story contained religious elements, then he would work them out in detail—complete with a vision of the Virgin Mary (played by Mary Pickford), modern miracles, and a rather unpleasant and realistically depicted sub-plot involving a leprosy victim who passes his affliction on to Fairbanks. However, to compensate for the grimmer elements of the film, Fairbanks' agile stunting (backed up by some astute doubling from Richard Talmadge), his ballet-like grace in moving, riding, or both, and some very funny comedy moments with a tempestuous girl friend (Lupe Velez) gave the film a joyous flavor, despite its serious undertones. It also contained some magnificently smooth and convincing glass shots and an extremely handsome production design. In a later period, when audiences were no longer confused by the sudden switching of mood and the ultra-rapid segues from slapstick to tragedy, *The Gaucho* would probably have been a much bigger hit.

Undoubtedly the artistic highlight of the mid-1920's, and still one of the most famous—or notorious—*cause célèbres* of film history was Erich von Stroheim's *Greed,* begun in 1923, put through a long editing process in 1924, and finally premiered in December of that year.

Stroheim's career had been stormy and somewhat desperate from the beginning. As an extra and bit player in early Griffith films (and in Fairbanks, Norma Talmadge, and other star vehicles produced under the Griffith banner), he had constantly sought to enlarge both his parts and his value to his employers as an assistant, research man, technical adviser, and general factotum. Although he would later develop an impressive and even warmly human acting style, subtlety was not a strong point in his early days. Apart from using grotesque make-up, scars, and eyepatches to make his often villainous characters more colorful, he over-acted outrageously. The sheer weight of his personality dominated scenes where his character was only a minor role and, as in *Old Heidelberg* (1916), he mercilessly upstaged Dorothy Gish and Wallace Reid.

Stroheim's initial film as a director (he also wrote it and starred) was a personal, artistic, and commercial success. Few careers have been launched as auspiciously as his was with *Blind Husbands* in 1919. It was strong material with an inherently sexual theme, yet also with a framework of melodrama that appealed to popular tastes. The unconventional yet straightforward plot line dealt with an American doctor vacationing in the Alps with his wife. The husband is a decent man, but dull, taking his marriage—and his wife—for granted. The wife, likewise an honorable person, is nevertheless sexually frustrated and thus prone to be receptive to the seductive advances of an Austrian army officer, played by Stroheim. There is considerable subtlety in the writing and in the juxtaposition of characters, and a powerful climax of confrontation and retribution atop a mountain peak. Its excessive "moral compensation," which called for the villain to more than pay for his sins, was not a sop to the still fairly liberal screen censorship. It was a trait of austere morality in Stroheim's own make-up that was to crop up time and time again in his films. Above all, it was a film that was made reasonably economically, and showed strong self-discipline. Stroheim's next film, *The Devil's Passkey* (1920), was apparently an equally adept film (its loss today is one of the major gaps in film history), well received critically and commercially. With *Foolish Wives* (1921), however, Stroheim embarked on a curious pattern of seeming self-destruction: deliberately flaunting instructions and contracts, and shooting reels and reels of material that, by virtue of both length and content, could never survive past a first rough cut. Its plot is virtually an extension of *Blind Husbands*, set this time in Monte Carlo, with an American diplomat and his bored wife prey to the attentions of the bogus Count Karamzin, again played by Stroheim. But whereas, in *Blind Husbands*, Stroheim's villain was merely a lecherous opportunist, here he is blatantly a criminal (involved in, among other shady deals, counterfeiting) and a degenerate, accompanied by cronies only slightly less degraded than himself. While there was a measure of sympathy for the Stroheim of *Blind Husbands*, here there was none.

Undoubtedly, many of Stroheim's excesses were magnified for publicity purposes. Others may well have been justified for the subliminally realistic effect they had on certain scenes or the actors playing them. But the long, involved sub-plots and the stress on degeneracy, depravity, sex, and specifically bordello scenes, were obviously futile elements to try to incorporate into film at that time. With the exception of *Greed*, not his own plot material, Stroheim seemed to have only one basic plot in him, and that a kind of wish-fulfillment fantasy of the aristocratic court-life of old Vienna. From *Merry Go Round* (1923) on, his major films other than *Greed—The Merry Widow* (1925), *The Wedding March* (1927), and *Queen Kelly* (1928)—were all variations on the same theme, and each one was approached as though it would be Stroheim's last chance. All of the previous themes and characters were refurbished and new excesses added. The story was the same in every case. Stroheim was either fired or removed from final control, or the pictures were simply abandoned prior to completion (in the case of the last two), and watered-down, salvaged versions prepared for release. Unlike Griffith, who was prepared to compromise—and had a long and productive career because of it, with many films produced and released wholly as Griffith conceived them—Stroheim was not prepared to compromise. Although he was doubtless hurt and frustrated, he probably also enjoyed the role of artistic martyr—and if his films were as near and dear to him as children, as he claimed, one wonders why he didn't take the precaution of making and preserving at least one full print of all of his films before the inevitable cutting began. Too, his one film that was released with minimal tampering, *The Merry Widow* (some extravagant bordello scenes were cut, along with some wedding night exotica, but the basic structure of the film was left relatively intact), was, although a commercial success, a bore.

Greed, based on the Frank Norris novel *McTeague*, was a story that had always obsessed Stroheim, who claimed to have read it while virtually starving as an extra in his early days with Griffith. He may have read it, or he may have seen the earlier version of 1915. The latter seems quite probable, since, while no copies of the film are known to exist, stills show a remarkable resemblance to images in the Stroheim film. His version, claiming to utilize every single aspect of Norris' novel (but also enlarging on it to add visual interpretations of his own), was made initially in forty-two reels, cut by Stroheim himself to twenty-four, further cut by Rex Ingram—a director Stroheim respected—to eighteen, and finally released in ten reels. Out of all this has come the legend of a "butchered masterpiece," and no doubt much powerful material has been lost. Certainly the extant stills of those missing scenes so indicate, and whet one's appetite. On the other hand, the ten-reel version as released is definitely a masterpiece, and one can have nothing but admiration for the editors (whom Stroheim dismissed with such contempt) who eliminated those final eight reels (after Stroheim's and Ingram's initial cuts) and still came up with such a powerful and coherent work. Admittedly, there are obvious gaps and a lack of subtlety and motivation. The one basic cut, in a narrative sense, which moves from McTeague's murder of his wife to his flight into the desert—eliminating a whole sub-plot and several months of time—is rather jarring. And the many subtle visual symbols that are used throughout (the two canaries in the cage, for example, that parallel the relationship between McTeague and his wife) are incomplete and sometimes rather heavyhanded when used arbitrarily.

On the whole, however, the theme of *Greed* is concentrated in a ten-reel version in a way that would have been impossible in the longer version that Stroheim conceived. Further, in its present version, the film has been hailed as a masterpiece of realism. "Naturalism" might well be a better word, and certainly the film tries to convey the raw naturalism of an Emile Zola. With the original version's long, nightmarish sub-plot and surrealist dream sequences,* the film's consistency and cohesion on a naturalistic level might have been drastically upset. And much as one would wish to see Stroheim's original version of the film (which is constantly being reported in unlikely corners of the world, like a nitrate Holy Grail), one must bear in mind that a number of film-makers *did* see the full forty-two reels in their initial screening. Apart from proclaiming themselves over-awed, as well they might be, none of them ever felt constrained to rush into print (then or later) to describe or defend what he saw. Given audience tastes and exhibitor requirements of the day, Stroheim's belief that an eight-hour version (possibly shown in two halves) or even a four-hour version would be feasible seems naïve indeed. Even today excessively long movies, from *Gone With the Wind* on, have had to have cast-iron star and entertainment values built into them—something that *Greed* most certainly did not have—and attempts to merchandise them (i.e., the Russian *War and Peace*) via either marathon one-night sessions or split over two days have not proved a success.

Even in its "butchered" version, however, *Greed* remains one of the milestones of the American cinema, and a remarkably modern one. One can trace its influences from routine American silents like *Death Valley* (1927) and *Leatherneck* (1929) through to John Huston's *The Treasure of Sierra Madre* (1948), where, quite apart from narrative content, the role played by Walter Huston seemed almost an homage to the performance of Gibson Gowland in the latter portions of *Greed*. Too, *Greed* is a modern film in its technique, which is often deceptive. Although Stroheim was an avowed disciple of Griffith, and was cer-

---

* A full description of *Greed* as shot, illustrated by stills from all the missing footage, is available in Herman Weinberg's *The Complete "Greed."* Weinberg also provided a similar record of the likewise edited *The Wedding March.*

tainly the most distinguished of all the American directors to emerge from a Griffith apprenticeship, his methods in every way seemed to be opposed to those of Griffith. Whereas Griffith, in his plots, liked to find hope and love amid poverty, Stroheim preferred to dwell on depravity and ugliness amid wealth and splendor. And while Griffith would use film technique (rather than plotting or acting) to tell his stories, often calling attention to that technique in the process, Stroheim put all the emphasis on the story itself, and on players (for the most part, actors rather than stars), to hide his technique. This has caused many critics to term him a "primitive" director and to liken him to Chaplin. Chaplin was perhaps simplistic rather than primitive. He understood technique but seemed to distrust it—or, perhaps out of ego needs, tended to shoulder the burden of narrative himself, as the star.

Greed, however, more than refutes the claim that Stroheim neither understood nor used technique. His use of deep-focus photography and groupings in *Greed* (particularly one shot of Gibson Gowland in a large head foreground shot, with Zasu Pitts on the stairway behind him in sharp focus) blueprints many similar shots hailed as revolutionary in Orson Welles' *Citizen Kane.* Some critics, too, have complained of the lack of camera mobility in *Greed,* although in 1923—between the declining influence of Griffith and the upcoming influence of Murnau—it had diminished in *all* American films. Actually the camera moves a great deal in *Greed,* but there is only one scene (the establishing shots of McTeague in the mine, where the camera tracks with him as he pushes his ore-wagon) where it is obvious. In other cases, the movement of the camera is so right and natural that one often just isn't aware that it *is* moving. Only by sitting through the film dispassionately (not an easy task), and looking for and counting the number of moving-camera shots, does one realize that it moves a great deal—far more, for instance, than it does in *The Iron Horse.*

Stroheim's understanding of film technique was so thorough that *The Wedding March* (1927) is structured around the editing process. The story deals (in part) with the apparently doomed love affair between an aristocrat (Stroheim) and a commoner (Fay Wray), and several sequences within the film underline the attempts to keep the two apart by literally *editing* them apart. In the sequence where the two first meet, they never once appear in the same frame, yet their attraction to each other is made warm and irresistible. *The*

Wedding March is arguably Stroheim's finest film. In purely film-making terms, it is his most sophisticated work, and in a sympathetic role, rather than as the lecherous villain of *Foolish Wives,* Stroheim's own humanity comes through. If his performance here reflects his *real* personality, then one can well understand the fierce loyalty of his crews and casts.

It was Stroheim's misfortune—quite apart from his unorthodox productions methods and the number of powerful enemies he made, with Irving Thalberg heading the list—to be at his creative peak at a time when Hollywood was undergoing its first major crisis. The year 1924 saw the establishment of radio as a new, *free* entertainment, and as with television in the early 1950's, it affected the movie box office. Theater attendance was way down in 1925, and Hollywood hit back with one of its strongest barrages of purely entertainment movies, cast-iron proof that films like *The Phantom of the Opera, Peter Pan, The Merry Widow* and *The Big Parade* could offer entertainment against which radio could not compete. It is significant that Stroheim's most commercially successful film in this period was *The Merry Widow,* which at least promised extravagant romantic escapism (and partly came through, despite Baron Sadoja and his foot fetishes!) and had an unbeatable box-office team in Mae Murray and John Gilbert. It's also typical of Stroheim's odd combination of obstinacy and integrity that he chose to repeat all his old excesses almost immediately. Having re-established his reputation, to a degree, and come up with a film that *was* making money—after three mutilated and controversial films in a row—Stroheim, instead of marking time and proving his reliability by making at least one more commercial film,† chose instead to throw himself into the ultimately aborted *The Wedding March.* With its bizarre plot and skyrocketing costs, it made enemies of potential friends like Pat Powers, who financed it.

With its determination to combat the competition of radio, Hollywood turned 1925–26 into two of its most outstanding years—if not in terms of classics, then certainly in terms of excellent and varied enter-

---

† *The Merry Widow* showed that Stroheim could combine his own rather bizarre style with a commercial property, although the key in this case may have been the box-office insurance of the two stars. Nevertheless, *The Merry Widow,* even after cutting, contained elements that were strong meat indeed, and Stroheim was not ashamed of the edited version as releasd.

tainment features, crafted with great skill and taste. But with the exception of Stroheim's films and Sternberg's debut feature, 1926's *Salvation Hunters*—a pretentious and rather silly film, equating art with the sordid underbelly of life, and one that Sternberg later admitted was purposely "arty" in an attempt to draw attention to himself—the Hollywood feature of those years was lavish and glossy, a "show" in every sense of the word. Despite size, however, the unpretentious desire to entertain—the quality of the pre-1920 movies—returned in large measure. Quite apart from the fact that the comedy film—with Lloyd, Keaton, and Chaplin at their peak, flanked by newcomers W. C. Fields, Harry Langdon, and Raymond Griffith—was enjoying its golden age, other genres relaxed and played for unsophisticated fun. The stately, rather stolid swashbucklers of previous years—*Scaramouche*, Frank Lloyd's *The Sea Hawk*—were replaced by *Son of the Sheik* and *Don Juan*, both of 1926, both tongue in cheek, reveling in their luxury and flamboyance, never taking themselves seriously, yet avoiding self-parody.

George Fitzmaurice's *Son of the Sheik* was a delightful romp, full of action and fun, much of it quite gutsy. It was easily Valentino's best and most relaxed performance, and by far his best film—a most fitting swan song to a meteoric career that would be cut short by his tragic death before the film went into general release. *Don Juan*, though longer, more elaborate, and serving the additional purpose of introducing the Vitaphone system via its music and sound effects, was another most engaging film. Concentrating on stylish romance and elegance for most of its considerable running time, it then switched into high gear in its last third with a rousing, prolonged climax of action— a superbly staged duel between John Barrymore and Montague Love (still the "definitive" screen duel, with its fast cutting, stylish angles, and camera mobility), leading to incarceration in a dungeon, escape from a torture chamber, horseback pursuit, and more swordplay. In this film, Barrymore established a particularly good relationship with director Alan Crosland, who seemed to know exactly how to harness the Barrymore exuberance and keep his basically slow films constantly on the move. Crosland would seem to have been an ideal director for Fairbanks, and it is a great pity that he did not, for example, direct *Robin Hood* or *Don Q, Son of Zorro* and bring those handsome but dead films to life.

Spearheaded by the stage success of *What Price Glory?*, the war film—absent from the screen for some years—became a useful addition to Hollywood's big "shows" of the period. Best of them all was King Vidor's *The Big Parade*, actually a 1925 film, though often cited as a 1927 production because its general release was delayed two years following extremely long-running road-show engagements. Like *The Covered Wagon*, it started relatively unambitiously and grew to epic status as it progressed. It is unfairly hampered today by the very qualities that made it important originally. Vidor re-created perfectly the flag-waving fervor and jubilant patriotism that sent America marching off to war without knowing what war was really like. He spends a great deal of time on training-camp cameraderie, and then on the behind-the-lines fun of drinking, carousing, and forming romantic attachments. When, after nearly ninety minutes of build-up, his unprepared recruits are thrown into the hell of combat, the impact is shattering. Vidor knew how essential this structure was, and, on being told that his film was too long and would have to be cut, went through it methodically, time and time again, snipping frames from the beginnings and ends of scenes, so that the overall rhythm would be unimpaired. Since then, of course, other films have covered the same ground, and we have been through a second world war that was far better documented than the first in terms of newsreel and other factual coverage. In the light of our own knowledge, *The Big Parade* now seems to take too long to make its points.

Too, *The Big Parade* is a "big" Hollywood film. Though some sequences—the superbly staged and timed march through the woods in the face of unseen snipers—have a documentary-like quality, others (particularly the night combat scenes) have the look of Hollywood art direction and expertise. The occasional glass shots, and the high-powered emotionalism of the parting and ultimate reunion of the two lovers (John Gilbert and Renee Adoree), are moving, but possibly a trifle artificial in light of the underplayed treatment such sequences were given in films about World War II. Nevertheless, the sincerity and the overall impressions of *The Big Parade* linger. One recalls the theatricality and the trick shots (the dirt trench caving in on an entire platoon of men) of *What Price Glory?* (1926), the magnificent staging and sheer excitement of the air-land combat material in *Wings* (1927), or the charm and vivacity of Clara Bow in that film, but somehow it is

The Big Parade that survives as the first really important film about World War I. For a film to assail the false values of the American people was an extremely rare and courageous undertaking in the 1920's. How well and honestly it does so can be recognized by studying America's World War I newsreels, which catered to those values and, for propaganda purposes, concentrated on fun behind the lines and victory parades as the troops pushed forward to occupy new positions. No World War I documentary captured the fear, futility, and senseless death as did John Huston's World War II documentary, *The Battle of San Pietro*.

Just as Hollywood used big screens and spectacle to combat television in the 1950's, it felt that size was the answer in the mid-1920's. Although audiences were certainly not short-changed by the expensive new films that resulted, sheer size—or length—in many cases hurt individual films. Mary Pickford's *Little Annie Rooney* (1925) was far too long and lugubrious for its own good. At six reels, it would have been snappy and enjoyable. At nine (and it seemed far longer), it milked its sentimental situations to the point where poignancy became mere bathos. *Ben Hur* (1927) was likewise hurt, if not by its size (which was both impressive and justifiable) then certainly by its length. Most of all, it was weakened by its basic construction, which placed both of its highlight sequences—a superbly staged full-scale sea battle and the even more impressive chariot race—into the *middle* third of the film, leaving nothing to look forward to in the final third but a singularly unstimulating visit to a leper colony. Apart from those two large-scale, prolonged action sequences, *Ben Hur* is a ploddingly directed film, but as with *Scaramouche*, it gains immeasurably from being seen in an original print. It may not become any faster or more dynamic, but it does take on the rich tapestry of good theater, with tinting and toning, and Technicolor sequences, adding visual elegance. By any standards, it is far superior to the abysmal 1959 remake, with its snail's pace and ineptly amateurish miniatures used in the sea battle. Its well-staged chariot race, full of brilliantly executed stunts, was certainly the saving grace of the film, but even it lacked the majesty and pomp of the original sequence. (The granting of a dozen Academy Awards to the remake was the final insult!)

Nor were American audiences willing to accept all that Hollywood offered, despite star and production value, and the lack of competition

other than radio. Whimsy and fantasy were ingredients that materialistic jazz-age audiences just weren't buying. Herbert Brenon's adaptation of Sir James Barrie's *Peter Pan* seemed to be a freak success, because it hit the theaters at an ideal time as a Christmas attraction.
Though essentially theatrical (deliberately and sincerely so, out of
respect to the form of the original), and only occasionally taking
advantage of the possibilities of the cinema (as in the shots of the mer-
maids lolling off the Catalina coastline, or the incredibly lovely shot of
the galleon taking off from the water and flying back to London), *Peter Pan* was an enchanting film. Barrie's text was condensed but undis-
torted (except for some sub-titles which, for the U.S. market, established the Darling children as Americans), and the beauty of his
original dialogue, which could so easily slip into fey or embarrassing
sentimentality, was handled by both performers and director with im-
peccable taste. Most of all, the film owed its success to the energetic,
sprightly, dancing, joyous performance by Betty Bronson as Peter.
Even if one can sense, occasionally, the off-screen guidance of this
then relatively inexperienced teen-age actress, it is a radiant performance, capable of shifting from joy to sadness with the slightest change
of expression or a nuance of body movement. Bronson should have become one of the major stars of the silent cinema, and for a while
seemed about to usurp Mary Pickford's throne. However, Paramount
was singularly inept at exploiting their unique personalities, as they
had proved with Valentino. Rather than carefully tailoring material to
a special talent, they would cash in on a particular star's popularity by
rushing him or her through as many films as possible, and in the manner of the nearest equivalent star. Ultimately Paramount decided to
turn Betty Bronson into a second-string Clara Bow—a role she was
qualified to fill competently and attractively, in modern comedies like
The Cat's Pajamas (1926) and *Ritzy* (1927).

Fortunately, the initial success of *Peter Pan* caused Paramount to re-
unite Bronson and director Herbert Brenon in another Barrie adaptation, *A Kiss for Cinderella* (1926), before the disappointing box-office
performance of *Peter Pan*, once it had left the Christmas holiday show-
cases, provided the tip-off that Barry whimsy was not a generally popular commodity. *A Kiss for Cinderella* was a masterpiece. Eminently
superior to *Peter Pan*, though lacking its popular appeal, it had a sophistication and an underlying sadness that meant that the more it was

understood, the less popular it was likely to be. This time Brenon took full advantage of the film medium, and the large stages of Paramount's Long Island studio enabled him to bring to life the exaggerated, luxury-for-its-own-sake view of royalty and court life as seen through the eyes of a Cockney slavey. Few films, perhaps only Jean Cocteau's 1947 *La Belle et la Bete,* have caught the genuine flavor of fairy-tale magic as beautifully as this one. The production design was stunning yet tasteful, full of lovely touches impossible in the theater: the lamp-posts bowing to Cinderella on her way to the ball, a transformation from pumpkins and mice to gold coach and horses that even outdid the galleon scene in *Peter Pan,* and the utilizing of a camera mounted on a moving and revolving platform to capture, first, the grace of the ball and then its speeded-up chaos as midnight strikes and Cinderella's spell is broken. The film contains a great deal of typically Barrie wit and humor, which Englishman Brenon understood and translated magnificently; but the overriding quality is one of pathos.

The acting, too, is superb. Betty Bronson had matured as an actress within the year, and the pure pantomime of *Peter Pan* was here transformed into a performance of subtlety and insight. Even Tom Moore, usually just an amiable leading man, a 1920's equivalent of Sonny Tufts, was able, under Brenon's direction, to create a character of enormous warmth. His final, long-held stare to the camera, with its suggestion that his Cinderella may in fact die, is one of the most moving yet underplayed scenes on film. A major tragedy connected with *A Kiss for Cinderella* is that the last surviving 35mm print—a richly toned, crystal-clear print that was itself a thing of beauty, thus conveying so much of the magical quality of Barrie—was allowed to deteriorate badly before a preservation copy was made. The only viewing print available today, in black-and-white and with splotchy hypo deterioration disfiguring and obscuring much of the highlight sequence of the ball, is only a shadow of the original. Failure to preserve the original while there was still time is virtually a cultural crime.

Hollywood's aggressive anti-radio campaign also indirectly served to sort out the newer directors and either elevate or reduce their status. Alan Crosland, unambitious artistically and clearly happy to dazzle audiences with his good humor and elegant style, rose to his peak in this period via such Barrymore films as *Don Juan, The Beloved Rogue, When a Man Loves,* the gloriously uninhibited melodrama *Old San*

Francisco, and Al Jolson's *The Jazz Singer.* Conversely, Elmer Clifton, a Griffith protégé and assistant who branched out on his own in 1922 with the outstanding *Down to the Sea in Ships,* never developed as that film suggested he would. *Down to the Sea in Ships* was distinguished by some brilliantly authentic whaling footage and by the fact that no other American film by another director looked so much like a Griffith film. In theme, characters, cutting, structure, and even in its racial attitudes, certainly in its pictorialism, it could have passed unchallenged as a Griffith film had his name been on it. But clearly, Clifton could not devote his career to pseudo-Griffith pictures, and it soon became clear that when he was *not* emulating Griffith, he had little else to offer. By the end of the twenties, he was working for deMille, turning out slick, efficient programmers like *The Wreck of the Hesperus* and *Let 'Er Go Gallegher.* In the sound period he was reduced even further to westerns, serials, and the cheapest of independent quickies. Occasionally, when a film such as Ida Lupino's *Not Wanted* (1949) contained Griffith-like qualities, he rose to the occasion quite remarkably, as though unable to perform at his best except in the manner of his original mentor.

Much has been written—and surmised—about the early twenties as representing Hollywood's first major attempt at self-censorship in order to avoid governmental censorship. Directors, writing their memoirs, have tended to be over-emphatic and perhaps unduly sarcastic about what they were not permitted to do on screen in that last decade of the silents.

Hollywood, it is true, did embark on a policy of "purification" following a trio of scandals that hit Hollywood in the very early twenties: the death of Wallace Reid and the revelation of his addiction to drugs; the murder of William Desmond Taylor (and the involvement of Mary Miles Minter and Mabel Normand); and the sensational Virginia Rappe case, which wrecked Fatty Arbuckle's career, even though he was proven innocent of her rape or death. Any one of these scandals on its own would probably have passed without undue furor; but the three coming together, and at a time when Hollywood was already being criticized for the sexual or other "objectionable" content in films as diverse as *Foolish Wives* and *The Sheik,* posed a real threat. Petty censorship had been a thorn in Hollywood's side even before there *was* a Hollywood—from the days of Edison's *The Kiss,* in fact. Here was enough ammunition for the press and all the individual reform groups to create a *cause célèbre,* to band together and call for government censorship. Aware of the problems that would bring, Hollywood turned to self-regulation as the preferable alternative, and brought in Will Hays to set up and enforce codes of conduct for players and codes of content for the movies themselves.

Arbuckle and Mary Miles Minter were almost immediate and very useful scapegoats. Completed Arbuckle films were totally abandoned and never released, and this extremely talented comedian, on the threshold of major stardom since he was in the vanguard of the comedy stars switching to features, found himself frozen out—able to work only under an assumed name as a director and banned from appearing entirely. (He did return in a rather good series of two-reelers in the early 1930's; but it was too late, and he died while the films were still in production.) Mary Miles Minter's involvement in the Taylor case was not severe enough to call for the junking of her completed films, but it was enough to tarnish her reputation and ease her into a premature retirement at the beginning of 1923.

Minter was a charming player, very much in the Mary Pickford tradition, both in her looks and in the vehicles in which she starred. However, she was less mannered than Pickford (at that particular stage in Pickford's career) and her films—especially *A Cumberland Romance* (1920)—were well produced and often stunningly photographed. Although it is unfortunate that she was eased out of films when at her peak, she had had a solid and quite lengthy career up to that point. The real tragedy is to film history, in that most of her films were made prior to the twenties, are only sparsely preserved, and certainly are not generally available, even in archives. Had she continued making films well into the 1920's, she would probably now be a name to rank alongside Pickford, Bow, and Moore, instead of an unknown entity remembered primarily as a footnote to a murder case.

The "changes" to Hollywood product resulting from its self-imposed purge were, however, more a matter of additions than subtractions. Hollywood polished its image by turning out more "wholesome" movies—but it was heading in that direction anyway, with the increased stress on feature-length comedy, and the cycle of religious and Biblical films, already tentatively under way since 1919's *The Miracle Man,* was emphasized. Directors and stars in the public eye were made aware that misconduct—at least, publicized misconduct—might well be sufficient grounds for cancellation of a contract. But there was no dramatic curtailing of adult subject matter. Changes—i.e., the substitution of a happy ending for Tolstoy's tragic one in Garbo's *Love* (1927), her first version of *Anna Karenina*—were dictated as much by the box office as by the censors. A "notorious" property such as Michael Arlen's *The Green Hat* was considered to be inviting trouble and reached the screen in a much-laundered version (as Garbo's *A Woman of Affairs,* 1929)—but these problems were not unique to the twenties. Generally speaking, tasteful directors like Clarence Brown were able to stick to approved scripts and still suggest the so-called adult material that they were unable to spell out. It may well be that the restrictions of the 1920's seemed major ones to writers and directors of that time, since the whole art of movie-making was advancing and maturing so rapidly; but in retrospect those restrictions seem far less frustrating today, when we have the later experience of the Production Code as a reference. Then, from 1934 through the beginning of 1939, Hollywood seemed bent on turning out nothing but Never-Never-Land entertainment. The relative lack of censorship exercised by Hollywood in the twenties is proven by the abrupt about-face caused by the coming of sound when Hollywood, convinced that films had to be "real" and "honest," plunged into stories of sex, crime, and amorality with such gusto and on such a large scale that, after four years of it, with relatively little interference, another and perhaps more understandable "purge" was called for.

The year of Hollywood's initial concern over radio, 1924, was also the year of *The Atonement of Gösta Berling* in Sweden (starring Lars Hanson and Greta Garbo under the direction of Mauritz Stiller) and *The Last Laugh* (starring Emil Jannings under the direction of F. W. Murnau) in Germany. Hollywood, alert for new talent as well as prestige at this particular moment, took note. The European invasion of Hollywood—or, perhaps more accurately, Hollywood's pillage of Europe—was about to begin.

17

Art Direction and Production Design

Art direction and its related field, production design, came to the motion picture somewhat late in the day. Careful, planned art direction for the movies cannot really be dated prior to 1915, and even then, it tended to be the exception rather than the rule.

The approximately twenty years of movie-making leading up to 1915 had little need for art direction, the principal functions of which were to evoke atmosphere and/or suggest as realistic a milieu as possible. Since the pre-feature films were necessarily limited by their telescoping of time, by minimal budgets, and by (for the most part) only gradually developing acting and directorial skills, realism was not (and not intended to be) a major factor. Indeed, many within the picture-making business still felt their wares to be a novelty of transitory value only, unworthy of being linked in any way with art.

Thus, the eventual function of the art director in the early films was usually shared by the director and his cameramen. The best of such teams, for example, Griffith and Bitzer, were often more creative in what they *suggested*—a cunning arrangement of people and props within the frame, implying an extension of on-screen "sets" or activity into off-screen space—than in what they actually *showed*. Nevertheless, the roots of art direction can be found in what *was* done on screen: the diminishing use of characterless flats; added elements of perspective; a decreasing use of painted props (it was common, for example, in kitchen "sets" for the stove, pots and pans, and other artifacts

299

to be painted on a background wall) in favor of actual objects; and attempts to match continuity and lighting styles from set to set or from interior to exterior. The progress made in these moves toward reality over a few short years is quite remarkable, especially since, at first, studio space did not get markedly larger. Some of the interior sets in Griffith's 1915 *The Birth of a Nation* have no more space than those in Griffith's Biograph one-reelers of several years earlier. Yet so carefully are they composed, so meticulously copied from (among other sources) the Mathew Brady photographs of the Civil War period, that on screen they look totally real. Production stills of the sequence of Lee's surrender to Grant show the "set" to be cramped, and little more than a few pieces of furniture were thrown in front of a few flats. On screen, however, there is no sign of such austerity. Indeed, the only tell-tale signs throughout the entire film of the primitive studio conditions are the violently flickering candles, the rustling tassles on drapes, or the suddenly disarrayed hair of a feminine player, all evidence of the gusts of wind blowing through the open-air roofless stages.

It was Cecil B. deMille who consciously brought art direction to Hollywood. His pre-1920 features were highly theatrical in origin or style, or both, and he brought in two men to exploit this quality visually. First was Wilfrid Buckland, a set-designer from Broadway, and a few years later, Paul Iribe, a successful French costume designer. De Mille's sets in this period were ornate but hardly spectacular, and his major effects were achieved through lighting and sets designed to make the most of that lighting. In *The Cheat* (1915), much of the action takes place in the home of a Burmese millionaire. The Oriental motif of his home allows for much use of transparent rice-paper shades and other decorations. Several key scenes, beautifully lit, are played in silhouette *through* rice-paper panels. In one climactic moment, the Burmese (Sessue Hayakawa) is shot and falls back against such a panel, and the spreading stain of blood on it as he sinks to the floor is far more dramatic (and theatrical) than a straightforward rendering of such a scene.

Interestingly enough, D. W. Griffith achieved outstanding results in these early years more by instinct than by applied research or artistic consultation, although he did accept the advice and collaboration of historians and architects. The Babylonian sequences of *Intolerance* (1916) were designed largely by Griffith himself. They can be said to represent almost a supreme example of "instinctive" art direction, since relatively little is known about Babylonian history or culture. Even such famous paintings as "The Feast of Belshazzar," on which Griffith based tableau-like effects in the film, were themselves the result of imagination. Yet so right were his instincts that the Babylonian story of *Intolerance* is far more convincing than many more carefully researched and art-directed historical spectacles of later years. Possibly the only major historical prop that might be disputed is Griffith's bestowing on the Babylonians a form of flame-thrower, which combined twentieth-century war apparatus with a surrealistic design of more indeterminate vintage.

Made concurrently with these early films of deMille and Griffith were the westerns of William S. Hart, which likewise owe their unerringly accurate detail of dress and architecture to Hart's own passion for realism. Admittedly, it wasn't difficult for a western of 1916 to be realistic. The Old West hadn't yet disappeared. Many of those who had lived through its pioneering days were still alive and on the spot, and those superb Mathew Brady glass-negative photographs of the West and its inhabitants, crystal clear in their detail, were easily accessible for reference. Place a Mathew Brady photo of cowboys lounging against a saloon bar side by side with a William S. Hart scene of the same thing, and it is often only by recognizing certain actors—Robert Kortman, Leo Willis, Robert McKim—that one can tell reality from movie reconstruction. Nor is there evidence that Hart *consciously* copied Brady, as Griffith admittedly did in his Civil War films. Brady photographed reality; Hart remembered and reconstructed it. Other than building sets in a certain relationship to landscape, or including ornamental or other props on the walls or tables of his saloons for possible (and simple) symbolic use in certain camera movements, the concern for reality was the only real form of art direction in the early Hart westerns. And if it was relatively easy to achieve this kind of unofficial art direction, then it was less easy to resist the temptation (sternly resisted by Hart, but not always by other western filmmakers) to distort the western "look" into something resembling the glossy, romantic images of the dime novels.

It was in movies with a contemporary locale that the lack of art direction was most apparent. Often the function would be shared by the director, the cameraman, and the property master. Their decisions were often colored by such considerations as how a standing set could be re-vamped or how a set to be constructed could later be used in another film. Looking at movies of the 1912–20 years, one often has few clues in the decor as to just when the film was made, and it is only the clothes—reliably contemporary, since they were usually the players' own clothes, and not supplied by a wardrobe department—that provide a guide to the year. Perhaps because of the profusion of available props and artifacts, sets in contemporary stories tended to be far more cluttered and inaccurate than those in period stories.

Maurice Tourneur, with his painter's eye, was able to evoke a completely convincing atmosphere of eighteenth-century rural England in his Fort Lee-filmed *The Wishing Ring* in 1914. Yet the interior sets in George Loane Tucker's *Traffic in Souls* of a year earlier, set in contemporary New York, are far less realistic. This may have been partially due to the hurried and even secretive conditions under which the film was made, and the possible need to adapt sets used for other films. Nevertheless, there is a Victorian look to many of the interiors of homes and offices: ultra-busy wallpaper and a plethora of vases and ornaments. Admittedly, this look of stuffy claustrophobia was not entirely inappropriate for 1913; many older people retained this link with the past well into the 1930's. But it *is* inappropriate for an essentially modern story of organized crime, such as *Traffic in Souls,* and the interiors clash rather notably with the exteriors shot in the busy streets of New York.

Even as late as early 1920, in an engaging and thoroughly modern comedy such as Douglas Fairbanks' *When The Clouds Roll By,* there are inconsistencies which applied art direction could have overcome. Clothes, and such props as a ouija board, do far more to pinpoint the period than do the sets. A hotel façade that Fairbanks scales is clearly in a California style of architecture, even though the film is set in New York. And the heroine, a struggling young artist who lives in Greenwich Village, resides in a remarkably ornate "apartment." One of the delights (though in a realistic sense, one of the curses) of silent films was the height that could be achieved in sets. Not only was the nearly square on-screen image more conducive to a stress on verticals than the later sound (and still later wide-screen) rectangular frame shapes, but the fact that many sets were built on roofless stages in order to take maximum advantage of the sun's light meant that there was much more vertical than horizontal space to play with. The heroine's apartment in this film, therefore, a far cry from the typical economical but cozy Greenwich Village apartment, again is designed far more in the California manner, with a second floor ringed by a balcony looking down on the ground floor. The freedom to use height created many architectural clichés in the silent period which were maintained through the sound era. For example, Elizabethan architecture is characterized by extremely low ceilings, yet virtually all movies set in this period—from the silent *The Sea Hawk* to the sound, from *The Private Lives of Elizabeth and Essex* to the British-made (but American directed and photographed) *Fire Over England*—persist in letting Queen Elizabeth, her ladies-in-waiting, and her dueling knights and treacherous enemies cavort in glossy, high-roofed, cathedral-like chambers, usually with black marble floors that reflect and thus intensify the artificial height.

To attack *When the Clouds Roll By* for such a trivial thing is unfair. It was and is a highly sophisticated film, with remarkable expertise in trick photography that could hardly be bettered today, and was exceptional for 1920. Yet its lack of concern for art direction in a basically realistic milieu is typical. On the other hand, when Fairbanks moved into his big costume spectacles of the early 1920's, he became so obsessed with art direction and design (almost for its own sake) that the essentially Fairbanksian qualities—enthusiasm, pace, wit, good humor, and the ability to make points quickly and pungently—were swamped in a mass of decor, costumes, and stylized design. Nevertheless, to Fairbanks probably goes the credit for recognizing the importance of design in film. Art direction in the pre-1920 years was essentially of theatrical origin, whether in the juxtaposition of sets with lighting styles so characteristic of deMille or in the deliberately artificial decor of Maurice Tourneur's *The Blue Bird*—a magnificent film pictorially, but not an essentially cinematic one. Even though combined with genuine exteriors, most of its studio-made sets, backed up by much silhouette work and use of painting, *could* have been duplicated without too much difficulty on any theater stage.

The 1920's, however, represent the peak of the art director's achievements in, and importance to, film, and also saw the creation of the role of production designer. It is difficult to pinpoint with any accuracy the functions of anyone in the field of art direction, since they vary so much from picture to picture and studio to studio. And even in the

later days of strictly unionized delegation of duties and responsibilities, there were inevitable overlappings and collaborations in any area
of design. In a basic sense, however, the art director's job began when
the script was finalized, and when the importance of a film and the
size of its budget were determined. The art director would design and
supervise construction of the sets or re-design existing sets. Costuming
and the collection (or construction) of props often came within his
jurisdiction, although usually these were assigned to specialists in
those particular fields.

Although the production designer had the same skills and performed
many of the same functions as the art director, he operated on a higher
plateau and usually only for much more important films. (Every film
had an art director, if only nominally; relatively few carried production designer credits.) In many ways, the production designer was a
director before the fact; indeed, some production designers, most notably William Cameron Menzies, did go on to careers as directors.

When a film of major importance needed a specific and consistent
stylistic "look" throughout (*Robin Hood, The Thief of Bagdad, Sunrise* in the silent period and *The Adventures of Tom Sawyer, Gone
With The Wind,* the remake of *The Thief of Bagdad* in the sound
era), a production designer was brought in well ahead of physical production, and usually ahead of script finalization, to block out a visual
style. The sets he designed might be conceived with a specific star in
mind, or to facilitate filming of a specific action sequence. Very often,
the production designer's ideas would themselves suggest a fresh
course of action, and the script would be changed accordingly to encompass them. In big spectacle sequences, particularly those involving
disasters, the work of the production designer would have to be well
coordinated with that of the cameraman, the special effects crew, and
the second-unit direction.

Few crafts in film-making have been as underrated (by critics) and
ignored (by the public) as that of art direction, which often has far
more influence on the style of the finished film than the work of the
director. Its influence is often longer-lasting, too. The style of Fairbanks' *The Thief of Bagdad* was determined long before any cameras
rolled. The decision to make Baghdad a city of whiteness and light,
spectacular but not solid, a city that was a backdrop to action and fantasy, not a city in which people really lived, was reached by Fairbanks

and his consulting artists, by designer William Cameron Menzies and cameraman Arthur Edeson. With the film's visuals pre-determined, its trick effects of flying carpet, flying horse, and other wonders firmly the responsibility of Edeson, and the narrative controlled by Fairbanks' gracefully choreographed performance, there was almost nothing for a director to add. Indeed, it is somewhat surprising that Fairbanks gave the directorial reins to Raoul Walsh, an expert, no-nonsense action director, but one who seemed somewhat out of his element amid such fairy-tale magic. Actually, Walsh would have been far more suited to the earlier (1919) Fairbanks film, *His Majesty the American,* which was full of the speed, irreverence, and casual, cheerful sadism that was so much Walsh's forte, as well as being partially concerned with Pancho Villa's depradations, an area in which Walsh had had personal experience. As it happened, neither *His Majesty the American* (directed by another old Griffith protégé, Joseph Henaberry) nor *The Thief of Bagdad* suffered through lack of guidance by a particularly suitable director, indicating once again that Fairbanks himself was the real presence both in front of and behind the cameras, and that directorial credits on his films were largely academic.

Some art directors carry the imprint of a director with whom they have had a particularly felicitous relationship. Others, in contrast, are so dynamic that they can permanently influence other directors. This fact again stresses how futile it often is to pinpoint credit for, or ownership of, a specific visual style. Ben Carré, one of the pioneers of early French cinema, went to work for emigré director Maurice Tourneur in Fort Lee in the pre-1920 years, as did apprentice director Clarence Brown. After they left Tourneur, Brown and Carré worked together for a while, creating films very much in the image of Tourneur, and then went their separate ways. Although Brown constantly acknowledged his debt to Tourneur, as a director he finally evolved his own style, still essentially visual but less pictorial than Tourneur's. Carré's set design always remained firmly rooted in the tradition of painting, however, though not necessarily one school of painting. Some of his best work, coincidentally, was also done in a Raoul Walsh film, *The Red Dance* (1928). Carré's superb sets for a Russian prison camp—stylized, expressionistic, and realistic, all at the same time—appeared early in the film and created a sober tone which was never erased, despite the speed and camera mobility which characterized Walsh's treatment of a basically straightforward action melodrama. Carré was one of the few genuine visual poets of the silent American film,* and the full impact and value of his contributions has yet to be assessed.

Anton Grot is typical of the art director whose work is so striking that it is often erroneously assumed to be the creation of the overall director. Although Grot came to film before 1920, was one of the first art directors to insist on three-dimensional qualities in movie sets, and contributed much of the magnificence to the huge sets of Fairbanks' *Robin Hood* (1922), his most important contributions were made in the sound era and thus are largely outside the scope of this book. In the 1930's and early 1940's he became something of a mechanic and an inventor as well as a designer. Although he created some of the dazzling, modernistic sets for the Busby Berkeley musical numbers, his real forte was in the somber, expressionistic European-localed sets, with their roots in both the silent German film and the Bauhaus school of architecture. His sets for the 1931 *Svengali* were largely responsible for making it the best of many versions, silent and sound, of the Du Maurier novel. He worked so well with Michael Curtiz that Curtiz (an incredibly accomplished and versatile craftsman, but hardly a major or even a very personal director) has been given credit for a style that was essentially Grot's.

Warner Brothers Studio in the early 1930's was essentially a super-efficient assembly-line factory. Directors frequently made six films a year, and had little time to think much about their upcoming projects until they walked onto the set and started work. Grot's sets were thus ready and waiting, without collaboration on Curtiz's part, and given the economy of the Warners operation, made maximum use of space and lighting to achieve effects. Production team-work may have given a certain uniformity to Warner product, but it was often a creative and certainly an efficient uniformity. Other art directors assigned to work on upcoming Curtiz projects knew how well the Grot design had worked for him and did their best to copy it. Cameramen, aware of the unique "look" of the Curtiz-Grot films, knew what Curtiz liked or was used to, and likewise copied the lighting style for which Grot's sets had been designed. As a result, Curtiz's films acquired a specific visual style that, understandably, came to be regarded as *his* personal

---

* Carré worked well into the sound period, too, and was one of many artists who contributed to the extraordinary titular sequence in the 1935 *Dante's Inferno*.

style.† The tremendous influence of Grot, not only on Curtiz but on Warner product of the 1930's as a whole, can be realized only if one goes back to Grot's work of the 1920's, which shows any number of precedents for the Warner/Curtiz style. Grot's use of space and shadows in deMille's *The Road to Yesterday* (1925) is typical of the kind of shot composition that came to be regarded as a Curtiz signature. A bank hold-up in *Walking Back* (1929), showing little more than the face of the bank-teller, the suggestion of the bank's design, and the figures of the gangsters all in shadows and silhouette, pre-dates many identical episodes in the Warner gangster films of the early 1930's. One can only conjecture how the validity of the auteur theory, as applied to specific directors, might be shattered if far more were known about the work of men like Ben Carré and Anton Grot.

There were many reasons for the suddenly increased importance given to the visual look of films in the 1920's and the corresponding employment (and often importation) of creative artists in the fields of painting, design, sculpture, architecture, and costuming. These craftsmen were given surprising leeway and freedom of experimentation, in some cases being paid high salaries for work that ultimately turned out to be too revolutionary to be practical.

For one thing, films were getting longer and slower. Plots were veering away from straightforward action and narrative to stories that were more complex, psychological, and sophisticated. Stars, directors, and producers became, in many cases, their own impressarios, using film self-indulgently to create monuments to their own talent—or vanity. The studio heads, most of them ex-immigrants and merchants, and aware of their own cultural shortcomings, tried to make up for it by loading their films with all the culture money could buy—not always

---

† Curtiz was essentially a loyal company man who took whatever assignments he was given and delivered according to studio specifications rather than personal preference. He was astute in being able to use stylistic innovations which helped the film, drew attention to his own initiative, and yet at the same time didn't "rock the boat" in an artistic sense. Rather surprisingly, almost at the end of his career, Curtiz became an impressively tasteful and personal director as well as a slick one. His 1950 *The Breaking Point* is possibly his one masterpiece, but it came too late in his career (and was too unsuccessful commercially) for it to open up new avenues for him. Moreover, shortly afterward, he moved from Warners to 20th Century Fox, where he was confronted with a different studio policy, a different kind of product, and was cut off from the expertise of the Warner team that he relied on.

to the films' advantage. Because silent films were, by their very nature, stylized and unrealistic, it was better to make them as much as possible within the studio, where all elements could be controlled and no clashes between a realistic on-location exterior and a studio set could occur. There were exceptions, of course. Establishing shots or sequences needing recognizable locations *were* done away from the studio, and certain naturalistic films, of which *Greed* (1923) is the prime example, were made entirely on location. But these were the exceptions —obviously, so were the westerns—and for the most part, the 1920's film was a studio-made entity.‡

The popular and critical success of many German imports, most of them almost obsessively made entirely within the studios, likewise had affected American film-makers, who liked to keep in vogue. Not least, the European market was tremendously important to Hollywood in the 1920's. Europe itself was slow in recovering from the effects of World War I. There was rebuilding to be done; inflation and unemployment were rampant. Entertainment was needed as never before, and most of the European countries, operating on shoe-string budgets, couldn't hope to compete with the opulence, entertainment values, and star power of the American film. Hollywood moved in with a vengeance, buying up large interests in European production and exhibition outlets. In some cases, intervention amounted almost to dominance, and many countries—especially Australia—later complained bitterly, and with some justification, that their own industries had been suppressed by Hollywood. And what Hollywood didn't control, it imported. The small but distinguished Swedish film-making industry was literally stopped in its tracks in 1924, when Hollywood took its two greatest directors, Victor Seastrom and Mauritz Stiller, its most promising new star, Greta Garbo, and the well-established Lars Hanson. Much the same thing happened in Germany.

Economics apart, however, there is no doubt that the audiences of

‡ There was a slight relaxing of this modus operandi in the 1930's and then an almost total return to it in the early 1940's, when gasoline rationing and other restrictions brought about by the Second World War confined film-making within studio walls once more. The wartime *Sergeant York*, in which Tennessee hills and battle-front trenches were all re-created in the studio, has *exactly* the look, in an art-direction sense, of a 1920's movie. The move to authentic locations did not begin until the late 1940's.

all these countries *wanted* Hollywood films and Hollywood stars, and flocked to see them. Hollywood, in turn, anxious to consolidate this market, saw to it that a large percentage of its films had European locales. (An even larger percentage of European-localed films were made in the very early 1930's, however, in a desperate attempt to maintain its dominance of the European market, which was sorely threatened by the coming of sound and its accompanying language barrier.) And European locales meant large-scale construction of sets, whose frequent inaccuracy was unnoticed by Americans, while their larger-than-life style was both pleasing and flattering to Europeans. The sets were solid-looking and impressive. Often whole streets were erected as standing (permanent) sets, to be neatly disguised when the setting switched from Paris to Berlin or Moscow. Small cottages and farmhouses (the real things could easily have been found in the still-rural areas of Hollywood) were constructed with all the meticulous care lavished on sets for palaces, nightclubs, or railroad stations.

The art of set design was at its height in these years, helped by the consistency of style achieved through staying in the studio. The system crumbled badly in the 1940's, when Hollywood tried to have the best of both worlds by constructing "exterior" sets in the studio and juxtaposing them with genuine exteriors conveniently found in the immediate countryside. The sets were sets and looked it, *without* stylization (except for the afore-mentioned *Sergeant York,* and certain other Warner Brothers films like *The Sea Wolf*), and the contrast with the real thing made the sets look doubly artificial. Most of Fox's *The Ox-Bow Incident* was shot in the studio—certainly all of the dramatic material relating to the lynching, and even scenes of a night encounter with a stagecoach. Yet the western street, and one or two scenes of the vigilante posse riding across the plains, were "real," and didn't match. Color lent even more artificiality: the barnyard in MGM's *National Velvet* was backed by one of the flattest and most characterless scenic backdrops ever. It could never have convinced, but it would have *worked* far better if so much of the film hadn't used genuine California land and sea scapes to simulate (quite effectively) England. The tremendous efficiency of art direction in the early 1940's was too often minimized by the inconsistency of its application. Warner Brothers was the one studio that emerged with honors in this period, and it is perhaps no coincidence that the redoubtable Anton Grot was in residence for many of their best (and *entirely* studio-made) films, ranging from *The Sea Wolf* and *The Sea Hawk* to *Mildred Pierce*.

Not only were the 1920's sets impressive (*The Red Dance*), decorative (John Ford's *Hangman's House*), or evocative (Josef von Sternberg's *Docks of New York*), but in many cases sets and decor were designed to give opportunities for specific bravura photographic effects. Typical was the pullback shot introduced by director Clarence Brown, cameraman George Barnes, and production designer William Cameron Menzies in the Rudolph Valentino vehicle, *The Eagle* (1925). The shot began with a close-up of the host of a banquet at the head of his table, and then pulled back, rapidly and smoothly, down the entire length of the table, past the animated guests and over tableware and other props that were adroitly removed (and replaced) to facilitate the camera's unimpeded passage. The next year, the Garbo vehicle *The Temptress* went the shot one better, first by pulling back from Garbo over a much longer and more heavily decorated table, and then by repeating the complete shot *under* the table, contrasting the sophisticated faces and mien above table with the more "honest" behavior of the feet below: one set of feet making advances to another, a lady easing her tired feet out of her shoes, a man scratching his ankle, and so forth. The shot remained a "showcase" fixture for directors throughout the 1930's, too, although perhaps because such luxury would have proved abrasive to a Depression-era audience, almost always in a European framework. Clarence Brown repeated the shot, in another Russian setting, for *Anna Karenina,* while Josef von Sternberg added such bizarre touches as a skeleton leaning over a cauldron in his pullback of Catherine of Russia's table in *The Scarlet Empress.* Most overpowering of all, however, and one of the few occasions when camera movement in a sound film surpassed its inspiration from a silent, was the pullback to end all pullbacks performed by James Wong Howe for the 1937 version of *The Prisoner of Zenda.* Starting on a tight close shot of Ronald Colman and Madeleine Carroll as they are about to make their entrance to the grand ball, the camera for a moment moves backward at their pace as they walk forward. Then its speed increases, and it pulls back—and back—*and back,* revealing more of the size and grandeur of the marble staircase they are descending, then a suggestion of the ballroom, then more and more of the ballroom itself with its milling throngs. The musical score matches the mounting majesty of the shot, and when the camera finally comes to a halt in mid-air, one hundred yards from its point of departure and in one uninterrupted shot, the figures of Colman and Carroll have become dwarfed by distance, and as a final clincher to the art director's magic, the spaciousness of the ballroom is made to seem even more so by the brief use of a glass shot.

Many films of the 1920's make rewarding viewing for their art direction alone, particularly the earlier swashbucklers of Douglas Fairbanks and the later films of Frank Borzage, Erich von Stroheim, Josef von Sternberg, and perhaps most of all, F. W. Murnau. Obviously not all silent films had the advantage of an Anton Grot or a Wilfrid Buckland. Many smaller films were cheaply made and showed it. Some had inappropriate art direction, or none at all. Yet the percentage of film with *negative* art direction—for example, those hurt by bad or careless design—was remarkably small. No silent films quite matched the ineptitude of the ultra-economy-conscious "B's" and serial quickies of Sam Katzman in the sound era, where art direction often consisted of nothing more than grabbing the handiest props to cover the paucity of set. One of the most deathless of Katzman gaffes occurred in his *Son of the Guardsman*, a Robin Hood derivation, in which the wall of a tavern was decorated with a large portrait of a cavalier who couldn't have existed, let alone been painted, for at least another 400 years. No wonder the cavalier was laughing, perhaps at the achievement of Katzman's "art" department in at least getting a portrait from the right country, if not the right period.

Further stimulating the visual aspect of 1920's films was the fact that, for perhaps the only time (thus far) in the history of film, a *popular* new form of art design was developing, on a world-wide basis, concurrent with film. Decorative art, popularly condensed to Art-Deco, was officially launched at an exposition in Paris in 1925. But this was merely the official recognition of an art that had been developing for some time. While it was basically new, simple, light-hearted, and streamlined, it contained elements from earlier and more serious forms of art. It incorporated much of German expressionism, no little surrealism, and even used symbols and motifs (particularly sunburst designs and ultra-simplified human and animal figures) that were a throwback to the ancient Egyptians. As if to emphasize that from the very beginning, film was an important aspect of Art-Deco, French avant-garde film was included in the exposition. Art-Deco's modernistic style also made it an inevitable adjunct to another 1920's phenomenon, jazz music, which could be expressed, in the visual abstract, far more effectively through Art-Deco design than through any other pictorial means. (It is significant that silent movies—ranging from the Swedish *The Golden Clown* to the American *Our Dancing Daughters* and the British *Moulin Rouge*—invariably suggested the *sound* of jazz by setting it against an Art-Deco background.)

The development of Art-Deco in film is not easy to trace. For one thing, even when new, there were few rules clearly defining the aims and boundaries of the art. There are even fewer today, when considerations of commercial nostalgia muddy the waters. At the yearly Art-Deco exhibitions begun in New York in the mid-1970's, many items listed for sale (at outrageously inflated prices) as authentic Art-Deco were actually third-rate approximations from a much later period. And nobody seemed to know or care! Furthermore, since it was a mass, popular art, many film art directors were scornful of it and used it only in a spirit of derision. There was a tendency for it to be used as an indication of decadence. In America, as late as 1934, some of the most extreme Art-Deco was presented (in *The Black Cat*) as being the design of one of the most horrendous of all screen villains: a sadistic and perverted devil worshipper, played by Boris Karloff. In his German thrillers of 1922–32, and particularly in his *Dr. Mabuse* films, Fritz Lang associated his villains and tyrant figures with modern art designs. One wonders whether Hitler, who had great regard for Lang's filmmaking abilities, took note. When he came to power, he officially banned modern art in Germany.

As if to stress their contempt for the movement, many art directors seemed to feel a greater freedom to use Art-Deco in retreating to the past or looking forward to the future, where they couldn't be accused of taking it seriously. Since Egyptian design was one of the ingredients of Art-Deco, it is perhaps not surprising that deMille's *Cleopatra* should use it extensively, while such futuristic films as *Things to Come*, *Men Must Fight*, *Just Imagine*, and *Flash Gordon* were equally enterprising.

While one can perhaps study expressionism (and its influence on film and other areas) as a single entity, the development of Art-Deco,

COMEDY

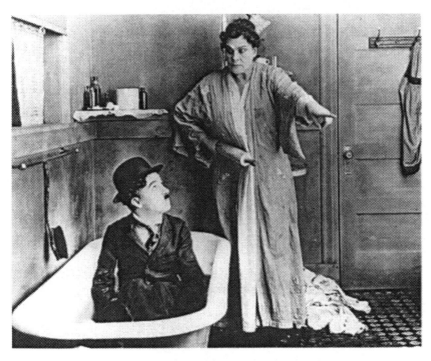

Payday (Chaplin, 1921) with Charlie Chaplin, Phyllis Allen

The Gold Rush (Chaplin, 1925)

Whispering Whiskers, a Sennett of the 20's with unchanged formula—Kewpie Morgan, Billy Bevan, Madeleine Hurlock

Chaplin's half-brother Syd was a talented comedian too, though often wasted in traditional Sennett knockabout like this

Max Davidson, endearing if stereotyped Jewish comic, in Hal Roach's *Call of the Cuckoo* (1927)

Wrong Again, a 1929 Hal Roach comedy that offered an up-to-the-minute satire of Buñuel's *Un Chien Andalou*, with Laurel and Hardy.

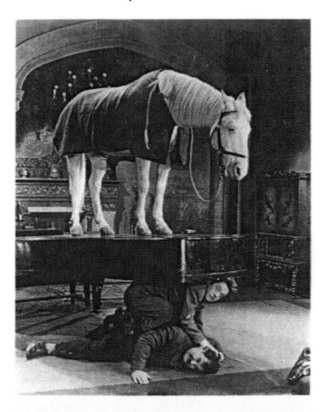

Liberty (1929): Laurel & Hardy—comedy of embarrassment

Sherlock Junior (1924), Buster Keaton

Raymond Griffith

The Navigator (1924), Buster Keaton and Kathryn McGuire

Movie Night (1928) with Charley Chase

Safety Last (1923), Harold Lloyd

The Cruise of the Jasper B (1927, directed by James Horne), Rod la Rocque
and Mildred Harris

For Heaven's Sake (1926), Harold Lloyd (with Noah Young, center)

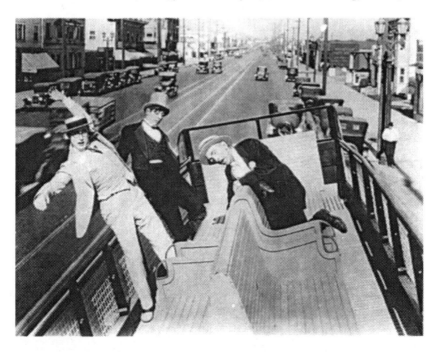

Long Pants (1927, directed by Frank Capra), Harry Langdon with Alma Bennett

Sunrise (1927, directed by F. W. Murnau) with George O'Brien, Janet Gaynor, and Margaret Livingstone. Arguably, the finest film of the silent era, but quite certainly the most beautiful pictorially.

Outstanding photography of Westerns was a major contribution of Dan Clark, one of the finest if least publicized cameramen.

Phantom of the Opera (1925)
with Lon Chaney and Mary
Philbin

Stella Dallas (1926) with Douglas Fairbanks, Jr., Lois Moran, Alice Joyce,
and (back to camera) Belle Bennett

Ben Hur (1926) with Ramon Novarro and Claire McDowell

The Night Cry (1926)
with Rin Tin Tin

The Tower of Lies (1925), directed by Victor Seastrom, with Lon Chaney, Norma Shearer, Claire McDowell

The Cat and the Canary, Martha Mattox, Tully Marshall

The Cat and the Canary (1927)

London after Midnight (1927), Lon Chaney

That Certain Thing (1928), Frank Capra's directorial debut at Columbia; with Viola Dana, Ralph Graves

The King of Kings (1927), directed by Cecil B. deMille, with H. B. Warner

White Shadows in the South Seas (1928), directed by W. S. Van Dyke

The Crowd (1928), directed by King Vidor, with Eleanor Boardman, James Murray

The Wedding March (1928), directed by and starring Erich von Stroheim

Street Angel (1928), directed by Frank Borzage, with Janet Gaynor

Beggars of Life (1928), Wallace Beery and Louise Brooks

Docks of New York (1928), directed by Josef von Sternberg, with Betty Compson and George Bancroft

Seventh Heaven (1927), directed by Frank Borzage

Wings (1927), directed by William Wellman

Four Devils (1928), directed by F. W. Murnau, with Janet Gaynor and Charles Morton

Peter Pan (1925), directed by Herbert Brenon, with Betty Bronson

A Kiss for Cinderella (1926), directed by Herbert Brenon, with Betty Bronson (right) and Esther Ralston

City Girl (1929), directed by F. W. Murnau, with Dick Alexander and Mary Duncan

Queen of the Northwoods (1929), one of the last silent Pathé serials; with Ethlyne Clair

Interference (1929), one of the first big talkie successes, with William Powell, Ruth Chatterton, and Clive Brook.

especially as it relates to film, has to be examined country by country, and then by individual company, since each aimed at a different market. France, with a far less marked division between its artistic and its purely commercial film product, was one of the first countries to incorporate Art-Deco design effectively in its films. *L'Argent* made in 1929 by the often experimental director Marcel L'Herbier, remains one of the best and most authentic examples of the art form from the country of its origin.

In America, MGM, under the leadership of resident art director Cedric Gibbons, was by far the most aggressive company, first in reflecting Art-Deco tastes and then in instigating new trends. MGM's films were always aimed at audiences that were rich—or (according to their own philosophy)—poor audiences that *envied* the rich and thus wanted to see glamor and elegance in films rather than reality. The "average" MGM family was usually independently wealthy and lived in a mad whirl of cocktail parties aboard yachts, with the source of such unlimited income usually unspecified but taken for granted. If nothing else, the MGM films of the late 1920's are a useful barometer of the extremes in Art-Deco tastes. Apart from matching the modernity and sophistication of MGM's tales of divorce, marital discord, and liberated youth, the decor was often used psychologically. In *The Kiss* (1929), Garbo and her husband (to whom she is loyal, but whom she does not love) live tense and virtually untenable lives. And the decor in which they live is equally untenable: the ceilings are low and claustrophobic, chairs and tables pointed, triangular, menacing. When, after one particular crisis, Garbo tries to relax, she is unable to do so. She is impelled to move restlessly from one uninviting chair to another, always "spied on" by a grotesque painting, light fixture, or sculpture. She can be at ease only with the two other (and chastely involved) men in her life, Conrad Nagel and Lew Ayres. Their meetings take place in an art museum or on a tennis court, both free from Art-Deco influence and menace. In the final courtroom-trial sequence, Garbo herself—photographed from below and gowned in a stark Adrian creation—is transformed into a film equivalent of the slim, chic figurines that served as decorative motifs for ash trays or automobile radiator "figureheads." *Our Dancing Daughters* (1928), one of the definitive jazz-age films, starts with a full-screen close-up of such a figurine, which dissolves into and is identified with the dancing figure of Joan Crawford. Space rather than furniture is used symbolically in this film. Joan Crawford plays "a free soul"; she enters and exits from scenes via wide, ornate staircases. The rooms of her mansion are free and uncluttered; groups of parents, girl friends, and male swains can gather in one of them and be dwarfed by space and height.

Universal, which owned no theaters in the big cities and therefore had to aim its films more at rural audiences—were Art-Deco, if not unknown was less highly regarded—showed far less interest in promoting the cause of this art form. Its films reflected, unobtrusively, general trends of the day. When everybody goes to a party in *Skinner's Dress Suit* (1925), the night-club is decked out Egyptian style, with tent motif and Nubian slaves, an acknowledgment of the enormous influence of Valentino and *The Sheik* on day-to-day living. However, Universal's use of Art-Deco was largely limited to its films of legend and fantasy and its big-city stories. Typical was *Broadway* (1929), Paul Fejos' successful screen version of the hit Broadway play. With an excellent set design by Charles D. Hall—and a traveling camera crane designed specifically for the occasion—the huge night-club set, in which the camera swooped and pounced from dizzy heights, represented a bizarre sign of Hollywood's recognition of this new pictorial art. Not only was it Art-Deco to an extreme degree, but it showed recognizable traces of German expressionism, too. The top of the set, where bizarre reality met surrealist infinity, was more than casually related to the night-club set in Fritz Lang's *Dr. Mabuse* of 1922. And when the camera had momentarily finished swooping and tracking, and came to rest backstage, the theatrical curtain pulled across the stage continued the expressionist flavor with a design of constantly staring eyes. (Again, one is reminded of Lang, and the montage of eyes as Brigitte Helm performs her erotic dance in *Metropolis* of 1926.)

There was an architectural inconsistency to the set, since the *exterior* of the night-club suggested no more than an unimposing two-story drug-store. Dramatically, it was even more inconsistent, since the hero, a hoofer (played by Glenn Tryon), spent the entire film bemoaning his lot of having to play cheap downtown clubs and looking forward to the time when he could move uptown to the big time and that perennial goal of all vaudevillians, the Palace. Even a command performance at Buckingham Palace would have been anti-climactic after an engagement at Universal's night-club.

But away from the big-city milieu, Universal had little time for Art-Deco. Clarence Brown's *Smouldering Fires* (1924), though set in a big city and the world of high finance, had virtually none of it. The film makes an interesting comparison with the similarly plotted *Female* (1933) from Warners. Warners was never on too secure a ground (that early) with stories of high living and millionaire financiers. They were much more at home with the working-class life of office girls and railroad workers. *Female* was an essay in the Art-Deco style of MGM, but without the stylistic consistency that made *The Kiss* workable. The heroine's backyard swimming pool looked like an artificial re-assembly of the parts of Busby Berkeley's waterfall ballet set in that same year's *Footlight Parade* (in fact, it may have been just that), while the lobby of her home—an area the size of any respectable railroad terminal—was graced by a supreme status symbol, an organist perched mid-way up one of the walls, with no way of access or escape. Presumably he was hoisted to his post every morning, or possibly he had a rope ladder hidden in the organ.

Paramount, with its European-flavored stories, directors (Lubitsch, Mamoulian, Sternberg), and stars, and a product aimed at the readers of sophisticated, high-society magazines, was perhaps the least flamboyant and most tasteful purveyor of Art-Deco on the screen, especially with Lubitsch's 1932 *Trouble in Paradise.*

Hollywood didn't really need the 1925 Paris exposition to discover Art-Deco, though that certainly gave it added impetus. Well before that date, and especially in the bizarre but often coldly beautiful creations of Natacha Rambova (a designer who worked closely with the equally bizarre actress Nazimova), Art-Deco existed in such early 1920's films as *Salome* and *Camille.* The gold-fish-bowl design of Camille's bedroom, and an opera house with *interiors* that looked like Caligariesque *exteriors,* are sets that still mesmerize. What Hollywood ultimately did was not to merely use or reflect Art-Deco but to transform it into a kind of design that could exist only in film and that relied for its effectiveness on camera trickery, lighting, and editing.

Authentic, reflected (if exaggerated) Art-Deco can be seen at its best in the Hollywood films of the late 1920's. But *filmic* Art-Deco, with an identity all its own, had to await the 1930's. Such films as deMille's *Madame Satan* and Schoedsack's *She* can perhaps be regarded as the definitive Art-Deco films of the 1930's, although the musicals (Busby

Berkeley and Astaire-Rogers in America, the Jessie Matthews vehicles, especially her 1934 *Evergreen,* in Britain) and even the animated cartoons (Warner's *Page Miss Glory* was both a celebration and a satire of Art-Deco) did their share to propagate it, even though limiting it to popular genres where it would not, at the time, be taken seriously. Art-Deco was already being replaced in the late 1930's by more practical and graceful forms of art, and the advent of World War II made it immediately obsolete. Whether one regards it as a serious art, a permanent art, or not an art at all, it's fortunate that its ascendency matched so exactly the movies' own pictorial zenith. The Art-Deco delights of *Our Dancing Daughters* and the more substantial stylistic design of *Sunrise* can stand side-by-side as representing the peak achievements of Hollywood's designers just before sound took over and, for a time at least, rendered design and pictorial beauty if not obsolete, then at least a victim to the immediate demand to *hear* rather than *see.*

18

European Influences

To a degree, American film had always demonstrated a certain amount of willingness to be influenced by Europe. Its early efforts in comedy certainly derived from the French, and one of the best of the early American serials, *The Exploits of Elaine* (1915), was as good as it was because of its close ties to the French serials of Feuillade. The success of *Quo Vadis?* (1912) may have prompted Griffith to concentrate much time and effort on the Babylonian episodes of *Intolerance,* and the popularity of the Lubitsch-Negri *Passion* (1919) may have suggested to him the commercial feasibility of *Orphans of the Storm* (although in both of those cases, influence was limited to the choice of subjects rather than to the way in which they were made). Although its expressionistic style was distrusted, the attention garnered by *The Cabinet of Dr. Caligari* in its U.S. release in 1921 caused it to be widely copied by American film-makers, but only in the most superficial way.

In 1924, however, Hollywood needed to strengthen its image in the fight against radio, and the acquisition of European "culture" was one of the ways in which it chose to do it. Fortunately, by this time, many European films had acquired a Hollywood gloss, although German film, strong in conception and in ideas, was often weak in execution (by Hollywood standards) until 1924–25.

When Hollywood brought over Greta Garbo, Mauritz Stiller, Lars Hanson, and Victor Seastrom in the mid-1920's, it virtually wiped out the Swedish film industry in terms of prestigious artists of more-than

317

local appeal. Good directors like Gustaf Molander remained, but there were not enough of them to maintain an international market. Oddly enough, Sweden, unlike Australia (which bitterly resented Hollywood involvement in its industry, and blamed it for its own industry's failure to develop), was flattered by Hollywood's attention—and, of course, the Hollywood films of the exported stars and directors were enormously popular in Sweden.

Although Ernst Lubitsch, Pola Negri, and Dmitri Buchovetski (despite his name, a director of *German* films in the early 1920's) had emigrated earlier, and Fox's negotiations to sign up F. W. Murnau were begun in 1924, it was essentially the success of two films—*The Last Laugh* (1924) and *Variety* (1925, but released in the United States in 1926)—that sold the American public on German films. Their commercial success has been vastly over-rated. One constantly hears generalizations about *Variety* "breaking box-office records everywhere," which was certainly not the case. But it did cause critics to vote it the best film of the year, and the point is that, while the number of showings in the United States could not begin to compete with native product, nevertheless, in those showings the films were accepted as at least the equal of Hollywood product. They were both exceptionally slick and glossy productions, in a technical sense well up to Hollywood standards. *The Last Laugh,* moreover, even though its subtleties may not have been fully understood by U.S. audiences, was a "different" story, an exceptionally dramatic one, and one without the sexual and/or political undertones that made so many European films suspect.

Variety, however, represented something of a cheat, since what made the film so successful in the United States was its total reshaping to the Hollywood pace and pattern. In the original version, Emil Jannings leaves his wife to run off with a sexy immigrant. They live together and ultimately become moderately successful circus performers, until they team with a big-name trapeze performer and become topline stars. Ultimately, the woman betrays Jannings with the trapeze star, and Jannings kills him, paying for his crime with a prison term from which, after ten years, he is pardoned. The first thing Hollywood did was to chop off the entire opening, thus turning Jannings' mistress into his wife, losing the subtlety of the ending, in which events come full circle, and tending to make the trapeze star the villain for having seduced the wife. Removal of the opening reels also eliminates the seedier, dockside sections of the story before Jannings becomes a star. The film now takes place against fairly well-to-do backgrounds resembling those of an American carnival, and later the big-time vaudeville review.

Apart from changing the shape and the morality of the film, the American distributor, Paramount, also changed its pace. The original, though faster than average, did maintain the lethargic pace of German films of the period and was roughly twice as long as the American release version. If there were three reaction shots of Jannings in the original, they would be cut down to one in the American prints. The brooding, introspective quality of the original was speeded up, yet cunningly, all of the outstanding photographic innovations of Karl Freund were retained. In a commercial sense, it was a magnificent job of keeping the outstanding characteristics of the original, yet so reshaping it to please American tastes that it became a totally different film. (It may even have become a better film. One hesitates to make that judgment, yet it is difficult to sit through the ponderous German original more than once or twice without boredom setting in, while the lightning-paced six-reel American version seems to gain in narrative cohesion what it loses in occasional subtlety. The two versions, side by side, offer an "instant" summing up of how the two versions of *Greed* might have fared if placed in a like juxtaposition.)

In any event, *The Last Laugh* and *Variety* paved the way for the coming German invasion, which was much more successful, on the whole, than the Scandinavian invasion—or kidnapping, depending on one's point of view. Victor Seastrom's eight American films are a remarkable showcase of Swedish temperament and extroverted puritanism. The best of them are so stark and austere that, if it weren't for the presence of Lillian Gish, Garbo, and other Hollywood names, they could pass as Swedish imports. Many of them seem interrelated, particularly *Name the Man* (based on a Hall Caine novel of sin and perhaps excessive redemption) and the beautifully photographed and acted *The Scarlet Letter* (based on the Nathaniel Hawthorne novel, which could be described in identical terms). Lars Hanson's impressive but far too stylized acting (in *The Scarlet Letter* in particular, though also in *The Wind*, in both of which "grand manner" acting is in marked contrast to the subtle and graceful underplaying of Lillian

Gish), further stresses the "non-American" quality of these films. Nevertheless, on the whole, Seastrom's American career can be considered a success. *The Scarlet Letter* (1926) was undoubtedly his masterpiece, an adaptation of the Hawthorne novel, in which the stark, puritanical fervor of the original novel was matched by the austere echoes of Scandinavian cinema. Even though the scenario somewhat muted and romanticized Hawthorne's original, Lars Hanson's extremely stylized playing and Hendrik Sartov's superb camerawork, full of delicate pictorial symbolism, restored the balance. Lillian Gish's mature and sensitive performance, in a role that was a far cry from the Victorian innocents that she had played for Griffith, was superb.

Gish, Hanson, and Seastrom were reunited by MGM for *The Wind*, a strange amalgamation of themes and elements from *Greed, White Gold,* and traditional westerns. A bizarre, shapeless affair, devoid of any real sense of period (even Lillian Gish's costuming seemed to exist in a vacuum), it was a monumental example of talent triumphing over scenario. Even changing the original tragic ending (in which the Gish character goes insane and wanders off into the desert) to a happy one (she kills the villain who has earlier raped her, buries his body in the desert, and is reunited with her previously estranged husband) seemed not to affect the film, except perhaps for its commercial betterment. The plot, though based on a 1925 story, seemed too old-fashioned and erratic to be taken seriously, and the switch from tragedy to happiness hardly represented a box-office sellout. The atmospheric photography (John Arnold), Seastrom's beautifully underplayed direction (the killing scene was a brilliant essay in suggestion, the whole act of the body falling to the floor being conveyed by a shot of a dust-laden plate jarring, and resettling), and the superb control exercised by Lillian Gish over potentially flamboyant theatrics, all represented the silk purse of silent screen art at its peak, despite the sow's ear on which it was squandered. Commercially, he was able to fall back on Hollywood stars (Gish, Chaney, Shearer, Gilbert, Garbo) to counteract his somewhat austere style. And in any case, while Swedish directorial styles (many of which derived from the German cinema) were not exactly emulated by other Hollywood directors, lesser imported directors like Sven Gade, and the use of Scandinavian-oriented material as vehicles for Swedish stars (Clarence Brown's *Flesh and the Devil,* from a Suderman story, starring Garbo, Gilbert, and Hanson, is a case in point), did tend to make the Swedish point of view, if not commonplace, then at least visible. Seastrom's Hollywood career was certainly more successful than Stiller's. The latter began to direct Garbo in *The Temptress* (1927) almost as though he were taking up when they had both left off in *The Atonement of Gösta* Berling. Even Garbo's hair style and gowns seemed to be from that picture. Stiller, however, was quickly removed and replaced by the more conventional Fred Niblo. Of Stiller's handful of American films, the best was undoubtedly the slow but impressive *Hotel Imperial* (1927), although the omnipresence of producer Erich Pommer and star Pola Negri undoubtedly helped to give it a look far more Germanic than Swedish.

It was, in any case, the German influence that dominated, not only in the United States but perhaps even more so in England, where there was often no indication that a film like *Moulin Rouge* (directed by E. A. Dupont, with Olga Tchekowa) or *The Informer* (directed by Arthur Robison, with Lars Hanson and Lya de Putti) was British. Following the success of *The Last Laugh* and *Variety*, Fritz Lang's *Metropolis* (1926) was another stunning welding of German artistry with American expertise and showmanship.

It is usually claimed that it was the huge success of *The Last Laugh* in the United States that caused William Fox to sign F. W. Murnau and give him carte-blanche on *Sunrise*. The facts are otherwise, although it is not known for sure what prompted Fox's initial interest. The contracts were signed January 1925, just a week or two after the Berlin premiere of *The Last Laugh*, and certainly long before it had a chance to establish a U.S. reputation. It seems likely that Karl Freund, cameraman on the film, and with Hollywood ambitions for himself, recognized during the shooting that the film would cause something of a sensation and urged Fox to sign Murnau before anyone else did. He undoubtedly assumed that he would be shipped to Hollywood along with Murnau, although as it happened, he would stay in Germany for the time being, though as a consultant to Hollywood interests. Some time later, he did move to Hollywood where he enhanced his already considerable reputation as a cinematographer and directed a handful of pictures, two of which (*The Mummy*, 1932, and *Mad Love*, 1935) are recognized as stylistic classics of the horror film.

Murnau's contract was a generous one, both financially and in terms of the freedom it gave him to use many of his German associates in scripting and production design. No individual titles or properties were specified within the contract. Much as Murnau looked forward to working in Hollywood, with all the facilities he needed, he didn't rush to move there. In fact, he remained in Germany long enough to make the film that was by far the best of his European productions, *Faust* (1926). By the time he arrived and made *Sunrise* for late 1927 release, German films had become both fashionable and reasonably profitable, and other German directors had preceded him into Hollywood production. The enormous critical success of *Sunrise*, however, caused it to be the single most influential picture of the period. From *Sunrise* on, German directors working in Hollywood, and Hollywood directors in awe of Germanic technique, consciously tried to imitate it. Prior to *Sunrise*, the imitation had been largely limited to superficial elements—an emphasis on the moving camera or on bizarre angles—while the German directors themselves usually tried, and often with surprising success, to absorb themselves in the Hollywood mainstream of production.

Typical of the pre-*Sunrise* films was Dmitri Buchowetski's *The Swan*, produced in late 1924 and released in 1925 for Paramount. The first of three versions of the Ferenc Molnar play (there was an early sound version with Lillian Gish and a much later remake with Grace Kelly), this one was produced only three years after the play's premiere in Budapest. Already there were substantial changes, for both commercial reasons and artistic ones, the latter fully explained by writer-director Buchowetski at the time. They caused no great waves of protest, however, and the only criticism that the *New York Times* had to make was that it might not go down with the flapper audience. Far more Lubitsch and Stroheim than Molnar (one whole episode seemed almost a spoof of a key *Foolish Wives* episode), it was a handsome and snappy production that bowled along far more rapidly than Molnar would have liked, and was dominated by Adolphe Menjou's perfectly styled and good-natured performance. At the time, before Menjou had come to specialize in such roles, it must have been a doubly-impressive performance, especially in comparison with the extremely wooden acting of Ricardo Cortez and Frances Howard. Miss Howard, a beautiful but lifeless creature, made only a handful of films before retiring, marrying Sam Goldwyn and devoting herself to the business side of film-making. Although in its speed and light-hearted flair the film was a typical mid-1920's Hollywood product, its Germanic roots were stressed in the sets, with their strong emphasis on perfect symmetry and balance. The film also made an apt comparison with the same director's earlier German version of *Othello* (with Emil Jannings and Werner Krauss), in which he frequently changed Shakespeare into Sennett while remaining faithful to the original text. Yet it was a thoughtful and interesting production, again highly decorative in terms of sets, and was thought quite highly of at the time—especially by Rene Clair.

Critical espousal of German films was by no means absolute. Ward Marsh, critic of the Cleveland *Plain Dealer,* was a reviewer who took films very seriously. He often championed worthwhile but sparsely shown foreign films (he was responsible for getting Seastrom's Swedish silent *Thy Soul Shall Bear Witness* shown in Cleveland) and frequently took issue against censorship. On the other hand, he did not underrate the taste of the public and felt himself to be fairly representative of that taste. Writing about the new fad for German films (in August 1926), he comments:

> The only thing we haven't stolen is *The Cabinet of Dr. Caligari,* and even that has had an effect on our lighting to achieve atmosphere and symbolism. *Variety* has taught us the use of camera angles in films like *You Never Know Women* and *Fine Manners.* But the Germans have never created a *Peter Pan* or a *Kiss for Cinderella* for the screen, and for imaginative quality, these along with *One Glorious Day* are superb. Have they ever done a *Covered Wagon* or an epic half so fine? Can you go over there and bring home a *Tol'able David,* a *Peter Ibbetson** or one with the simplicity of *A Woman of Paris?* Can they furnish us with a *Big Parade* or *Marriage Circle* or *Four Horsemen of the Apocalypse* or a *Miracle Man?* Could you ask for a mother-love tale from them which would in any way approximate Norma Talmadge's *The Lady?* I would not treat lightly such pictures as *Deception, Passion, The Cabinet of Dr. Caligari* or even *Variety.* They are fine pictures, excellently made, but we are too eager to make a great deal of importations and less liable to give credit to some of our not only talented but hard-working directors and cameramen.

Such fair-minded but essentially timid enthusiasm for German technique vanished, however, as well it might, with the release of Mur-

---

* Marsh makes a minor slip here. The adaptation of *Peter Ibbetson* to which he refers was actually titled *Forever.*

nau's *Sunrise*. One would hesitate to call *any* film the finest of its era, though as a climax to the art of silent film, one could certainly defend that statement if it were applied to *Sunrise*. But quite certainly, it is a textbook illustration not only of what the silent film could achieve despite the lack of dialogue, but, on the contrary, what it could achieve *because* of it.

Based on (and changed from) Herman Suderman's mystical story, *Sunrise* is, as its sub-title states, "a song of two humans." A hard-working farmer strays from his wife and is seduced by a woman from the city. She urges him to murder his wife in a way that will make it look like an accidental drowning, and run away with her to the city. At first horrified, he finally agrees. But in the trip across the lake, he cannot go through with his plan, although he tries to. His terrified wife runs from him. He pursues her, begs forgiveness, and in the course of a day in the city, wins back her love and trust. On the journey back across the lake, a sudden storm wrecks their little boat. The husband gives his wife the bundles of bullrushes with which he had planned to keep himself afloat after killing her. In the aftermath of the storm, she cannot be found and is presumed dead. In sudden fury, the husband attempts to kill the temptress—but at the crucial moment, his wife is found alive. They are reunited for an even happier life.

A bald synopsis can give no hint of the incredible beauty and sense of joy and love that pervade the film, and much of it is due to the fact that the film is silent (though equipped with an evocative score and sound effects that are used extremely creatively). The very lack of dialogue gives it a timelessness and a universality that would have been impossible in a sound film. Although based on a European story by Suderman, *The Trip To Tilsit*, the film is ambiguous as to its setting. Certain aspects suggest Europe, but it could just as well be taking place in Canada or Georgia. Even the time period is arguable. Clothing is certainly not of the mid-1920's, and if the automobiles are, then the stylized city set and the futuristic amusement park further—and deliberately—muddy the waters. Yet dialogue (quite apart from rendering its sweep of emotion in commonplace terms) would automatically have tied it to a period and a country, and the universality would have gone. Possibly films need a kind of fairy-tale or fable structure to achieve this universality. In varying degrees, *Love Me Tonight* (1932) and *King Kong* (1933) achieved it, even though both films *had* to be precise about their location. A good example of a sound film which *tried* for that universality was Sternberg's *Crime and Punishment* (1935), which was quite ingenious in achieving it *visually* but was totally defeated *aurally* by the anachronisms, the modern and wholly American expressions, and the accents themselves.

Sunrise creates that universality not only visually, but because its emotions are likewise timeless and know no geographic borders, and because each member of the audience is able, in a sense, to "regulate" the emotion of the film without having dialogue spell it out for him. Too, the film will obviously mean far more depending on one's own experience of life. A married couple who have drifted apart and been re-united would undoubtedly find it a far more moving film than happy young newly-weds. The lack of dialogue helps in other ways, too. By supplanting speech with music and *sound*, the track is able to use sounds both dramatically and symbolically. At each climactic juncture in the plot (the attempted killing, for example), church bells signify the moment of catharsis. In one of the closing sequences, the wife sleeps peacefully in her husband's arms as they sail across the lake—and *continues* to sleep while the storm blows up, rages about them, and makes the little boat rock on the waves. In the realistic medium of the sound film, it would be absurd to suppose that she could sleep through such a tempest. In the stylized medium of silence, it works as a symbol of her total trust in the man.

Despite the naturalistic qualities of the occasional lake and woodland scenes, *Sunrise* is an extremely stylized and unreal film, made real by the humanity of its protagonists. The city sets, done in forced perspective to make them look larger and more spacious than they are (even to using midgets in the background!), represent a city as it *would* look to peasants seeing it for the first time, or after a long period of anticipation. Yet it is amazing how often film students, so completely caught up in the film's spell, ask whether the city was a studio creation or shot on location. Likewise, nobody ever seems to question the validity of George O'Brien's performance, despite the curious nature of the role. O'Brien himself was hardly a major actor, having specialized essentially in breezy western and action roles under John Ford. His whole personality, normally optimistic and extroverted, here became brooding and introspective. He even used his body in a stylized way, hunched forward as though literally carrying the weight of the world on his shoulders—as he is, until the spiritual reunion with his wife. (One can follow this typically Germanic acting method across at least two oceans: from Jannings in *Variety* in Germany to O'Brien in *Sunrise* in Hollywood, thence to England via Lars Hanson in *The Informer*, and well into the sound period with Charles Laughton in *St. Martin's Lane* (1938), which, coincidentally, was made by Erich Pommer, producer of *Variety*, thus bringing the style full circle.

Sunrise must be one of the very few films clearly intended and mathematically planned as a "prestige" and "art" production all the way, which still comes off with warmth, humanity, and seeming spontaneity. (Usually films thus planned emerge, like John Ford's *The Fugitive* in 1947, as academically impressive but cold and heartless.) The poignancy and humanity of some sequences of *Sunrise* has never been surpassed in any movie, sound or silent: the husband trying to calm his wife's fears and win back her trust, taking her to a restaurant and ordering cake which neither of them want or can eat; or their witnessing of a marriage ceremony, where the husband finds himself repeating, and perhaps understanding for the first time, the marriage vows, to collapse in his wife's arms and be comforted by her.

In terms of production design and photography, *Sunrise* not only represents the very best of Hollywood, but stresses the gap that still existed between the capabilities of Europe and the expertise of Hollywood. It is amazing to think that there were only five years between this film and Murnau's *Nosferatu*.† For all its depth and visual virtuosity (and the camerawork was by two of Hollywood's finest, Charles Rosher and Karl Struss), *Sunrise* is an essentially simple film. The basic scenario by Carl Mayer is lyrical and poetic, but uncomplicated—assuming complications only when one compares it with other Murnau films (*City Girl*, 1929, or *Tabu*, 1931) and realizes that, despite disparate plot lines, there were certain motifs and patterns that Murnau wove into all of his films. Even the camerawork is deceptive. One sequence, in which the husband goes to meet his mistress in the swamp at night, looks as though a vast set was created and then criss-crossed

† *Nosferatu*, Murnau's version of *Dracula*, was, in 1922, a refreshing break from the studio-bound qualities of other German fantasies, its expressionistic style tempered by natural locations. It was and is an outstanding film, better than Murnau's immediately subsequent German films, yet is undeniably primitive when compared with his final German works and his American films that followed between 1924 and 1929.

with camera tracks. When one studies the movement of the camera carefully, one realizes that a simple T-shaped track was used, and that the mobility of the camera on that track, plus the movements of O'Brien, create an amazing sense of motion and space in what is actually a fairly small and limited area.

Even though its commercial success was limited by the competition of the new talkies, *Sunrise* was an enormous critical success, the kind of prestige item of which all studio heads dreamed. (Studio prestige was highly sought after, and most studios aimed at making at least one such film a year, regardless of possible short-range losses. The enormous profits from the Tom Mix westerns more than paid for *Sunrise*, just as over at Warner Brothers the slick and highly enjoyable Rin Tin Tin actioners underwrote the John Barrymore specials that were usually unsuccessful outside of key metropolitan areas.)

The impact of *Sunrise* as a film, and of Murnau as a new artistic leader, was enormous, especially at Fox. There directors, out of genuine homage, tried to emulate his style. And writers, art directors, and cameramen who came in contact with him used the techniques they learned from him in their next films, and the influences became crossbred. Particularly illustrative of this process was Frank Borzage's *Street Angel* (1928), which came out just a few months after *Sunrise* and attempted the well-nigh impossible task of re-creating the *commercial* success of Borzage's earlier *Seventh Heaven* (a 1927 film with the same stars, Janet Gaynor and Charles Farrell) and linking it to the *artistic* concept of *Sunrise*. Its slight and unlikely romantic story was drawn out to undue length and lacked both the classic simplicity of *Sunrise* and the larger-than-life bravura qualities of *Seventh Heaven*. But its opening fifteen minutes were pure UFA, its heavy, oppressive lighting and stylized groupings in Bauhaus architectural design recalling not only *Sunrise* but even specific images from Lang's *Metropolis*. The later portions of the film suggested that Borzage had also taken the trouble to study Murnau's *Tartuffe* (1924). Borzage's subsequent *The River* (1929), virtually a two-character story in a very restricted setting, was also thoroughly Germanic in its studio-bound reconstruction of an exterior (river and mountains and the coming of winter snows) environment.

Virtually all of the basic Fox directors—William K. Howard, Howard Hawks, Raoul Walsh, and spectacularly (but in the early sound period) William Dieterle—embraced Murnau's visual style, with some, like Howard, retaining strong traces of it permanently. Even so American a director as John Ford, whose basic influence came from Griffith, and who would return to a particularly strong recapitulation of Griffith themes and methods in his films of 1933–36, temporarily changed (and slowed) his whole style to match that of Murnau. His *Four Sons* (1928) even used the sets of the small European village from *Sunrise* and worked from an (uncredited) stream-of-consciousness screen treatment by Herman Bing, the Murnau assistant who had also worked as an intermediary between Mayer's original scenario of *Sunrise* and the final shooting script. (Incidentally, despite meticulous pre-planning and story-boarding, some of the best cuts and moments of pure technique of *Sunrise* appear *only* in the film, and in none of the several written treatments, confirming, if it were needed, Murnau's very positive contributions.)

Ford's *Hangman's House* (1928), which might have been a fairly conventional Irish melodramatic romance, became a very strange mixture of German-dominated visual stylistics reminiscent of *Warning Shadows* (1922), with foreshadowings of Ford's later talkies *The Informer* (1935) and *The Quiet Man* (1952). If nothing else, *Hangman's House* totally repudiates Ford's oft-stated claim that he was not an artist but merely a worker doing a job the best way he knew how. It is full of scenes and compositions that only an artist would use, including a long tracking shot through the mist of a studio-made river—a scene that could have been dispensed with for its small narrative value, and probably would have been replaced by a fade or a title *if* Ford had been merely "doing a job."

Murnau's own later work at Fox hardly measured up to the stunning success of *Sunrise*. However, it is perhaps difficult to assess it fairly since his second film, *Four Devils* (1928), has long been missing (and in view of Murnau's stature, may thus be the single most important and frustrating "lost" film, with Stroheim's *The Devil's Passkey* (1920) running a close second). His final film for Fox, *City Girl*, 1929 (made under the title *Our Daily Bread*), was sabotaged by the coming of sound. It is something of a miracle that *City Girl* was made at all, since in 1929 a silent—and a slow, lyrical silent, at that—was already an anachronism. Moreover, it followed the theme of city versus country life that had already fascinated so many directors, including William Beaudine (*The Canadian*, 1926), Victor Seastrom (*The Wind*, 1928), and William K. Howard (*White Gold*, 1927), so that its one basic dramatic theme—man (or woman) versus the elements—was an overly familiar one in 1929. Rumor has it that while Murnau sincerely wanted to make the film, envisioning it as a kind of "woodcut," the reason it was sanctioned was that a Fox executive wanted the film as a vehicle for his current girl friend. Murnau threw himself into it whole-heartedly, renting an entire ranch in Oregon for the wheat-farming sequences, but when it was finished, Fox was dismayed by its lack of commercial sales angles and performed a curious hatchet job on it. The first five reels were left relatively intact; the second five were cut down to two, and re-shot in sound, making the most of opportunities for bunk-house singing and story-telling. Although many of Murnau's superb establishing shots and documentary scenes of wheat-harvesting were retained, the latter portions of the film were now clearly no longer his, and the unmotivated acceleration of pace must have played havoc with the film's structure. The reviews were not bad, doubtless out of respect for Murnau, but the film received only sparse exhibition and soon disappeared. Ironically—and for once, happily—this butchered version has now vanished, and Murnau's original version—or at least, a cut that approximates his original version—does still exist. Although an unspectacular film after the emotionalism and visual dexterity of *Sunrise*, it gains strength via repeated viewings and is a much stronger and subtler film than initial contact with it suggests—just as Welles' *The Magnificent Ambersons*, for so long in the shadow of *Citizen Kane*, is now emerging as a far more substantial film than we first thought. Murnau's final film, *Tabu* (1931), made independently for Paramount release, used music and sound effects but was otherwise a silent film, closer in spirit to his earlier German fantasies (and *Nosferatu* in particular) than to his Fox films. He died in an auto accident in Hollywood prior to its release, before having had a chance to demonstrate what he might have been able to do with talkies.

Away from Fox, the German influence was less concentrated but equally pronounced. Paramount, with Lubitsch, Pommer, Negri, Stiller, Stroheim (temporarily!), and Sternberg on their talent roster, and such German imports as Joe May's *Homecoming* on their release schedule,‡ reflected a considerable European influence. In a visual sense, Sternberg's films were the closest to the German school, though they were glossier and more romantic. His *Docks of New York* (1928) represented something of a high point in his personal style and was also one of his best pictures—perhaps because for once it was about real people, and because Sternberg handled his actors (George Bancroft and Betty Compson in particular) as intelligent individuals rather than as puppets. Photographically, it is still one of the glories of the American cinema, though often in an extremely self-indulgent way, weakening its already slim story line to accommodate visual effects. At one point, George Bancroft's departure to procure a glass of water for the stricken heroine seems to serve no narrative purpose other than that of allowing him to stroll through fishnet-strewn outdoor stairways, down through a picturesque saloon, and back again. A farewell scene is prolonged almost to epic proportions as the heroine sews a button on her lover's coat, threading the needle via subjective gauzed close-ups seen through tear-stained eyes.

The influence on style wasn't all in one direction, however. William Wellman's extremely powerful story of hoboes in the pre-Depression era, *Beggars of Life* (1928), opens magnificently with a hobo (Richard Arlen) accidentally discovering the body of a dead farmer and then listening to the explanatory story of the girl (Louise Brooks) who killed him to escape rape. It's a dynamic opening, with the beautiful Brooks relating her story while the action, via striking yet casual images, is superimposed. One suspects that G. W. Pabst must have studied this sequence carefully when he used Brooks subsequently in two 1929 German films, *Diary of a Lost Girl* and *Pandora's Box*. (Incidentally, *Beggars of Life* seems to have been a key inspirational film for Preston Sturges' 1941 *Sullivan's Travels*.)

At MGM, King Vidor—a director almost as American as Borzage and Ford—certainly paid homage to German style in what is still probably his finest work, *The Crowd* (1928). A moving story of two ordinary people struggling to find happiness and success in New York, and not being quite up to the pressures and the competition, *The Crowd* has

---

† In the late twenties, UFA, Paramount, and MGM formed an amalgamation known as Parufamet, and Paramount and MGM released most of the major UFA films in the United States, though frequently taking two-part, four-hour movies and reducing them to streamlined eighty-minute versions.

certain affinities with De Sica's post-World War II classic *The Bicycle Thief,* most especially in the almost indefinably tender relationship between the father and his son. Yet for all of its realism, the sets and lighting (particularly the scenes in the hospital) are often unreal and stylized in the German manner. It was a style that Vidor would return to periodically, one of the most striking instances being his 1949 *The Fountainhead.*

Some directors, newly arrived from Europe, were so obsessed with stylistic virtuosity (an obsession shared by the studio heads who imported them) that they tended to run amok with their visuals. Typical was Michael Curtiz, whose first American film, *The Third Degree* (1926), was a dazzling display of filmic pyrotechnics—eccentric angles, constant mobility, fanciful lighting—all smoothly executed for him by cameraman Hal Mohr. Curtiz, however, never (even much later, when he was more familiar with Hollywood scripting processes) achieved the ability to cut through the dramatic entanglements that a too-wordy script, or his own fascination with pictorialism, led him into. *The Third Degree* backs itself into so many dramatic corners that even when its plot is virtually told, it still takes Curtiz two reels to tidy up and dispose of all the dramatic loose ends. A few American directors *did* resist the lure of German stylistics, and retained their own deceptively simple but actually sophisticated style. Clarence Brown, a director of extreme taste and sensitivity, was one. Always under-rated as a director because his style was unobtrusive, and because his films tended to be elaborate star vehicles (Garbo, Valentino, Gable, Crawford), he was taken for granted, respected for his reliability, but his unique personal style was too often unrecognized.

Beneath the gloss and decor that accompanied his big MGM specials lay an interesting method of telling much of his stories via three-shots—grouping his three principals into compositions which of themselves told much of the story. It was a form of silent-day narrative that extended into his sound films as well; his talkie *Anna Karenina* with Garbo conveyed so much of the various conflicts via three-shot compositions that it can almost be played as a silent, with the sound turned off. (Such an experiment is easily made, since the film is quite regularly shown on television.) A demonstration of Brown's subtle simplicity can be illustrated by comparing Curtiz' *The Third Degree,* with all of its plot intricacies, with Brown's *Smouldering Fires* of 1924. The plot of that one (an intelligent soap-opera) likewise winds up with many problems unresolved. Brown even sweeps away some of the poetic but cluttered sub-titles of the original script, and where Curtiz would have had to use two reels of narrative, Brown settles for a *single shot*—an expressive three-shot in which the imaginative grouping and the nuances of facial expression not only sum up the situation *as it is,* but also pinpoint its resolution.

Undisputed headquarters of German gothic was Universal, which in the sound period would utilize its Germanic style and craftsmen in a long series of horror films. But, at the end of the 1920's, Carl Laemmle imported top talent from Europe, welcomed them to Universal with characteristic parades and brass bands, and set them to work creating high-class essays in the macabre and vehicles for Conrad Veidt. Paul Leni's *The Cat and the Canary* (1927) was filled with atmospheric tricks and photographic innovations, as was its only slightly less impressive follow-up, *The Last Warning* (1928). Leni and his brethren may have been artists with traditional temperament, but they had no qualms about adapting themselves to Hollywood formulas. The German sense of humor has always been rather weak and leaden (except to German audiences), and yet the German directors (Lang among them) who used humor least, and certainly least effectively, always prided themselves on having a great sense of humor. Therefore, it was with no sense of "slumming" that they confronted the obligatory comedy relief in films like *The Cat and the Canary,* and evoked it with the same gusto that they gave to the film's qualities of horror and menace. Somehow, this enthusiasm for pallid comic material became its saving grace.

The only time this extended utilization of humor (often farce and slapstick) really grated was in *The Beloved Rogue,* the 1926 film which might be considered the cornerstone of Hollywood gothic. Magnificently photographed by Joseph August, with stunning sets by William Cameron Menzies, the artistic collaboration of Alan Crosland and Paul Bern, and one of John Barrymore's finest and subtlest silent-screen portrayals, backed up by Conrad Veidt in a thoroughly stylized and Germanic interpretation of King Louis, the film certainly did not need the slapstick caperings of those two Mack Sennett graduates, Slim Summerville and Mack Swain.

Paul Leni's other work at Universal included the magnificently sumptuous *The Man Who Laughs* (1928), from the Victor Hugo novel. It didn't have quite the humanity that it might have had if Lon Chaney rather than Conrad Veidt had played the grotesque central role. Also, it was hindered somewhat by the introduction of a *vocal* voice-over love-song in otherwise tender moments, and its sets were certainly far more reminiscent of Germany than the England it was supposed to evoke. Photographically it contained many echoes from *Nosferatu*, emphasized by the villains' constant emergence from low-ceilinged, tomb-like edifices. The stark opening reel, with bodies swinging from gibbets in a snow storm, was pictorialism of a high order. Paul Fejos was another emigré addition to the Universal directorial ranks, his particular claim to fame (accomplished with the help of cameraman Hal Mohr and designer Charles Hall) being the bizarre, surrealist Art-Deco night-club set from *Broadway*. Even the program westerns at Universal reflected German inspiration. *Wild Blood* (1929) was photographed by George Robinson, who later did *Son of Frankenstein* (1939) and some of the best of Universal's sound horror films. It contained some remarkable visual effects: the villain tempting the heroine with visions of city glamor, à la *Sunrise*, and an astonishing sequence, done via subjective shots, hand-held camera, and superimpositions, of the heroine's near-descent into madness when she is driven to despair by the boredom and frustration of western life.

The wholesale artistic leadership of Hollywood (and British) films by German style (and stylists) in this period has been noted in the past, but usually via the simple expedient of quoting *Sunrise*. The reduction of this whole process to a single film is, in a way, understandable, since so many of the key films involved—*Street Angel*, *Hangman's House*, *The Beloved Rogue*, *The Man Who Laughs*—were not available for study. Without them, the emphasis in the late twenties seemed to shift from artistry to technology: the talkies, which had been tried experimentally almost since movies began, were now approaching commercial and mechanical feasibility. First via *Don Juan*, with its music and sound effects, supported by shorts in which people spoke and sang, and then in 1927, via *The Jazz Singer*, with its songs and limited dialogue, climaxed by the development of the Movietone system—sound on film as opposed to sound on disc—it became apparent that the silent cinema, though not yet dead, was certainly dying.

19

Transition to Sound:

Early Talkies

Although *Don Juan* in 1926, and far more significantly, *The Jazz Singer* in 1927, clearly signaled the ultimate end of the silent era, the years 1927 and 1928 represented a curious phenomenon. While the silent film as an industry was dying, it was still growing as an art. Its peak achievements in those two years were accelerated by the need to reach the screen before the form in which they had been made was obliterated for all time.

For once, art was left to the artists—with relatively little supervision during production, though occasionally with a great deal of post-production interference in order to adapt completed material to one or another of the new systems. Not only was Hollywood up to its neck in conversion to sound, and unable to decide, initially, whether sound on disc or sound on film was the better method—a decision that affected theaters as much as it did production—but there were other mechanical problems to be solved. The European version of a Hollywood film was no longer the same film with appropriate sub-titles. It was frequently a totally different and separate production, with its own script and its own European actors and director. Wide-screen processes—ranging from the Magnascope process, which merely enlarged the screen for key climactic and spectacular sequences, to the use of 70mm film— were in a new experimental stage. So was the more widespread use of color, spearheaded by the recently improved two-color Technicolor system. When a film was to be made in two or more foreign versions,

334

and possibly with a color or wide-screen process involved as well, the logistics—considering the total lack of experience with sound—were enormous. When the Wall Street financial crash came in 1929, Hollywood had its survival problems, too, and some of its solutions involved a stress on the novelty values of these recent innovations. Economics and mechanics seemed to take precedence over artistry, and if the latter was pushed into third place in terms of importance, it was not necessarily a bad thing. The artists were often left alone, with a freedom of function that they had rarely encountered before.

Thus, in a strange, convoluted way, the period of motion pictures most dominated by technology and profit considerations also became one of the most creative periods in all film history. First of all, it was clear that the silent movie had no future but was still a temporary necessity. It would be a long time before all the theaters, especially the smaller ones in the hinterlands, had converted to sound. They still needed product; and although audiences were quickly sold on the idea that talkies were modern and silents old-fashioned, they were still loyal to favorite stars, many of whom were not yet ready to take the plunge into sound. Further, many silents had been in preparation for a long time. To abandon them would be a total loss, but to go ahead and produce them, as economically as possible, would entail a lesser loss and possibly even a small profit.

There was a glorious kind of fatalism in the last days of the silents. The films were being produced purely for the moment; in a year or two, they would be dead for all time. Producers, directors, stars, and studio heads all seemed united in an unofficial and unspoken mass conspiracy to create one great Last Stand of the silent film, to show what it could do before the ultimate death at the coming of the microphones and sound tracks.

What it could do was considerable; the silent film was at its peak of visual sophistication. Directors and cameramen had virtually abandoned color tones and tints, achieving the effects they wanted through subtle camerawork. Inter-titles were shorter and sparser than ever, usually merely a back-up to the visuals instead of a narrative equal partner. Moreover, the influence of the European and especially the German cinema was still flourishing and would remain in Hollywood through the early thirties. It would never really wane even then, but would become so thoroughly absorbed into the Hollywood talkies of directors (usually of German origin) like Fritz Lang and later John Brahm and Robert Siodmak that one almost ceased to regard it as a European "influence."

While sure-fire theater fodder—westerns, action pictures, comedies—were certainly not abandoned, there was still a feeling that, even if silent films that had to be made would live for only a year or two, they might as well be made the way the film-makers wanted. The only recognizable concession to the economics of the period was a stress on simplicity where possible. Von Sternberg's *Docks of New York* and Vidor's *The Crowd*, both of 1928, were both relatively uncomplicated films: contemporary stories, few big stars, no star egos to be coddled. An artistic undertaking as grandiose as Murnau's *Sunrise* was still permissible in 1927, but in 1929 he had to settle for the less expensive design of *City Girl*, in itself no minor achievement.

The stars with either direct or indirect control over their vehicles disregarded box-office formulas and the kind of films their fans expected. They brought their silent careers to a close with films that may have been self-indulgent in their displays of style—acting, directorial, visual—but were certainly climactic, in terms of showcasing both their own work and the silent film in general. Barrymore's *Beloved Rogue* (1927) and *Tempest* (1928) are particularly illustrative of this trend, as was Gloria Swanson's *Sadie Thompson* (1928), which, despite being directed by the normally rough-and-ready Raoul Walsh, achieved an almost Carl Dreyer-like austerity and pace, and, like Dreyer's upcoming *Le Passion de Jeanne D'Arc* (1929), told much of its story through close-ups. Even away from Swanson's control and supervision, Walsh, as commercial a director as one could envision, tried to inject almost overpowering visual art into another of his late silents, 1928's *The Red Dance*. Although its story was a novelettish excursion into the then-fashionable though little understood (by Hollywood) Russian Revolution, its camerawork (primarily by Charles Clarke) and its sets and overall art direction (by Ben Carré) were outstanding.

Nor can one overlook the too-often-maligned studio heads, who not only interfered *less* at this particular time but also sanctioned these essentially uncommercial projects in the first place. The studio heads, too, saw a chance for prestige and glory, even if it was virtually forced on them. Many of them, like Louis B. Mayer of MGM and Carl Laemmle of Universal, were acutely aware of their own intellectual shortcomings and educational gaps. They weren't ashamed of them, and in many cases regarded their own non-intellectual tastes as reliable barometers of how the vast majority of the movie-going public felt. But they were frequently envious of the men of wit, taste, and learning whom they hired to write or direct for them. This "lost cause" period of 1927–28 gave them a chance to show that they, too, appreciated art by instigating and promoting films like *Lonesome* and *White Shadows in the South Seas.* Too, the studio heads saw a chance to make statements of their own as well. It is no coincidence that in this period one finds an unusually large number of films celebrating, often in unashamedly sentimental fashion, the glories of Jewish ritual and tradition. The success of *The Jazz Singer* may have been a partial catalyst, but since it was the songs and the sound that created attention for that film, its story usually being dismissed (somewhat unfairly) as old-fashioned and hokey, it would not have created a cycle of Jewish generation-conflict stories. The most typical of these films was probably 1925's *His People,* made for Universal well before the sound revolution; but as a cycle, it was particularly prolific in the post-1926 period. Universal probably contributed more to the genre than any other studio, ranging from 1927's *Surrender* to the Jewish-Irish comedy of the "Cohens and the Kellys" series.

Most of the top silent directors—Borzage, Ford, Stroheim, Sternberg, Vidor—were sad to see the onrush of sound, feeling that it would both destroy a unique art form and lessen the commercial value of Hollywood films in the European market. To a large extent, their feelings were correct, though their predictions of what the sound film would become were often way off target. None of them were anxious to rush into talkies, partly because they disliked them and partly for the more practical reason that their reputations might be lost easily and quickly. They were happy to leave the experimenting to the lesser studio hacks and to move into the new medium when the obvious problems had been licked.

Interestingly enough, some of these directors, working on silents well after talkies had been established, evolved ingenious methods for approximating dialogue. Of all the major stars, Garbo was the last hold-out, afraid of venturing into sound because of her thick Swedish accent. Her last silent, *The Kiss,* was released in late 1929 and continued to circulate through 1930. From an artistic point of view, it was probably her best silent, but it was relatively short, lacked a dynamic male co-star, and certainly didn't have the popular appeal of her more exotic earlier works. It contained one quite remarkable sequence in which Garbo, cross-examined by detectives on the accidental death, murder, or suicide of her husband (an event in which she was implicated, but to what extent the audience does not yet know), constantly changes her story, halts in mid-sentence, recollects, and fabricates. All of it is conveyed by visuals that virtually fill out her own uncompleted sentences or, in some cases, substitute for them entirely.

Between *The Jazz Singer* of 1927 and such landmark early talkies as *Applause* and *Hallelujah,* both of 1929, lies a vast no-man's-land of hybrid productions, neither wholly silent nor wholly sound. Some films, conceived as pure silents, such as Michael Curtiz's *Noah's Ark,* were given last-minute doctoring to include long and usually unnecessary dialogue sequences. *Noah's Ark,* told in the framework of a World War I story, occasionally came to a dead halt for comic banter between army buddies. Even the totally lyrical *White Shadows in the South Seas* spent undue footage on an episode in which the hero (Monte Blue) teaches the native girl (Racquel Torres) to whistle, a fairly obvious plagiarism from the chewing-gum lesson in *The Big Parade.* Ken Maynard's westerns at Universal, all trick riding and mobile camerawork, suddenly became static when the action moved into the saloon and the story was advanced by dialogue for a full half-reel—usually twice per film. Some films, like *Broadway* (1929), were designed to be released in both silent and sound form—not a difficult process, since the extreme camera mobility retained the "look" of a silent film and made cutting easy. The musical numbers were trimmed down to emphasize size and spectacle rather than the songs themselves, and dialogue exchanges were likewise shortened by the use of titles. Although there were problems with the new sound equipment, it *was* possible to design a film for release in both versions, the silent one usually being one to two reels shorter than the sound.

On the other hand, many early talkies were *all* talk—especially those like *The Sophomore* and *Sailors' Holiday.* Both of these films were made in late 1929 by Pathé, one of the smaller companies, which merely took their dialogue-ridden films and released them intact, but with most of the none-too-inspiring dialogue replaced by footage-consuming titles. Since even westerns—and Paramount's *The Virginian* and

The Light of Western Stars are typical—tended to substitute dialogue, sound, and singing for the more traditional action, they suffered rather badly in silent form.

The most interesting and experimental of the early talkies—for example, Robert Florey's *The Hole in the Wall*—tended to be the crudest. The advanced ideas often could not be matched by current technology, and because they were usually unimportant films, their lesser stature or star did not justify the kind of budget that could give them a little extra polish.

To the part-talkies, dual versions, and other hybrids was added a sudden rush of imports from Great Britain and Europe. With the value of silent European films virtually nil, European producers unloaded their unreleased product at giveaway prices. And even though the market for them was small, independent American distributors could afford to buy them cheaply and show a quick profit, especially as a number of them featured stars and directors (Jannings, Negri, Lubitsch, Stiller) who had become big Hollywood names in the five or six years since they had been produced. It would have been a fascinating and stimulating period for film students, had they existed then; there has never been another period of total change quite like it.

One wonders, however, how the average film-goer, brought up on fast action and lush Hollywood magic, reacted to the change. The best Hollywood films were now virtually "art-house" pictures, slow and self-indulgent, with even Chaplin, Keaton, and Lloyd reflecting the change. The new talkies still appeared fairly ragged and untidy.

The afore-mentioned gap between *The Jazz Singer* and *Applause* existed largely because the interim experimental films were fairly weak commercially (and thus not studied very seriously at the time or revived thereafter), and because film history has always been considered in terms of major directors. Since the major directors did not embrace sound until 1929, the lesser directors who did—and the films they made —have been ignored.

For the most part, the sound films of 1928 and early 1929 were made for two reasons: first, to make money, and so to cash in on the sheer novelty of sound—the second Al Jolson film, *The Singing Fool*, grossed five million dollars—and, second, to see just what could or couldn't be done in the new medium. In one sense, it was a happy period to work in. The lazy or untalented director could grind out five or six reels of talk or song, reasonably assured that the sheer novelty (for a while) would bring in a profit. Conversely, the director prone to experimentation could try just about everything with the same assurance; even if his ideas went wrong, they'd still be new and could tap the same profitable market. It was an incredibly complex period, however far removed from the simplistic satirization of it that was depicted in the delightful musical *Singin' in the Rain* (1952). And it provided some rare moments of largely unrecognized glory for routine studio directors whose prior—and later—work was standard and uninspired, but who here found themselves assigned to projects where they could tinker, experiment, and test the welding of sight and sound to the limit. If they failed, any damage to their reputation would be negligible, whereas to a Ford or a Borzage, a critical mauling could be serious. To their credit (and undoubtedly to the credit of their cameramen and other technicians), some of these journeymen directors came through with flying colors, making films that deserve to be far better known than they are.

Some of the most interesting work was done at Fox, where the Movietone system of sound on film permitted greater flexibility than the sound-on-disc system espoused by Warner Brothers. John Blystone, earlier a director of Tom Mix westerns, directed an unusual little programmar for Fox entitled *Thru Different Eyes* (1929), somewhat of a forerunner of the Japanese *Rashomon* in its structure—a murder trial in which totally different viewpoints are presented by various witnesses. The sound of off-screen shots plays an important role in the ultimate denouement, and the continuous use of the mobile camera through dialogue and sound scenes is both notable and unusual. Camera mobility was an outstanding feature of another 1929 film, the David Butler-directed *Sunny Side Up*. The charmingly relaxed playing and singing of Janet Gaynor and Charles Farrell, and the exceptionally strong score of hit songs, enable the film to hold up very well even today, although the thirteen-reel length and protracted story which later became standard stuff to be repeated by Alice Faye and Betty Grable, does seem excessive. However, the camerawork, frequently involving a crane, is constantly on the move. The long opening sequence is almost Max Ophuls-like in the way the camera explores a tenement set, panning, tracking, raising and lowering itself from one level to another, and pausing only to let dialogue register before moving on in long, cut-free takes. Even tricky scenes—such as dialogue exchanges in a speeding motorcycle and sidecar—feature direct rather than post-synched sound, with the shadow of the traveling microphone right there on the road to prove it!

Films like *Sunny Side Up* and *Thru Different Eyes* paved the way for the prestige directors to make their sound debuts once many of the bugs had been ironed out. Ford and Vidor still made mistakes in their early films, but these were essentially artistic mistakes, and they learned fast, making remarkable progress from film to film. A usefully illustrative film is *The Valiant,* made for Fox in 1929. It was director William K. Howard's first talkie and stage actor Paul Muni's first film, a downbeat *film noir* forerunner about a man who kills another, refuses to say why or to identify himself, and takes his secret with him to the electric chair. Howard, a strong, visual, silent director, obviously had trouble adapting to the sound medium, though not as much as other directors of a similar style. *The Valiant* starts out with much more camera mobility than most 1929 films, especially those based on plays. Its use of street exteriors with direct sound, its cutting, and its lighting suggest that it is going to be quite a picture. Then, however, the nature of its story forces it to concentrate more and more on restricted settings and to force on Muni a great deal of dialogue. Howard doesn't exactly throw in the towel, but he does adjust to the fact that the focus must be on Muni rather than on an abstract directorial style, and at the mid-way point virtually turns the film over to Muni. It's not the kind of role that Muni did best, being an introverted rather than an extroverted characterization. Moreover, Muni was obviously unfamiliar with film technique and screen make-up. Under the circumstances, Howard does well, and Muni does better than might be expected. The slow, deliberate pacing makes the film seem longer than its brief sixty minutes, but in its own way its plot is quite gripping, and even today its values are not purely academic.

With all its flaws, *The Valiant* does help to show how much further ahead than Europe Hollywood was in its transition to sound. The British film *Atlantic*, made the same year, directed by E. A. Dupont and photographed by the great Charles Rosher, seems incredibly primitive when juxtaposed with it. Moreover, Howard (and other directors like him) learned fast. His 1932 *The Trial of Vivienne Ware* is a minor masterpiece of style and pace. It was unquestionably the fastest-paced film made to that time, and one might argue that in many ways it still is. Since both it and *The Valiant* were melodramas made by the same director for the same company, together they provide an invaluable lesson in the problems of sound and the rapidity with which they were overcome—a lesson that covers four years of Hollywood history in less than two hours!

Far too many generalizations and misconceptions exist concerning the abandonment of the grammar and art of the silent film in favor of sound. As generalizations, obviously they contain some truth: 1929 had *no* films of the caliber of *The Beloved Rogue* or *Sunrise*, and a great many films like *Disraeli*. But the specifics that accompany the generalizations are usually quite wrong—for example, the oft-repeated statement that the camera was totally immobilized and imprisoned within a static "sweat-box." Obviously there were mechanical problems, and the possibility of sound equipment picking up the noise of camera machinery was very real. It was *easier* to employ a static camera, and since so many of the early talkies were actionless stage derivations, there was no need for the camera to be as agile as it had been. But the point is that it was a matter of personal choice for the director. Despite the opposition of crewmen, he *could* move his camera if he so chose, and in order to overcome the static quality of dialogue-controlled narratives, some 1929 films have a good deal more camera mobility than silents of a year or two earlier.

Significantly, one finds far more use of the moving camera at Fox, with its Movietone system, than at Warners, with its disc system. Using long-playing discs, running the equivalent of a reel in order to facilitate synchronization, Warners tended to divide its films into "acts"—not terribly difficult, since many of them were based on plays—and it was not uncommon for one set and one basic conversation to last for an entire reel. If the particular set-up happened to run for just seven minutes, then that was often the arbitrary end to that particular reel. (This explains why so many films of the period are listed as being ten or twelve reels in length, but in actual running time correspond to only seven or eight reels.) Sound recording on the disc system was of extraordinary good quality, as well it might be. The record industry was flourishing and had achieved high standards, whereas the sound-on-film process was much newer. On the other hand, apart from the artistic restrictions of the disc system, there were mechanical problems. One or two breaks and repairs in the film itself could destroy synchronization unless the missing frames were replaced or "padded" by blank leader, either method being tricky, untidy, and, in the long run, impractical.

One of the major changes in the structure of the early talkies was caused by the fact that a whole new art of screenwriting had to be developed. In many cases, early sound films were constructed like silents, and dialogue was merely added. Alternately—and more often—Hollywood fell back on novels, plays—and *unproduced* plays—where the writing and the dialogue were already a *fait accompli*. Producers owning properties based on novels or plays that had already been made as silents had somewhat of an edge, using the earlier films as models to which pre-written dialogue could be grafted. Typical of these were *The Green Goddess,* which George Arliss did for the second time in 1929, and *The Locked Door* (made earlier as a Norma Talmadge silent, *The Sign on the Door*), which served as the first major starring vehicle for Barbara Stanwyck. Although full of entrances and exits, pauses on stairways for dramatic theatrical effect, and with too much stress on slowly delivered, clearly enunciated dialogue, it was quite an interesting mixture of old and new, with director George Fitzmaurice breaking up the excessive dialogue by adroit editing. Nor was there anything essentially wrong with filmed theater if it was good theatre. George Arliss' *The Green Goddess* was and is a delight, a bravura showcase for that theatrical giant and an improvement on the silent version in that dialogue allowed for subtler development of the tongue-in-cheek approach.

Some of the unproduced plays deserved their fate, but they provided a useful transitional source for Hollywood. Furthermore, the unfamiliarity with smooth screenwriting produced, for a while, a naturalistic style of dialogue that has always proved impossible to duplicate (as witness the later works of John Steinbeck or Paddy Chayevsky). Since dialogue was itself a novelty, and audiences did not expect wit or sophistication, many of the early talkies had dialogue which was so casual and unpolished as to seem both honest and spontaneous. The charmingly direct boy-girl dialogue in Mamoulian's *Applause* (1929) had this quality.

In many areas, the echoes of the silent film lingered—particularly in the realm of musical scoring. Early talkies, such as *Lights of New York* (1928) and *The Squall* (1929), featured virtually non-stop scores, as in the tradition of the silents, and still used sub-titles as informational and transitional devices, despite the dialogue. Apart from being a stylized and unrealistic device, the music constantly battled the dialogue, often literally. The scoring was usually done live on the set. In these early days, before the use of mixes and re-mixes, actors had to pitch their voices to overcome the musical competition. Critics quickly assailed the music as an unrealistic device, and almost immediately Hollywood went to the other extreme and abolished music entirely. When "mood" music was thought to be essential, it had to be introduced from a logical source, which invariably meant the radio. Before launching into a long, emotional discussion with Gloria Swanson in *Indiscreet*, Ben Lyon first turns on the radio, which, minus commercials, conveniently delivers a passage of dramatic music that matches all the moods and nuances of their conversation. The episode concluded, the radio is pointedly turned off. Even Bebe Daniels' seduction of Ricardo Cortez in the first *The Maltese Falcon* (1931) is preceded by the turning on of the radio. Not until 1932, with horror films such as *The Most Dangerous Game* and such Lubitsch films as *Trouble in Paradise*, was the art of scoring for films revived seriously and very effectively.

So much was going on in film in this transitional period that virtually every genre could itself be broken down into sub-genres. The musical, for example, went through virtually half-a-dozen different stages between its birth in 1927 and its apparent demise in 1931. *The Jazz Singer* inspired sentimental dramas; the gangster films with night-club backgrounds (*Broadway*); the all-star revues (*The Show of Shows, The King of Jazz*); the operettas (*The Vagabond King, Golden Dawn, The Love Parade*); the adaptations of hit Broadway musical comedies (*Whoopee, Animal Crackers*); and the creation of original Hollywood musicals (*Sunny Side Up, Just Imagine*).

Hollywood undoubtedly made a mistake in this period by assuming that, since its films were now "real" because they talked, they had to be "realistic" in all other aspects, too. This judgment was reflected in its treatment of musical scoring, and in the virtual elimination of qualities of poetry and lyricism. (Such French films as Duvivier's 1932 *Poil de Carotte* earned at least part of their deserved reputations by going against Hollywood strictures and daring to incorporate elements of fantasy or poetry into otherwise realistic narratives.) Hollywood's use of color in this period seems a spectacular example of bad judgment. The early pastel shades of two-color Technicolor were charming but unrealistic, and therefore were used almost exclusively for the musical and, a little later, the horror film. Although color had been used in such silent westerns as *Wanderer of the Wasteland* (1925) and *Redskin* (1929), it was considered too unreal to be used in the near-documentary early sound westerns, such as *The Virginian* and *The Big Trail.* Aesthetically, the decision may have been right, but in a box-office sense, the use of color might have salvaged the genre in that commercially unsuccessful flurry of big-scale westerns of 1929–31. Oddly enough, the operettas were hugely popular. With their color, music, and deliberate artificiality, they were about the only films that somehow captured the magic and romance of the silents.

Five films of 1929 perfectly sum up the differing approaches used to find the most successful route for talkies. Unquestionably the most successful film of the year, with both critics and audiences, was *Disraeli—* stodgy, all-talk filmed theater, saved only by the charisma of George Arliss, and a much lesser film than his *The Green Goddess* of the same year. Clearly, theater was what seemed to loom largest in the future of the film.

William Wellman's now forgotten melodrama *Chinatown Nights* is a perfect example of what Hollywood directors themselves envisioned as the talkie of the future. In pacing, mobile camerawork, and overall design, it is essentially a silent film, still using a constant musical score and narrative sub-titles. Much of the dialogue is merely superimposed over medium or long-shot scenes where the characters are either in motion or in semi-darkness, concealing the lack of dialogue synchronization, with occasional direct-sound dialogue exchanges in close-up.

King Vidor's powerful *Hallelujah* represents the old-guard Hollywood director converting to sound without sacrificing visual style. It uses sound, *exploits* sound, and is perhaps a grimmer and more realistic subject than would have been attempted during the silent period.

Representing the advance-guard of the new Hollywood, Rouben Mamoulian, from the stage, tried imaginatively to weld picture and sound creatively in *Applause.* He was not wholly successful. Technique had not yet caught up with inspiration, and some of his innovations, involving combined sound tracks, did not work smoothly. Other ideas, especially some involved moving camera shots, were sabotaged by crews that wanted to put this upstart in his place and *prove* to him that what he asked for couldn't be done. Nevertheless, despite technique which today calls attention to itself, *Applause* is a major achievement—as important a film in 1929 as Welles' *Citizen Kane* was in 1941.

The fifth, and in some ways most successful, example is the delightfully sophisticated tongue-in-check romp, *Bulldog Drummond*, which among other things is a reminder of how outrageous yet tasteful films could be in the free-wheeling days before the censorship of the Production Code. *Bulldog Drummond*, directed by F. Richard Jones, maker of such thoroughly enjoyable silents as Mabel Normand's *Mickey* (1917) and Douglas Fairbanks' *The Gaucho* (1927), is one of the best 1929 films, but it has been down-played because it is purely an "entertainment." With its superb sets and art direction by William Cameron Menzies and outstanding camerawork (by George Barnes and Gregg Toland), *Bulldog Drummond* combines the great visual elements of the silents (including a decided gothic influence) and their larger-than-life sense of fun with the advantage of good sound-scripting and beautifully delivered dialogue. Ronald Colman's breezy, assured performance not only made him a major star of sound films, magnifying his already considerable popularity, but also reshaped the rather dour image of Drummond into a model that would be followed in succeeding decades. Yet, while Colman's performance dominates, it does not do so at the expense of the film. The dialogue adds immeasurably to the fun, but in a story-telling sense, *Bulldog Drummond* could play with its sound track removed and titles substituted.

These five films are admittedly high spots and exceptions. Many others tried and failed. Many more didn't try at all, and still succeeded quite well within the limited audience expectations of 1929. Nevertheless, while *Bulldog Drummond*, *Applause*, and *Hallelujah* might seem an inadequate replacement for the glories of the late silents of 1927–28, Hollywood was learning fast. The years 1930–31 were a period of improvement and retrenchment, and in 1932, Hollywood burst forth with an invigorating and fresh amalgamation of the best of the silents with the best of sound. Lubitsch, Ford, Vidor, Wyler, and others from the silent period were still young. Having mastered the new medium, they were starting out again, bursting with ideas and the same delight in what the movies could do that had characterized the earliest silent films. New directors from the stage—James Whale,

George Cukor, John Cromwell, Mamoulian—and new faces from the stage—Cagney, Muni, Robinson, Bogart, Tracy, Gable—added to this fresh approach. The year 1932 was stunning, offering so many "definitive" films in so many genres—western, musical, comedy, gangster—that it has remained one of the key years in the history of cinema. Above all, it was the year in which Hollywood learned to harness sound and use it, but not be dominated by it. Some of the films of that year, especially Mamoulian's *Love Me Tonight* and Lubitsch's *Trouble in Paradise,* restored all of the joyous pictorial elegance of the silent film backed up by an exuberant celebration of sound. In fact, in many ways the pictorial/aural sophistication of that year has never been equalled since. The silent cinema, progressing steadily, peaked late; the sound cinema, learning from the silent, peaked early. The reasons are complex, debatable, and perhaps ultimately a little depressing—but belong in another book.

Appendix:

The State of Film Scholarship in America

The Silent Film: Books, Films, Archives and Other Reference Tools

It would be a graceless gesture indeed for one book on film to attempt to pass judgment on all the others. Fortunately, it is not needed, since a book already exists which does that job for us. But before describing it, and certain other books which are essential for a study of the silent film, it is perhaps necessary to sum up the current status of books on film.

The market for film books, boosted partially by scholarly and student interest but more by an overall boom in nostalgia-oriented material, has increased incredibly since the fifties. Supply, however, has more than exceeded demand or need.

In the thirties and forties, only a comparative handful of film books—historical, critical, or autobiographical—were written. Because of the limited resources then available to the writer, they weren't always totally accurate. On the other hand, writing on film wasn't taken seriously enough for accuracy to be either contested or regarded as very important. Nevertheless, the sincerity and passion for cinema evident in these books—by Gilbert Seldes, Paul Rotha, and Lewis Jacobs—have enabled them to withstand the test of time and to become standards.

Before either film history or nostalgia became big commercial markets, but when there were signs that they might, a number of veteran show business personalities issued their own autobiographies, secure in the belief that "old" cinema was a dead language that could never be resuscitated. Mack Sennett, in his autobiography, wrote detailed descriptions of the plots and working conditions surrounding the production of a whole series of mid-1920's films that W. C. Fields starred in for him—films that were neither made nor even contemplated. Mae West, in her autobiography, carefully describes ego and initiative-building scenes in her movies that don't tally at all with the actual scenes, never dreaming that within a very short period, those films would be back on theater screens, and then on television all over the country, for comparison with her story.

Even at the peak of their popularity, film books have never been potentially big money-makers, not even those written by big stars and directors. To their credit, most authors of books on film write not because they dream of huge royalties and a life of ease, but because they love film and want to pass on their knowledge to the reader in a way that will stimulate a similar love—or at least, a desire for further investigation. But as more has been written (not only in books, but in the proliferating film magazines too), more accessible (and public domain) material has thus become available to the carpet-baggers and freebooters, who have swarmed into the field much as Griffith described them swarming into the Reconstruction South in *The Birth of a Nation*. One way to make money in a dubious commercial field is to print quickly, beating the other author to the punch, and to print cheaply, using shoddy and often murkily unrecognizable still photographs to illustrate one of the richest pictorial arts of all. Those publishers so keen to get a book out quickly are usually not trying to protect an original idea but rather to cash in on somebody else's idea before another competitor can do so. Very often the initial book on a personality or a genre is *not* the definitive work, and a second, more thoughtful and carefully researched book is called for. And the author assigned may be admirably equipped to produce such a work, but the deadline pressure—often to turn in a finished manuscript within three months of accepting the project—is too intense to enable him to do anything like his best work. The result: another salable, moderately successful, but totally unnecessary book.

Often, the haste to publish proves futile. Certain genres, such as the horror film, and certain stars, such as Humphrey Bogart, have proved to have such enormous appeal that virtually *any* book dealing with them will sell. Much film-book publishing is thus safe but unoriginal, the effort and money put into it depriving some far more worthy area of a place in the market. It is incredible that there should be more than half-a-dozen books apiece on Bogart, John Wayne, Clark Gable, and Boris Karloff, a dozen on July Garland, certainly two or more on the barely begun careers of Liza Minelli, Barbra Streisand, and Clint Eastwood, yet not one (other than his own autobiography) on that unique actor George Arliss. Directors likewise run in fashionable cycles. Hitchcock probably holds the record, but books on Ford, Griffith, deMille, Bergman, Welles, Hawks, Stroheim, and Kubrick are proliferating too, each of these directors having accumulated anywhere from three to a dozen books on his career. Yet there is not one to date on Clarence Brown, Carol Reed, James Whale, Victor Saville, Robert Siodmak, Herbert Brenon, or William Dieterle, all of them directors of major interest and importance, whose careers spanned many years and often more than one country.

Needless to say, not all publishing houses are devoted to the immediate profit. Many have a strong sense of integrity, and with libraries and universities as a major customer source, realize that quality and reliability will, in the long run, be justified. Nor can one condemn those publishers who do not have such an attitude. Book publishing is, after all, as much of a profit-geared industry as the making of movies; with no profits, there'd quickly be no movies, and no books about them. Further, the segment of the public that wants only nostalgia and fan-magazine trivia is surely entitled to buy what it wants, without having to read serious tomes on film history or aesthetics as the only means of satisfying their casual interests. Nonetheless, the frequent and unwise attempts to cater to both markets simultaneously has resulted in a great deal of mediocrity. Some of the books so offered are dangerously close to illiteracy, hardly readable because of their clumsy grammar and heavy-handed prose. Others are almost monuments of misinformation, not only repeating all the errors of previous works but fabricating entirely new ones. *Some* of the errors in film books of the sixties and seventies are literally beyond belief, since there is absolutely no way that such misinformation could have been gleaned or misinterpreted from either the actual facts or prior comment on them. They can only be the product of guesswork or deliberate distortion. Hollywood, it must be admitted, is equally guilty of such distortion in films about its own past; the gross inaccuracies and rank *impossibilities* in Hollywood "tributes" to its own past greats—*The Buster Keaton Story* and *Gable and Lombard* being two especially stomach-churning examples—transcend any charitable claims of "dramatic license."

Further adding to the glut of books on film are those characterless quasi-reference books: collections of stills accompanied by the sparsest of texts or the assembly-line lists of star careers and credits. This is a lazy kind of film history: most of the information contained therein, though scattered, can be tracked down by the assiduous scholar. Further, the speed of production and regularity of issuance of such books prevents their containing any sense of perspective, or serious critical or historical analysis. One writer manages to bring out a five-hundred-page volume of this type almost every month, putting film history on the same kind of assembly line that turns out automobiles or television sets.

Nor is this just a transitional, temporary problem. True, the really bad books may make little headway. They won't be absorbed into university-level reference libraries or be reprinted. But as part of a gigantic block of writing on film, they will always be with us. Just as films of the 1920's are often (and misleadingly) considered a primary source of information for writers and historians dealing with that period, so will the great mass of film history written in the 1960's and 1970's (when many of the original directors, cameramen, stars, and other participants in the movies' earlier days were still alive and available, if not always too reliably, for consultation) be regarded a hundred years hence as the most authoritative written material on film. Admittedly, the many gaps in film history have to be filled in *now,* while we still have those all-important direct links to the past. But unfortunately, the ideal timing is off by many years.

Today's serious film historian has advantages undreamed of by his pioneer predecessors, not the least of them being the knowledge that he is not alone in his passion, and that his discoveries will find a small but growing and eager readership. In the thirties, and even into the forties, the film historian was very much of a trail blazer. Little had been published, and the best source material—trade publications, the better fan magazines—were usually not considered of sufficient interest or importance to be kept on file by libraries. Archives were virtually non-existent; the few theaters specializing in older films were usually concerned only with the immediate and fairly commercial past. Rental libraries of 16mm films were limited in what they offered. Production and distribution organizations were suspicious, uncooperative, and totally unsympathetic to any proposals to record the history of their industry and art. The efforts involved in tracking down a single elusive film were prodigious and often expensive. Frequently, out of sheer frustration—physical inability to do his job as thoroughly as he wished, coupled with the knowledge that virtually no one cared anyway—the potential historian would shift gears in mid-stream and divert his energies to running a film society. This was also an uphill fight, but at least he saw films and had the satisfaction of re-discovery, the sharing of pleasure, and the knowledge of having stimulated new "converts" to the cause of film history. (A surprising number of today's best film-makers and writers came to their careers from the film society movement, an activity that they were usually introduced to in the early teen years of their school days).

Today's film historian is backed by such enormous advantages—mainly developed since the mid-1950's—that comparing him with his predecessor of thirty-five years ago is almost like comparing the horse-and-buggy and the jet plane. Film schools and film courses at universities give him far more than just basic background, and guide him in methodology for research and study. Although television is a poor tool for the serious study of film, since it so distorts the true value of a film, at the same time it must be admitted that merely by switching channels any night, one can come across a dozen films that thirty years ago would have been totally unavailable, or accessible only after much searching, cajoling, and expense. If nothing else, the mere *presence* of television has meant the preservation, and availability, of thousands of film titles. Commercial theaters, at least in the bigger metropolitan areas and in college towns, now frequently play retrospectives that not too long ago would have been physically and commercially impossible.

The proliferation of books on film includes any number of reprints that form invaluable research tools: reviews, advertising campaigns, and fan magazine articles, which may not be of prime historic interest but do provide an exceptional barometer of public taste. Archives throughout Europe and the United States are certainly not casually or easily accessible, but there is usually one within the range of the average working scholar, who tends to gravitate toward Hollywood, New York, or Washington, D.C., where most of the research material lies. In recent years, too, the American Film Institute has not only secured industry cooperation, screening prints, and documentation, but has also issued fellowship study grants and has funded many research projects. One of the most valuable of these has been an Oral History program, through which lengthy and in-depth interviews with industry pioneers and craftsmen have been recorded on tape, and in some cases have already been published.

Older historians who had no such doors opened to them, and who had to finance all of their own research, could be forgiven for being a little envious of all these riches. But there is still no real short-cut to becoming a film historian. One still needs passion, devotion, and above all, a childhood and adolescence devoted to film, so that one has had the prolonged viewing experience needed to form perspectives and judgments. The greater resources available today merely means that the student no longer needs to spend excessive time and energy in research; he can now turn directly to recording and analyzing. The enormous pool of information gathered, for example, by the American Film Institute's Oral History program is now being studied, compared, and combined with other findings, and is beginning to serve as a launching pad for original, meticulously detailed, and authoritative writings on film by such outstanding young film historians as Richard Koszarski and Anthony Slide. Evidence already exists that this new writing on film, combining perspective with reliability, is extremely important and will set new standards in chronicling the movies' past. Unfortunately, however, it will still take some years for this movement to become established, and by then, many first-class writers may find the going rather rough because of a market glutted by earlier, if inferior, works on parallel subjects.

Another and perhaps more serious reason to lament the overall standards of film literature today is that these generally low standards leave the field open to insidious attack by the educational forces that seek to over-intellectualize the film. The film has been treated with scorn far too long, and attempts to impart intellectual, cultural, and artistic intent to an essentially entertainment medium have frequently been minimized and suppressed. But now the pendulum seems to be swinging in the other direction, led by the advocates of film theory rather than film history. Obviously there must be room for both, and in truth, it is difficult to separate them. If there were no film theorists among directors, there could be no advancement of film art, and thus no film history. In some ways, the most dangerous of the new intellectualized approaches to film are those of the related fields of structuralism and semiotics. No detailed analysis of these theories will be attempted here, since even the structuralists seem unable to agree among themselves. All of the initial books on film structuralism devote themselves not to applying their theories to specific films, but instead to dissecting, and disagreeing with, the theories outlined by other structuralists. Basically, however, structuralism holds that film study and critical analysis have never been adequately performed, and can succeed *only* when based on observations of signs, symbols, and visual language within the film itself. It argues, inflexibly, that the signs fall into only two camps: those that were intended by the director, and usually indicated by the script; and those that are there subconsciously. Thus, even if a director repudiates a specific structuralist interpretation of a given image, or explains it as being an accident or a mistake, the structuralist critic will still insist that it is a totally valid if subliminal symbol, and must be considered as such in analyzing the meaning of the film. Obviously this approach can be defended, and possibly even developed usefully, in the more contemporary films, where knowledge of production information is easily obtained, and even more so in the cases of individual and unsupervised directors such as Ingmar Bergman and Federico Fellini, who can be credited with total and autonomous control of their films.

But the approach falls totally flat when one does *not* have access to such information. Many films of the past have been worked on by more than one director, and do not, therefore, present a consistent point of view. Mistakes have been made and covered up. Several widely differing versions of the same film can exist. Stock footage or montages may have been interpolated by the editor, without the consultation or approval of the director. The "meaning" of some scenes may be economy, compromise, or carelessness rather than inspiration. Yet the structuralists tell us that a film can be studied solely on its internal evidence, without recourse to any knowledge of the director's other films (which may be closely related via a continuing theme) or to the period in which the film was made, and which it must inevitably reflect. The most minutely detailed analytic essays have been offered by the structuralists on Griffith's Biograph films of 1908. It takes longer to read them than it does to see the films, and undoubtedly it took the authors longer to formulate them than it took Griffith to make the films. The interpretations placed on the choice of angle, or on a single simple bit of "business" stagger the imagination. Some observations are quite good, but could have been arrived at by any competent critic or historian. Others are—pure and absurd—fabrication, and by burdening a 1908 work with a 1975 interpretation, the original intent of the film is perverted and distorted. Typical of the structuralists' contempt for history as a basis for any kind of film study is a recent (1976) statement in the writings of Christian Metz, both the leader and the figurehead of the film-structuralist movement. In analyzing Fellini's 8½, Metz makes the incredible statement that only about three films (all European) have ever been made about the *making* of films, and that only 8½ did it properly. Quite apart from the fact that there have been hundreds of films about the making of films, most of them from Hollywood, at least two of them— Preston Sturges' *Sullivan's Travels* and Helmut Kautner's German *Film Ohne Titel*—did *exactly* what 8½ set out to do, did it better, and did it twenty-five years earlier!

Structuralism, as a theoretical approach to criticism, obviously has its place as an important adjunct to contemporary film criticism. But it needs to discipline itself and prove itself. So far, it has yet to show that it can teach us anything about a given film that we didn't already know. A structuralist analysis of one sight gag in Buster Keaton's *Cops* takes far longer to read than the gag does to play, and all it achieves is to confirm the information, in pompous rhetoric, that Keaton was able to convey instinctively, visually, and amusingly in a few seconds. It does one more thing: in peeling away the "layers" of the gag, it gives it a somber importance that Keaton never intended, and effectively destroys it for future viewing.

Some of the film structuralists are well experienced in other fields of film history and criticism, and clearly see it as a new science to be studied and applied. But others possibly see it as a route to power and dominance. They have almost resented it when their theoretic gods—Eisenstein, Vertov, Resnais—have become more widely understood and accepted, and thus have escaped from their eclectic control. Structuralism, with its ambiguities and self-imposed boundaries, gives them a chance to re-create that quasi-intellectual control, and to that end they have created a virtually undecipherable language*—surely the ultimate proof of their basic lack of involvement with an essentially visual and communicable medium. Reading a structuralist essay, one all too often comes across paragraphs in which no three consecutive words make sense (except to other structuralists, perhaps) and where language becomes a kind of masturbatory exercise. This kind of super-intellectualization of film is in some ways even more dangerous than mediocrity because it is *dull*, deadening interest instead of stimulating it. It is as real a danger to the cause of film history as the deterioration of color stock—and a much more difficult one to combat.

Books

Of major reference importance is *Cinema Booklist*, compiled by George Rehrauer for Scarecrow Press in 1972, indexing and describing well over 1,500 books on film—histories, criticism, biographies, scripts, etc.—as well as containing a reference section on periodicals. Due to the rapid proliferation of film books, it was out of date within a year, but a second, revised edition

---

* As an illustration of this exclusive vocabulary of concealment and confusion, cited below is a typical one-sentence excerpt from structuralist writing. Significantly, the author is writing about *other* writer's opinions. Its source is deliberately withheld, since it is not from a published work, and it is admittedly unfair to the author to tear a piece of prose from a lengthy piece of theoretical writing. The intention is neither to ridicule nor to criticize the views expressed, merely to stress the jargon in the writing itself and the fact that the point of view could have been put forward in simpler and shorter terms:

"Metz's and Williams' distinctions between metaphor and metonym placed in paradigm or syntagm that develop the discourse of the diegesis and those that comment connotatively on the denotative of the narrative are particularly helpful in understanding how metaphor and metonymy work in the dream."

has been prepared, and presumably will be updated periodically. Exceptionally thorough, it is also admittedly a trifle over-generous in its appraisals; a book must really plumb the depths of mediocrity before the author becomes severely critical. But in its listings and cross-indexing of material covered, and in its descriptions of the *contents* of each book, it performs an admirable service. Several new books are also concerned exclusively with indexing material already written, one of the best and most useful being *The New Film Index* (Dutton, 1975), compiled by Richard Dyer MacCann and Edward S. Perry, a bibliography of English-language magazine articles published between 1930 and 1970.

By far the most indispensable book for any study of the silent film is Kevin Brownlow's *The Parade Gone By* (Knopf, 1968). Only indirectly a history of the silent film—although a completely reliable one, and covering much fresh ground—it is instead a series of impressions of the period, zeroing in on specific craftsmen—directors, cameramen, title-writers, scenarists, stars—with in-depth interviews. "Interviews" is perhaps the wrong word, since Brownlow is content to prod their memories, inject the right question at the right time, and then leave them alone until it is time to wrap up and summarize. Brownlow is a film-maker as well as a historian, and is much concerned with the technical expertise behind the emotional and visual qualities of the silent film. There are some stunningly good stills, expertly chosen and beautifully reproduced, to illustrate the topics (e.g., glass shots) that he talks about at length, and the chapter on *Ben Hur* is a model of concise crystallization of technical data, historical background, and critical acumen into a most readable and informative whole. Although *The Parade's Gone By* has been issued in paperback form, the hard-cover original is recommended, since the layout of the stills, the quality of the printing, and the texture of the paper are deliberately designed to capture the pictorial elegance of the silent film. It's doubtful that there will ever be a better book on the silent film; certainly there can never be another one produced with close cooperation from the pioneer artists involved. At least thirty-three of Brownlow's interview subjects have died in the eight years since the book was published.

Next to Brownlow's, the most handsome and evocative book on the silent film is Walter Kerr's *The Silent Clowns* (1975), also published by Knopf. There have been a number of books on individual comedians, comedian-directors, and comedy-directors, some (like Rudi Blesh's *Keaton*) quite admirable, but there has been a long-felt need for an overall survey of screen comedy. One, which attempted to encompass both silent and sound, was useful but inadequate. *The Silent Clowns* will clearly remain the definitive work on the genre and has arrived in the nick of time, since the structuralists are already seeking to embroil Keaton, the most intellectual of comedians, in their crushing tentacles. Kerr's preference is clearly toward Keaton and Langdon, and his acute analysis of their work more than justifies it; but he plays no favorites. Chaplin and Lloyd are treated fairly, too, as are Laurel and Hardy and such lesser-known comedians as Charley Chase and Lloyd Hamilton. If there is a flaw in the work at all, it is that the stills—well chosen, often rare, and beautifully reproduced—tend to distract one's attention from the text, which is bountiful, well-informed, and so well constructed that one *should* stay with it, without interruption. Yet stills are obviously a necessary adjunct to any work on visual comedy, and in addition, illustrate Kerr's points in a way that too many film-book illustrations do not. Perhaps there is no solution to such a problem, although one might have been to concentrate the stills into one or two major pictorial sections.

George Pratt's *Spellbound in Darkness* (New York Graphic Society, 1966) is an admirable (and quite different) companion volume to Brownlow's *The Parade's Gone By*. It *is* a chronological history of the silent, and primarily American, film, but it is told largely through contemporary reviews, editorials, and script excerpts. However, Pratt's perspective, and his skill in selecting exactly the right illustrative material and surrounding it with his own brief but perceptive commentary, make it as great a contribution as Brownlow's, even though at first glance it seems a simpler and less ambitious work.

Somewhat less important than the three foregoing volumes, but nevertheless still one of the best books on the silent screen, is Edward Wagenknecht's *The Movies In The Age of Innocence* (University of Oklahoma Press, 1962). Wagenknecht is a prolific and authoritative writer in areas other than film, but one senses that film—and especially the Griffith films—is his first love. He is honest about his biases and makes no bones about dealing with what he loved best in the silent era. But he is a critic of great taste and has *seen* all that he writes about; if it is not necessarily a book about the best silent films, it is certainly about the best *in* silent film. Highly recommended, though, it can be savored and enjoyed more if regarded as a back-up to the Brownlow, Kerr, and Pratt books, and read *after* them.

Books on the early history of the film often tend to be both eclectic and suspect. More than one writer has chosen to concentrate on the formative years knowing that he'll face neither competition nor argument. However, some of them are invaluable. Terry Ramsaye's *A Million And One Nights*, reissued by Simon and Schuster in 1964, was originally written in 1926. It was then, in two volumes, one of the most concise and reliable accounts of the birth of the movies as a novelty, as an art, and as an industry. Further, it was written early enough for its facts to be checked and confirmed. Flaws, generalizations, and errors have become more apparent in later years, but it is still both an invaluable and a very readable work. Rather more academic, and certainly the product of a more precise methodology, is C. W. Ceram's *Archaeology of the Cinema* (Harcourt, Brace, 1965). The title tells all; it deals with the apparatus and inventions that led up to the cinema, and it cuts off at 1900. It dwells in details on exactly the kind of material that most books understandably gloss over, condense, or ignore altogether.

Books on directors, happily, have become much more popular—and marketable—than they once were, though there is still a tendency for the popular directors to be re-hashed and re-analyzed time and time again, at the expense of less commercial but equally interesting directors who have not, as yet, been given a single volume. For the most part, the director-books fall into one of three categories: the autobiographical entries by the directors themselves, the critical analyses, often combined with lengthy interviews with the directors involved, and the "objective" biographies. There are so many of these that it would be unfair to deal with them here, not only because space precludes their being dealt with adequately but because some of the best of them deal with non-American directors, or more essentially with the sound period. However, one should cite one book as a model of what this kind of writing *should* be: Karl Brown's *Adventures with D. W. Griffith* (Farrar, Straus and Giroux, 1973). Brown was a young cameraman who worked with Griffith on *Intolerance* before becoming one of the top cameramen at Paramount in the 1920's, a director of note, and something of a writer, though on increasingly less important films in the 1930's. He writes with accuracy and charm, combining the experience of sixty years earlier and the perspective of all that has happened since. Not all cameramen can write, but several have, and more should, for their histories are often the most reliable of all. Cameramen were technicians and artists, unconcerned with and uninvolved in the financial side of the industry. They rarely got the blame for failures or the credit for successes. As long as they knew their job and did it, they had no concern about cycles or fads; their job was as constant and assured as a restauranteur's in a large city. They had no time for the prima donna temperaments of stars; if they put on those kinds of airs, they usually didn't last very long—as Hendrik Sartov found to his cost at MGM. Because they've never had to justify mistakes or rationalize failures (perhaps among themselves, but never to the public), they've had few axes to grind and no bucks to pass. Their sense of film history tends to be far more impartial than that of stars or directors. Since they have seldom been lionized in print, there is perhaps an understandable tendency to make the most of a rare opportunity and occasionally to claim a little more credit for a specific cinematographic innovation than is entirely their due. But even these moments are usually presented without a sense of boasting and are backed up by sufficient technical data to make them seem basically truthful. The lack of concern about status or box office is undoubtedly largely responsible for the lack of tension in their lives and working methods. It is hardly coincidental that the cameraman enjoys a far longer professional life than that of star or director, and usually keeps at it until he retires—at the peak of his earning power and creative abilities—somewhere in his seventies.

The validity of cameraman Brown's book about a director contrasts quite strikingly with one director's book about himself. Frank Capra's career spanned the silent and sound periods. During the years of World War II, he worked on documentaries and training films. He worked with major stars and major companies, was responsible for turning Columbia from an independent into a major studio, and produced films which are regarded as both commercial and artistic classics. Yet his book, *The Name Above the Title* (Macmillan, 1971), is almost the exact model of what a historical book should *not* be. Capra (in his lecture appearances, as well as in his writing) knows a good story, and knows the kinds of stories that will get a laugh or a gasp—regardless of truth. His autobiography is full of anecdotes that are clearly fabricated, of dates, places, people, and title that just cannot jell because too many historic facts are against them. (One story juxtaposes into one happening events that were several years apart!) Moreover, Capra is egotistical and unwilling to share credit. He boosts already highly successful films by imparting to them qualities they didn't have and don't need; and less amusingly, he is vindictive. Many old scores are settled in the book, and his treatment of Harry Langdon, long dead, is both cruel and inaccurate. Ironically, in spite of all this, *The Name Above the Title* is still one of the most useful of all film books. Despite Capra's bad memory, to be charitable, it is a wonderfully evocative and accurate picture of *how* a director worked at various stages, and under varying conditions of power and freedom, throughout the history of film. It outlines realistically many of the problems and pressures a director had to face, and, by implication, many of the problems and pressures that his co-workers had to put up with from him. Books like this make one wonder anew that out of such chaos and turmoil emerged films that made sense and sometimes were even masterpieces.

Two earlier survey books are still classics of their kind and remain essential additions to any library: *The Rise of the American Film*, by Lewis Jacobs (Harcourt Brace, 1939; reissued, Teachers College Press, 1968), and *The Film Till Now*, by Paul Rotha (Funk and Wagnalls, 1929, revised and reissued 1949). Jacobs' book is concerned only with the American film principally until the coming of sound. Rotha's (with added material by Richard Griffith in an updated later edition) is much more ambitious, attempting a *chronological* coverage of *world* cinema. Today one can argue over certain omissions and certainly question certain statements and opinions; but in both cases, the validity of the whole is unimpaired by time, and the judgments made then are still sound.

No attempt will be made here to cover all the books on genres (western, horror, science-fiction, detective, gangster) or on individual crafts (camerawork, special effects, art direction, music, editing), let alone the many books devoted to non-American cinema. Even so small and generally undistinguished an industry as Australia's has produced over half a dozen books on its history. Worthy of mentioning in passing, however, is the *"Focus On . . .* series of paperbacks published by Prentice-Hall in the 1960's and 1970's. Each issue is devoted to a genre, a director, or a specific film, and is a compilation of the best material written on its subject. Particularly useful are the two issues on D. W. Griffith and *The Birth of a Nation*, since they pull together often violently opposing viewpoints.

Two lesser-known but eminently worthwhile books are *Hollywood, The Golden Era* (A. S. Barnes, 1971), by Jack Spears, and *The American Film Heritage* (Acropolis Publications, 1972). Despite its nostalgia-oriented title, the former book is an excellent collection of meticulously accurate historical essays by one of America's most thorough researchers, many of them revised, updated versions of articles that originally appeared in *Films in Review*. Some of these articles contain collated information that can be found in no other source—for example, surveys of the depiction of the Doctor or the Indian on the screen. The chapter on the Indian offers far more reliable and complete information than a whole later book on the same subject. There are also some freshly-approached career articles, and an exceptionally good essay on Mary Pickford's directors.

The American Film Heritage was published by the American Film Institute to celebrate the conclusion of a major phase in its film preservation program. It deals primarily with films, directors, and genres that have been in need of reappraisal, and which now *can* be reappraised through the material rediscovered. The stills, some illustrative of early color tints, are well chosen and reproduced, and the text was contributed by more than a dozen specialists in the particular fields represented. The value of film books like this one, *The Parade's Gone By*, and *The Silent Clowns* is that, despite their obvious reliability, increasingly they do not *have* to be taken on trust. More and more, the films they describe are becoming available, in some cases for rental, in others through periodic screenings via archival outlets. Seven final titles have been relegated to last position *only* because of the need to keep an open-ended space for the inclusion of important titles at the last minute before going to press. Actually, these are all key books.

A History of the Cinema (from its origins to 1970), by Eric Rhode (Hill and Wang), is just what its title suggests, an updated and chronological survey of world film history, similar in design to *The Film Till Now*, perhaps, but done with critical insights and film availability denied to that earlier work.

Hollywood Directors, 1914–1940, by Richard Koszarski (Oxford University Press), is a particularly useful, readable, and unique film history, done via the writings of the directors themselves as they commented on current fashions, problems, the transition to sound, and their own particular style. Much of it reveals them to be better film-makers than prophets, but its wider-than-usual scope makes it an invaluable book, not just for the pleasure of its reading but for virtually any film history or appreciation class. Each director represented is also introduced by Koszarski via a succinct and astute summing up of his career.

Caligari's Cabinet and Other Grand Illusions, by Leon Barsacq, revised and edited by Elliot Stein (New York Graphic Society), is far and away the best book yet (of all too few) on production design and art direction. Covering history, theory, and practical matters, it is superbly illustrated and absolutely indispensable. Stein's additions include a section of 341 biographical sketches and credit listings for leading art directors. Much stress is placed on the silent period.

Harold Lloyd: The King of Daredevil Comedy, edited by Adam Reilly, with contributions by a number of critics and historians (Macmillan), is the first book that *really* does justice to this hnique comedian. An *Encyclopedic History of the American Movie Studio* by Mark Wanamaker (McGraw-Hill, 1978) is exactly what its title suggests, and the climax of years of research and the collection of hundreds of rare photographs of early and late studios all over the United States, and production stills of films being made there. Each studio is dealt with individually, and the information amassed concerning the progress and frequent ownership change of even the smallest studio (including all the non-Hollywood ones) is quite staggering. Few works on the really early period of films have been so well documented. This is a unique and long-needed work.

Finally, two invaluable sets of reference volumes. *The New York Times'* six-volume set of reprints of its reviews (and film editorials and news commentaries) from 1913 to 1968 is an obvious primary source for any study of the film. Admittedly, the standards of its critical analysis are surprisingly low and bland. One often finds much more perceptive writing in the review columns of *Photoplay*, particularly under the guidance of James Quirk in the 1920's, when the magazine transcended the traditional role and expectations of the "fan" magazine. Nevertheless, for their systematic coverage of most films, their informational content, their reliability as a barometer of contemporary taste, and their meticulous cross-indexing system, the *Times* reviews are essential.

The American Film Institute Catalogue, 1921–30 is the first of a number of publications (this one a two-volume set) to be devoted to individual decades, and is as complete as is humanly possible in its listing of *all* the feature-length films of its ten-year period, with full cast, credits, and other production and distribution information, and a good synopsis. The volume has been criticized for not being much more than that, for not—for example—indicating which films are important and why, pointing out innovations, or commenting on the evolution of a directorial style. But such complaints seem to miss the point. Trying to combine objectivity of fact with the ambiguities of a critical stance would not only result in a "loaded" and one-sided book—if for no other reason than that the majority of the films described no longer exist for reappraisal—but would double the already prodigious size, production time, and price. Admittedly, there are flaws which refined researching methods will probably minimize in later editions. *Some* extant films have escaped the researchers' net; certain synopses appear to have been compiled from a combination of reviews and press handouts, and are not totally reliable; and one or two British and Australian films have crept in, presumably because the cast and production names give no immediate clue to their origin. Nevertheless, it is a monumental work, designed to be a corner-cutting tool for the historian who knows how to use it, and a useful adjunct to the researcher from non-film fields. For example, the cross-indexing is so arranged that *content* of films—ranging from sheep-farming to the Bible, from locomotives to prostitution—is listed separately, indicating to a researcher in any given field what films are worthy of investigation.

Magazines and periodicals tend to be transient and often very short-lived. An admirable little magazine called *The Silent Picture*, never very large or ambitious, but full of useful research and interview material, just couldn't make a go of it even within its unspectacular limits, and died quietly in 1975. Another only semi-commercial magazine, *The Velvet Light Trap*, much larger and more ambitious, is particularly valuable in career articles on directors, cameramen, art directors, and others from the Warner Brothers "family," a predilection based partially on the personal taste of the editors, but also largely on the fortuitous depositing of the Warner library at the nearby University of Wisconsin at Madison, making prints and documentation readily available for reference. *The Velvet Light Trap* is becoming so ambitious in scope that, frankly, it is difficult to see it surviving, and this mention may well be more of a tribute than a realistic reference, though one hopes not.

Australia in the mid-1970's launched an elaborate, all-purpose film magazine, *Cinema Papers*, which sought to be all things to all readers—part trade journal, part historical and critical review, part fan magazine—and with enough space (and pictures) devoted to current sex, nudity, and pornography to woo a less dedicated clientele as well. Its historical pieces understandably veer to the Australian film, but other areas are covered as well, and the magazine deserves to survive. However, there is ample documentation (in Rehrauer's *Cinema Booklist*, mentioned earlier, and in sundry other indexes) on the state of film magazines, so at this point one needs only to mention three well-established, durable, and presumably permanent film magazines which do provide unique, well-documented, and invaluable material on the silent American film: *Films in Review* and *Film Comment*, both published in New York, and *Focus on Film*, published in London.

Film Rentals and Film Purchasing Outlets

The period 1974–76 has seen many major upheavals in these two areas. Because of widespread (and increasingly blatant) film piracy and copyright violations, resulting in losses of millions of dollars to Hollywood each year, the film industry joined forces with the Federal Bureau of Investigation in tracking down and indicting illegal traffickers in film. This has resulted in many companies going out of business, and in perfectly reputable companies changing their policies. Too, 1976 saw the beginning of a revolutionary new form of film sales—the transformation of film onto video-disc, enabling a complete feature film to be sold outright for only a few dollars—far less than the increasingly high rental fees, and cheaper still, of course, than the prices charged for outright purchase. (A feature that could be *bought* for $300 and *rented* for $85 can be bought in video-disc form for about $6.oo!)* Obviously, universally compatible systems have to be worked out, and the present restriction of being able to play the disc only through a television set will doubtless, in time, be relaxed to allow for projection on a larger screen. But since this represents a big new source of revenue, the industry is behind it one hundred percent, and clearly this is not an area about which one can give guidance with any guarantee of permanence. However, it is unlikely that the video-disc market will pay much attention to all but the obviously commercial silent films, and key distributors in that field will doubtless continue in operation.

Rental of 16mm films varies a great deal according to location, the films shown, and the restrictions imposed by the distributor. Many can be shown only if no admission charge is made and no advertising is issued. Rentals can, in some cases, be as high as those for commercial engagements. Colleges and universities, assured of big audiences, frequently have to pay percentage rates, and often provide a more profitable source of revenue for the distributors than normal commercial theaters.

Films Inc. has branches throughout the country, and their silent library includes many of the most important MGM films: Vidor's *The Big Parade* and *The Crowd*, all but one of the Garbo films, many of the Tod Browning and Lon Chaney vehicles, and such representative silents as *Our Dancing Daughters, The Merry Widow, White Shadows in the South Seas*, and *The Patsy*. Wellman's *Wings*, a Paramount film, is also included in their release schedule. Universal 16, likewise with offices in most key cities, has fewer silent films but is gradually strengthening that area. Among its more important silent releases are Pabst's *The White Hell of Pitz Palu*, Stroheim's *Foolish Wives*, and Leni's *The Man Who Laughs*.

The Museum of Modern Art, in New York City, though more restrictive in that it is not a commercial film distributor and must limit its rentals largely to educational and cultural groups, has the best single collection of American silent films, with most of the basic and milestone films. (Their catalogue extends to European films too, of course.)

One of the most useful distributors of American silents is Killiam Shows Inc., a New York company that owns the D. W. Griffith estate, the Edison and Biograph groups, and many other unique packages of silent film. Initially their activities were limited to television, but in the mid-1970's they entered the 16mm non-theatrical field, too, with virtually all of the Griffiths, plus many Fairbanks, Keaton, Barrymore, Sennett, Valentino, Chaplin, and Chaney films. Initially the stress was on star personalities rather than directors (other than Griffith), but a leasing arrangement with 20th Century Fox brought major classics from the 1920's into their fold, including key works

---

* Prices of course vary considerably depending on the type of film and the distributor involved. The prices quoted are merely representative of current figures, and will doubtless be out-of-date very quickly.

by Murnau, Ford, Walsh, Hawks, and Howard. Print quality of the Killiam releases is exceptionally good. Where necessary, sections have been optically treated to restore the original speed; good, carefully arranged musical scores (but no narrative intrusions) have been added; and best of all, the original rich color tints have been restored, so that modern audiences can see in these films at least an approximation of their original visual elegance.

The American Film Institute in Washington, D.C., is also investigating ways to make much of its restored material more widely available. Their entry into the 16mm distribution field will add a tremendous new bloc of important silent American films to those already accessible.

Archives

The words "archive" and "cinematheque" began to be used rather loosely in the seventies, and most universities that possessed any kind of a film collection appropriated one of those two words to dignify their holdings. Nevertheless, the number of basic reference collections in America has increased considerably, thanks to the newly created "archives"—actual, or by designation—at Yale, Harvard, Berkeley, UCLA, New York University, Madison, Columbia, Dartmouth, and other universities. The basic archives in the United States, however, remain the George Eastman House at Rochester (quite possibly the best archive anywhere in the world), the American Film Institute and Library of Congress collections in Washington, D.C., and the Museum of Modern Art in New York. These institutions all offer varying degrees of hospitality, depending on current activities and staff capabilities. Twenty years ago, when staff and budgetary problems were less serious, and when film history researchers were far fewer in number, the archives would *welcome* students, almost as a justification for their existence and offer the most cordial cooperation. Today their resources are smaller and the demands made upon them are much greater. And alas, too many historians seem to feel that because their cause is a just one, they should have carte blanche access to everything and unlimited cooperation. But the *attitude* and the *purpose* of the archives hasn't changed. They *want* to help and usually will, provided they are given as much flexibility and notice as possible. If charges are made for screening facilities, they are usually nominal and very reasonable.

American students are often given quite remarkable assistance in the European archives of London, Brussels, Copenhagen, Stockholm, and other capital cities. In fact, visiting students often fare much better than residents. Having to dole out their screening and research time carefully, the European archives rationalize that anyone spending the time and money to get there from a distant land is obviously dedicated and worthy of support. They admit the dedication of the natives, too, but argue that, in time, the resident *can* get to see everything in regular screenings for the public. The theory is certainly true on paper, but is rather hard on the local student who may need to see and compare all of a given director's work—and may have to wait years before they are all shown on the archive's normal schedule.

Film Courses

The number of courses given at American universities (and film series open to the public via schools and museums) has been proliferating throughout the 1970's. Many universities offer an astonishing variety of subject matter, ranging from aesthetics and highly intellectualized approaches to specific directors, to essentially "popular" surveys of the work of stars or genres. Still, even "popular" areas can be both stimulating and informative when handled by an instructor who knows how to relate them to their period and to other arts. Since hundreds of courses are offered each year, and the list of participating institutions varies (and grows), the best single source for up-to-date information on such courses is the American Film Institute (at the John F. Kennedy Center for the Performing Arts, in Washington, D.C.), which every year issues a printed booklet outlining all of the courses currently offered, with pertinent information as to addresses, faculty, and other data.

The Movies in America:
Art and Industry

A Chronological Survey of Highlights
of the Silent Period

1893   Edison's "Black Maria," the world's first movie studio, opens in February in East Orange, New Jersey. Its first product: *Fred Ott's Sneeze*, running a few seconds, and being a near-close-up record of an employee sneezing.

1894   At 1155 Broadway, New York's first Kinetoscope peep-show opens.

1895   American Mutoscope, the forerunner of Biograph, is formed.
The "Latham Loop" camera device, allied with the Armat Projector, creates an intermittent movement that reduces the period of darkness, expands the period of light in its shutter-action, and thus makes for smoother projection.

1896   Theatrical showing of movies at Koster and Bial's Music Hall.
The Kiss provides precursor for many battles based on censorship.

1897   The Corbett-Fitzsimmons fight is filmed; eleven reels of footage shot.

1898   Edison's *Cripple Creek Bar Room* is, by locale if not by content, the movies' first western.
Edison's patents suits move into high gear via his suit against Biograph.
The Passion Play is filmed, and runs for more than two reels; a major if premature advance.

1899   Vitagraph (the ancestor of Warner Brothers) is formed.

1900   The invention of the three-bladed shutter further improves projection quality.

1902 In Los Angeles, the Electric Theater opens: the first theater designed for the exclusive showing of movies.

1903 Huge success of *The Great Train Robbery* spurs production of more ambitious though still single-reel films.

1905 Phrase "Nickelodeon" coined regarding small movie theater opened in Pittsburgh.

1906 First color photography system, Kinemacolor.

1907 David Wark Griffith enters industry as actor/writer.

Ben Hur copyright infringement case.

1908 Edison builds new studio in the Bronx, New York.
Production proliferating; Kathlyn Williams, Harold Lockwood, Wilfrid Lucas, Owen Moore, Hobart Bosworth, Arthur Johnson, Florence Lawrence among players appearing regularly in film, though without billing or star status.
Griffith directs *The Adventure of Dollie.*
Motion Picture Patents Company formed.

1909 An estimated 9,000 movie theaters in operation.
Mary Pickford enters movies.
Gertie the Dinosaur first major animated cartoon.
Key films: *The Lonely Villa, A Corner in Wheat,* both by Griffith.

1910 Pathé inaugurates weekly newsreel.
Star system under way via exploitation of Florence Lawrence.
Key films: *A Tale of Two Cities, Life of Moses, Uncle Tom's Cabin, The House With Closed Shutters, Ramona.*

1911 Experiments with sound movies. Films moving into two- and three-reel stage.
Key films: *Vanity Fair, David Copperfield, Enoch Arden.*
Thomas H. Ince directs first films.

1912 Year of changeover to feature films of five reels and more.
Adolph Zukor forms Famous Players; imports Sarah Bernhardt's *Queen Elizabeth* from France, spurs production of big-name, theatrically styled features.
Mack Sennett forms Keystone to specialize in comedy.
13,000 theaters showing movies in the United States.
Key films: *Cleopatra, A Girl and Her Trust, Barney Oldfield's Race for Life, The New York Hat, Man's Genesis, Musketeers of Pig Alley.*
Lillian and Dorothy Gish enter movies via Griffith's *An Unseen Enemy.*

1913 Public acceptance of nine-reel (imported) *Quo Vadis?* accelerates changeover to longer domestically produced films.
Charles Chaplin joins Keystone.

The Adventures of Kathlyn establishes format of the serial film.
Key films: *The Battle of Elderbush Gulch, Judith of Bethulia, Traffic in Souls.*

1914   *The Perils of Pauline* solidifies popularity of serial format. Major new personalities: Cecil deMille, William S. Hart.
Expansion of "deluxe" theaters.
Mary Pickford's $104,000-a-year salary opening wedge in steady escalation of star system and attendant salaries.
Key films: *Tillie's Punctured Romance, The Spoilers, The Squaw Man, Neptune's Daughter, The Avenging Conscience, The Wrath of the Gods, The Wishing Ring, The Italian.*

1915   The year of *The Birth of a Nation*.
Number of film theaters in the United States reaches 17,000.
Patents Trust dissolved by legal order.
Major new screen personalities: Theda Bara, John Barrymore, Hal Roach, Harold Lloyd, William Farnum, Douglas Fairbanks.
Chaplin joins Essanay. Griffith-Ince-Sennett form Triangle.
Key films: *The Cheat, A Fool There Was, The Mother and the Law, The Battle Cry of Peace, Ghosts, The Tramp, Juggernaut.*

1916   The year of *Intolerance*.
Famous Players-Lasky-Paramount formed as producer/distributor combine.
Star salaries continue to spiral with Chaplin's $675,000-a-year deal with Mutual.
Foreign imports continue but lose ground to ever-improving domestic product.
Key films: *Civilization, A Daughter of the Gods, Oliver Twist, Joan the Woman, Romeo and Juliet, The Snow Bird, Easy Street, Hoodoo Ann, The Aryan, Manhattan Madness, Hell's Hinges, The Cossack Whip.*

1917   Exhibitors form production group as Associated First National. Goldwyn Pictures formed.
Griffith, Ince, and Sennett leave Triangle for Paramount, taking key stars with them. John Ford directs first feature.
Key films: *Wild and Woolly, Poor Little Rich Girl, Snow White, The Narrow Trail, Cleopatra, A Tale of Two Cities, Thais, Straight Shooting, The Immigrant, Mickey, Raffles, Blue Jeans, The Girl Without a Soul, Pride of the Clan.*

1918   Robertson-Cole Company, forerunner of RKO Radio, formed.
Anti-German propaganda films at peak.
Old-established companies—Edison, Selig, Mutual, Essanay—unable to meet competition from newer, bigger studios, and being forced out of business.

Chaplin moves to First National.
Key films: *Hearts of the World, The Blue Bird, The Heart of Humanity, Shoulder Arms, Tarzan of the Apes, A Dog's Life, Stella Maris, Whispering Chorus.*

1919   Post-war boom in theater construction and studio expansion.
United Artists formed by Griffith, Pickford, Fairbanks, and Chaplin.
Move toward elimination of smaller independent companies, gathering of stars into a concentration of fewer but bigger studios.
William Randolph Hearst creates Cosmopolitan Productions, releasing initially through Paramount (later MGM and Warners).
Famous Players-Lasky undertakes construction of (still extant and active) major studio in Astoria, Long Island.
Production continues expansion of theatrical holdings.
Key films: *Broken Blossoms, True Heart Susie, Blind Husbands, His Majesty the American, Male and Female, The Miracle Man, Victory, Prunella, Eyes of Youth, Daddy Long Legs, The Outcasts of Poker Flat.*

1920   C.B.C. Film Sales Co. formed (ultimately, Columbia Pictures).
Metro Pictures Corp. bought by Marcus Loew.
Theodore Case patents photoelectric cell.
Paramount extends theatrical holdings.
Key films: *Way Down East, The Kid, Pollyanna, Last of the Mohicans, The Greatest Question, Kismet, The Devil's Passkey, The Woman and the Puppet, Dr. Jekyll and Mr. Hyde, Treasure Island, Huckleberry Finn, Conrad in Quest of his Youth, One Week.*

1921   Release of Germany's *The Cabinet of Dr. Caligari,* together with popularity of Lubitsch-Pola Negri films imported the year earlier, helps create small art-house market.
Key films: *Tol'able David, The Four Horsemen of the Apocalypse, Camille, The Sheik, Over the Hill, The Three Musketeers, Little Lord Fauntleroy, Disraeli, The Mark of Zorro, The Affairs of Anatol, Sentimental Tommy.*

1922   Trio of sex, murder, and drug scandals create excessively bad public relations for Hollywood, causing it to establish own censorship and regulation code to ward off possible government-imposed censorship.
Will Hays appointed head of the Motion Picture Producers and Distributors of America to oversee on-screen and off-screen morality.
Technicolor demonstrates their new two-color process.
Key films: *Foolish Wives, Orphans of the Storm, Nanook of the North, Manslaughter, Oliver Twist, Blood and Sand, Salome, Robin Hood, Tess of the Storm Country, When Knighthood was in Flower, Grandma's Boy, The Prisoner of Zenda, Smilin' Through, Broken Chains.*
Ernst Lubitsch arrives from Germany.

1923 Irving Thalberg leaves Universal to join Louis B. Mayer.
Fox allocates two million dollars to building new Hollywood studio.
Lewis J. Selznick out of production after bankruptcy action; son David O. Selznick announces entry into production.
Super-western cycle introduced by *The Covered Wagon*.
DeForest Phonofilm, a sound-on-film device, demonstrated at Rivoli Theatre in New York.
Commercial radio on the horizon.
Pola Negri, familiar through importation of German films, signed by Paramount.
Metro and Sam Goldwyn combine.
Key films: *The Covered Wagon, Anna Christie, The White Sister, The Christian, Merry Go Round, Cameo Kirby, The Ten Commandments, Trail of the Lonesome Pine, The White Rose, The Hunchback of Notre Dame, Rosita, Safety Last, Scaramouche, Down to the Sea in Ships, A Woman of Paris.*
Technicolor in commercial use.

1924 New merger produces the powerful MGM company.
UFA, leading Germany company, opens New York offices to further plans for German-Hollywood co-production.
Key films: *Greed, The Iron Horse, The Thief of Bagdad, Beau Brummel, Smouldering Fires, Sherlock Junior, The Sea Hawk, Monsieur Beaucaire, Isn't Life Wonderful?, America, He Who Gets Slapped, Romola, The Enchanted Cottage, The Marriage Circle, Forbidden Paradise, Manhandled, Janice Meredith, Girl Shy.*

1925 Free entertainment provided by radio produces Hollywood's first period of real fear of outside competition.
Sound experimentation continues.
Cecil B. deMille leaves Paramount, joins the small Producers Distributing Corp.
Warner Brothers buys Vitagraph assets, including two studios and fifty exchanges.
Sam Goldwyn joins United Artists.
Key films: *Peter Pan, The Eagle, The Road to Yesterday, Seven Chances, The Freshman, The Gold Rush, Salvation Hunters, Stella Dallas, Little Annie Rooney, Don Q, Son of Zorro, Lady of the Night, The Vanishing American, The Goose Woman, Are Parents People?, Skinner's Dress Suit, Sally of the Sawdust, The Merry Widow, The Big Parade, The Tower of Lies, The Unholy Three, Soul Fire, The Phantom of the Opera, The Sea Beast.*

1926 *Don Juan*, with sound (music and effects), on disc, and supporting shorts with direct dialogue and singing, launches serious attempt to win support for wholesale changeover to sound. Warner process called Vitaphone.

Debt-ridden D. W. Griffith closes own studio, sacrifices independence, goes to work for Paramount.

Joseph P. Kennedy assumes control of F.B.O. Productions.

Fox-Case announce Movietone, sound-on-film system, to rival Vitaphone.

Columbia, expanding, buys its own studio.

Key films: *A Kiss for Cinderella, Beau Geste, The Kid Brother, La Boheme, Don Juan, Tramp Tramp Tramp, What Price Glory?, Son of the Sheik, The Black Pirate, Sparrows, The Beloved Rogue, Mare Nostrum, Tumbleweeds, The Winning of Barbara Worth, The Bat, The Volga Boatman, The Sorrows of Satan, The Scarlet Letter, Mantrap, The Torrent, The Temptress, For Heaven's Sake, Dancing Mothers, Ben Hur.*

1927 *The Jazz Singer* gives Warner Brothers lead in sound, although Fox's Movietone system is the more practical and ultimately wins out.

Academy of Motion Picture Arts and Sciences formed in Hollywood; 1927 first year of Academy Awards.

Federal Trade Commission declares block-booking system to be illegal.

6,200 seater "palace" theater, the Roxy, opens in New York with *The Loves of Sunya.*

Key films: *The General, It, Wings, Flesh and the Devil, Long Pants, The Strong Man, Underworld, When a Man Loves, Uncle Tom's Cabin, The Gaucho, Night of Love, Man, Woman, Sin, Barbed Wire, Chang, The Unknown, The King of Kings, Stark Love, College, Sunrise, Seventh Heaven, The Cat and the Canary, White Gold.*

1928 *Lights of New York,* the first all-talkie, produced by Warner Brothers.

Key films: *Street Angel, The Wedding March, The Crowd, White Shadows in the South Seas, Lilac Time, The Circus, The Last Command, The Patriot, Our Dancing Daughters, Four Sons, Hangman's House, Tempest, Sadie Thompson, The Case of Lena Smith, The Wind, The Cameraman, The Singing Fool, The Way of the Strong, That Certain Thing.*

1929 Silents virtually ousted by talkies; many hybrid versions (part talkie, silent with sound effects, etc.).

Key films (silent): *Wild Orchids, The Kiss, Women of Affairs, Four Devils, City Girl* (latter two both released with sound sequences).

Key films (sound): *Broadway, Sunny Side Up, The Virginian, The Valiant, Applause, Hallelujah, Bulldog Drummond, Broadway Melody, Disraeli, The Green Goddess, Alibi, Laughter, The Coconuts, The Hole in the Wall, The Love Parade.*

Chronological Survey Listing

Many of the films listed are referred to within the basic text of this book, but others are not. In earlier years, not to have identified each title by at least giving the director, the stars and a genre classification would have been both lazy and frustrating. Today, however, one has merely to refer the researcher—who might find such a year-by-year list a useful springboard—to the *American Film Institute Catalogue of Feature Films* from 1921–30, wherein all films of that period are recorded with detailed cast and credits and synopses. A similar volume covering the pre-1920 features is also in the assembly stage for near-future publication.

It should be emphasized that the list of "key films" supplied for each year is an arbitrary and non-definitive selection, chosen to be a reliable cross-section of the important films of that year, combining both the innovative, the artistic, and the influential with the most representative popular releases. Undoubtedly, personal preferences creep into the area of interesting films made by worthwhile if not yet major directors (such as William K. Howard and Frank Capra).

Nevertheless, the list makes an interesting comparison with another list of top-grossing films, compiled in the mid-1930's by the trade paper *The Motion Picture Herald*, and covering all films up to that point. Admittedly, any list compiled that late must be far from completely reliable, especially where independent and states-rights films are concerned. Nevertheless, even if the exact figures quoted are open to question, the fact that these films were the most popular with audiences *cannot* really be doubted. Since far and away the biggest money-maker was *The Singing Fool*, with a gross of five million dollars, it can be seen at a glance that many of the somewhat extravagant claims made for individual films are highly suspect. (Mack Sennett, for example, claimed an eighteen-million-dollar gross for this 1917 *Mickey!*) Also, the list indicates grosses, not profits, and in that sense is a little misleading. If Douglas Fairbanks' *The Thief of Bagdad* cost even half the two million dollars claimed for it, then at best it broke even and probably showed a loss. And while *Ben Hur* was undoubtedly a top grosser, MGM's deal with the owners of the property was such that they paid out an inordinate amount in royalties; for them, the film was a success of prestige rather than dollars.

The thirty-one films in the list were made between 1915 and 1929. It is noteworthy that seven of them are full talkies, and three more are silents that were, however, released with music, songs, and effects. Thus, a third of the films come from the last three years of the silent period. Also, the remainder of the *full* list, extending to the mid-1930's is much longer, though covering a shorter period of time. All that this really proves, however, is that the sound films made more money because by then theater tickets cost more. The only reliable guide to any film's grossing capabilities is the number of admissions sold.

The list of box-office champions—those with receipts between a million and a half and five million dollars—up to the end of the silent period, in approximate order of money-making importance, consists of *The Singing Fool, The Four Horsemen of the Apocalypse, Ben Hur, The Big Parade, The Birth of a Nation,** *The Covered Wagon, The Jazz Singer, Sunny Side Up, The Broadway Melody, The Cockeyed World, The Freshman, The Gold Rush, The Kid, Rio Rita, The Ten Commandments, The Gold Diggers of Broadway, The Sea Hawk, Way Down East, What Price Glory?, Seventh Heaven, Street Angel, Girl Shy, Beau Geste, Four Sons, The Hunchback of Notre Dame, The King of Kings, The Merry Widow, Safety Last, Secrets, Stella Dallas, The Thief of Bagdad.*

While statistics are largely meaningless, this listing would seem to suggest that Harold Lloyd, Janet Gaynor/Charles Farrell, and directors Raoul Walsh and Frank Borzage were the box-office champions of the fifteen-year period under review, since they are the only personalities to be represented by three films apiece, with Griffith, Chaplin, deMille, Ronald Colman, Al Jolson, John Gilbert, and Edmund Lowe/Victor McLaglen runners-up with two films apiece. One notices, with some surprise, the absence of some of the biggest box-office stars of all: Mary Pickford, Rudolph Valentino, Gloria Swanson, Lon Chaney.

In some ways, the list *is* a vindication of the Hollywood system that claimed to know what the public wanted. With the single exception of *The Birth of a Nation,* which was very much of a financial gamble when it was made, all of the films—many of them, such as Ford's *Four Sons,* of high artistic quality—are essentially popular entertainments which must have been considered sure-fire propositions. Nowhere in sight are the innovative or purely artistic films made without compromise to the box office: *Greed, Nanook of the North, Sunrise, Stark Love, Isn't Life Wonderful?,* or *A Woman of Paris.* Equally significant, the best of the early talkies (*Hallelujah, Applause*) are overlooked in favor of no less than *six* somewhat primitive musicals. (Had we extended the coverage to 1930, this trend would have been sustained.)

Hollywood, as always, writes its own history in terms of gross receipts. Yet it is somewhat ironic that *Ben Hur,* one of the top grossers of the silent period, was actually a financial loss (due to production costs and contractual obligations), whereas *Greed,* usually written off as a total disaster, did actually show a small profit!

---

* Putting *The Birth of a Nation* in fifth place is open to question, since it is generally conceded to be the top-grossing film of all time. However, it has always been difficult to obtain reliable box-office figures for this film, and it may have been even more difficult in the mid-1930's. After listing it until the mid-1970's as *the* top grosser, though finding it impossible to quote exact figures, *Variety,* the trade journal, suddenly repudiated the claim but without giving specific details or reasons. On the basis of the number of paid admissions, and *continuous* exhibition, its number one position seems justified.

Index

Other titles of interest

Available at your bookstore

OR ORDER DIRECTLY FROM

DA CAPO PRESS, INC.

1-800-321-0050